UK Divers' Source

THE GUIDE TO SPORTS DIVING AND ASSOCIATED SUPPLIERS IN THE UK

Stephen M...

Advertisement Executive
Gary Conlan

Design & Typesetting
Neal Klyman

Printer
Ken Greener Print

Publisher
Inigo Press Ltd
24 Poland Street
London W1V 3DD
Telephone: 071 434 3807
Fax: 071 434 3799

ISBN 0 9521978 0 4

Introduction

Welcome to the first issue of the *UK Divers' Source.*

The publication was conceived barely six months ago, as a direct result of a lack of readily available information.

We have sourced expert articles on the sport that we hope will make interesting reading and researched and listed information that we trust will prove valuable reference material for all UK divers, irrespective of their affiliations. The book has been printed on high quality paper, to the highest standards, and should stand up well when you take it out into the field. Finally we have kept the price to a bare minimum as we believe that everybody should have their own copy.

We are pleased to say that the idea has found favour with the industry as demonstrated by the kind support of our advertising clients. We realise that we may not have got everything right in this issue and, with such a rapidly evolving sport, we probably never will. However we recognise the dangers of complacency and believe that achieving excellence is a continuous process that needs constant monitoring and improvement. We would therefore greatly value your comments, criticisms and suggestions as to how we can improve future publications. So please do take the time to complete the competition and questionnaire on page 381 - there is no need for a stamp if you send it to the address on the form and you could win £1000 in vouchers to spend with any of our display advertisers. This means that you could start the next season with a complete new kit, further training or the Caribbean holiday you have been dreaming of.

Diving is made that much safer in the UK by the search and rescue infrastructure that we enjoy. In recognition and support of the often unsung efforts of these services we are pleased to announce that we will be donating 3% of profits from the sale of this book to be shared between the RNLI and the DDRC.

All that remains now is for us to thank our clients, contributors and staff for their tireless support in helping to make the idea a reality. We hope that this and future publications will be of use and look forward to your continuing support.

Happy Reading.

All photographs facing titles pages by Dr Paul Naylor, unless otherwise stated.

Plumose anemone - Metridium senile

Sea anemone - Actinothoe sphyrodeta

Certification Agencies

The British Sub-Aqua Club (BSAC)

BSAC membership is open to anyone aged 14 or over. Applications are made to one of the BSAC's branches, which are self-governing groups of members of the club. Upon acceptance, the applicant becomes a member of the BSAC (and, of course, of the Branch).

The annual charge for membership comprises of a fee payable to the club and one payable to the branch. The total cost therefore varies from branch to branch.

Although virtually all of the BSAC's members are Full Diving Members, there are other categories of membership (such as Snorkelling and Associate) which are subject to different subscription rates.

Full Diving Members receive upon joining a copy of Sport Diving, the BSAC's diving manual, and every month each Full Diving and Associate Member receives a copy of Diver, an independently published magazine which serves as the non-technical journal of the club.

All members of the BSAC are automatically covered by a policy of third-party liability insurance carried by the club. This protects each member (and guests, under certain circumstances) to the extent of £2 million from any claim made against him or her in respect of loss allegedly suffered by others as a result of the member's diving and related activities.

The BSAC has had an active publishing programme for almost 35 years, and in 1985 it embarked on the publication of a unique set of sport diving manuals.

The set was introduced by a completely revised and up-dated edition of the club's basic manual, Sport Diving which was followed by Seamanship for Divers. The third volume in the series, Safety and Rescue for Divers appeared in late 1987, with Advanced Sport Diving added to the list in the autumn of 1989.

Snorkelling For All was launched in autumn 1991 to enhance the range. BSAC members receive a significant discount when purchasing any of these manuals.

The club also publishes a range of diver training materials and manuals to support its system of instruction, as well as the NDC Bulletin - which is the technical publication of the club's National Diving Committee, and the BSAC Wreck Register series for those members interested in exploring shipwrecks around the British Isles.

The BSAC has a national coaching network which is without parallel in any other country.

A full-time principal national coach, heads a team consisting of 15 part-time regional coaches, and some 50 assistant regional coaches.

This team conducts conferences and runs courses in diving and diving-related skills for the benefit of members of the club and assists branches with their training activities.

Their work contributes greatly to the maintenance of the club's high standards of training and safety. The instructor training scheme is also available to suitably qualified divers to qualify to teach others in their branches and is becoming an increasingly important aspect of the BSAC.

In addition to conducting its own international operations, the BSAC is active abroad through membership of the World Underwater Federation (CMAS). The club is the federation's member organisation in Britain, and as such its diving qualifications are officially recognised in 66 independent countries around the world.

BSAC members are accordingly entitled to obtain CMAS diving qualification certificates, cards and wetsuit badges for use when diving in those countries.

To provide essential services to its members, the club maintains a headquarters in Ellesmere Port, Cheshire. Under the direction of the club's office manager, a staff of 15 employees deal with membership requirements, meets the organisation's administrative needs, and runs a mail order operation selling BSAC publications and other items stocked for the benefit of members.

The club's headquarters is also responsible for maintaining relations with appropriate government agencies, local governmental and regulatory organisations, sport governing bodies, conservation groups, etc. in order to ensure that members' interests as divers are safeguarded and that full account is taken of the views and legitimate needs of the country's sport diving community.

The Professional Association of Diving Instructors (PADI)

In 1966 John J Cronin and Ralph Erickson founded PADI - the Professional Association of Diving Instructors (in the USA) - to raise an organisation of instructors offering the most progressive and the safest diver training available.

Cronin and Erickson determined that PADI diver courses would be developed and taught by professionals, making them quite distinct from courses offered by amateurs and hobbyists.

PADI has since grown into a worldwide organisation issuing diver certifications in 110 countries.

When asked about PADI, people in the diving industry will usually describe the association as "a training agency" or say "they teach people how to dive".

While these reflect a prevailing view, they actually fall short of describing PADI's full function. Considering the association's involvement in retail education, business support, legal defence, lobbying, dive travel, professional insurance, hyperbaric science and other aspects of the dive business that reach well beyond a "training agency" niche, it is clear that PADI has established itself as much more than this.

Having said that, PADI is still without doubt the leader in diving education.

For more than 25 years PADI has set the standard for quality, fun and excellence in diver education. More divers worldwide participate in PADI programs than any other (500,000 in 1992 alone), making PADI diver credentials the most recognised and respected in the world.

The PADI system of diver education has been developed by instructional and subject matter experts, and consists of the only courses to successfully qualify for college credit recommendations from the American Council on Education (in the US) and UK government recognition as valid evidence of competence in training and development (instructor) and sport and recreation (other courses) for use in the work place (NVQ's).

Due to PADI's world-wide network of dive centres you are able to both start or complete your chosen PADI course in 110 different countries, one of which is the UK.

With an excess of 90 professional PADI dive centres and 1500 Instructors situated throughout the UK we are able to offer a service unequalled within the industry (in 1992 18,983 people living in the UK participated in PADI courses).

PADI dive centres throughout Britain offer:

- A training schedule that can be tailored to meet your needs.
- An educational system that is both modern in concept and educationally valid.
- A course that leads to a certification card that is recognised in 110 countries.
- Courses that you can start in this country and complete while on holiday if you wish.
- Tuition from an Instructor who's professional qualifications (HSE approved) are evaluated and updated on a regular bases.
- The opportunity through training to turn your hobby into a career move that could change your life.
- An opportunity to have fun learning something you have always wanted to while gaining a National Vocational Qualification.

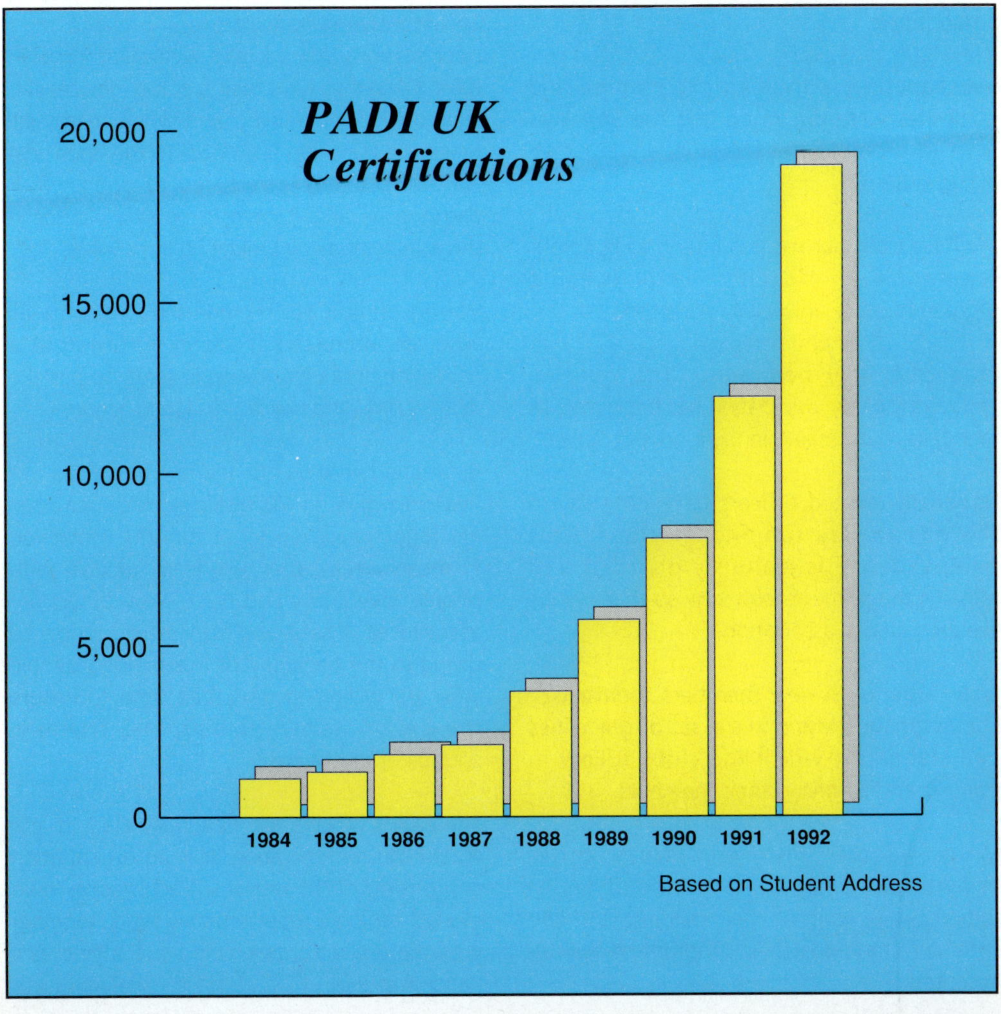

The Sub-Aqua Association (SAA)

The Sub-Aqua Association was founded in 1976 because independent diving clubs in Britain felt the need for a strong voice in the country's diving affairs.

Originally this union took the form of a diving register of non-affiliated clubs, but demand grew quickly for a more formal organisation.

Subsequently, a training programme and guidelines were drawn up and the SAA was born to promote the UK independent club diving system.

We have clubs abroad and intend to build our reputation worldwide. Our training programmes are universally accepted.

From the very beginning, the guiding philosophy of the association has been that, as members, clubs maintain their independence.

Nationally elected officers have little say in the day to day running of clubs. This independence is jealously guarded and remains the prime reason why so many clubs seek to join our association.

SAA clubs teach new members themselves. The association lays down a set of guidelines and standards, which the clubs follow in training and certifying their members.

Many people who join from other organisations may have varying styles of tuition but as long as their training is in line with our standards their programme will be accepted.

The SAA training programme has been devised to ensure that the novice moves through the grades of competence in an enjoyable and progressive way, each new level of training building on what has previously been learnt.

This means that the novice learns to dive using an extensive system of evening classes and pool sessions spread over weeks rather than days. Once they have their medical, novices can start their diver training and when ready will make the transition from pool to the open sea. Naturally, being introduced to open water diving in an area known to be safe will make this as easy and unintimidating as possible.

We encourage our members to welcome all who are interested in taking up diving as a recreation, including the opportunity to partake in a 'try dive' and watch the club in action.

By training with a club new members will not 'learn to dive' in 20 minutes. Most courses are taught over weeks or months. However, in those weeks, they will learn to dive with people they know and trust. Newcomers are assured of a safe and fun introduction to diving in the company of like-minded people who are willing to give their time to ensure the best possible training in a friendly, sociable atmosphere.

The SAA's officers are nationally elected and receive no remuneration. It is an organisation comprising of 14 regions. Each has its own elected regional representative who, together with the executive, assemble twice a year as a national council.

The association holds an annual conference each autumn including the annual general meeting and a large trade show. This has become a major business and social event within the Sub-Aqua Association's diving calendar.

The SAA offers International recognition for our members and has the strength to support and protect members as well as offering third party insurance. It can also offer standardisation and assistance with training techniques, and access to a full range of national courses.

SAA national and regional courses take place up and down the UK throughout the year. They are often advertised in the association's magazine Scuba World and cover a wide variety of subjects including dive master, basic boat-handling, diver coxswain (recognised by the RYA with an equivalent crossover available), diver rescue (recognised by RLSS), marine life identification (with the MCS), nautical archaeology (with the NAS), underwater photography, VHF including licence, O_2 administration, chartwork and navigation, plus all the various instructor and examiner qualifications.

There are two annual subscription payments to the SAA which are made by clubs in January each year:

- Annual Club Registration Fee, paid by the club each year to register as a SAA club.

- Members Individual Fee, paid by the club for each individual member to cover SAA membership and third party insurance indemnity.

Many divers come to the SAA because their needs within diving are unfulfilled. Firstly, it has earned a reputation of being the friendliest to divers, no doubt because it has contact with the membership on a day to day basis. The officers are only a phone call or letter away. Secondly, the SAA pride themselves in their follow-up training and ancillary courses. By providing these facilities members remain stimulated within the sport and are unlikely to become bored.

Members are encouraged by their club diving officer to take courses when they feel ready to progress or if they show a strong inclination to a particular aspect of the sport.

SUB-AQUA SAA ASSOCIATION

SAA membership prices enable those on low budgets the chance to take up diving as a recreation. The association welcomes disabled trainees and divers provided their medical practitioners are happy, and age is immaterial provided the required fitness test and medical are passed (plus snorkel training for younger members).

The association's slower training system compares favourably with other diving schools. It allows novices time to absorb information and practice the more difficult skills at a comfortable pace matched to their individual needs.

Scuba diving is a recreation that can be enjoyed by anyone. Offered by a friendly, amateur organisation with a professional attitude, who could ask for anything more?

Scottish Sub-Aqua Club (SSAC)

The Scottish Sub-Aqua Club is recognised by the Scottish Sports Council as the governing body of the sport in Scotland.

The SSAC represents the interests of it's members and those of Scottish divers generally, with all official interested bodies including sports councils and tourist bodies as well as local councils.

Scottish diving is recognised as being among the most diverse and interesting in the world with temperate waters and areas such as St Kilda and Scapa Flow which are internationally renowned diving holiday destinations. The SSAC is actively involved in protecting this resource.

The association also provides it's members with third party liability insurance cover, and medical advice from our team of medical advisors, recently strengthened by a close association with the Diving Diseases Research Centre.

The club, through it's national diving committee, maintains and develops the training standards required of its members.

The heart of the club is the 70 plus branches based in many towns or areas of the big cities, as well as special branches at institutions such as colleges and universities.

These branches are well supported by 14 regional coaches, which ensures regular contact and support.

The SSAC's magazine - Scottish Diver - is delivered to all members, and is produced by an editor who is elected by the members at the AGM and served on the general committee.

The club also organises a range of diving and diving related courses both regionally and nationally as well as diving expeditions.

On the competitive side there are regular fin swim competitions and there is an annual diving officers' conference and a bi-annual diving conference with many eminent speakers.

The club maintains an extensive library which is available for use by its members.

SSAC remains at the forefront of developments in the diving world and has already agreed in principle to allow the use of Nitrox by members.

The SSAC is also preparing to introduce its own Nitrox endorsement towards the end of 1993.

The SSAC is the leader in the UK on training instructors in the skills necessary to teach diving to the disabled.

The first course of this type was attended by instructors from SSAC, BSAC and other diving organisations.

The Scottish Sub-Aqua Club is the oldest diving club in the UK (by two months) and celebrated its 40th anniversary in 1993.

Comhairle Fo-Thuinn (The Irish Underwater Council)

The Irish Underwater Council was founded in 1963 and now has an affiliated club in practically every county in Ireland.

We are affiliated to the world body - CMAS. In 1991 the council achieved a major objective when our club diver training module was adopted by CMAS as the standard for all countries worldwide.

Diving courses are run at club level up to the international two-star diver grade and at a national level from three-star diver to three-star instructor.

Inter-club competitions are organised in various events (octopush, underwater photography, underwater navigation, fin swimming etc) and national teams are selected to compete abroad in some events.

Junior snorkelling sections are a part of some clubs and snorkelling is recognised as a sport itself.

A technical commission meets regularly under the national diving officer and, in conjunction with the technical commission of CMAS, ensures that diving safety and standards in Ireland compare with the best in the world.

Subsea is the official magazine of the Irish Underwater Council and is posted free to every member four times per year. It is also available from larger bookshops and dive shops. It covers news, information, stories, articles, photographs etc of diving from all over the world. It is also posted to many overseas subscribers.

Diving a wreck for the first time is exhilarating, and finding one is a dream come true. One of our divers from the City of Derry Sub-Aqua Club discovered the *'La Trinidad Valencers'* in Kinnagoe Bay.

Once trained you will want to photograph those magical moments or the unbelievable underwater sights. Taking photographs underwater is now almost as easy as on land. Ireland has a wealth of underwater sites, most yet to be studied - our underwater archaeology society welcomes new members. The fauna and flora of Ireland is unique, the creatures and plants who inhabit our underwater world are beautiful and are not at all disturbed by the human interloper.

The west coast of Ireland from Cork to Donegal offers some of the best diving in Europe. There are several dive centres located along the coast and information on local dive sites can be obtained from the regional dive officers in each area, as well as information on accommodation etc. Some of the islands of the west coast offer complete diving packages.

Handicapped Scuba Association (HSA)

The Handicapped Scuba Association was formally organised in the USA in 1981 by Jim Gatacre, a NAUI Instructor, although the HSA had been teaching scuba diving to people with physical disabilities since 1975.

Working closely with the leading sports diver training organisations, a set of standards were developed which resulted in specialised physical performance standards.

These standards evolved around one central issue: the degree of buddy dependency required for a handicapped person to safely scuba dive.

The physical performance standards, therefore, had to challenge the student sufficiently to bring out their degree of buddy dependency as well as the ability to help a fellow diver who may be experiencing some difficulty, and to do so in a non-discriminatory manner.

Over the years the Handicapped Scuba Association has become the worldwide authority on sport diving for the handicapped. One of the concepts that makes this programme so unique is that handicapped and able bodied students receive the same training and are taught together, mastering aquatic skills from novice to advanced.

Another innovation, the multi-level certification system, was developed during the disabled diver workshops, conducted during the early eighties.

The multi-level certification system aims to provide a method based on physical performance, for an instructor to certify people with a wide range of physical disabilities. This method makes possible diver certification without having to evaluate unfamiliar 'disabilities'.

The scuba instructor is therefore able to conduct the course of training within the confines of the familiar physical performance standards, and issue diver certification knowing that the necessary precautions for safe diving are inherent to the certification level achieved by the handicapped student diver.

In response to the international popularity of handicapped diving over the past few years, the HSA has pioneered the Instructor Training Course (ITC).

This course, the only one of its kind, is an intensive three day course of theory and application that certifies qualified instructors as HSA Instructors capable of training and certifying their own classes of handicapped divers.

The HSA Instructor Training Course is a programme without equal. It provides the instructor candidates with specialised medical knowledge during eight hours of lectures on disabilities and sensitises instructors by 'handicapping' and placing them in situations typically problematic for the real handicapped scuba student. Finally, in open water, each instructor is required to co-ordinate and conduct a dive with two simulated handicapped students.

The HSA now offers the only comprehensive underwater educational programme in the world for students with physical disabilities and for instructors eager to accept the challenge of sharpening their teaching skills by excelling in the specialisation of handicapped diver training.

The internationally recognised qualification gained by the successful instructor candidate on completion of the HSA ITC indicates to potential handicapped students that their instructor is able to conduct their diving education to help each of them achieve their goal.

In the UK, the first HSA ITC was conducted at Diving Leisure, Hanworthy in June, 1988. It was attended by instructors from all the UK agencies as well as a group of Italian instructors.

More recently, at the end of June 1993, 12 instructors, again from BSAC, PADI and SAA in the UK as well as one from Austria and three from the Netherlands, took part in the latest HSA ITC conducted by Jim Gatacre.

This course was conducted at Stoney Cove, the leading inland diver training site, and was sponsored and organised by Ian Purvis of OK Diving Services Swindon.

In addition to the introduction of the Handicapped Scuba Association into the UK, a group of interested representatives both instructor and disabled, from BSAC, SAA, SSAC and PADI have formed a group under the name of Dolphin (Diving Organisations Link With The Physically Handicapped and Instructors Network).

Promoting safe diving for the disabled, Dolphin aims to educate existing diving instructors in the techniques for teaching diving to the disabled; be an advisory body for all; set up an information network.

Dolphin is affiliated to the Diving Diseases Research Centre (DDRC) Fort Bovisand.

For more details contact the founder and chairperson, Susie Shelley, DOLPHIN, c/o DDRC, Fort Bovisand, Plymouth, Devon PL9 OAB.

HSA Instructors course group.

UK Certifying Agencies

BRITISH SUB AQUA CLUB (BSAC)

TELFORD'S QUAY
ELLESMERE PORT
SOUTH WIRRAL, CHESHIRE L65 4FY
051 3571951
FAX: 051 3571250

SCOTTISH SUB-AQUA CLUB (SSAC)

THE COCKBURN CENTRE
40 BOGMOOR PLACE
GLASGOW G51 4TQ
041 4251021
FAX: 041 4251021

HANDICAP SCUBA ASSOCIATION INTERNATIONAL (HSA)

63 FARLEIGH CRESCENT
LAWN ESTATE, SWINDON
WILTSHIRE SN3 1JY
0793 695479
FAX: 0793 695479

SUB AQUA ASSOCIATION (SAA)

BRYSLAN HOUSE
UPPER STEET
FLEET,
HAMPSHIRE GU13 9PE
0252 622415
FAX: 0252 620729

PADI INTERNATIONAL LTD

UNIT 9, THE 306 ESTATE
BROOMHILL ROAD
BRISLINGTON
BRISTOL, AVON BS4 5RG
ENGLAND
0272 711717
FAX: 0272 710400

THE IRISH UNDERWATER COUNCIL (COMHAIRLE FO-THUINN)

78A PATRICK STREET
DUN LAOGHARIE
COUNTY DUBLIN
IRELAND
010 3531 2844601
FAX: 010 3531 2844602

International Agencies

BRITISH INTERNATIONAL LTD (BSAC)

TELFORD'S QUAY
ELLESMERE PORT
SOUTH WIRRAL,
CHESHIRE L65 4FY
051 3571951
FAX: 051 3571250

COMMITTEE MONDIAL ASSOCIATION SCUBA (CMAS)

SIEGE ADMINISTRATIF
VIALE TIZIANO 74
00196 ROME, ITALY
010 396 37517478
FAX: 010 396 36858480

HANDICAP SCUBA ASSOCIATION INTERNATIONAL (HSA)

1104 EL PRADO
SAN CLEMENTE
CA 92672 USA
010 1 714 4986128
FAX: 010 1 714 4986128

*** NATIONAL ASSOCIATION OF UNDERWATER INSTRUCTORS (NAUI)**

PO BOX 14650
MONTCLAIR
CA 91763-1150 USA
010 1 714 6215801
FAX: 010 1 714 6216405

PROFESSIONAL ASSOCIATION OF DIVING INSTRUCTORS (PADI)

1251 EAST DYER ROAD #100
SANTA ANA
CA 92705-5605
USA
010 1 714 5407234
FAX: 010 1 714 5402609

*** SCUBA SCHOOLS INTERNATIONAL (SSI)**

2619 CANTON COURT
FORT COLLINS
CO 80525 , USA
010 1 303 4820883
FAX: 010 1 303 4826157

** Of the numerous agencies certifying divers around the world (apart from those listed on page 18), NAUI and SSI are the only ones with a presence in the UK.*

Snakelocks anemone - Anemone viridis

Equipment

The arguments for ownership

by Steve Warren

The cost of diving equipment compares favourably with that of many other hobbies such as golf, or adventure activities such as snow skiing.

Nevertheless, many newly trained divers continue to question the benefits of owning their own gear and feel that they may be better off renting. This is a perspective that appears particularly true of people trained abroad who plan to dive exclusively on overseas holidays, often just once or twice a year.

Equipment ownership however, may provide important safety, comfort and cost benefits.

Safety is clearly the most important issue for responsible, defensive divers. There are various potential drawbacks to personal safety inherent in renting, for example, that most fundamental item, the regulator.

On the surface you may take breathing for granted. Underwater you can't. While a cheap, low performance regulator may work very well on a shallow easy going and relaxed dive, expecting it to deliver sufficient air freely and easily under increased demand may simply be asking to much.

What exactly constitutes demand? Swimming against a mild current, finning fast to catch up to your buddy or diving deep (and depth is relative - it's possible to feel uncomfortable swimming at a moderate pace in just 10m) all require more air. If your tank pressure is low the problems can be exacerbated.

Perhaps the worst scenario is one in which you are sharing air with your buddy, using an octopus. Two divers will clearly demand more air than one. Stress will increase that demand further. Throw in any of the other factors and you begin to see the problem. Who can guarantee that all of these factors will be avoidable on any given dive?

Why then do dive centres not rent out high performance regulators? Some do, but their investment in equipment and servicing will be higher and that will be reflected in their rental fees.

Other centres who are not so reputable may not be so fussy about what they offer or about all important maintenance.

Owning your own regulator means that you can choose one matched to your own diving needs with an appropriate alternate air source and have complete control over it's service history.

Buoyancy Control Devices are designed to provide greater safety and comfort in the water. Two major problems can occur with rental jackets. The first is fit. If the dive centre doesn't have the right size for you, you're going to be compromised. An overly large jacket may cause your tank to roll from side to side upsetting your trim and will tend to leave the diver hanging low in the water at the surface as the BCD rides up. BCDs' that are to small may have inadequate lift and poor positioning of the buoyancy chambers can adversely affect the way the diver floats on the surface.

The second problem is with inflation and deflation controls and releases. Their modes of operation and their positions on the jacket differ greatly between manufacturers and can make a diver all fingers and thumbs until, with practice, he or she learns to locate controls and releases instinctively, which takes time and must be relearned with each change of jacket. This delay in locating jacket functions can contribute to diver discomfort and stress reducing the ability to manage a problem. Clearly this is a situation best avoided!

If personal safety lies in personal responsibility then it does not make sense to fully entrust the responsibility for planning and monitoring dive profiles to a third party. You must be able to monitor your own depth and times and your surface intervals. Depth gauges and in particular dive timers or watches are not always available for rental.

Travelling divers may also find that they cannot choose metric or imperial which can be confusing if you have to mentally convert air pressure and depth from a system that you are unfamiliar with to one that you are. Self reliance rather than buddy dependence increases safety and is a powerful endorsement of equipment ownership.

Diving equipment is not cheap. But then neither is rental. The cost of hiring equipment regularly (and that includes hiring it for 10 days on holiday) soon adds up and the equipment is never yours.

Owning your own equipment means that you have gear that satisfies your own personal requirements and fits correctly, which you can operate instinctively and can maintain to your own satisfaction. If you like to upgrade your equipment regularly there is a ready market for secondhand gear and while you will not get back what you paid for it, the rental fees you have avoided may well exceed the shortfall.

Bulk and weight are often a concern for dive travellers. However warm water divers will find compact BCDs designed for their specific needs which take up very little space and in any case regulators do not weigh much.

Many airlines overlook minor weight transgressions and the more enlightened carriers consider diving equipment to be sporting goods and make special concessions.

Diving is most enjoyable when you dive without being distracted by your equipment. You should dive in harmony with it, barely aware that you are using it and able to operate it virtually subconsciously.

If you have to stop and think to use your ever changing rental gear perhaps it's time to spare a thought for the benefits of ownership.

Adam Parkes - Properly equipped for diving.

Selecting a Snorkelling Kit

by Steve Warren

Many divers get their first taste of underwater exploration through snorkelling, often on an overseas holiday. Young people often start off this way before moving to scuba as they mature. For many divers snorkelling is an activity they pursue in addition to scuba, for others a fulfilling sport in it's own right whilst for some, such as spearfishermen or film makers, it is a means to an end allowing them to approach wary marine life without announcing their arrival through the bubble noise of scuba.

Equipment for snorkelling is inexpensive to buy, is lightweight for travelling and can be used with scuba as well. It is very personal gear and to ensure fit, comfort and performance it is best to own a set. This consists of just three items - a mask to let you see clearly underwater, a snorkel to let you breathe comfortably with your face submerged and a pair of fins to provide propulsion and mobility with minimum exertion.

Masks provide an airspace between your eyes and the surrounding water that allows them to work properly in the medium they were designed for. A mask also covers your nose allowing you to prevent uncomfortable pressure build up during descents by equalising or to expel any water that may enter the seal by simply exhaling through your nose. Masks may be available in different sizes depending on the model and younger divers could find that an adult mask will fit them perfectly, avoiding the necessity of replacing masks as they grow older. For longevity and comfort most mask skirts are made from silicone which is more resistant to chlorine and saltwater than ordinary rubber and is more supple which increases comfort and provides a better seal against the water. Tempered glass is used for the faceplate. It is scratch resistant, easy to demist and, if smashed (very hard to do), breaks into relatively large, blunt pieces. Various approaches are used to provide maximum peripheral vision. Although a single lens can be used, two lenses may improve overall vision as they can be set closer to the eyes giving a wider field of view. Adding side windows helps some people as can panels in the base of the mask. You need to try a range of styles before making a decision. A purge valve is an option on some masks and can make evacuating water easier.

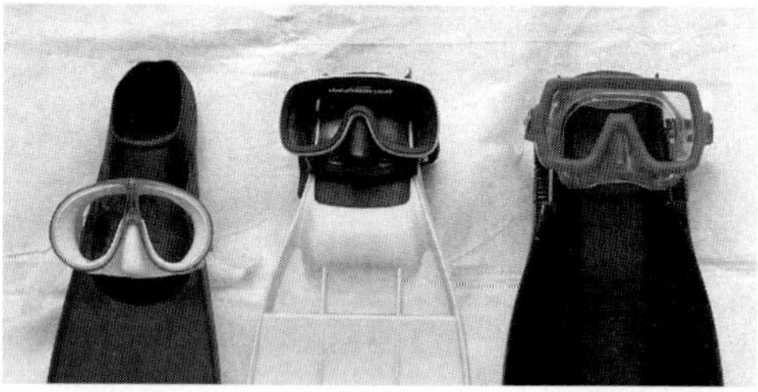

The centre mask is neoprene, the others are silicone.
Equipment: Courtesy, Ocean Leisure and Mikes Waterfront Warehouse.

Checking a mask for fit is quite straightforward. Firstly, fold the strap over the faceplate so it's out of your way. Push your hair well back so it will be clear of the skirt and looking up towards the ceiling press the mask gently onto your face. It should make a four point seal at your forehead, both sides of your face and under your nose. A SLIGHT sniff through your nose with your mouth closed should seal it easily. It should stick firmly to your face for as long as you continue to inhale. If you have facial hair you may have to try several masks to get a good seal. Next check your field of view. Peripheral vision is useful for locating your buddy. Downward vision helps you find chest and waist releases.

Check that you can reach your nose to equalise your ears. I prefer to teach students to block their nostrils from underneath, rather than pinching them shut which can be uncomfortable.

Choosing a mask is very subjective and deserves more time than most people devote to it. Sight is our primary sense underwater and a mask should be selected with that fact firmly in mind. Fortunately many dive centres appreciate the problems of choosing the "perfect" mask and will willingly let you pool test a mask and return and replace it if it's wrong. Divers with eyesight problems can use certain types of contact lenses or can usually have their mask fitted with corrective lenses. Your optician or dive shop can advise you on this, however, if you will be using prescription lenses in your mask I strongly recommend you give it a shot in the pool (or even the bath) for leakage before committing to having them installed. Many masks are provided with travel cases to protect them in your dive bag. This is particularly valuable if you have a corrective mask, not just because of the cost of it but because you're going to have serious problems if you have to borrow an ordinary mask having broken yours.

A spare strap is a good investment. Sooner or later you'll break a strap. This only ever seems to happen when your are putting the mask on - ie just as you are about to enter the water. This can foul up both your day and your buddy's. It is not a case of will your strap break but when and where. Will you have a spare? A bottle of defog is a cheap, effective and hygienic way of stopping mask mist up, I keep a bottle in my BCD for convenience.

Snorkels allow you to cruise comfortably on the surface and observe your surroundings without the constant irritation and effort of lifting your head to breathe. Scuba divers use them to conserve their air during surface swims and for additional safety in the event of having to swim to the boat or shore when low or out of air. Snorkels come in three main variations ; those you have to blow all the water out of yourself; those you only have to blow a little water out of and those which don't let any water in anyway.

The most basic are the cheapest but clearing a flooded snorkel after a surface dive is a learned technique and can require a little practice. Failing to completely clear the snorkel can lead to the irritation of trapped water sloshing about in the mouthpiece. If you are going on holiday and will not be taking snorkelling tuition and do not want to spend time acquiring snorkel clearing skills this type of snorkel may be best avoided.

Self draining snorkels clear most of the water from the tube automatically as you break surface through one or two valves. Experience has proven these valves to be very reliable. Minimal effort is required to clear any remaining water. Some models also handle unexpected duckings from the odd wave passing overhead very well by directing the water into a sump away from the divers breathing space where the next exhalation usually clears it. Non-flooding snorkels are designed to prevent water from entering the tube altogether. But just in case some does anyway they have self draining valves. This helps to expel water that might enter as you replace the mouthpiece after chatting to your buddy at the surface.

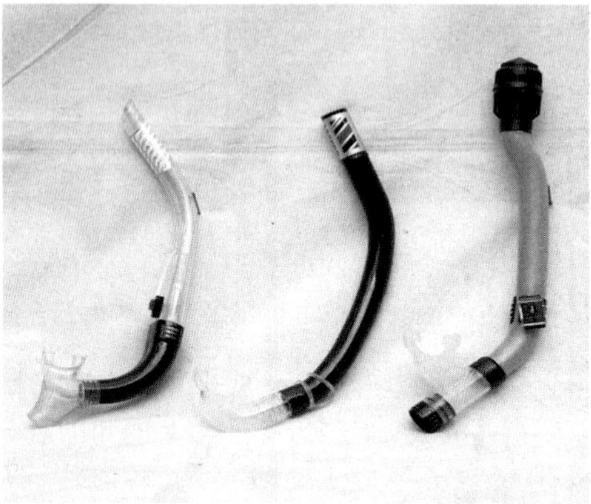

Left to right: Self draining snorkel, non self venting snorkel, and dry snorkel.
Equipment: Courtesy, Ocean Leisure and Mikes Waterfront Warehouse.

For your own comfort it's important that the barrel is wide enough to breathe easily through with minimal effort. Self drainers and dry snorkels are good for this as their wide bore can pass a lot of air but a wide barrel can make basic snorkels difficult to clear and divers with lower lungpower can find this a problem. A swivelling mouthpiece allows you to set the angle of the mouthpiece to match your jaw. A soft mouthpiece will be kinder on your gums than a hard one and should be sized to fit you. A quick release connector makes it easy to attach and remove the snorkel from your mask strap so that you can keep your mask in its case.

Fins provide propulsion and mobility. It is not speed that is the aim here, but covering maximum distance with minimum effort - in other words going as far as possible with the fewest number of kicks. Small bladed full foot fins are okay for pottering about in calm, currentless conditions and are used by some scuba divers in pools. More serious snorkel divers will want larger, stiffer blades for diving in a wider range of conditions and for making deeper breath hold excursions. Their needs are similar to those of a scuba diver and the same pair of fins will usually serve both purposes.

Fins come in two types of fitting. Full foot fins fit like slip-on shoes and are designed to be worn over bare feet - they are usually the cheapest and have flimsy blades being aimed very much at the holiday snorkeller. Better models have firmer, larger blades and can be used for scuba in warm waters when thermal foot protection is unnecessary. Slip ons are sized like shoes and need to fit snugly. Open back fins are designed to be worn with wet or drysuit boots.

Sizing is less critical with these than with slip ons. They are usually available in a range of sizes from extra small to extra large. If a diver is comfortable with two sizes I usually recommend they take the larger pair as they provide a little surplus room for a larger boot in the future. A diver may change from a wetsuit to a dry suit later on and this can make the difference between using the existing fins or having to buy a new pair.

An adjustable heel strap provides some leeway for extra comfort. Modern fin straps can usually be tightened or slackened with one hand and many feature quick releases which aid removal. A spare fin strap should be carried as a bare minimum though as straps get equal wear you can expect them to break around the same time. I prefer to carry one spare strap and one complete spare strap and buckle assembly so that if a strap parts I can simply snap in the replacement assembly

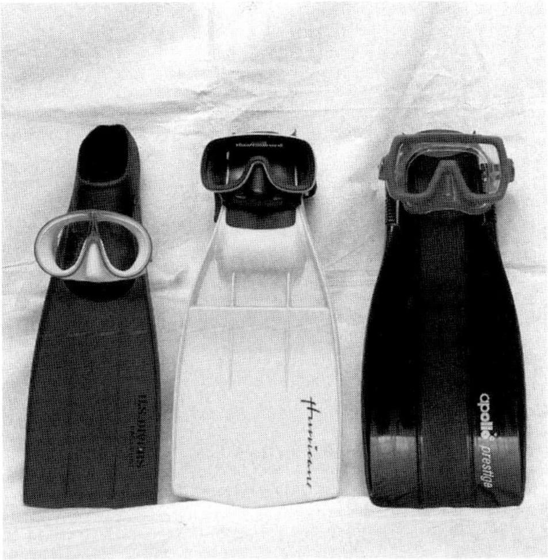

Left to right: Full foot fin, vented power fin, and power fin with membrane centre panel.
Equipment: Courtesy,Ocean Leisure and Mikes Waterfront Warehouse.

in seconds rather than having to rethread a strap into the old buckles which can take some time, is no fun in a crowded pitching boat, could delay my partner or students and could mean we miss slack tide. Later, in my own time I can thread my spare strap onto the old buckles ready for action and buy a new strap.

Blades vary. Some are vented to make the recovery kick easier, a feature that was introduced at a time when fins were fairly inflexible which made them hard work. Modern synthetics have enabled manufacturers to produce fin blades that flex in all the right places and vents have become less common. Some fins enhance performance by using membranes that "cup" the water and force it backwards to provide extra thrust. Incidentally, most modern fins take very little getting used to and as blade size is not proportional to foot size there is no problem with younger divers having adult fins. As with all equipment, if you need it for the environment you are diving in and your kids will also be diving in those conditions then they need appropriate gear too!

To check your fins for fit try slip ons with bare feet, sitting down and with your foot outstretched in a finning position. The fin should fit snugly with no loose edges around your foot which can chafe and your toes should not overhang the front. If they are still comfortable after a few minutes they are probably fine.

Open back strap fins are tried in the same position wearing appropriate boots. A perfect fit is less important here. However the sole of the fin should extend behind your arch and if someone holds the fin blade steady and you try to move your foot from side to side within the foot pocket there should be minimal movement.

These then are the three pieces of equipment that make up a basic snorkelling kit. Other items that may make your snorkelling more enjoyable are a manual to help you master some basic skin diving skills together with some safety advice, waterproof marine life identification cards or books so you know what you are looking at and an underwater camera to record your adventures.

Shallow water recyclable underwater cameras are available very cheaply and can provide surprisingly good prints in clear conditions. A mesh bag will keep your kit together and at the end of the day the whole outfit can simply be dunked in a rinse tank or bath and left to dry.

Finally, most diver training organisations offer snorkelling courses. These are usually fun, quick and easy and are well worth seeking out. A little basic training will go a long way towards making sure that you enjoy your snorkelling activities to the full.

Choosing the right Regulator

by Nick Rumble

A regulator is arguably the most important piece of scuba equipment a diver will buy. It enables him to breathe underwater by reducing the pressure of the air in the tank to a suitable level.

This is achieved through a two-stage system. The first stage reduces the pressure of air in the tank (which usually ranges from 150 to 300bar) to an intermediate pressure of between 7.5 and 12.5bar. The air is then carried through to the second stage demand valve (DV) via a low pressure hose, to the diver.

Regulator models differ primarily in the internal designs of both their first and second stages.

When choosing a piece of equipment of this importance advice should be sought from someone with an in depth knowledge of the many types of valve available. Somebody who either sells or services regulators would be a good source as they would be able to explain the many differences that may benefit you as an individual.

Any good salesman or technician will first enquire into your personal diving requirements. Whether for deeper diving or for cold water diving, each regulators has its own characteristics which will eventually determine the DV that you buy.

THE OPTIONS

Unbalanced piston first stage

(See figure 1.)

This is a reliable design, often used in dive schools as it requires little servicing. Its level of performance however, is the price paid for a cheaper regulator and minimal servicing bills. It is a useful first stage for a beginner, although it can be easily outgrown with the need for higher flow rates eg. dry suit feeds and other low pressure outlets, especially octopus rigs. This first stage's restriction lies with calibrating it for accurate intermediate pressure changes at depth and also low tank pressures.

It is a relatively simple design. Air enters the first stage and is immediately reduced to an intermediate pressure, which is regulated by

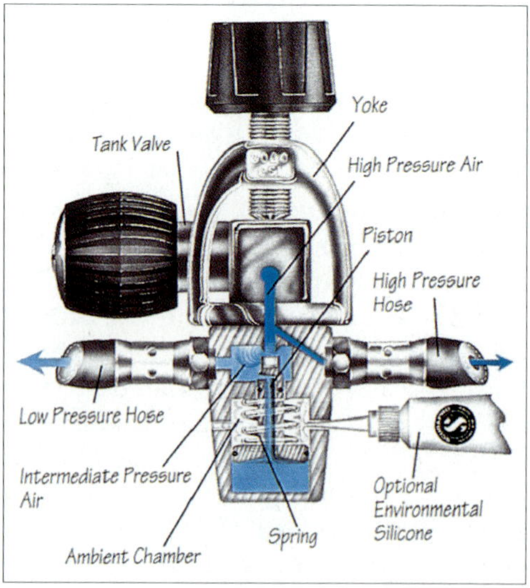

Figure 1. *Scubapro MK200*

a main spring. The piston - within the spring's coil - does not have a direct flow-through effect, allowing only low volume flow rates. Air then flows down the piston into the ambient pressure chamber where counter-acting water pressure regulates the air delivered to the diver.

Balanced piston first stage
(See figure 2.)

This is a good performer with highly accurate ambient pressure calibration, which means good capability at depth. It is also good for use with an alternate air source as it is capable of delivering high flow rates, even at depth and low tank pressures. Increased service bills over its unbalanced counterpart should be expected, but it is worth the extra cost for its superior performance. Most models run the risk of freezing-up in cold waters unless they have been environmentally sealed, though some manufacturers are adopting a modern technological approach to overcome this problem.

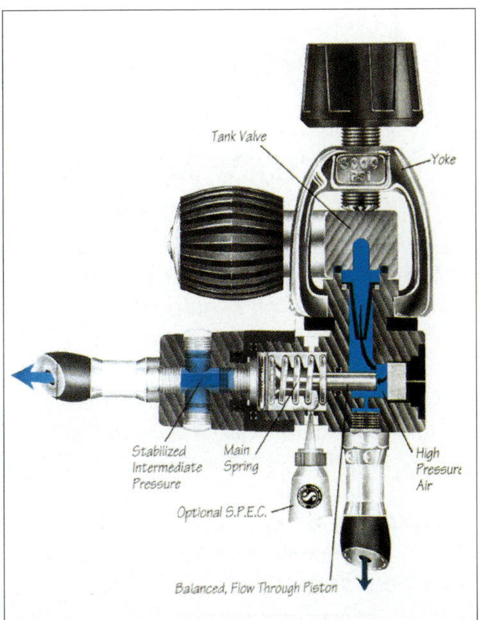

Figure 2. *Scubapro MK10*

As with the unbalanced model, the balanced piston first stage is a simple design. Air enters from the cylinder and flows past the filter, into the high pressure chamber which surrounds the stem of the piston. Air then passes through the piston and into the intermediate pressure chamber. When the pressure in the intermediate chamber equals the compression strength of the main spring the piston is forced shut - closing off any air flow until there is a demand from the second stage. On demand, the intermediate pressure drops and allows the piston and spring to recoil. While open, air can flow continuously to the diver through the piston. Ambient pressure is detected by the water pressure in the balance chamber, counter-acting the piston.

Balanced diaphragm
(See figure 3.)

This is another good performer with the benefit of total balancing and, even without environmental sealing, it has good cold-water capabilities as the ambient pressure chamber is completely sealed from any of the moving

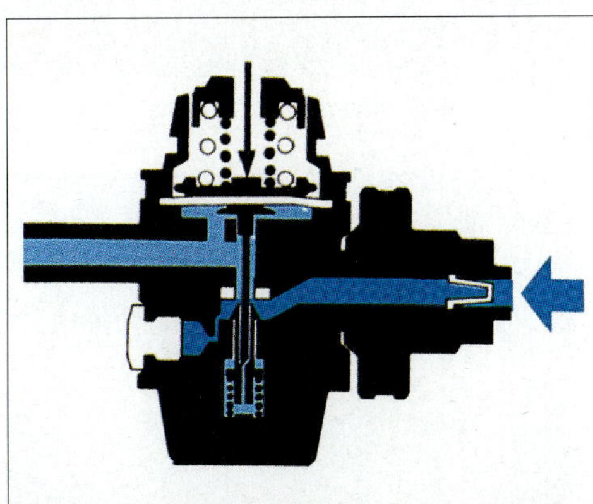

Figure 3. *Poseidon Jetstream/Odin Nr 2960*

parts likely to cause a freeze-up. Moderate to high service bills can be expected with this DV.

Air enters the first stage and flows into the high pressure chamber. It then passes through the already open valve and into the intermediate chamber, where the air acts against the flexible diaphragm. When the pressure in the intermediate chamber matches that of the spring tension, the pushrod attached to both the diaphragm and the valve seat is forced downwards, closing the valve until the diver inhales, reopening the valve.

SECOND STAGES

There are many second stage designs available, with performances varying greatly. The three types of second stage are the unbalanced, the balanced and the servo assisted second stage. Each has several variations but all rely on the same principles. All second stages currently on the market utilise the downstream effect ie. if it were to fail the regulator would go into a free flow as opposed to cutting off the air supply.

The air is delivered to the second stage via a low pressure hose, where the flow is controlled by a low pressure demand valve.

Unbalanced second stage

(See figure 4, page 32.)

As you can see the air has reached a point in the second stage where it has been stopped. This point - the poppet - is a neoprene rubber seat. Air cannot pass this point until the poppet is released from the orifice (a circular knife edge onto which the poppet seals). This is activated by the diver breathing-in, which causes a vacuum inside the second stage, pulling the diaphragm onto the lever. The poppet is then pushed away from the orifice, causing the air to flow at a rate determined by the diver's inhalations.

Balanced second stage

(See figure 5, page 32.)

The principles of this second stage are similar to that of the unbalanced version. However, instead of just employing a spring to retain the air pressure, it also uses a balance chamber. This additional feature means that the diver's exertion is counter-acting against the spring together with a small lower tension spring and a small pocket of air. This is commonly used on upper range models designed for high performance.

This stage is also known as a pneumatically balanced second stage.

Servo assisted second stage

(See figure 6, page 32.)

Once the air enters the second stage it flows through to a small chamber. As the pressure increases it causes a rubber cap to expand and shut-off against the side wall, closing off the air flow.

When the valve situated at the end of the chamber is depressed a very small amount of air is allowed to escape - enough to reduce the chamber pressure sufficiently for the rubber cap to return to its original state and allow the air to flow to the diver. Servo assisted second stages are usually associated with high performance regulators.

SERVICING

There are obvious and simple reasons for servicing a regulator. After all, the wearing

Scubapro MK 10 first stage. (Cutaway).

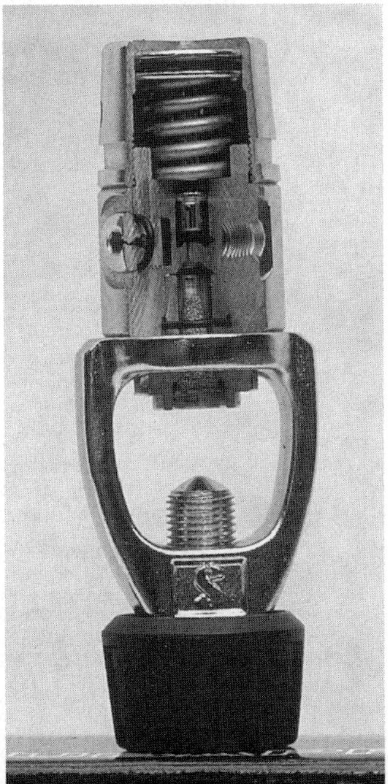

Scubapro MK 2 first stage. (Cutaway).

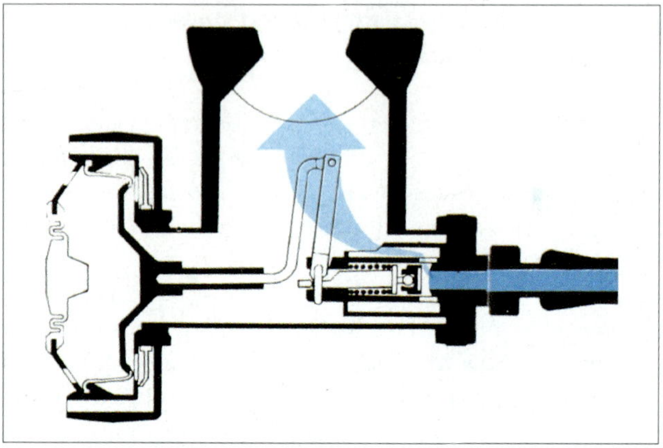

Figure 4. *Poseidon Cyklon 300*

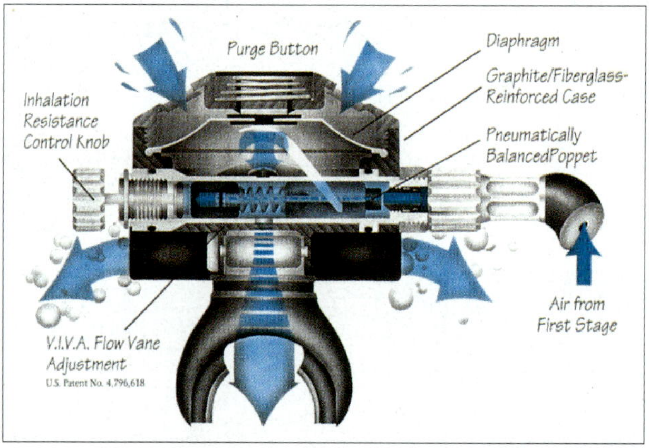

Figure 5. *Scubapro G250*

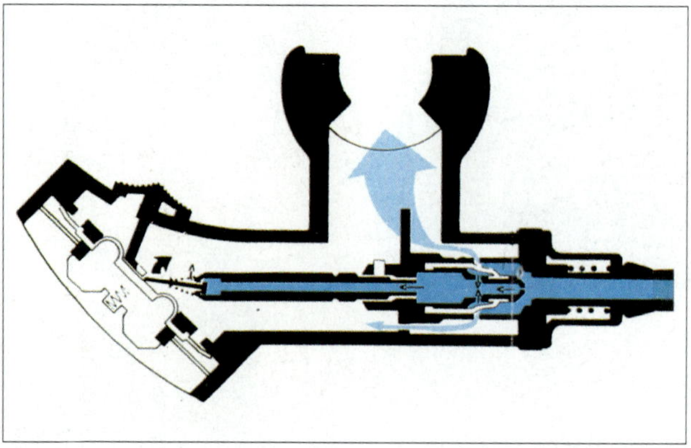

Figure 6. *Poseidon Jetstream/Odin*

parts of a demand valve cannot be expected to last indefinitely.
Unless otherwise stated, a demand valve needs servicing every 40 to 50 dives, or annually, whichever is first.

This servicing should be undertaken by a qualified and authorised technician. A factory trained engineer will also realise the need for using special tools such as intermediate pressure gauges or magnahelic gauges. The availability and correct use of these tools will ensure that the equipment is safe to use.

• *The diagrams used to illustrate this article have been reproduced by kind permission of Poseidon Industri AB, and Scubapro.*

Selecting a BCD

by Steve Warren

The buoyancy control device - BCD - has evolved from the simple airman's Mae West of the 1950s into the sophisticated purpose designed jackets of the 90s.

The essential role that the BCD plays in making diving easier, more comfortable and safer means that selecting the right BCD for your particular needs is all important. In this article we will review the uses of the BCD and suggest criteria to help you to choose the BCD that is best for you.

The buoyancy control device has made a significant contribution to diver safety and it is used by virtually all recreational divers. As with other diving equipment there is now a wide range of BCDs to choose from as manufacturers offer their customers increasingly specialised models to meet very specific diving requirements. The choice of BCDs available coupled with this increasing specialisation can be bewildering.

To help decide which BCD is best for you it would be useful to review their applications. The BCD provides the diver with the ability to control his or her buoyancy underwater.

Remaining neutral allows the diver to move through the water column with the minimum of effort, avoiding overexertion and conserving air, resulting in a more enjoyable and relaxing dive. Staying off the bottom protects delicate marine life from contact with the diver ensuring that future generations of divers will enjoy the same unspoilt sites that we did.

At will the diver can settle on the bottom (having first checked to ensure that the area contains nothing that will be damaged in the process of course!) to make equipment adjustments or to stabilize to shoot underwater photographs or video.

Skilled divers can also control their descent rate to a comfortable speed or ascend effortlessly using their BCD as an elevator.

On the surface the BCD supports the diver with their head clear of the water enabling them to see and be seen clearly by, for example, the dive boat.

In the event of a problem underwater the BCD can be used to assist a distressed diver to the safety of the surface. Divers in difficulties at the surface can use the BCD to keep the face clear of the water or an assisting diver can pass a diver or swimmer who is in difficulties a BCD to provide immediate buoyancy.

The BCD is not a lifejacket. It is not designed as such. It makes a significant contribution to personal diver safety by enabling divers to avoid situations such as overexertion which could lead to an incident.

BCDs are available in four main styles;

Horsecollar
Stabilizing Jacket
Advanced Design Vest
Wings

Depending on whether you will be diving with a full wet suit or dry suit or just a swimming costume or dive skin, you will want to select either a high or low buoyancy BCD.

The horsecollar, which is worn over the head, is the least expensive type of BCD. Underwater horsecollar jackets tend to bring the divers head up and force his feet down, making the diver unstreamlined. On the surface they place the diver on his back which can make it difficult for him to see the shore or an approaching boat without finning hard to remain vertical. As the horsecollar jacket isn't attached to the scuba tank a separate harness has to be worn. Some dry suit divers who usually use their suit to control their buoyancy wear horsecollar jackets for back up as a precaution underwater and for surface flotation. Special horsecollar jackets are available for this purpose.

The stabilising jacket is worn like a waistcoat. Underwater a correctly weighted and balanced diver will assume a horizontal position. Being streamlined reduces the effort needed to swim. On the surface a stabilizing jacket should float the diver either vertically or tilted slightly backwards. This makes it easy to take compass bearings or to locate the shore or dive boat without working to stay upright.

The air chambers over the shoulders of most "stabs" provide more buoyancy than other jackets. This makes them particularly suitable for larger divers or those planning to use twin cylinder sets. The scuba tank or tanks attach directly to the jacket.

The Advanced Design Vest evolved from the stabilizer jacket and shares many of its benefits. ADVs provide the diver with streamlined trim underwater and float a correctly weighted and adjusted diver vertically at the surface. ADVs differ from stabilizer jackets by adding adjustable quick release shoulder straps which many divers find provide a better fit and also make donning and removing the jacket easier. Advanced Design Vests are currently the most popular style of BCD with recreational divers.

Wings are horseshoe shaped and are worn on the back where they surround the tank or tanks. They were primarily developed to overcome the dead weight of heavy twin cylinder sets while supporting the diver in a horizontal position underwater or upright with the divers face clear of the water on the surface. They are used chiefly by the Cave and Technical diving communities at present.

Wings were developed for specialised diving activities and provide mounting points for carrying extra stage and decompression gas cylinders as well as penetration reels and attachment points for propulsion units. Wings often accept an additional set of wings worn piggy-back to provide additional buoyancy or a completely independent BCD in the event of a problem occurring with the first set. More basic wing style BCDs for ordinary recreational divers are also being introduced.

As well as choosing the style of BCD that best suits your diving requirements you will want to consider the available inflation options. All jackets can be inflated orally though this feature is rarely used by modern divers.

Most are supplied with a direct feed as standard which permits convenient push button inflation from your scuba tank. This is how most divers routinely control their BCD, avoiding the complications associated with removing their regulator to blow up their jacket, especially if encumbered with cameras, lamps or other hand held or wrist mounted accessories.

A Scubapro Master Jacket Advanced Design Vest.

European jackets are sometimes fitted with or can be adapted to use small compressed air cylinders that can be refilled from your scuba tank before diving. These are usually used to provide emergency inflation if the diver's direct feed fails or more controversially as a small reserve of air that can be breathed by an out of air diver. The use of spare air sources such as octopus rigs and pony sets and concerns about the difficulty of breathing from a BCD in an emergency has seen this idea largely abandoned.

Small one shot CO_2 cylinders are another option on some jackets. These are designed to provide instant buoyancy in the event of a surface problem. The lift that they provide diminishes rapidly with increasing depth. Divers are reminded that jettisoning the weight belt is an effective way of gaining buoyancy in a emergency.

When shopping for your own BCD it helps to define exactly what you want it to do for you. A temperate water diver will want to consider jackets that provide plenty of buoyancy or lift to offset the weight needed with full wet or dry suits, taking into account the type of cylinder set he uses. Extra lift will be required to support a diver using twin cylinders. Since a properly maintained BCD will last many years it's important to plan for your future interests as well as the diving activities you enjoy today. This saves you the expense of having to replace the jacket later on to meet your changing requirements or more importantly pre-empts you making dives that you are inadequately equipped for thereby compromising both your personal safety and that of your buddies.

Warm water divers who use thin wetsuits or dive skins do not require the buoyancy provided by temperate water jackets and can use smaller, more streamlined models. They may need additional comfort features such as soft or padded backpacks to prevent the BCD chaffing unprotected skin. A jacket that folds easily and is both lightweight and compact for travelling may be important.

Women may want to look at jackets designed for the female figure. These will have a more accommodating cut and may use cross bust straps which many women divers prefer. Young divers who are still growing may prefer a jacket with adjustable harnesses that allow for changes in build or interchangeable air cells to increase buoyancy as the youngster gets heavier or moves onto larger tanks.

Some BCDs integrate a quick release weight system. These are claimed to offer greater comfort and may benefit divers whose waistline challenges ordinary weight belts. However the combined weight of jacket, tank and weights may make handling the set more difficult.

Aftersales service is an important factor. Ask questions at the dive store. You are about to make an important investment, both financially and safety wise. The dive store will want to help you to choose the BCD that is right for you. They thrive on satisfied customers who bring in repeat business and recommend the store to others.

Is the BCD manufactured by a reputable and well established company? If the jacket is marketed by an importer or distributor ask about their reputation for customer service. If you have a problem will it be solved expediently? Will spares be available for the life of your jacket. If you plan to dive overseas find out if the BCD is likely to be repairable on site in the event of a breakdown abroad.

It is often useful to talk to other divers to find out which BCDs they use and recommend. However it is the dive store personnel who will probably be your best source of advice as their position in the diving industry gives them a unique vantage point from which to evaluate products and aftersales and they will have insights unavailable outside the trade.

When you have narrowed your choice down to several suitable models you need to try them on. The sales advisor will help you choose the correct fit.

Most BCDs are available in a range of sizes. To check for comfort you should ask the sales advisor to attach a scuba tank. Try inflating the jacket to check it doesn't squeeze. Try to push the jacket upwards by the shoulder to ensure that it won't ride up. Check freedom of movement by rotating your arms and try the pockets for accessibility. Make sure that the controls and releases fall easily to hand.

There are a number of useful accessories that can increase your comfort, personal safety or prolong the life of your jacket which you may want to invest in when you buy your BCD.

Padding can make your jacket and tank more comfortable in and out of water, especially in warm locations or pools where you are not using a suit.

Some companies offer back up second stages that incorporate or mount onto the direct feed which some divers prefer over normal octopus rigs. Air horns used to indicate a divers position or call up assistance can be fitted to most BCD and are far more effective than ordinary whistles.

Disinfectants and conditioners can prolong the life of the jacket and its fittings and it is a good idea to have it thoroughly inspected by a trained service technician annually to avoid problems.

Finally, a BCD is not a crutch to support poor diving technique. It does not excuse the wearer from acquiring good diving skills. Proper training in buoyancy control is necessary. New precision buoyancy control workshops are increasingly available for divers who wish to advance their personal diving skills beyond the levels taught during entry level classes which is often the ONLY BUOYANCY CONTROL TRAINING MOST DIVERS RECEIVE.

Higher levels

Some resorts now require their clients to be trained to these higher levels before inviting them to dive on the better sites. This is done to conserve the reefs and many resorts make no charge for the additional training.

Responsible divers enhance their diving and increase their personal safety by using their Buoyancy Control Device. Relying on it to attempt to overcome weak skills is merely an abuse with little long-term chance of success.

UNDERWATER KINETICS PERFORMANCE AND STRENGTH FROM

DiveTeam

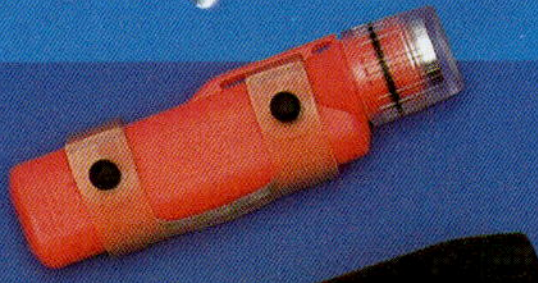

With the best selection of torches on the market, the Underwater Kinetics range includes the UK400, UK400R and UK800R. The rechargeable torches feature Nicad batteries and Halogen bulbs to give a staggering 100 watts of power!

Our hand held torches include the UKE 2AAA, Mini Q20 Lithium and Mini Q40 with hands free illumination.

SEA & SEA

Soon to be launched the SL4 and SL6 both with lanyards.

Underwater Kinetics offers a large selection of high impact, tough waterproof cases available in a variety of colours.

- From emergency grab bags to medical and camera cases. Built to take anything, because anything can happen!

SEA & SEA · THE TEAM TO DIVE WITH

SEA & SEA

DISTRIBUTORS OF QUALITY WATER SPORTS EQUIPMENT

INCLUDING

SEA & SEA

Quality water resistant cameras which enable water sport enthusiasts to take great pictures above or below the water.

SEAPEKS

Robust buoyancy compensators offer more comfort and safety features than any other jacket.

IST

A full range of quality masks, fins, snorkels, gloves and footwear in exciting styles and fashion colours.

UNDERWATER KINETICS

The go anywhere, take anything diving case, supported by a comprehensive range of underwater torches and accessories.

WENOKA SEASTYLE

A full range of top quality knives, fins and dive bags proven to be a divers friend.

DiveTeam

Complete range of diving accessories together with colour co-ordinated consoles and gauges.

AVAILABLE FROM ALL LEADING DIVE SHOPS

SEA & SEA

Trade enquiries to:

Sea & Sea Ltd., Philip House, Aspen Way, Paignton, Devon TQ4 7QR. Telephone: (0803) 663012, Fax: (0803) 663003

Keeping out the cold

by Dick Long

Dick Long is president of DUI, Inc. California, and has been a major contributor in the development of thermal protection for divers.

The risks to divers multiply as the water temperature falls but we have the technology to supply adequate thermal protection. However, as the encumberence of this equipment gets greater, the skill level required by the diver to operate the gear rises. In addition, the impact of equipment failure increases in colder water.

It is a well established fact that people work best at normal temperatures. Should the heat loss exceed heat production, the temperature of the human body will fall and with it goes strength, endurance, the sense of touch, the ability to make accurate observations and sound judgements, and detailed memory.

An adequate level of body heat equals good physical and mental powers. An inadequate level of heat results in poor performance and unreliability. Most divers lose more heat from their bodies than they generate during their dive. This is their first mistake and it can lead to others.

Whenever we place the human body in water temperatures below $93^{o}F$ ($34^{o}C$) it loses more heat to the environment than it manufactures. This is well established.

To prevent this, the amount of thermal protection required by the diver will vary with the water temperature, the exercise rate, and the structure of the diver's body. To ensure their personal safety, the diver must make sure that their body remains at operating temperature, in thermal equilibrium. In most diving situations this is rarely the case.

The onset of hypothermia, though often acknowledged and discussed, is rarely given adequate dive planning consideration. Among the problems encountered is 'unearned fatigue' the result of the lowering of the temperature in muscle and body tissues below the body's operating norm over a period of time.

This reduces the ability of the body's biochemical processes to operate at normal efficiency and by-products start to accumulate in the system. There is also an accumulation of thermal debt caused by repeated submersions in water and the reduction of the body temperature over a period of time. The body does not return to its normal temperature between dives. This is most pronounced in same day multidive operations.

There is not currently a quantitative monitoring method for easy recognition and diagnosis of this condition. Its symptoms are tiredness and a general feeling of fatigue without having done a large amount of work. A diver suffering from unearned fatigue is susceptible to a variety of illnesses.

There are adequate thermal protection systems available including a variety of wet suits and dry suits and strategies for their use. **THE BOTTOM LINE IS: IT IS JUST AS DEADLY TO RUN OUT OF HEAT AS IT IS TO RUN OUT OF AIR.**

All technical diving should be treated as cold water diving. It is common for technical divers to dive at depths over 50m and stay submerged for over one hour.

If the exercise rate (the heat production rate) is high enough, then the body temperature drop may be low enough for the diver to run out of air and/or time before their body cools to a dangerous point.

For example: If the diver feels chilled or shivers, it is reasonable to assume that he is operating at a significantly diminished capacity. Should an emergency occur at this point, the diver has less strength, endurance and mental agility to respond.

For those divers who would like to extend their time underwater or take up technical diving, the consequences are even greater. When the diver comes to his decompression stops, by the nature of the activity, he is at rest and heat production reduces dramatically - by as much as 75%. But the rate of heat loss remains constant. The diver's body loses temperature particularly in the major muscle masses and the muscle capacity decreases.

At this point, the body is not decompressing normally because the bloodflow patterns are not normal. Almost nothing is operating normally. The diver is now at much greater risk. Any diver who reaches the shivering point and stays in the water for whatever reason is at an unacceptable risk.

Both the serious recreational diver and technical diver must avoid this situation if they want acceptable safety margins.

We have the knowledge, technology and equipment to eliminate cold as a factor in most diving. All we need is training on how to apply it to the task at hand and we are working on that now.

Thermal Protection for Divers

Humans are poorly designed to operate in and underwater and so must rely on equipment to adapt them to explore inner space. The brevity of each visit is often thought of as being limited by air or bottom time for recreational divers. In fact with the advent of larger tanks, new tables, computers and the opportunity to make multi-level and repetitive dives, dive time may well run out, not because the diver is out of air or bottom time, but because he runs out of heat.

In all but the warmest waters around the globe, divers are likely to benefit from some type of suit that will provide protection from heat loss. This can range from a sport diver wearing a diveskin in the Caribbean to a saturation diver using a hot water suit in the North Sea.

The suits worn by recreational divers do not generate heat in the way that commercial suits do. They act instead to reduce or slow down heat loss. If the suit reduces heat loss sufficiently, air duration and your tables or computer will dictate the limits of your dive time. If the suit does not, you will get cold first and safe diving practices dictate that you must leave the water. How effective a dive suit will be at conserving body heat is dependant on a range of factors.

The first of these is the water temperature itself. Water absorbs heat from the divers body some 25 times faster than air. This is why on the beach still air at 21 degrees feels pleasantly warm and water at the same temperature soon feels chilly to an unprotected person.

Secondly, the activity level of the diver has a tremendous influence. A wreck diver swimming at speed to explore a large wreck will generate more heat than a macro photographer who is stationary or barely moving as he photographs tiny animals.

Thirdly, an individual's personal tolerance to the cold will vary and there are always some who are willing to tough it out.

The fourth factor is depth. Usually the deeper you go, the cooler it gets. Heat loss through respiration will also increase.

The fifth is the number of dives made in a given period. Chilling can be cumulative and once chilled it can take many hours for the body to return to its normal temperature.

The final factor is, of course, the type of thermal protection employed.

Just as the conditions people choose to dive in vary, so too does the choice of dive suit used. Not surprisingly given all the different factors that a diver may expose himself to, no single dive suit can be considered to be all purpose, it will have been designed with particular needs in mind. Suits break down into three main groups; dive skins, wetsuits and dry suits.

Dive Skins

Dive skins originated in Australia and were conceived to protect the diver against jellyfish stings rather than heat loss. They are usually made from lycra and are body hugging with excellent mobility characteristics. For people who feel the chill laminates are added to provide insulation equivalent to a 3mm wetsuit. Protection from windchill is a feature of some skins. They usually have no effect on a divers buoyancy and their insulation qualities are unchanged by depth.

Wet Suits

Wet Suits are constructed from foam neoprene rubber which contains tiny nitrogen bubbles. Warmth is retained in two ways. Firstly the neoprene provides a physical barrier between the water and the wearer which the heat has to cross. The nitrogen bubbles are a poor heat conductor and lose heat slowly. Secondly a layer of water is trapped between the suit and the diver which the diver's body warms up. Whilst the thickness and quality of the neoprene used will determine the level of heat transmission through the suit, the warm layer of water will be lost through flushing if the suit is not cut to fit closely - like a second skin.

Wetsuits are sold in a range of styles for use in most diving conditions ranging from 3mm shorties for warm water use to 8mm longjohns and jackets for temperate water enthusiasts. Semi Drys are simply wet suits that have seals added to the face, wrists and ankles to further reduce flushing.

Wet suits become less supple with thickness.

The gas in the suit means that they are quite buoyant and that with increasing depth the diver will lose both buoyancy and insulation. Most suits have a nylon finish on the outside and, when wet, windchill becomes a problem. Using a windcheater between dives will help.

Dry Suits

Dry suits completely isolate the diver from the water and can broadly be divided into suits that are designed to provide insulation in themselves and those that are designed to be worn with insulating undergarments.

Foam neoprene dry suits are made from the same material as wet suits and rely on the thickness of the neoprene barrier to reduce heat loss and on the air trapped inside to insulate the diver. As with wet suits insulation and buoyancy will decrease with depth.

The thicker the suit (usually 6-8mm) the more restrictive it is.

Membrane suits are usually made from thin rubber, pack cloth or nylon/rubber laminates and are designed to keep the wearer dry, but not warm. Undergarments made of foam rubber, polyester pile or thinsulate are worn underneath to suit the specific dive in much the same way as a person selects streetwear according to the weather.

A membrane dry suit.

The buoyancy and insulation characteristics of membrane systems is not normally affected by depth. They are usually quite baggy to allow for stretching as the materials used normally do not stretch. The flexibility of the suit is dictated by the undergarments used.

Dry suit divers may want to use a windcheater during surface intervals to reduce the effects of windchill, depending on the type of suit used.

Dry suits are fitted with inflation and deflation valves, much like a BCD, to admit and release air to prevent suit squeeze and to permit buoyancy control. Before using a dry suit training should be sought on how to use it from an instructor who is SPECIFICALLY qualified to teach dry suit diving.

For warmth a diver wears thermals and a thinsulate jumpsuit under his membrane suit.

With the right insulation it is possible for recreational divers to sport dive virtually everywhere. Indeed amateur divers operate from the Tropics to the Arctic. In the United Kingdom recreational diving is enjoyed year round, in comfort, by many enthusiasts. As in any equipment intensive adventure activity, being adequately equipped is essential and for safety, comfort and enjoyment underwater proper thermal protection is imperative.

Dive Computer Models, Algorithms

by Dr. Paul Heinmuller

Dr Paul Heinmuller was instrumental in the development of the dive computer and was a founder of Orca Industries in the United States. Orca computers are distributed in the UK and Europe by Coral Marine.

The only way to absolutely eliminate DCS from diving is not to dive in the first place. Be safe. Always add safety margins to the numbers provided by your dive computer. Don't rely on the computer to think for you. Computers don't make decisions, people make decisions based upon the information provided.

1983 saw the rise of the first commercially successful dive computers - the EDGE by ORCA and the DecoBrain by DiveTronics. Previously, other manufacturers had tried their hand at building a 'decompression meter' but the electronic technology did not exist to achieve their visions. The rise of microcomputers in the early 1980s brought lower microchip prices and power previously unavailable to the designers of 'decompression meters'.

While both the EDGE and DecoBrain were designed to monitor a diver's nitrogen loading, they each took a very different approach. The DecoBrain was a table based dive computer while the EDGE was a model based dive computer.

A table-based computer has a set of dive tables built into it and it tries to fit the dive profile onto the table. Or, in other words, it saves the user time by looking up the tables for him/her. As a rule, table based dive computers tend to be a lot more limiting (conservative) than model based computers and because they provide no benefit beyond manual use of the tables, they were unsuccessful. Only model-based dive computers currently exist in the marketplace.

There is often much confusion over the difference between a model based dive computer and a table based dive computer. Simply stated, a model based computer has an actual algorithm programmed into it. Each dive with a model based dive computer results in unique data that is generated by the data input to the algorithm. The algorithms (or models) differ from one computer manufacturer to the next, but all are based on extensive research.

Interestingly enough, algorithms are also used when generating a set of recreational tables. The algorithms used in dive computers (DCs) are usually more conservative than the algorithms which generate air tables. Divers can usually dive for longer, and more safely by following the model based dive computer since it is constantly updating the algorithm. A table based diver must consider their entire dive to be at their deepest depth.

Consider the dive shown in *figure 1 (see page 49)*. The deepest point on the dive was to 30msw, yet we can see that most of the dive was spent above 22msw. A diver using tables would have to calculate their nitrogen loading as though they had spent the entire 40 minutes of dive time at 30msw, whereas the computer diver is constantly having their nitrogen information updated.

ANALOG AQUALAND

Main features: ● Analog depth meter up to 55m in 0.1m increments (unisex type, on the left, reads depths in 1.0m increments)
● Maximum depth indicator ● Depth alarm ● Rapid ascent warning

PROMASTER

Venture Beyond Experience

For further information, please contact:
CITIZEN WATCH(U.K.)LTD. QUOIN HOUSE, FISHPONDS ROAD, WOKINGHAM BERKSHIRE, RG11 2QJ, U.K. TEL:0734-890333

Background

Nitrogen is inhaled as part of the air breathed from the SCUBA cylinder. During a descent, the nitrogen and oxygen are being breathed at a higher ambient pressure. While the oxygen is metabolised by the tissues, the nitrogen is forced into solution and absorbed by the tissues.

As the dive continues, more nitrogen is absorbed. During the ascent, the ambient pressure exerted on the diver is reduced and because of this, the partial pressure of dissolved nitrogen is greater inside the human body than outside.

Ideally, the diver would like to ascend at a rate that allows for the elimination ('out-gassing') of nitrogen without forming bubbles. Ascending too quickly or in too little time, will cause the pressure differential between the inside and the outside of the body to be too great. The nitrogen will come out of solution, form bubbles within the body and the diver will be diagnosed as having Decompression Sickness (DCS).

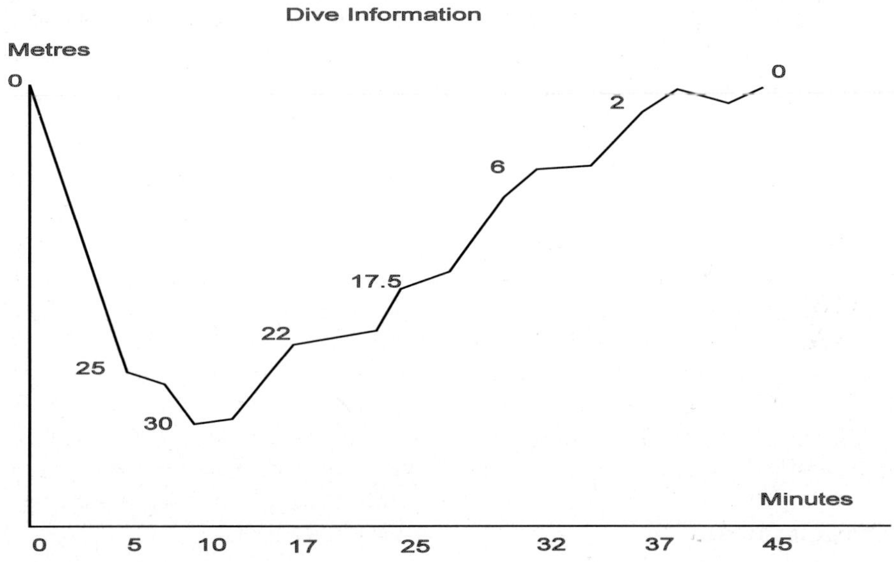

Diver : Blumenthal, Michael
Date : 28 th May 1993
Location : Cozumel, Mexico

Coordinates :
Buddy : Juan Fangio
Ait Temperature : 30C
Water Temperature : 22C

Tank Size :
Tank pressure. Start : 208 Bars End : 42 Bars
Dive Time : 40 minutes Maximum depth : 30metres

Notes :
Wall diving is rather like looking out of a lorry going past Harrods except with fish.

Even if the diver has ascended to the surface without forming any bubbles within their body, they will still have dissolved nitrogen in their tissues. If the diver wishes to make another dive within 24 hours, they must factor this 'residual nitrogen' into the equation.

If a diver stays too long at depth their tissues will absorb too much nitrogen to allow a direct ascent to the surface. If this occurs he must decompress, or reduce the ambient pressure slowly by ascending to prescribed depths that prevent the nitrogen from forming bubbles within the body.

To complicate things further, the human body does not absorb and release nitrogen uniformly. Each human being is different and each has a separate physiological and metabolic make-up that can change the way they absorb and release nitrogen daily.

The factors that influence nitrogen absorption and release include: age, gender, body fat content, hydration or dehydration, blood circulation, physical fitness, drugs, body temperature, exertion level and fatigue. To make matters more complicated, the tissues distributed throughout a human are not homogeneous either.

Dive Computer Models

Dive Computers attempt to determine nitrogen absorption and release within the human body based upon depth and time. The algorithms programmed into a computer are an attempt to model the different tissue groups within the human body.

These models divide the human body in terms of fast and slow tissues. A slow tissue is one that absorbs and releases nitrogen slowly - such as bone marrow or scar tissue. A fast tissue is one that absorbs and released nitrogen quickly, such as lung tissues and capillaries.

The ORCA model uses 12 tissue groups, with half-times from five to 480 minutes. A tissue half-time is the time it takes for a tissue group to fill or empty with nitrogen 50% of the way from the old tissue pressure to the new ambient pressure.

Tissue group No 1 has a half time of five minutes, which means that after five minutes it is 50% filled. After another five minutes (10 minutes total) it is 75% filled. After a further five minutes (15 minutes total) it is 87.5% filled . . .and so on until it reaches 98.4% (six half times), the traditional point which the tissue group is considered 100% loaded.

For the same dive, lets look at a tissue group with a half-time of 30 minutes. After 30 minutes it is 50% loaded, after 60 minutes it is 75% loaded, after 1.5 hours it is 87.5% loaded . . .etc. On the ascent, just the opposite occurs.

Keep in mind that most dive tables consider all tissues free of nitrogen after 12 hours, since the longest tissue has a 120 minute half-time. Most computers have a 480 minute tissue group that can take 48 hours to clear completely.

The Models

Most of the computers on the market are based on one of three models:

Spencer Model
Rogers Model
Swiss Model

Each breaks down the human body in terms of different tissue groups and all have their advantages and disadvantages.

The Spencer Model has the greatest amount of dive history logged against it and is the most used algorithm. It is based upon Dr Merrill Spencer's recommended no-decompression limits.

Spencer's revolutionary research using doppler technology to detect 'microbubbles' (usually the precursor to decompression sickness) within human subjects was hailed as 'far superior' to the US Navy research since it was based upon the precursor to DCS and not the ambiguous 'pain' of research divers experiencing DCS.

Computers using this model (ORCA Marathon, ORCA Phoenix and Suunto Solution) generally have more tissue compartments than the others and thus provide a greater amount of information to the model.

Pelagic computers (Oceanic DataMax, Sherwood Source, US Divers DataScan IV, Dacor Omni) use the Rogers Model. This is based upon research done by the Powell-Rogers group in their development of new recreational diving tables. It has been in use since 1988 and typically divides up the human body into 12 tissue groups.

Variations on Buhlmann's Swiss Model are typically used in European-built computers. They have, as a starting point, the ZHL-12 algorithm of A A Buhlmann. This model was originally developed for high altitude lake diving by A A Buhlmann but was later changed after reports of type 1 DCS. Subsequently, the model was adapted for dive computers built by Uwatec for distribution as US Divers Monitor, Parkway Legend, and Beuchat Aladin.

Independent adaptations are used in the Ocean Edge Computek and ScubaPro DC-11. In use, it typically uses only six tissue groups out of the complete set of 16 in the original ZHL-12 model.

Overview

In a dive computer, the diver never sees any of the models, the calculations or electronic circuitry. He only sees the numbers that are generated.

For example, the computer informs the user that the tissue group (the group that is presently controlling the dive) is 20% loaded, and they have 26 minutes remaining no decompression time (RNDT) at a certain depth. If the diver is currently at 24.5 msw and has been below the surface for a total of five minutes, the tank pressure is at 180 bar, the water temperature is 20°C, and they have 52 minutes remaining at this depth based upon the air consumption rate.

The differences between the models may appear to be few on paper, but in performance many are quite apparent. Over the years many computers and models have come and gone, based upon consumer satisfaction and dive data.

The ultimate decision of which is right depends upon you alone.

Underwater Video Equipment

by Philip Payne

If your friends do not understand your passion for diving, or should you wish to show them what it is like to swim with a Napoleon Wrasse, then perhaps you should consider taking up underwater video.

When choosing a video system for use underwater the obvious place to start is with the camcorder you wish to use. This, however, is a dangerous way of going about things as there are video housings available for very few of the camcorders on the market.

The first thing to do then, is to check with as many outlets as possible to find out which housings are available and what camcorders they hold.

You will then need to learn about the various housings offered. With regards to the depth rating, it is no good buying a housing waterproof only to 10m if your main interest is wreck diving. Similarly if you only want to snorkel with your video then there is no need for the extra weight of an aluminium housing.

A metal housing will not necessarily go deeper than a plastic housing. This is normally the case but is not a universal rule although a metal housing will almost certainly be stronger than a similar plastic case and is more likely to dent rather than to crack if if is knocked.

The material used will also affect the weight and buoyancy of the housing. If you want to take it on holiday think of that already strained baggage allowance. The buoyancy of the system will depend on the weight and the volume of the housing. A system that is too buoyant will need to be heavily weighted to make it neutral in the water.

The benefits of multipurpose housings are fairly obvious but I would recommend that you selected a housing that is specific to a single camcorder model. This will mean that all the controls are in exactly the right place so that modifications will not be necessary.

Model

A specific housing will normally be as small as possible to accommodate the relevant camcorder. This will insure that the camcorder and housing will be easier to transport and will not be unnecessarily buoyant. The most important reason for having a specific camcorder housing is that the optical system will be set up exactly for your camera and so you will get the best possible results.

Consideration should also be given to the type of front port on the housing. In general you will need a dome port for wide-angle work and a flat port for macro work. Ideally you should be able to change from one to the other depending on the type of filming you are doing though unfortunately all but the most expensive housings have only a single port available. It is possible however, to film through the wrong type of port but do expect a drop in quality.

At the other end of the housing is the viewfinder. Mostly these just allow you to look straight onto the camcorder viewfinder which will be adequate with a low volume mask. It is possible to get housings with a magnifying viewfinder or even a monitor screen but these will, almost invariably, increase the cost.

The controls on most video housings are fairly limited which is quite reasonable considering the number of other things there are to think about when diving. As a bare minimum there should be a start/stop record switch. Other controls which can be very useful are a zoom control and an on/off switch which will allow you to save battery power.

Moving down the list to less essential but still useful controls come colour balance and focus. The former will allow you to correct, to some extent, for the blueness of the light in shallow waters. The latter may take the form of either a manual focus control or a switch to allow you to turn off the camcorder's autofocus.

Consider whether you would prefer mechanical or electronic controls. Electronic controls are physically simple but if you have a problem at a dive site it can be easier to fix a mechanical control as you can see what is happening.

Another item becoming more common on video housings is the external microphone. This is a nice idea but just think about what you can hear underwater and ask yourself if it is really important for the sort of films you intend to make.

It is likely that you will have to compromise on your choice of housing as there will be no single one that meets all your requirements. Assuming you are left with a choice of two or three housings you should now consider your choice of camcorder.

The best format for domestic use is Hi8. There are several reasons for this. The tapes are small and so typically are the camcorders. It is possible to buy tapes with a running time of 90 minutes (or 180 minutes in long play). This will give you enough film for most dives. The tapes are available from any high street photographic shop. The use of Hi8 will give the best image quality available without using a professional system and the price difference over standard 8mm equipment is minimal.

The only disadvantage of using Hi8 equipment is that you cannot put the tape directly into your home VCR, but it is a simple matter to plug into a television and play the tape back directly from the video camcorder itself.

It is possible to buy batteries to power camcorders for an hour or more and at least two of these batteries should be placed high on your shopping list. You must, of course, check that your intended housing will allow you to fit these larger, high power batteries.

The lowest light level in which you can film varies from camcorder to camcorder. The figure you are interested in is the lux rating. Normal room lighting is several hundred lux and most camcorders will film in light levels below 10 lux so there is little to worry about. That said, the lower the lux rating the better.

All modern camcorders have zoom lenses with a wide-angle view of about 50°. This means that you will need to buy a wide-angle converter to double the angle of view for use in the housing. It is best to get this converter with the housing to make sure it fits. In some cases it may come with the housing.

There are numerous facilities on most camcorders that are of no particular use when filming underwater but as you may well want to use your camcorder on land as well it is worth checking these functions out. The best place to get further information is from a good shop dealing in videos. Two particularly good outlets are Tecno Retail and Jessops Photo Centres.

Regarding both camcorder and housing it is important to buy both within a fairly short space of time as video manufactures have a habit of discontinuing their lines with frightening speed. It is important then not to buy a housing for which you can no longer find the camcorder and vice versa.

Once you have your camcorder and housing you can start filming underwater, but for the best results there is one other essential item: lighting.

The lowest power lights that are practical to use are 50 Watts. Most video lights come in a range of powers from 50 to 250 Watts. It is better to buy two 50 Watt lights than one 100 Watt light for two reasons. Firstly using two lights will give you a more even spread of light than one. Secondly with two lights you will still have one working if the second one fails.

Two things to consider about the lights themselves are their charge times and the sort of bulbs they take. The quicker you can charge the lights the better so you can do as many dives as possible. It may even be possible to buy a quick charger for your lights. The bulbs for your lights should be readily available and not too expensive.

Most underwater video lights are sold with handles so that they can be used as high power diving torches but this means that you will need to buy separate arms to attach the lights to the camcorder housing.

Once you have everything together you can get into the water and start filming. As this is covered by other articles and a plethora of books I will give but one piece of advice - keep filming. The film is cheap and can be reused. A 90 minute tape should be full when you surface.

When you return home, edit your tape ruthlessly - this will make your film as interesting as possible.

When you have finished you may not have a box office hit but you should have something that will make your friends gasp and help them to understand your passion for diving.

by B. Hugo

Alternate Air Sources

by Simon Potter

Simon Potter is a PADI Master Instructor and Dive Director of midlands based "The Diving Initiative" . He began diving with Plymouth Polytechnic in the 1970's, qualified as an instructor in 1984 and has worked in that capacity in the UK, Cyprus and Egypt. He is actively involved in the linking of National Vocational Qualifications to PADI Instructor Development Courses.

Most divers would agree that running out of or low on air should never happen. Until recently training has emphasised the technique of buddy breathing. The skill of sharing one regulator however is one which requires good training and regular practice to maintain efficiency and low anxiety levels and in reality few people either relish or cope with buddy breathing under stress. This is where an alternate air source can make the difference between an unfortunate experience and a serious incident. Authorities now agree that alternate air sources should be part of standard equipment. They can be divided into two groups: those that require assistance from another diver and those that are independent of a buddy.

THE OCTOPUS RIG

This is probably the most common device currently employed by recreational divers. The Octopus Rig is a spare second stage attached to the first stage by a slightly longer than normal low pressure hose. There are several benefits to this system. They are inexpensive, their use is easily understood and training is simple. To reduce problems the hose should be marked with either a colourful plastic wrap or electrical tape for easy identification and attached to the front of the BCD by a quick release clip for instant access. The down side of the Octopus Rig is that divers are dependent upon their buddy for help. Divers need to be close enough underwater at all times to reach each other in an emergency and procedures need to be discussed during the buddy check. Some regulators may even fail in extreme conditions with the high air flow rates demanded in anxious moments.

THE ADAPTED BCD CONTROL

Several forms of this device are currently available on the market and include the Scubapro Air II, the Apeks Octaplus and AP valves Autoair as well as several others. The device doubles as the BCD inflator/deflator and as a regulator. A similar system is employed by Sherwood and Mares whereby the BCD controls are standard but there is a regulator attached to the hose feeding the low pressure inflator. In the event of an emergency the donor needs to offer the regulator from his own mouth to the air casualty and take control of the alternate air source for himself. The advantages are that the number of hoses are reduced and the system is inexpensive. Disadvantages are that to facilitate the system there is a point during the exchange at which neither diver has an air supply and, unless the donated regulator is attached to a long hose, its use can be a little uncomfortable.

PONY CYLINDER

This system utilises an entirely separate scuba system commonly comprising of a 2L or 3L cylinder complete with its own regulator. The pony cylinder is then attached to the diver's primary cylinder. A distinct advantage is that air can be supplied to either diver from the pony cylinder at a moments notice. The supply is of a known amount which may even allow stops to be conducted on the ascent. This is a system well worth considering if you are contemplating dives where buddy separation is a risk. Again there are a few disadvantages to weigh up. A larger investment in equipment is necessary and this carries an increased annual service bill. The system is bulky, weighs more, and the weight is unevenly distributed.

BIFURCATED SCUBA SYSTEM

This system is probably nearest to an ideal. The diver actually wears two separate cylinders and regulators. The amount of air available is usually ample, is of a known quantity and available to anyone low on air. Because the cylinders are of equal size the wearer is now balanced in the water and on land, although at the cost of a lot more weight. A further advantage is that buoyancy can be provided to the diver via either cylinder. Often the diver will have a low pressure feed to the dry suit from one regulator and the BCD fed from the other. The Bifurcated System is the most expensive option. It can cost little more than a pony cylinder if all the expenses are taken into account although it is the heaviest alternate air source available. This system allows easy access to air by any diver and well worth consideration if planning dives such as wreck penetration which again have a high risk of buddy separation.

SPARE AIR

Spare Air is a unique lightweight device comprising of a neat, small regulator attached to a small aluminium cylinder. It can be filled from the divers primary cylinder or directly off a compressor. Should a diver or buddy need it, it can be pulled quickly from its elastic holster and breathed from in an instant. It has some of the advantages of the pony cylinder and bifurcated scuba systems without the bulk though the volume of air it contains is very limited but is arguably sufficient to get someone out of trouble in an emergency.

RESERVE MECHANISM

This is simply a tank valve which has a pressure sensing device to indicate when air pressure is low. The diver must set the device before diving and accesses his reserve air by a pull rod. There are several problems inherent in a device of this kind and reserves have become virtually extinct in sports diving.

There are many configurations of alternate air sources to consider and one diver's preference will not necessarily be another's choice. The diver has to make a selection based upon his diving requirements, budget and conscience. Which ever style is adopted it is good practice to ensure that the alternate air source is clearly marked for easy identification, the regulator secured by a quick release clip and in clear view to facilitate immediate access. In order to reduce confusion it is also imperative during the pre-dive buddy check to discuss its use in the event of an emergency. Good quality training, continuous practice and awareness should ensure that a diver need never run out of air. However even during the best planned dives things can go wrong and in this situation you may well consider your alternate air source one of your wiser investments.

Inspectorate for Diving Equipment Servicing & Testing (IDEST)

by Mike Todd

Mike Todd, C-Eng, B-Met, MIE-E, is chairman of IDEST and may be contacted for further details (full addresses, telephone numbers, names etc) on (0689) 826820.

From time to time, cylinder tests produce a strange result. Very rarely, thankfully, is there a cylinder explosion and injury to a diver/compressor operator when an "in test" cylinder fails. The words "in test' are deliberately in quotes because it has often been difficult to determine just how or when the test had been carried out.

In several cases that have been recorded, the cylinders had, according to the test house, been properly tested. In two such instances however, this was subsequently found not to be the case and the test house concerned was successfully prosecuted. So, just how should a diving cylinder be tested? How can a diver be sure that his/her diving cylinder has been properly tested?

All UK diving organisations recommend that cylinders should be tested to BS5430. This calls for a visual inspection every two years. The external and internal surfaces of the cylinder are checked for flaws/damage and the threads of the cylinder and its valve checked for form and wear.

Every four years, the cylinder should be subjected to a visual inspection and a hydraulic test. The latter usually consists of filling the cylinder with water and then pressurising it to its test pressure, measuring any permanent expansion that might occur. There should be none, but up to 5% is permitted by the specification to allow for inaccuracies in the test equipment.

BS5430 also requires test houses to be equipped to a specified minimum standard - BCGA CPI 1 - and that the test should be carried out by "competent personnel".

A watchdog or independent inspection authority would be able to check test houses, their equipment and their personnel and issue a Certificate of Approval. This would assure the diver that a particular test house can, and does, test cylinders to BS5430.

In 1985, the Inspectorate for Diving Equipment Servicing and Testing (IDEST) was set up. The organisation set its sights on cylinder testing as the first objective and intends, eventually, to also take on board other important safety aspects - regulator servicing, supply of pure air, etc.

The aims of IDEST are to:

- set standards for servicing and testing.
- provide inspection of premises, equipment and personnel.
- grant approval to those meeting the required standards.
- maintain a register of Approved Test Houses
- provide training to produce "competent personnel".
- provide advice for Approved Test Houses.
- produce publicity about IDEST and Approved Test Houses.

IDEST currently enjoys the support of the UK diving agencies, the diving trade (DTA - Diving Trades Association) and the Society for Underwater Technology (SUT) as well as UK cylinder manufacturers and distributors.

Another important consideration is that IDEST is completely independent. No-one carrying out inspections, giving approvals or making decisions is actually employed in the diving industry, either as a tester, servicer or supplier.

There are currently 42 IDEST Approved Test Houses for testing diving cylinders to BS5430 and several others are awaiting Inspection/Approval. The BSAC, in its publications, actually recommends its members to use only IDEST Approved Test Houses!

The benefits generated by IDEST should be that the diver will know that his expensive equipment is being serviced and tested to a uniform, accepted high standard.

The test house receives confirmation that work, equipment and personnel are of the correct standard, gains "consensus" opinions on difficult cases and gets publicity for the high standards being employed. Manufacturers and distributors benefit from knowing that their equipment is getting the correct service.

IDEST REGISTER OF APPROVED TEST HOUSES

1A - THE DIVING LOCKER, Chiswick, London.

1B - S E DIVING SUPPLIES, Gillingham, Kent.

1C - KENT DIVING & WATERSPORT SUPPLIES, Orpington.

1D - AIR TESTING SERVICES, Orpington.

1E - STONEY COVE MARINE TRIALS, Stoney Stanton, Leics.

1G - LIFE SUPPORT ENGINEERING, Storrington, W. Sussex.

1H - ROBIN HOOD WATERSPORTS, Heckmondwike, W. Yorks.

1J - HULL SCUBA CENTRE, Hull.

1K - SAFETY AIR SERVICES, Woolton, Liverpool.

1M - EDINBURGH DIVING CENTRE, Edinburgh.

1N - G SQUARED ENGINEERING, Burgess Hill, Sussex.

1P - LUXFER RETEST, Colwick, Nottingham.

1Q - GILDENBURGH WATER, Whittlesey, Peterborough.

1R - SEAWAYS, Falmouth, Cornwall.

1S - AIR SERVICES, Maidstone, Kent.

1T - NEW HAW AQUARIA, Weybridge, Surrey

1U - DIVERS AIR, Holt, Clwyd.

1V - SCUBA WORLD WATERSPORTS, Collumpton, Devon.

1W - UPPERFIELD MARINE & DIVING, Rotherham, S. Yorks.

1X - MIDLAND DIVING EQUIPMENT, Leicester.

1Y - KENMORE TECHNICAL SERVICES, Newcastle on Tyne.

2A - SCEPTRE WATERSPORTS CENTRE, Lincoln.

2B - SOUTHERN CYLINDER SERVICES, Foreham, Hants.

2C - T H DIVING SERVICES, Hooe, Plymouth.

2D - DIVE FORCE MARINE, Cheapside, London.

2E - WIRRAL SPORTS & LEISURE, Merseyside.

2G - DIVELINE, Ipswich.

2H - SOLENT DIVERS, Portsmouth, Hants.

2J - REMAR SAFETY SERVICES, Caerphilly, Mid.Glam.

2K - PUFFIN AIR SERVICES, Cold Norton, Essex.

2L - DEEP DIVE DIVING SERVICES, Luton, Herts.

2M - SCUBA TECH (WATERSPORTS), Lancaster.

2N - LANDEX LTD, Radstock, Bath.

2P - PETER'S LTD, Bristol.

2Q - MIDLAND AQUA SUPPLIES, Birmingham.

2R - DIVING SERVICES (ANGLESEY), Anglesey.

2S - WALSALL DIVING SERVICES, Walsall, W. Midlands.

2T - RUNNYMEDE DIVE SERVICES, Egham, Surrey.

2V - G & H DIVING SERVICES, Feltham, Middx.

2W - YEADON HYDRAULICS, Yeadon, West Yorks.

2X - SLATERS AQUA SPORTS, Preston, Lancs.

2Y - CORMETON FIRE PROTECTION, Whitley Bay.

Minute Finder

Minute Finder charts can provide a simple solution to an important problem.

Removing the complexity of air calculation for the new diver and designed as a handy 'look up' table for the more experienced, the charts show minutes of air available, in accordance with pressure gauge reading and anticipated depth.

Cylinder specific, the charts are available for 10, 12 and 15 Ltr. cylinder sizes. Based on a 25 Ltr. per minute surface breathing rate, (the generally accepted figure for air calculation) the charts show total minutes minus any seconds, for clarity and safety.

In view of the fact that the charts will be subjected to the normal brutalities of the divers world, each chart has been produced on a flexible pvc plate, 480 microns thick and printed both sides, with anti-saline/solvent resistant PY inks (polymer bound to the facia).

Designed as a surface aid to dive planning, a chart measures 150mm by 122mm and fits easily into the divers stab/ABLJ pocket.

Developed to reduce the risk of mis-calculation, the chart is easy to use and it can take less than 30 seconds to plan your air requirements, for a square profile dive.

Using the correct chart for your cylinder, look under the corresponding BAR pressure to find minutes available, at chosen depth, from this you simply allow for reserve (suggested 50 BAR minimum, indicated in RED on the chart), ascent times and any decompression stop times.

Multi-level dives are just as easy to plan, using a series of addition in BAR. For second dives at shallower depths, decompression requirements and reserve permitting, the chart allows optimum use of cylinder capacity.

Following requests from instructors of various diving persuasions the charts have been produced in an acetate format, for over-head projection use. Instructors can now build their own lectures around the chart, as it visually displays the relationships between breathing rates, ambient pressure and cylinder parameters to the new diver. As one instructor commented "anything that makes air calculation simpler, can only be good!"

Four-wheel drive Discovery

The Land Rover range has been extensively developed in recent years, with the result that the marque currently sets the standard in all three sectors of the four wheel drive vehicle market.

With the introduction of new engines, improved transmission, suspension and interiors and major exterior revisions, the Defender is now the ultimate working/utility vehicle.

In the personal transport and leisure vehicle sector, the Discovery has won many awards for both its design and off road capability.

After more than 22 years the Range Rover remains virtually unchallenged in the luxury sector.

Production of the original Land Rover started in 1948 and since then 1.8 million vehicles have been produced. It is estimated that more than two thirds are still running.

The Solihull-based company is the only dedicated four wheel drive vehicle manufacturer in the world, with sales of 55,000 annually. Exports account for 70 per cent of production.

DEFENDER

The Defender was launched at the beginning of 1991 and is based on the Land Rover 90 and 110 range.

The four wheel drive Defender is known throughout the world as a tough workhorse able to venture into areas impassable to other vehicles.

The Defender is available in 90 and 110in wheelbase form with a choice of body styles: hard top; soft top; station wagon and pick up.

Whatever type of working vehicle a customer requires a Defender model will provide the answer, whether it is for carrying bales of hay around a farm or for taking a group of 10 people on an outward bound course.

Many customers specify the 200 Tdi engine which produces 107bhp and 188 lbft of torque at a very low 1800 rpm making this engine ideal for off road and towing work.

Some models, with the powerful V8 3.5 litre petrol engine with 134bhp and 187 lbft torque, are available, while predecessors of these engines - 2.5 litre petrol and the naturally aspirated diesel can still be ordered via the factory.

Land Rover places great importance on its range of Defender optional equipment and accessories to ensure that customers can tailor their vehicles to their exact requirements.

DISCOVERY

The Discovery is available as a three or five door model fitted with a 111bhp, 195 lbft of torque version of the 200 Tdi engine and two fuel injected petrol units - a 2 litre and a 3.5 litre V8.

Land Rover 'Discovery'.

Like the Defender, all models use a permanent four wheel drive system, simple to use high and low ratio gearbox and differential lock.

Suspension is engineered to allow maximum axle articulation ensuring that the Discovery lives up to Land Rover's off road pedigree.

The interior has unusual features such as storage pockets in the roof lining above the rear seating area and fascia mounted radio controls. A raised roof line provides spacious headroom and luggage capacity.

The 1993 line-up sees improvements including a sophisticated security system fitted to all Discoverys. A catalyst also comes as standard equipment on petrol variants.

A four speed automatic transmission option on models fitted with the V8 petrol engine has been introduced. Other options include rear air conditioning; higher levels of in-car entertainment; and the Freestyle Choice package which includes wider section tyres, specially designed alloy wheels and anti-roll bars front and rear.

The five door models are fitted with items such as electric windows, alloy wheels, central locking and two additional rear passenger seats.

RANGE ROVER

In the 22 years since the Range Rover was launched it has become a classic, due to its design and Land Rover's policy of continual improvement. It remains virtually

Range Rover.

unchallenged at the luxurious end of the four wheel drive market.

During the past five years, an extensive development programme has seen changes in all areas. The new Range Rover Vogue LSE went on sale in autumn '92. Its 108in wheelbase and auto transmission, provides a smoother, quieter and more refined on-road ride.

The vehicle's off-road capabilities are also improved by a combination of the new 200bhp 250lbft torque 4.2 litre V8 engine, electronic air suspension (EAS), and a new electronic traction control system.

EAS has five height settings spanning a range of 130mm. They are Access Mode, which makes getting in and out of the vehicle easier; Low Profile, for cruising over 50mph; Standard, for normal road use; High Profile for off-road and wading; and extended profile to regain traction when the bottom of the vehicle is grounded.

The Range Rover Vogue SE is also fitted with EAS and electronic traction control as standard, and all other petrol Range Rovers are fitted with a high compression version of the 3.9 litre V8 catalyst engine.

In addition to the two V8 fuel injected engines, the Range Rover is also sold with Land Rover's own 200 Tdi turbocharged diesel engine.

In November 1992 a standard Range Rover Tdi was driven 832 miles from John O'Groats to Lands End and was officially recorded as returning 53mpg.

This gives a potential range of more than 920 miles without having to refuel The 200 Tdi engine provides Range Rover Tdi with 111bhp, improved refinement and driveability and a top speed of more than 94mph.

On the Vogue LSE and SE models cruise control, anti-lock braking, leather upholstery, heated front seats, electric sunroof, colour-keyed alloy wheels and air conditioning represent just some of the equipment fitted as standard.

Land Rover 'Discovery'.

Buying equipment for you and your boat

by Jason MacIntosh

Jason MacIntosh, 22 years of age, is a specialist in marine electronics. A sailor since he was 10, Jason is an RYA qualified Day Skipper and is manager of Tolley Marine's Ocean Leisure branch in London.

In the past decade the marine electronics market has grown at incredible pace. As a result of this growth it has become increasingly accessible to the leisure market. The cost of equipment has come down dramatically and reliability has improved.

I would like to describe to you, the customer, the three main products need to dive safely and efficiently from boats - Navigators, Fishfinders and VHF radios.

There are three main types of navigation systems. Loran-C, which is not available in this country; Decca, the traditional system in the United Kingdom and GPS (Global Positioning System) which is a worldwide navigation system. GPS has only been on the open market for the past three or four years is the subject of a great deal of conversation. The vast number of makes and models available for all of these systems can make choosing the right one for you and your boat a difficult task.

Selecting only those units which are waterproof soon brings down the numbers. You will also need a system that is easy to use and understand. The main categories of information you will require are longitude, latitude, speed of ground (SOG), course over ground (COG), range (RNG), bearing (BRG), cross track error (XTE) and estimated time of arrival (ETA) as well as a memory for storing a number of waypoints. Most units give you all this information graphically but some display it numerically. Your choice is a matter of personal preference.

The best way to choose a Decca or GPS is to make a checklist of your requirements:

1. Is the unit Waterproof?
2. Can you interface to other equipment?
3. Is it easy to use and understand?
4. Is the display clear?
5. Is it easy to install onto your boat?

A Lowrance GPS consul.

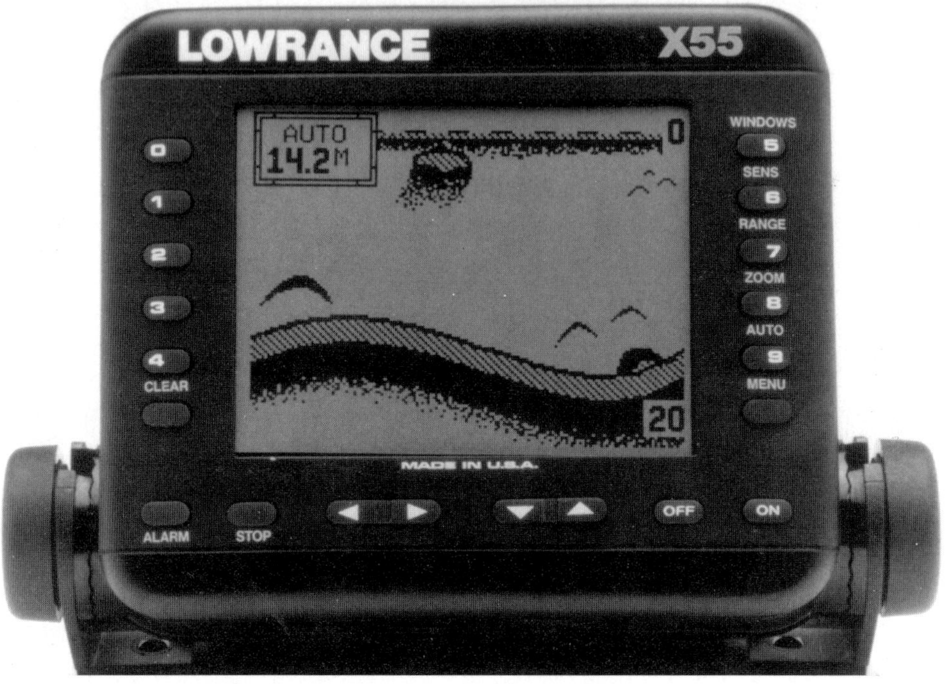

A Lowrance X55 fishfinder

The cost of Decca and GPS systems vary considerably. This is normally a result of the information that it gives you. Prices start at present from about £265 to £550 for Decca while GPS units range from about £600 to over £2000.

Fishfinders are very useful pieces of equipment to have on a diveboat. Not only do they tell you the depth of the water you are in, they also give you a good idea of the nature of the sea bed you are over.

When choosing a fishfinder you must consider the situation you will be in when using it, the information that you require from it and how these details will be displayed. All makes of fishfinders will tell you how many vertical pixels make up the display. This will give you a very good idea of the quality of picture. 60 pixels renders a very blocky picture and you will find it very difficult to pick out any real detail. 100 pixels plus will give you a clear picture and you will be able to discern all the contours of the sea bed.

An important feature to look for on a fishfinder is Grayline. Grayline shows you the type of seabed you are on - whether it be silt, mud or rock. This works by measuring the strength of the return signal from the transducer. If it hits rock the signal is very strong on return. If it hits silt or mud the return signal is relatively weaker because it has penetrated the softer bottom. Zoom is another good option to have. As you might expect, zoom enlarges the picture displayed on the screen which can prove very useful over a divesite as you will be able to see a lot more bottom detail. The best units to buy are those with both a x2 zoom and x4 zoom.

Once again it is always best to make a checklist of the features you are looking for.

1. Always make sure the unit is waterproof.
2. How many vertical pixels does it have?
3. Does it have grayline?
4. Check that it has a good zoom.

Prices of fishfinders varies from a basic unit at about £180 to a more advanced one at around £700.

V.H.F radios are also very important to have onboard as you will need to communicate with other boats or a land base and may also need to radio for assistance in an emergency. There are two common types of VHF radio; the handheld portable unit and the fixed station unit. Handhelds are useful for coastal waters as they are easy to carry from boat to boat. However, they do have a limited range; normally around six miles on a good day with no land or hills in the way, though in bad conditions it may only reach two or three miles. Remember also that a portable relies on batteries and must be used sparingly.

Fixed stations run off the boat's batteries and you can normally use them more liberally. Their range is a considerably greater too, normally 15-20 miles on high power. You should look for a set with 55 international channels, dual watch and channel 16 override. Make sure that the set has passed the appropriate UK type approval tests and that you apply to the Radiocommunications Agency for a licence.

There are three categories of licence:

The Ship Radio Licence allows the installation or use of all maritime radio equipment including MF, HF, VHF, satellite communications equipment (Ship Earth Stations), radar, low powered on board communications and emergency position indicating radio beacons (EPIRBS) for use on international maritime frequencies.

The Ship Radio (VHF) Licence allows the installation or use of VHF maritime radio on the international VHF maritime frequencies on board a particular vessel. It also covers radar and EPIRBS.

The Ship Radio (Transportable) Licence allows the use of particular VHF maritime radio on the international maritime frequencies on DIFFERENT vessels.

Always make a checklist of what you need from the set.

1. Is it waterproof?
2. Has it all 55 channels?
3. Is it approved to British standards?
4. Is it easy to use (remember that in an emergency someone who has never used one before may have to operate it).

Prices for handhelds currently start at around £150 for a basic set with waterproof sets costing around £450. Fixed units range from about £150 to £400.

For product key codes see reference page 347

Equipment Manufacturers and Distributors

ADVANCED DIVING PRODUCTS
TINDLE ENTERPRISE CENTRE
1-3 PETERSFIELD ROAD, WHITE HILL,
HANTS GU35 9AR
0420 479606 FAX: 0420 475500

BASIC: BD
SPECIAL PRODUCTS: DECO BOY

AP VALVES
WATER MA TROUT INDUSTRIAL EST
HELSTON, CORNWALL TR13 OLW
0326 561040 FAX: 0326 573605

BASIC: BCD, BD, ACC
AIR SOURCE: AA, TNK
INSTRUMENTATION: CSL
OTHER PRODUCTS: TANK & DRY SUIT VALVES
SPECIAL PRODUCTS: BUDDY JACKETS

APEKS MARINE LTD
UNIT 4, WATERY LANE INDUSTRIAL ESTATE, DARWEN, LANCASHIRE BB3 2EB
0254 873655 FAX: 0254 773919

AIR SOURCE: REG, AA
OTHER PRODUCTS: TANK & DRY SUIT VALVES

APOLLO SPORTS CO., LTD
905 SHAKE
EBINA CITY, KANAGAWA, JAPAN 243-04
010 81 462 334111
FAX: 010 81 462 335886

BASIC: BCD, MFS, LT, BD, ACC
AIR SOURCE: REG, AA, TNK
INSTRUMENTATION: CSL, WCH
CLOTHING: WET, DRY, BTS, GLV
SPECIAL PRODUCTS: DIVER PROPULSION VEHICLES
DISTRIBUTED BY OCEAN LEISURE

APOLLO SPORTS CO.,LTD
KOWA COMPANY LTD
NO 4-14, 3 CHOME,
NIHONBASHI-HONCHO, CHUO-KU
TOKYO, JAPAN 103
010 81 3 32797241
FAX: 010 81 3 32425856

EXCLUSIVE EUROPEAN DISTRIBUTOR

AQUA-LUNG LTD
57 SPARKENHOE STREET
LEICESTER, LEICESTERSHIRE LE2 OTD
0533 514200 FAX: 0533 511161

DISTRIBUTES: SEA QUEST, SPIRO, US DIVERS, TECHNISUB, FENZY, NIHON

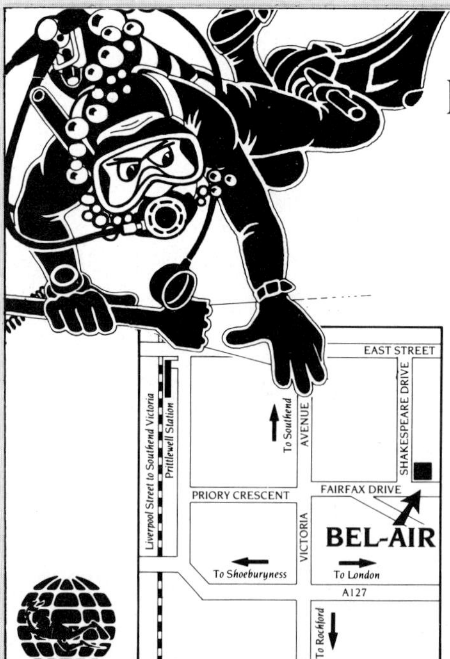

AQUARIUS SPORTS LTD
24 BROWNLOW SHOPPING CENTRE
BROWNLOW WAY, BOLTON, MANCHESTER
BL1 3UR
0204 365120 FAX: 0204 365120

CLOTHING: DRY, SEMI, GLV

AVON TECHNICAL PRODUCTS DIVISION
BATH ROAD
MELKSHAM, WILTSHIRE SN12 8AA
0225 791823 FAX: 0225 705585

CLOTHING: DRY, GLV

BEAVER SPORTS (YORKS) LTD
FLINT STREET
FARTOWN, HUDDERSFIELD, WEST
YORKSHIRE HD1 6LG
0484 512354 FAX: 0484 434995

CLOTHING: WET, SEMI, DRY, BTS, GLV

BEL-AIR SUB AQUA SUPPLIES
82 FAIRFAX DRIVE
WESTCLIFF-ON-SEA
ESSEX SS0 9AF
0702 353205

BEUCHAT SUB INTERNATIONAL
4 AVENUE BOIS BAUDRAN
13015 MARSEILLE, FRANCE
010 33 91 607070
FAX: 010 33 91 600694

BASIC: BCD, MFS, LT, BD, ACC
AIR SOURCE: REG, AA, TNK
INSTRUMENTATION: CSL
CLOTHING: WET, SEMI, BTS, GLV
OTHER PRODUCTS: SPEAR FISHING EQUIPMENT
NO UK DISTRIBUTORS

BF AQUASPORT
19 MAPLE WAY
EARL SHILTON, LEICESTER,
LEICESTERSHIRE LE9 7HW
0455 846505 FAX: 0455 848094

CLOTHING: WET, DRY, CTM, GLV

BIRCHLEY PRODUCTS
7 BUSH HAY
CHURCHDOWN, GLOUCESTER,
GLOUCESTERSHIRE GL3 2QR
0452 855312 FAX: 0452 855312

BASIC: LT, BD, ACC
OTHER PRODUCTS: TANK TESTING EQUIPMENT

BLANDFORD SUB-AQUA
BLANDFORD HOUSE
UNIT 7
MILL HILL INDUSTRIAL ESTATE
FLOWER LANE,
MILL HILL
LONDON NW7 2HU
081 9596013 FAX: 081 9593001

BASIC: MFS, ACC
INSTRUMENTATION: WCH
CLOTHING: BTS, GLV
DISTRIBUTES: MARES, SUUNTO, PELICAN CASES

BLUE WATER TECHNOLOGY
24 POLAND STREET
LONDON W1V 3DD
071 7348152 FAX: 071 4343799

SPECIAL PRODUCTS: PERSPEX SCREEN GUARDS FOR ALADIN DIVE COMPUTERS

BOUYANCY TRAINING SYSTEMS
236 SW 171ST STREET
SEATTLE,
WA 98166 USA
010 1 206 2412634
FAX: 010 1 206 2418051

SPECIAL PRODUCTS: PRECISION BOUYANCY TRAINING SYSTEMS
NO UK DISTRIBUTORS

BOWSTONE DIVING PRODUCTS
BELPER ROAD
HEATON MERSEY INDUSTRIAL ESTATE
STOCKPORT,
CHESHIRE SK4 3QP
061 4420272 FAX: 061 4431508

BASIC: BD, ACC
CLOTHING: THM, OUT

BUDDY SYSTEM KNIFE
CHARLES CLIFFORD & ASSOC.
6610 SNIDER PLAZA
DALLAS, TX 75205 USA
010 1 214 3738722

BASIC: ACC
SPECIAL PRODUCTS: BUDDY SAFETY KNIVES
NO UK DISTRIBUTORS

CASIO WATCHES
UNIT 6
1000 NORTH CIRCULAR ROAD
LONDON NW2 7JQ
081 4509131 FAX: 081 4526323

INSTRUMENTATION: WCH

CAVALERO
DIVISION DE MAREQUIPEMENT SA
BOULEVARD DEL LA GARE
13821 LA PENNE SUR HUVEAUNE
FRANCE
010 33 91 361000 FAX: 010 33 91 248276

BASIC: BCD, MFS, LT, BD, ACC
AIR SOURCE: REG, AA, TNK
INSTRUMENTATION: CSL
CLOTHING: WET,SEMI, BTS, GLV
OTHER PRODUCTS: SPEAR FISHING EQUIPMENT
DISTRIBUTED BY SOLENT DIVERS

CIRCLE ONE
MARSH LANE
LORDS MEADOW INDUSTRIAL
ESTATECREDITON, DEVON EX17 1ES
0363 773005 FAX: 0363 774289

CLOTHING: WET, SEMI, GLV

CITIZEN WATCH (UK) LTD
QUION HOUSE
FISHPONDS ROAD,
WOKINGHAMBERKSHIRE RG11 2QJ
0734 890333 FAX: 0734 890536

INSTRUMENTATION: WCH

CORAL MARINE
BROADWAY HOUSE
21 BROADWAY, MAIDENHEAD
BERKS SL6 1JK
0628 810654 FAX: 0628 810669

BASIC: BD, ACC
CLOTHING: GLV
DISTRIBUTES: ORCA COMPUTERS, SCUBA TOOL, BOOKS ON DIVING

CRESSI-SUB S.p.A.
VIA G ADAMALI
501-I-16165, GENOA, ITALY
010 39 10 8301315
FAX: 010 39 10 804743

BASIC: BCD, MFS, LT, BD, ACC
AIR SOURCE: REG, AA, TNK
INSTRUMENTATION: CSL
CLOTHING: WET, SEMI, OUT, BTS, GLV
OTHER PRODUCTS: SPEAR FISHING EQUIPMENT
DISTRIBUTED BY INTERNATIONAL DIVING & WATERSPORTS

D2 (MARINE) LTD
UNIT 15A
BALMAKEITH INDUSTRIAL ESTATE, NAIRN
GRAMPIAN IV12 5QW
0667 54882 FAX: 0667 54873

CLOTHING: WET, SEMI, OUT, CTM, BTS, GLV

DACOR CORPORATION
161 NORTHFIELD ROAD
NORTHFIELD, IL 60093 USA
010 1 708 4469555
FAX: 010 1 708 4467545

BASIC: BCD, MFS, LT, BD, ACC
AIR SOURCE: REG, AA, TNK
INSTRUMENTATION: CSL, CMP
CLOTHING: WET, SEMI, BTS, GLV
DISTRIBUTED BY HYDROTECH

DARLINGTON FABRICS CORPORATION
1359 BROADWAY
NEW YORK, NY 10018 USA
010 1 212 2797733
FAX: 010 1 212 5645325

PRODUCTS: MANUFACTURERS OF DARLEXX FABRIC

DIAMOND WETSUITS LIMITED
NORTHOLT DRIVE
BOLTON, MANCHESTER BL3 6RE
0204 28225 FAX: 0204 361549

CLOTHING: WET, SEMI, DRY, SKN, BTS, GLV

DIVE LINE LTD
ST JOHNS WORKS
ST JOHNS ROAD, IPSWICH, SUFFOLK IP4 5DQ
0473 715533 FAX: 0473 271815

SPECIAL PRODUCTS: SCREEN GUARDS FOR DIVE COMPUTERS

DIVE RITE MANUFACTURING
PO BOX 498
LONDON SW19 6BX
081 7890961 FAX: 081 7802018

DISTRIBUTES: DIVE RITE

DIVE RITE MFG. INC
ROUTE 14 BOX 136
LAKE CITY, FL 32055 USA
010 1 904 7521087
FAX: 010 1 904 7550613

BASIC: BCD, LT, ACC
INSTRUMENTATION: CMP
OTHER PRODUCTS: FILL STATION ACCESSORIES
SPECIAL PRODUCTS: TECHNICAL DIVING EQUIPMENT
DISTRIBUTED BY DIVE RITE, UK

DIVE SKINS (OZTEX INC)
15455 NW GREENBRIAR PARKWAY
210, BEAVERTON, OR 97006 USA
010 1 503 6455146
FAX: 010 1 503 6455276

CLOTHING: SKN
NO UK DISTRIBUTORS

DIVING & RESCUE SUPPLIES LTD
PARKGATE BUSINESS PARK
UNIT B2, RAIL MILL WAY
ROTHERHAM, YORKSHIRE S62 6JQ
0709 780666 FAX: 0709 780550

BASIC: BD, ACC
CLOTHING: DRY, THM
DISTRIBUTES: TUSA, AQUION

DIVING UNLIMITED INTERNATIONAL
UNIT 7
WELLSHEAD CRESCENT, DYCE
ABERDEEN, GRAMPIAN AB2 0GA
0224 724093 FAX: 0224 725335

DISTRIBUTES: DUI, ZEAGLE

DIVING UNLIMITED INTERNATIONAL
1148 DELEVAN DRIVE
SAN DEIGO, CA 92102-2400 USA
010 1 619 2361203
FAX: 010 1 619 2370378

BASIC: ACC
CLOTHING: DRY, THM, GLV
OTHER PRODUCTS: COMMERCIAL DIVING SUITS
DISTRIBUTED BY DUI, UK

DMS WATERWARE
TONEDALE INDUSTRIAL ESTATE
WELLINGTON, SOMERSET TA21 0AN
0823 662918 FAX: 0823 662394

CLOTHING: DRY, GLV
OTHER PRODUCTS: INFLATION VALVES, HOSES

DREAM MARINE LTD
UNIT 1
6-10 CONVENT STREET
NOTTINGHAM
NOTTINGHAMSHIRE NG1 3LL
0602 506622 FAX: 0602 418925

CLOTHING: WET, SEMI, DRY, BTS, GLV

ELLESSE WATCHES
STELUX HOUSE
BIRD STREET, LITCHFIELD
STAFFORDSHIRE WS13 6PW
0543 414211 FAX: 0543 258233

INSTRUMENTATION: WCH

FORCE FINS
28 ANACAPA STREET
SANTA BARBARA, CA 93101 USA
010 1 805 9669628
FAX: 010 1 805 5648240

BASIC: MFS
NO UK DISTRIBUTORS

GREENAWAY MARINE
BROAD HINTON
SWINDON, WILTSHIRE SN4 9PA
0793 731666 FAX: 0793 731644

BASIC: ACC
SPECIAL PRODUCTS: UNDERWATER COMMUNICATION SYSTEM

GRYPHON DRYSUITS
UNIT 49
KETLEY BUSINESS PARK, TELFORD
SHROPSHIRE TF1 4JD
0952 253664 FAX: 0952 253664

CLOTHING: DRY

GUL INTERNATIONAL
WALKER LINES INDUSTRIAL ESTATE
BODMIN, CORNWALL PL31 1EZ
0208 72382 FAX: 0208 75218

CLOTHING: WET, SEMI, CTM, BTS, GLV

GYBE
10 WATERLOO COURT
WATERLOO ROAD
STALYBRIDGE
CHESHIRE SK15 2AU
061 3048471 FAX: 061 3048471

CLOTHING: WET, SEMI, DRY, GLV

HARPER DIVING EQUIPMENT
UNIT 21
THREE SPRINGS TRADING ESTATE
VINCENT ROAD
WORCESTER
HEREFORD WR5 1BW
0905 351528 FAX: 0905 351528

CLOTHING: DRY, SEMI, GLV

For product key codes see reference page 347

HELIOS (SAFETY & RESCUE PRODS)
UNIT 6
THE OLD SMITHFIELD
ASTON STREET, SHIFNAL
SHROPSHIRE TF11 9DT
0952 461541 FAX: 0952 462948

BASIC: ACC
CLOTHING: GLV

HENDERSON DIVEWEAR
1 WHITALL AVENUE
MILLVILLE, NJ 08332 USA
010 1 609 8254771
FAX: 010 1 609 8256378

CLOTHING: WET, DRY, SEMI, SKN, BTS, GLV
NO UK DISTRIBUTORS

HYDROTECH
STONEY COVE
SAPCOTE ROAD, STONEY
STANTON
LEICS. LE9 6DW
0455 273089 FAX: 0455 274646

BASIC: ACC
AIR SOURCE: TNK
CLOTHING: WET, SEMI, DRY, CTM, BTS, GLV
DISTRIBUTES: DACOR

IDEATIONS DESIGN
4257 24TH AVENUE WEST
SEATTLE, WA 98199 USA
010 1 206 2810067
FAX: 010 1 206 2856897

BASIC: BD, ACC
SPECIAL PRODUCTS: DIVE ALERT
DISTRIBUTED BY SEACURITY

IKELITE UNDERWATER SYSTEMS
50 W 33RD STREET
INDIANAPOLIS, IN 46208 USA
010 1 317 9234523
FAX: 010 1 317 9247988

BASIC: LT, ACC
INSTRUMENTATION: CSL
SPECIAL PRODUCTS: UNDERWATER DIVER RECALL SYSTEMS
DISTRIBUTED BY OCEANIC, UK

INTERNATIONAL DIVING & WATERSPORTS
1 NEW ROAD
SHOREHAM BY SEA
WEST SUSSEX BN43 6RA
0273 455892 FAX: 0273 465149

CLOTHING: WET, SEMI, CTM, BTS, GLV
DISTRIBUTES: CRESSI-SUB

IRVINGTON ENTERPRISES LTD
WITTINGTON HOUSE
764-768 HOLLOWAY ROAD
LONDON N19 3JG
071 2819477 FAX: 071 2819478

CLOTHING: SEMI, SKN, GLV

IST SPORTS
15705 ARROW HWY #7A
IRWINDALE, CA 91706 USA
010 1 818 3375598
FAX: 010 1 818 9605211

BASIC: BCD, MFS, BD, ACC
AIR SOURCE: REG, AA
INSTRUMENTATION: CSL
CLOTHING: SKN, BTS, GLV
DISTRIBUTED BY SEA & SEA, UK

JW AUTOMARINE
HEMPSTEAD ROAD INDUSTRIAL ESTATE
HEMPSTEAD RD, HOLT , NORFOLK NR25 6DL
0263 713522 FAX: 0263 711152

BASIC: LT, BD, ACC
DISTRIBUTES: TOSHIBA DIVE LIGHTS

KENT DIVING
7 OASTHOUSE WAY
ORPINGTON, KENT BR5 3PT
0689 875521 FAX: 0689 877246

CLOTHING: SEMI
DISTRIBUTES: TRIDENT

MARES S.p.A.
VIA CERISOLA BORGHETTO
37-16035, RAPALLO, GENOA ITALY
010 39 185 6821 FAX: 010 39 185 669984

BASIC: BCD, MFS, LT, BD, ACC
AIR SOURCE: REG, AA, TNK
INSTRUMENTATION: CSL, CMP
CLOTHING: WET, SEMI, OUT, BTS, GLV
OTHER PRODUCTS: SPEAR FISHING EQUIPMENT
DISTRIBUTED BY BLANDFORD SUB-AQUA

MARLIN LEISURE LTD
51 SHANNON SQUARE
CANVEY ISLAND, ESSEX SS8 0PW
0268 698333 FAX: 0268 510340

CLOTHING: WET, DRY, GLV

MIDLAND DIVING EQUIPMENT LTD
57 SPARKENHOE STREET
LEICESTER, LEICESTERSHIRE LE2 0TD
0533 624262 FAX: 0533 512227

AIR SOURCE: TNK
OTHER PRODUCTS: TANK VALVES
DISTRIBUTES: LUXFER TANKS, WHIRLWIND COMPRESSORS

MOBY DIVING EQUIPMENT LTD
UNIT 1, BANBURY ROAD, BYFIELD
NORTHANTS NN11 6XJ
0327 62274 FAX: 0327 60363

CLOTHING: WET, SEMI, DRY, CTM, GLV

NAMRON (AQUA PRODUCTS) LTD
CANKLOW MEADOW INDUSTRIAL EST.
WEST BAWTRY ROAD, ROTHERHAM
SOUTH YORKSHIRE S60 2XL
0709 371006 FAX: 0709 367295

BASIC: ACC
CLOTHING: WET, SEMI, DRY
DISTRIBUTES: SHERWOOD SCUBA, SALVAS, TOOL MASTER, MULTIPLIER

NORTHERN DIVER
OFFSHORE COMPONENTS
THE STANDISH CENTRE, CROSS STREET
WIGAN, LANCASHIRE WN6 0HQ
0257 421330 FAX: 0257 427049

AIR SOURCE: TNK
CLOTHING: DRY
DISTRIBUTES: FABER TANKS

OBAN WETSUITS LTD
TORRAN GORM INDUSTRIAL ESTATE
LOCHAVULIN, OBAN, ARGYLL PA34 4PL
0631 64118 FAX: 0631 667641

CLOTHING: WET, SEMI, DRY, OUT, CTM, BTS, GLV

OCEAN EDGE
7992 MIRAMAR ROAD
SAN DIEGO, CA 92126 010 1 619 6959130
FAX: 010 1 619 6959402

BASIC: BCD, MFS, LT, BD, ACC
AIR SOURCE: REG, AA
INSTRUMENTATION: CSL, CMP
CLOTHING: BTS, GLV
DISTRIBUTED BY POLAR BEAR

OCEAN LEISURE
11-14 NORTHUMBERLAND AVENUE
LONDON WC2N 5AQ
071 9305050 FAX: 071 9303032

DISTRIBUTES: APOLLO

OCEAN TECHNOLOGY SYSTEM (OTS)
2950 AIRWAY AVENUE (D3)
COSTA MESA, CA 92626 USA
010 1 714 7547848
FAX: 010 1 714 9661639

SPECIAL PRODUCTS: UNDERWATER COMMUNICATION EQUIPMENT - BUDDY PHONE
NO UK DISTRIBUTORS

OCEANIC
14275 CATALINA STREET
SAN LEANDRO, CA 94577 USA
010 1 415 3525001
FAX: 010 1 415 3524803

BASIC: BCD, MFS, LT, ACC
AIR SOURCE: REG, AA
INSTRUMENTATION: CSL, CMP
CLOTHING: WET, SEMI, SKN, BTS, GLV
DISTRIBUTED BY OCEANIC, UK

OCEANIC (SW) LTD
LANGLANDS BUSINESS PARK
UFFCULME
CULLOMPTON
DEVON EX15 3DA
0884 840001 FAX: 0884 841770

DISTRIBUTES: OCEANIC, SPARE AIR, IKELITE

ORCA, DIVISION OF EIT
45625 WILLOW POND PLAZA
STERLING, VA 20164 USA
010 1 703 4780333
FAX: 010 1 703 4780815

INSTRUMENTATION: CMP
DISTRIBUTED BY CORAL MARINE

OTTER WATERSPORTS
29 WALKER TERRACE
WAKEFIELD ROAD
BRADFORD
WEST YORKSHIRE BD4 7HP
0274 307555 FAX: 0274 307555

CLOTHING: WET, SEMI, DRY, GLV

PARKWAY SYSTEM
241 RARITAN STREET
SOUTH AMBOY, NJ 08879 USA
010 1 908 7215300
FAX: 010 1 908 7214016

BASIC: BCD, MFS, BD, ACC
AIR SOURCE: REG, AA, TNK
INSTRUMENTATION: CSL, CMP
CLOTHING: WET, SEMI, DRY, CTM, BTS, GLV
NO UK DISTRIBUTORS

PELICAN PRODUCTS INC
2255 JEFFERSON STREET
TORRANCE, CA 90501 USA
010 1 213 3289910
FAX: 010 1 213 5338160

BASIC: LT, ACC
SPECIAL PRODUCTS: HARD EQUIPMENT CASES
DISTRIBUTED BY BLANDFORD SUB-AQUA

POLAR BEAR DIVING EQUIPMENT LTD
UNITS B1-B2
PENNYGILLAM INDUSTRIAL ESTATE
LAUNCESTON
CORNWALL PL15 7ED
0566 773654 FAX: 0566 776065

BASIC: BD, ACC
CLOTHING: DRY, THM, CTM, GLV
DISTRIBUTES: OCEAN EDGE

POSEIDON INDUSTRI AB
AKEREDSVAGEN 1
BOX 8050, 421 08 VASTRA
FROLUNDA
SWEDEN
010 46 31 498440
FAX: 010 46 31 474368

AIR SOURCE: REG, AA
CLOTHING: DRY, GLV
DISTRIBUTED BY UWI

PREMIER DIVE CASES
435 RIVERSIDE AVENUE
MERRITT ISLAND, FL 32953 USA
010 1 407 4520817

SPECIAL PRODUCTS: HARD CASES FOR DIVING EQUIPMENT
NO UK DISTRIBUTOR

RITE BITE MOUTHPIECES
2525 16TH STREET #7
GREELEY, CO 80631 USA
010 1 303 3531324
FAX: 010 1 303 3521402

SPECIAL PRODUCTS: MOUTHPIECES
NO UK DISTRIBUTOR

ROBIN HOOD WATERSPORTS
152 LEEDS ROAD
HECKMONDWIKE,
WEST YORKS WF16 9BJ
0924 443843
FAX: 0924 474529

BASIC: LT
CLOTHING: DRY, THM, GLV

SCUBA TOOL
11526 GRISSOM LANE
DALLAS,
TEXAS, TX 75229 USA
010 1 214 2438016
FAX: 010 1 214 2438016

BASIC: ACC
SPECIAL PRODUCTS: SCUBA TOOL
DISTRIBUTED BY CORAL MARINE

SCUBAPRO (UK) LTD
UNIT J, ROAN INDUSTRIAL ESTATE
LAVENDER AVENUE, MITCHAM
SURREY CR4 3HH
081 6403122 FAX: 081 6403123

DISTRIBUTES: SCUBAPRO

SCUBAPRO UNDERSEA IND. INC
3105 E. HARCOURT
PANCHO DOMINQUEZ, CA 90221 USA
010 1 213 6397850
FAX: 010 1 213 6050293

BASIC: BCD, MFS, LT, ACC
AIR SOURCE: REG, AA, TNK
INSTRUMENTATION: CSL, CMP, WCH
CLOTHING: WET, SEMI, DRY, OUT, BTS, GLV
SPECIAL PRODUCTS: DIVER PROPULSION VEHICLE,
PERSONAL DIVE SONAR
DISTRIBUTED BY SCUBAPRO, UK

SCUBATEK UK
77 ROCHFORD GARDENS
SLOUGH, BERKS SL2 5XA
0753 538103 FAX: 0753 676130

BASIC: ACC
SPECIAL PRODUCTS: SCREEN GUARDS FOR DIVE COMPUTERS
DISTRIBUTES: GAGE GUARD, UNIQUICK, AQUALOCK,
ABOSLUTELY CLEAR

SEA & SEA LTD
PHILIP HOUSE, ASPEN WAY
PAIGNTON, DEVON TQ4 7QR
0803 663012 FAX: 0803 663003

BASIC: BCD, ACC
CLOTHING: THM
SPECIAL PRODUCTS: SEAPEKS, DIVE TEAM
DISTRIBUTES: SEA & SEA, IST,
UNDERWATER KINETICS, WENOKA

SEA CURE
PO BOX 559
MONROE, WI 53566 USA
010 1 608 3288008

SPECIAL PRODUCTS: ORTHODONTIC MOUTHPIECE
NO UK DISTRIBUTORS

SEA QUEST
2151 LAS PALMAS DRIVE
CARLSBAD, CA 92009 USA
010 1 619 4381101
FAX: 010 1 619 4383142

BASIC: BCD, MFS, ACC
AIR SOURCE: REG, AA
INSTRUMENTATION: CSL, CMP
CLOTHING: WET, SKN, OUT, BTS, GLV
OTHER PRODUCTS: SPEAR FISHING EQUIPMENT
DISTRIBUTED BY AQUA-LUNG

SEACURITY
PO BOX 966
POOLE, DORSET BH17 9YF
0202 658645 FAX: 0202 693234

BASIC: ACC
DISTRIBUTES: DIVE ALERT

SEAFLEX LTD
SAMUEL WHITE
COWES, ISLES OF WHITE PO31 7DU
0983 290525 FAX: 0983 295853

BASIC: BD

SEAPRO, INC
21612 SURVEYOR CIRCLE
HUNTINGDON BEACH, CA 92646 USA
010 1 714 9601905
FAX: 010 1 714 9695588

BASIC: BCD, BD, ACC
AIR SOURCE: REG, AA
SPECIAL PRODUCTS: TECHNICAL DIVING EQUIPMENT
NO UK DISTRIBUTORS

SEIKO (UK) LTD
HATTORI HOUSE
VAN WALL ROAD, MAIDENHEAD
BERKS SL6 4UW
0628 770001 FAX: 0628 770655

INSTRUMENTATION: WCH

SHARK SPORTS LTD
NORDSTROM HOUSE
NORTH BROOMHILL
MORPETH
NORTHUMBERLAND NE65 9UJ
0670 760365 FAX: 0670 761343

BASIC: BD, ACC
CLOTHING: WET, SEMI, DRY, THM, GLV
OTHER PRODUCTS: COMMERCIAL DIVING SUITS
SPECIAL PRODUCTS: SHARKS INTERGRATED
SURVIVAL SYSTEM

SHERWOOD SCUBA
120 CHURCH STREET
LOCKPORT, NY 14094 USA
010 1 716 4333891
FAX: 010 1 716 4331275

BASIC: BCD, MFS, LT, ACC
AIR SOURCE: REG, AA, TNK
INSTRUMENTATION: CSL, CMP
CLOTHING: SKN, OUT, BTS, GLV
DISTRIBUTED BY NAMRON

SOLENT DIVERS
122-128 LAKE ROAD
PORTSMOUTH, HANTS PO1 4HH
0705 814924 FAX: 0705 291538

DISTRIBUTES: CAVALERO

SPIROTECHNIQUE
BP 14806517
CARROS CEDEX, FRANCE
010 33 93 290835 FAX: 010 33 93 087531

BASIC: BCD, MFS, LT, BD, ACC
AIR SOURCE: REG, AA, TNK
INSTRUMENTATION: CSL, CMP
CLOTHING: WET, SEMI, DRY, SKN, BTS, GLV
DISTRIBUTED BY AQUA-LUNG

SPORASUB
99 CHEMIN DE LA MURE
13015 MARSEILLE, FRANCE
010 33 91 030000 FAX: 010 33 91 032531

NO UK DISTRIBUTORS

SPORTS SUITS OF AUSTRALIA
7625 HAYVENHURST #35
VAN NUYS, CA 91406 USA
010 1 818 3760402
FAX: 010 1 818 3737721

CLOTHING: SKN
NO UK DISTRIBUTORS

SUB AQUA PRODUCTS LTD
63-65 TWYFORD ROAD
EASTLEIGH, HANTS S05 4ZG
0703 612144 FAX: 0703 611634

BASIC: MFS, LT, ACC
CLOTHING: WET, BTS, GLV
DISTRIBUTES: MARINOX OXYGEN UNITS

SUUNTO OY
JUVAN TEOLLISUUSKATU 8
SF-02920 ESPOO, FINLAND
010 358 0 847033 FAX: 010 358 0 843810

INSTRUMENTATION: CSL, CMP
DISTRIBUTED BY BLANDFORD SUB-AQUA

TAG HEUER WATCHES
16-18 HARCOURT STREET
WORSLEY
MANCHESTER M28 5GN
0204 862179 FAX: 0204 862146

INSTRUMENTATION: WCH

TECHNISUB SpA
PIAZZALE KENNEDY 1/D
16129, GENOA, ITALY
010 39 10 530051 FAX: 010 39 10 541483

BASIC: BCD, MFS, LT, BD, ACC
AIR SOURCE: REG, AA, TNK
INSTRUMENTATION: CSL
CLOTHING: WET, SEMI, OUT, BTS, GLV
DISTRIBUTED BY AQUA-LUNG

THE GATES RUBBER COMPANY LTD
EDINBURGH ROAD
HEATHHALL, DUMFRIES DG1 1QA
0387 69591 FAX: 0387 50995

CLOTHING: DRY, GLV
OTHER PRODUCTS: COMMERCIAL DIVING SUITS

THE ROLEX WATCH COMPANY
3 STRATFORD PLACE LONDON WIN 0ER
071 629 5071 FAX: 071 495 0888

INSTRUMENTATION: WCH

TIKI LTD
VELLATOR INDUSTRIAL ESTATE
BRAUNTON, DEVON EX33 2DX
0271 812442 FAX: 0271 816570

CLOTHING: WET, GLV

TRIDENT DIVING EQUIPMENT
9616 OWENS MOUTH
CHATSWORTH, CA 91311 USA
010 1 818 4072980
FAX: 010 1 800 6979516

BASIC: ACC
DISTRIBUTED BY KENT DIVING

TUSA
TABATA USA INC
2380 MIRA MAR AVENUE
LONG BEACH, CA 90815 USA
010 1 310 4983708
FAX: 010 1 310 4981390

BASIC: BCD, MFS, LT, ACC
AIR SOURCE: REG, AA
INSTRUMENTATION: CSL
CLOTHING: BTS, GLV
DISTRIBUTED BY DIVING & RESCUE SUPPLIES

TYPHOON INTERNATIONAL LTD
MORTLAKE COURT
28 SHEEN LANE, EAST SHEEN
LONDON, LONDON SW14 8LW
081 8769818 FAX: 081 8769223

BASIC: ACC
CLOTHING: WET, SEMI, DRY, GLV

UNDERSEA LTD
1 FLORELLE CENTRE
EBBLAKE INDUSTRIAL ESTATE, VERWOOD
DORSET BH31 6AX
0202 822025

BASIC: ACC

UNDERWATER KINETICS
1020 LINDA VISTA DRIVE
SAN MARCOS, CA 92069 USA
010 1 619 7447560
FAX: 010 1 619 7447320

BASIC: LT, ACC
DISTRIBUTED BY SEA & SEA, UK

US DIVERS AQUA LUNG
PO BOX 25018
SANTA ANA, CA 92799-5018 USA
010 1 714 5408010
FAX: 010 1 714 4329340

BASIC: BCD, MFS, LT, BD, ACC
AIR SOURCE: REG, AA, TNK
INSTRUMENTATION: CSL, CMP
CLOTHING: WET, SKN, BTS, GLV
DISTRIBUTED BY AQUA-LUNG

UWATEC Ag
ENGENBUHL 130
5705 HALLWIL, SWITZERLAND
010 41 64 542940 FAX: 010 41 64 542280

INSTRUMENTATION: CSL, CMP
SPECIAL PRODUCTS: ALADIN
DISTRIBUTED BY UWI

UWI
12-13 NEWMAN LANE INDUSTRIAL EST
ALTON, HANTS GU13 2QR
0420 544422 FAX: 0420 544795

CLOTHING: DRY, GLV
OTHER PRODUCTS: COMMERCIAL DIVING PRODUCTS
DISTRIBUTES: UWATEC\DIVE DYNAMICS, POSEIDON,
BAUER COMPRESSORS

WENOKA SEASTYLE
1134 53RD COURT NORTH
W. PALM BEACH, FL 33407-0238 USA
010 1 407 8456155
FAX: 010 1 407 8424247

BASIC: MFS, LT, ACC
CLOTHING: BTS, GLV
DISTRIBUTED BY SEA & SEA, UK

WEST WALES DIVERS
HASQUARD CROSS
HAVERFORD WEST
PEMBROKESHIRE SA62 3SJ
0437 781457 FAX: 0437 781093

CLOTHING: WET, GLV

ZEAGLE SYSTEMS INC
37150 CHANCERY ROAD
ZEPHYRHILLS, FL 33541 USA
010 1 813 7825568
FAX: 010 1 813 7825569

BASIC: BCD
AIR SOURCE: REG, AA
DISTRIBUTED BY DUI, UK

COMPRESSORS

AEROTECNICA ITALIANA
20094 CORSICO (MI)
ITALY
010 39 2 48601240
FAX: 010 39 2 4502844

DISTRIBUTED BY SUBMARINE MANUFACTURING & PRODUCTS

BAUER KOMPRESSOREN GMBH
PO BOX 710260
D-81477 MUNICH, GERMANY
010 49 89 780490
FAX: 010 49 89 78049167

DISTRIBUTED BY UWI

COMPAIR REAVELL LTD
PO BOX 44
IPSWICH, NORFOLK IP2 OA4
0473 602222 FAX: 0473 601704

HASKEL ENERGY SYSTEMS LTD
NORTH HYLTON ROAD
SUNDERLAND, TYNE & WEAR SR5 3JD
091 5491212 FAX: 091 5490911

SPECIAL PRODUCTS: GAS MIXING & PRESSURE BOOSTING SYSTEMS

HAMWORTHY COMPRESSOR SYSTEMS LTD
CHEQUERS BRIDGE
GLOUCESTER, GLOUCESTERSHIRE GL1 4LL
0452 528431 FAX: 0452 507394

HYMATIC ENGINEERING
11 WILLIAMS WAY
WOLLASTON, NORTHANTS NN5 7QR
0527 64931 FAX: 0527 591117

SPECIAL PRODUCTS: HYPRESAIR COMPRESSORS

MARINE SURPLUS SUPPLIES LTD
UNIT 8A
THE WATERFRONT MARINE IND. EST.
DOCK RD, LYTHAM, LANCASHIRE FY8 5AQ
0253 794433 FAX: 0253 794596

SPECIAL PRODUCTS: USED & RECONDITIONED COMPRESSORS AND PROFESSIONAL EQUIPMENT

MIDLAND DIVING EQUIPMENT LTD
57 SPARKENHOE STREET
LEICESTER, LEICESTERSHIRE LE2 0TD
0533 624262 FAX: 0533 512227

AIR SOURCE: TNK
OTHER PRODUCTS: TANK VALVES
DISTRIBUTES: LUXFER TANKS, WHIRLWIND COMPRESSORS

SUBMARINE MANUF. & PRODS. LTD
UNIT 8A
THE WATERFRONT MARINE IND. EST.
DOCK ROAD
LYTHAM, LANCASHIRE FY8 5AQ
0253 794433 FAX: 0253 794596

OTHER PRODUCTS: DECOMPRESSION CHAMBERS & OTHER PROFESSIONAL EQUIPMENT
DISTRIBUTES: AEROTECNICA-COLTRI COMPRESSORS

UWI
12-13 NEWMAN LANE INDUSTRIAL EST
ALTON, HANTS GU13 2QR
0420 544422 FAX: 0420 544795

CLOTHING: DRY, GLV
OTHER PRODUCTS: COMMERCIAL DIVING PRODUCTS
DISTRIBUTES: UWATEC\DIVE DYNAMICS, POSEIDON, BAUER COMPRESSORS

SAFETY

ADVANCED DIVING PRODUCTS
TINDLE ENTERPRISE CENTRE
1-3 PETERSFIELD ROAD
WHITE HILL
HANTS GU35 9AR
0420 479606 FAX: 0420 475500

PRODUCTS: SMB-DECO BOY

AP VALVES
WATER MA TROUT INDUSTRIAL EST
HELSTON, CORNWALL TR13 0LW
0326 561040 FAX: 0326 573605

PRODUCTS: SMB

BIRCHLEY PRODUCTS
7 BUSH HAY
CHURCHDOWN, GLOUCESTER
GLOUCESTERSHIRE GL3 2QR
0452 855312 FAX: 0452 855312

PRODUCTS: SMB

BOWSTONE DIVING PRODUCTS
BELPER ROAD
HEATON MERSEY INDUSTRIAL
ESTATESTOCKPORT, CHESHIRE SK4 3QP
061 4420272 FAX: 061 4431508

PRODUCTS: SMB

COMPASS MARITIME
OLD SARUM AIRFIELD
SALISBURY, WILTSHIRE SP4 6DZ
0722 338155 FAX: 0722 332852

PRODUCTS: UNDERWATER DIVER RECALL SYSTEM

DIVING & RESCUE SUPPLIES LTD
PARKGATE BUSINESS PARK
UNIT B2, RAIL MILL WAY
ROTHERHAM
YORKSHIRE S62 6JQ
0709 780666 FAX: 0709 780550

PRODUCTS: SMB, ETC

GREENAWAY MARINE
BROAD HINTON
SWINDON, WILTSHIRE SN4 9PA
0793 731666 FAX: 0793 731644

PRODUCTS: UNDERWATER COMMUNICATION SYSTEM

HELIOS (SAFETY & RESCUE PRODS)
UNIT 6, THE OLD SMITHFIELD
ASTON STREET, SHIFNAL
SHROPSHIRE TF11 9DT
0952 461541 FAX: 0952 462948

PRODUCTS: OXYGEN KIT, ETC

IDEATIONS DESIGN
4257 24TH AVENUE WEST
SEATTLE, WA 98199 USA
010 1 206 2810067
FAX: 010 1 206 2856897

PRODUCTS: DIVE ALERT
DISTRIBUTED BY SEACURITY

IKELITE UNDERWATER SYSTEMS
50 W 33RD STREET
INDIANAPOLIS, IN 46208 USA
010 1 317 9234523
FAX: 010 1 317 9247988

PRODUCTS: UNDERWATER DIVER RECALL SYSTEMS
DISTRIBUTED BY OCEANIC, UK

JW AUTOMARINE
HEMPSTEAD ROAD INDUSTRIAL ESTATE
HEMPSTEAD ROAD, HOL
NORFOLK NR25 6DL
0263 713522 FAX: 0263 711152

PRODUCTS: SMB

LAERDAL
LAERDAL HOUSE
GOODMEAD ROAD, ORPINGTON
KENT BR6 0HX
0689 876634

PRODUCTS: RESUSCITATION MANIKINS, POCKET MASKS

LIFE SUPPORT ENGINEERING LTD
ROBELL WAY
STORRINGTON, WEST SUSSEX RH20 3DN
0903 742322 FAX: 0903 745923

PRODUCTS: OXYGEN KIT, ETC

PAINS WESSEX LTD
HIGH POST, SALISBURY, WILTSHIRE SP4 6AS
0722 411611 FAX: 0722 412121

PRODUCTS: FLARES, UNDERWATER DIVER RECALL SYSTEM

SABRE SAFETY LTD
MEDICAL DIVISION
MATTERSON HOUSE, ASH ROAD
ALDERSHOT, HANTS GU12 4DE
0252 334581 FAX: 0252 21993

PRODUCTS: OXYGEN KIT, ETC

SEA & SEA LTD
PHILIP HOUSE
ASPEN WAY, PAIGNTON, DEVON TQ4 7QR
0803 663012 FAX: 0803 663003

PRODUCTS: OXYGEN KIT

SEAFLEX LTD
SAMUEL WHITE
COWES, ISLES OF WHITE PO31 7DU
0983 290525 FAX: 0983 295853

PRODUCTS: SMB

SEMS LTD
UNIT 13, OLYMPIC BUSINESS CENTRE
PAYCOCKE ROAD, BASILDON
ESSEX SS14 3EX
0268 534427 FAX: 0268 281009

PRODUCTS: SMB

SHARK SPORTS LTD
NORDSTROM HOUSE, NORTH
BROOMHILL
MORPETH
NORTHUMBERLAND NE65 9UJ
0670 760365 FAX: 0670 761343

PRODUCTS: SHARKS INTERGRATED SURVIVAL SYSTEM

SOS PRODUCTS
198 HIGHER ROAD
URMSTON
MANCHESTER M31 1BH
061 7484190 FAX: 061 7468359

PRODUCTS: GENERAL

SUB AQUA PRODUCTS LTD
63-65 TWYFORD ROAD
EASTLEIGH, HANTS S05 4ZG
0703 612144 FAX: 0703 611634

DISTRIBUTES: MARINOX OXYGEN UNITS

SUBMERSIBLE SYSTEMS INC
18112 GOTHARD STREET
HUNTINGDON BEACH
CA 92648 USA
010 1 714 8426566
FAX: 010 1 714 8424626

PRODUCTS: SPARE AIR
DISTRIBUTED BY OCEANIC, UK

TRADE ASSOCIATIONS

DIVING TRADE ASSOCIATION (DTA)
BRITISH SPORTS AND ALLIED INDUSTRIES FEDERATION
23 BRIGHTON ROAD
SOUTH CROYDON, SURREY CR2 6EA
081 6811242 FAX: 081 6810012

THE DIVING EQUIPMENT MANUFACTURERS ASSOCIATION (DEMA)
PO BOX 217
TUSTIN, CA 92681, USA
010 1 714 7445287
FAX: 010 1 714 7445294

For product key codes see reference page 347

Photographic and Video Manufacturers and Distributors

UNDERWATER CAMERA SYSTEMS

KONICA
PLANE TREE CRESCENT
FELTHAM,
MIDDLESEX TW13 7HD
081 7516121 FAX: 081 7550681

CAM, ACC

NIKON UK LTD
NIKON HOUSE
380 RICHMOND ROAD
KINGSTON UPON THAMES
SURREY KT2 5PR
081 5414440 FAX: 081 5414584

CAM, FSH, ACC

SEA & SEA
3-2-20 SAIWAICHO KAWAGUCHI-SHI
SAITAMA 332, JAPAN
010 81 482 562251
FAX: 010 81 482 562276

CAM, FSH, ACC
DISTRIBUTED BY SEA & SEA, UK

SEA & SEA LTD
PHILIP HOUSE
ASPEN WAY, PAIGNTON
DEVON TQ4 7QR
0803 663012 FAX: 0803 663003

DISTRIBUTES: SEA & SEA, UNDERWATER KINETICS

LAND CAMERA & VIDEO SYSTEMS

CANON PHOTO DIVISION
BRENT TRADING CENTRE
NORTH CIRCULAR ROAD
LONDON NW10 0JF
081 4591266 FAX: 081 4594202

CAM, VID, FSH, ACC

KONICA
PLANE TREE CRESCENT
FELTHAM,
MIDDLESEX TW13 7HD
081 7516121 FAX: 081 7550681

CAM, ACC

KYOCERA YASHICA
4 BENNETT COURT
READING, BERKS RG2 0QX
0734 311919 FAX: 0734 311240

CAM, FSH, ACC

MAMIYA CAMERAS
JOHNSONS PHOTOPIA
HEMPSTALLS LANE, NEWCASTLE
STAFFORDSHIRE ST5 0SW
0782 717100 FAX: 0782 717707

CAM, ACC

MINOLTA UK
1-3 TANNERS DRIVE, BLAKELANDS NORTH
MILTON KEYNES, BUCKS MK14 5BU
0908 211211 FAX: 0908 613497

CAM, FSH, ACC

NIKON UK LTD
NIKON HOUSE
380 RICHMOND ROAD
KINGSTON UPON THAMES, SURREY KT2 5PR
081 5414440 FAX: 081 5414584

CAM, FSH, ACC

OLYMPUS
2-8 HONDURAS STREET, LONDON ECIY 0TX
071 2532772 FAX: 071 2516330

CAM, FSH, ACC

PANASONIC
INTROPHOTO LTD
PRIORS WAY, MAIDENHEAD, BERKS SL6 2HR
0628 74411 FAX: 0628 771055

CAM, VID, FSH, VLT, ACC

PENTAX UK
PENTAX HOUSE
SOUTH HILL AVENUE
SOUTH HARROW, MIDDLESEX HA2 0LT
081 8644422 FAX: 081 8641861

CAM, FSH, ACC

SONY (UK) LTD
CUSTOMER INFORMATION CENTRE
C/O NATIONAL OPERATION CENTRE
PIPERS WAY, TATCHAM
NEWBURY, BERKS RG13 4LZ
081 7841144

VID, CSE, VLT, ACC

UNDERWATER CASINGS, LIGHTING AND ACCESSORIES

ACCU GEAR
724 7TH AVENUE
NEW YORK, NY 10019 USA
010 1 212 2477605
FAX: 010 1 212 3071858

CSE, VLT, ACC
NO UK DISTRIBUTORS

AMPHIBICO INC
9563 COTE DE LIESSE, DORVAL, CANADA
010 1 514 6369910
FAX: 010 1 514 6368704

CSE, VLT, ACC
DISTRIBUTED BY EYEWITNESS LTD

AQUATICA
AQUA VISION SYSTEMS
7730 TRANS CANADA HWY
MONTREAL, CANADA
010 1 514 7379481
FAX: 010 1 514 7377685

CSE, ACC
DISTRIBUTED BY EYEWITNESS LTD

BENNY SUTTON
THE IMAGE CENTRE
216 UXBRIDGE ROAD, SHEPHERDS BUSH
LONDON W12 7JD
081 7433788 FAX: 081 7431369

DISTRIBUTES: SEACAM

BIRCHLEY PRODUCTS
7 BUSH HAY, CHURCHDOWN, GLOUCESTER
GLOUCESTERSHIRE GL3 2QR
0452 855312 FAX: 0452 855312

CSE, FSH, VLT, ACC

DIVE RITE MANUFACTURING, INC
ROUTE 14, BOX 136
LAKE CITY, FL 32055 USA
010 1 904 7521087
FAX: 010 1 904 7550613

VLT, ACC
DISTRIBUTED BY DIVE RITE, UK

DIVE RITE
PO BOX 498, LONDON SW19 6BX
081 7890961 FAX: 081 7802018

DISTRIBUTES: DIVE RITE

DRY TECH
THE STUDIO
OLD HOUSE, ST ANNES STREET
GRANTHAM, LINCOLNSHIRE NG31 9AG
0476 592724 FAX: 0476 592734

DISTRIBUTES: EWA MARINE

EWA MARINE
GOEDECKE & CO
POSTFACH 1362, 8011 KIRCHHEIM
GERMANY
010 49 89 9044063
FAX: 010 49 89 9035808

CSE
DISTRIBUTED BY DRY TECH LTD

EYEWITNESS LTD
THE DROVE
SHERFIELD ENGLISH ROAD, PLAITFORD
ROMSEY, HANTS SO51 6EF
0794 22500 FAX: 0794 23601

DISTRIBUTES: AMPHIBICO, HMI, AQUAVISION(AQUATICA)

GREENAWAY MARINE INT LTD.
BROAD HINTON
SWINDON, WILTSHIRE SN4 9PA
0793 731 667 FAX: 0793 731 644

CSE, ACC PRODUCT: SEAPRO
DISTRIBUTES: SEAPRO, UN, SUBTRONIC

HAMA
POSTFACH 80
8855 MONHEIM 45, MONHEIM, GERMANY
010 49 90 915020

FSH, VLT, ACC
DISTRIBUTED BY HAMA, UK

HAMA PVAC LTD
UNIT 4 CHERRYWOOD
CHINEHAM BUSINESS PARK, BASINGSTOKE
HANTS RG24 OWF
0256 708110 FAX: 0256 708112

DISTRIBUTES: HAMA

HARTENBERGER
REINER HARTENBERGER
RENNEBERGSTRASSE 19, D-5000 KOLN 41
GERMANY
010 49 221 415000
FAX: 010 49 221 415050

CSE, FSH, VLT, ACC
NO UK DISTRIBUTORS

HUGYFOT.SCHWEIZ
RENE HUGENSCHMIDT
ZURICHSTRASSE 62, CH-8700 KUSNACHT
SWITZERLAND
010 41 1 9105886 FAX: 010 41 1 9108086

CSE, FSH, VLT, ACC
NO UK DISTRIBUTORS

IKELITE UNDERWATER SYSTEMS
50W 33RD STREET
INDIANAPOLIS, IN 46208 USA
010 1 317 9234523
FAX: 010 1 317 9247988

CSE, FSH, VLT, ACC
DISTRIBUTED BY OCEANIC, UK

ISOTECNIC
VIA MILANO 177
30714 CASTELNUOVO, D/GARDA ITALY
010 39 45 6450480
FAX: 010 39 45 6450477

FSH, VLT, ACC
DISTRIBUTED BY OCEAN OPTICS

NAU TECHNIK
MICHAEL WITHAUS
SACHSTRASSE 29, D-54781 MUNCHEN
GERMANY
010 49 89 3789217
FAX: 010 49 89 3782166

CSE, ACC NO UK DISTRIBUTORS

NIMAR
PLASTOMECCANIE
VIA MARTINI, D-CHERBARBO 9
COREGLIO, REGGIO EMILIA ITALY
010 39 522 692015
FAX: 010 39 522 693629

CSE, VLT
NO UK DISTRIBUTORS

OCEAN OPTICS
11-14 NOTHUMBERLAND AVENUE
LONDON WC2N 5AQ
071 9308408 FAX: 071 9303032

ACC
DISTRIBUTES: ISOTECHNICS, SUBAL, MORRIS

SEACAM
HARALD HORDOSCH
CV HOTZENDORF-STRASSE 40, A-8570
VOITSBERG, AUSTRIA
010 43 3142 22885
FAX: 010 43 3142 62958

CSE, ACC
DISTRIBUTED BY BENNY SUTTON

SEALUX
PETER DORFLER STRASSE 28
D-87437 KEMPTEN, GERMANY
010 49 831 79427 FAX: 010 49 831 71865

CSE, FSH, VLT, ACC
NO UK DISTRIBUTORS

STROMM UNDERWATER INC
PO BOX 188 PLACE DU PARC
MONTREAL, CANADA
010 1 514 9820050
FAX: 010 1 514 9829225

CSE
NO UK DISTRIBUTORS

SUBAL
ARNOLD STEPANEK
LEOPOLD-WERNDL-STRASSE 31
A-4406 STEYR, AUSTRIA
010 43 7252 46424
FAX: 010 43 7252 52651

CSE, ACC
DISTRIBUTED BY OCEAN OPTICS

SUBATEC
ROUTE CONVERSION 247
1093 LA CONVERSION
SWITZERLAND
010 41 21 7912777
FAX: 010 41 21 7915777

FSH, VLT, ACC
NO UK DISTRIBUTORS

SUBTRONIC
STEIGLESACKER 9
D-73230 KIRCHHEIM/TECK
GERMANY
010 49 70 2146480
FAX: 010 49 70 2149448

VLT, ACC
DISTRIBUTED BY GREENAWAY MARINE

TECHNICAL LIGHTING CONTROL
238 LAS ALTURAS ROAD
SANTA BARBARA, CA 93103 USA
010 1 805 9622833
FAX: 010 1 805 9622833

OTHER PRODUCTS: STROBE ARMS
NO UK DISTRIBUTORS

TUSSEY UNDERWATER SYSTEMS
4878 CASS STREET
SAN DIEGO, CA 92109 USA
010 1 619 5512600
FAX: 010 1 619 5518778

CSE, ACC
OTHER PRODUCTS: STROBE ARMS
NO UK DISTRIBUTORS

UK-GERMANY
HERMANN LONS STRASSE 9
D-6251 BESELICH 1, GERMANY
010 49 6484 6621 FAX: 010 49 6484 6889

CSE, ACC
NO UK DISTRIBUTORS

UN COMPANY LTD
NO 17-9, 2-CHOME
MISUJI, TAITO-KU, TOKYO 111, JAPAN
010 81 3 38660195
FAX: 010 81 3 38669608

CSE, VLT, ACC
DISTRIBUTED BY GREENAWAY MARINE

UNDERWATER KINETICS
1020 LINDA VISTA DRIVE
SAN MARCOS, CA 92069 USA
010 1 619 7447560
FAX: 010 1 619 7447320

VLT, ACC
OTHER PRODUCTS: STROBE ARMS
DISTRIBUTED BY SEA & SEA

FILM MANUFACTURERS

AGFA UK LTD
27 GREAT WEST ROAD
BRENTFORD, MIDDLESEX TW8 9AX
081 5602131 FAX: 081 2314951

EASTMAN KODAK CO
343 STATE STREET
ROCHESTER, NY 14650 USA
0101 716 7244000

FUJI PHOTO FILM (UK) LTD
125 FINCHLEY ROAD
LONDON NW3 6JH
071 5865900 FAX: 071 7224259

IIFORD PHOTO
14-22 TOTTENHAM STREET
LONDON W1P 0AH
071 6367890 FAX: 071 5804095

KODAK UK
195 EUSTON ROAD, LONDON NW1 2BN
071 3871717

KONICA
PLANE TREE CRESCENT
FELTHAM, MIDDLESEX TW13 7HD
081 7516121 FAX: 081 7550681

Boating Equipment Manufacturers and Distributors

RIBS AND INFLATABLES

AVON INFLATABLE BOATS LTD
DAFEN, LLANELLI, DYFED SA14 8NA
0554 770371 FAX: 0554 774997

BAY INFLATABLES
TRADE STREET
CARDIFF, SOUTH GLAMORGAN
0222 222216 FAX: 0222 222813

BLUE WATER MARITIME LTD
DOLPHIN QUAY
QUEEN STREET, EMSWORTH
HANTS PO10 7BJ
0243 379216 FAX: 0243 375088

PRODUCT: BWM

CAPALDI MARINE
GREEN LANE
CLANSFIELD, PORTSMOUTH
HANTS PO8 0JU
0705 599666 FAX: 0705 599511

DISTRIBUTES: MAXXON INFLATABLES, RIMINI RIBS

CARSON MARINE LTD
HAMBLE POINT
SCHOOL LANE, HAMBLE
SOUTHAMPTON SO3 5NB
0703 844413 FAX: 0703 844413

MADE TO ORDER

CHINOOK INFLATABLES LTD
FARM ROAD
OAKMERE, NORTHWICH
CHESHIRE CW8 2HB
0606 888781 FAX: 0606 889036

DATELINE POWERBOATS LTD
46 BRIDGEGATE
RETFORD, NOTTINGHAMSHIRE DN22 7UZ
0777 708777 FAX: 0777 860236

DELTA POWER SERVICES
UNIT 17
SCHOOL STREET INDUSTRIAL ESTATE
HAZEL GROVE
STOCKPORT, CHESHIRE SK7 4RA
061 4566588 FAX: 061 4566588

EASY RIDER RIBS
82 NORTH ORMESBY ROAD
MIDDLESBOROUGH, CLEVELAND TS4 2AJ
0642 247145

MADE TO ORDER

FLATACRAFT LTD
1183 MELTON ROAD
SYSTON, LEICS LE7 8JT
0533 608468 FAX: 0533 640652

HUMBER INFLATABLES LTD
246 WINCOLMLEE
HULL, HUMBERSIDE HU2 0PZ
0482 226100 FAX: 0482 215884

NARWHAL UK
UNIT 12
HERONSGATE TRADING ESTATE
PAYCOCKE ROAD
BASILDON, ESSEX SS14 3EU
0268 524470 FAX: 0268 289385

NORTHCRAFT
UNIT 2A/2B
HULL ROAD INDUSTRIAL ESTATE
WITHERNSEA
EAST YORKSHIRE HU19 2XX
0964 613815 FAX: 0964 613815

OFFSHORE LTD
UNIT 4, BRADLEY HALL ESTATE
BRADLEY LANE, STANDISH
WIGAN, LANCASHIRE WN6 0XQ
0257 472800 FAX: 0257 427409

PRODUCT: OSPREY

PEPE BOATYARD
MILL RYTHE LANE
HAYLING ISLAND, HANTS PO11 0RG
0705 461968 FAX: 0705 462181

RED BAY BOATS LTD
COAST ROAD
CUSHENDALL, CO. ANTRIM BT44 0TE
0266 771331 FAX: 0266 771474

MADE TO ORDER

RIBTEC LTD
HAMBLESIDE
SWANWICK SHORE ROAD, SWANWICK
SOUTHAMPTON, HANTS SO3 7EF
0489 885773 FAX: 0489 885845

SEAHOG BOATS
FRECKLETON CREEK
NR PRESTON, LANCASHIRE PR4 1HB
0772 633016 FAX: 0772 633016

SELACRAFT
1A WITHERNSEA STREET
HULL, NORTH HUMBERSIDE HU8 8BQ
0482 215689 FAX: 0482 26269

SOUTH COAST RIBS
25 SHOREFIELD WAY
MILFORD ON SEA, LYMINGTON
HANTS SO41 0RW
0590 645655 FAX: 0590 645655

TEMPTRESS RIBS LTD
BEACON WORKS
RIGGS HEAD, SCARBOROUGH
NORTH YORKSHIRE YO12 5TG
0723 863205 FAX: 0723 862326

THANETCRAFT LTD
CREST HOUSE
102 CHURCH ROAD
TEDDINGTON, MIDDLESEX TW11 8PW
081 977 1100 FAX: 081 943 3151

THE WELSH RIB CENTRE
PICTON BOATS LTD
THE BOAT YARD, BRYNMENYN ESTATE
BRIDGEND, MID GLAMORGAN CF32 9TD
0656 724444 FAX: 0656 721709

PRODUCT: PICTON, COBRA

TORNADO INFLATABLE BOATS LTD
DAIRYCOATES INDUSTRIAL ESTATE
HULL, NORTH HUMBERSIDE HU4 6PA
0482 53972 FAX: 0482 572475

WINSOR BROS
UNIT 13-14
WICKERMARINE, CRANLEIGH ROAD
PORTCHESTER, HANTS PO16 9DR
0329 829100 FAX: 0329 829100

ZODIAC UK LTD
2 EDGEMEAD CLOSE
ROUND SPINNEY, NORTHAMPTON
NORTHAMPTONSHIRE NN3 4RG
0604 648124

OUTBOARDS MOTORS

EP BARRUS LTD
LAUNTON ROAD, BICESTER, OXON OX6 OUR
0869 253355 FAX: 0869 321485

PRODUCT: FORCE, MARINER
DISTRIBUTES: FISHPORT, MAXON

HERON SUZUKI
46 GATWICK ROAD
CRAWLEY, SUSSEX HR10 2XF
0293 518000 FAX: 0293 545315

HONDA UK LTD
POWER ROAD
CHISWICK, LONDON W4 5YT
081 7471400 FAX: 081 7469104

MITSUI MACHINERY SALES (UK) LTD
SOPWITH DRIVE
WEYBRIDGE, SURREY KT13 0UZ
0932 358000 FAX: 0932 385030

PRODUCT: YAMAHA

OUTBOARD MARINE (UK) LTD
8 HARROWDEN ROAD
BRACKMILLS, NORTHAMPTON
NORTHAMTONSHIRE NN4 0PD
0604 765131 FAX: 0604 769477

PRODUCT: EVINRUDE, JOHNSON

RON SCOTT MARINE LTD
HIGH STREET
TARPORLY
CHESHIRE CW6 ODX
0829 732257 FAX: 0829 733413

SELVA (UK) LTD
NEWMARKET ROAD
RISBY
BURY ST. EDMUNDS
SUFFOLK IP28 6RD
0284 811001 FAX: 0284 811021

PRODUCT: SELVA

SOWESTER
STINSFORD ROAD
NUFFIELD INDUSTRIAL ESTATE, POOLE
DORSET BH17 7SW
0202 667700 FAX: 0202 668585

PRODUCT: MERCURY OUTBOARDS

SPECIALIST OUTBOARD SERVICES
PO BOX 16
AYLESBURY, BUCKS MP17 8XS
0844 292528

TOHATSU MARINE
UNIT 2
BRIDGE ROAD WORKS, LYMINGTON
HANTS SO41 9BZ
0590 670787 FAX: 0590 670520

INSTRUMENTATION

ABB NERA
20 IMPERIAL WAY
CROYDON, SURREY CR0 4RR
081 6865701 FAX: 081 6866811

DISTRIBUTES: SKANTI

AMERICAN MARINE
PO BOX 6000
RINGWOOD, HANTS BH24 1FL
0425 476000

AMPRO DISTRIBUTION LTD
11 KINGSCLERE PARK
KINGSCLERE, NEWBURY
BERKSHIRE RG15 8SW
0635 299348 FAX: 0734 820337

DISTRIBUTES: PHILIPS AP NAVIGATORS

AUTONNIC RESEARCH LTD
WOODROLFE ROAD
TOLLESBURY, ESSEX CM9 8SE
0621 869460 FAX: 0621 868815

BROOKES & GATEHOUSE LTD
INTERNATIONAL MARINE HOUSE
ABBEY PARK, ROMSEY, HANTS SO51 9AQ
0794 518448 FAX: 0794 518007

PRODUCT: NAVSTAR

BURMARC LTD
UNIT 12
BEAVER INDUSTRIAL ESTATE, LIPHOOK
HANTS GU30 7EU
0428 724777 FAX: 0428 724652

DISTRIBUTES: KVH, QUADRO, NAVIONICS

CAS UK LTD
PO BOX 50
HORNCHURCH, ESSEX RM11 3PW
0708 437666 FAX: 0708 437667

PRODUCT: SHAKESPEARE

CJ INTERNATIONAL
ELLBRIDGE PARK
HATT, SALTASH
CORNWALL PL12 6PU
0752 845375 FAX: 0752 845375

DISTRIBUTES: MICROLOGIC, LORAN

COLNBROOK ELECTRONICS
CRABBS ABBEY
STOWBRIDGE, KINGS LYNN
NORFOLK PE34 3PE
0553 810161 FAX: 0553 810161

PRODUCT: WASP

COMMUNIQUE
COMMUNICATIONS HOUSE
PURLEY AVENUE
LONDON NW2 1SB
081 4509755 FAX: 081 4506826

DISTRIBUTES: STANDARD

FIRDELL RADAR REFLECTORS
THE GROVE
WARREN LANE
STANMORE
MIDDLESEX HA7 4LY
081 4203306 FAX: 081 4203306

PRODUCT: BLIPPER

FURUNO UK LTD
OCEAN HOUSE
ST. GEORGES ROAD
SOUTHSEA,
HANTS PO4 9QS
0705 295122 FAX: 0705 732405

GARMIN (EUROPE) LTD
FALCON HOUSE
FLEMING COURT, ALMA ROAD
ROMSEY, HANTS SO51 8ED
0794 519944 FAX: 0794 519222

ICOM (UK) LTD
SEA STREET
HERNE BAY, KENT CT6 8LD
0227 741741 FAX: 0227 741742

INCASTEC ASSOCIATES LTD
75-77 CHRISTCHURCH ROAD
RINGWOOD, HANTS BH24 1DH
0425 476211

DISTRIBUTES: BOTTOMLINE

MAGELLAN SYSTEMS (UK) LTD
ELMCROFT
3 ELMHURST ROAD, GOSPORT
HANTS PO12 1PG
0705 585200

MAGNAVOX
LANCASTER HOUSE
7 CHURCH STREET, SLOUGH
BERKS SL1 1TL
0753 538025 FAX: 0753 824633

MARCONI MARINE
WATERHOUSE LANE
CHELMSFORD
ESSEX CM1 2QX
0245 353221 FAX: 0245 358776

DISTRIBUTES: KODEN

MARINE SURVEY SYSTEMS
217 DEREHAM ROAD
NORWICH, NORFOLK NR2 3TE
0603 664028 FAX: 0603 664028

PRODUCT: MAGNETOMETERS-MX500

MARINEX LTD
1 FACTORY ROAD
UPTON, POOLE, DORSET BH16 5SJ
0202 632116 FAX: 0202 631980

PRODUCT: CELTREX, RIGEL, SEA STAR

NASA (1992)
BOULTON ROAD
STEVENAGE, HERTS SG1 4QG
0438 354033 FAX: 0438 741498

NAUTECH LTD
ANCHORAGE PARK
PORTSMOUTH, HAMPSHIRE PO3 5TD
0705 693611 FAX: 0705 694642

PRODUCT: AUTOHELM

NAVICO LTD
STAR LANE
MARGATE, KENT CT9 4NP
0843 290290 FAX: 0843 290471

PLASTIMO MANUFACTURING
SCHOOL LANE
CHANDLERS FORD INDUSTRIAL ESTATE
EASTLEIGH
HANTS SO5 3DG
0703 262211 FAX: 0703 266328

RAYTHEON MARINE SALES
ELIZABETH WAY
THE PINNACLES, HARLOW
ESSEX CM19 5AZ
0279 444244 FAX: 0279 444223

PRODUCT: APELCO, RAYTHEON
DISTRIBUTES: JRC

RITCHIE
4 MARKET SQUARE
AMERSHAM, BUCKS HP7 0DQ
0494 433077 FAX: 0494 726363

PRODUCT: COMPASSES

ROBERTSON STOWE
PARKLANDS BUSINESS PARK
FOREST ROAD, DENMEAD
WATERLOOVILLE, HANTS PO7 6XP
0705 230885 FAX: 0705 230665

PRODUCT: DATALINE, STOWE

S.M. INTERNATIONAL LTD.
SALT QUAY HOUSE
NORTH EAST QUAY
SUTTON HARBOUR
PLYMOUTH, DEVON PL4 ORA
0752 662129 FAX: 0752 222717

PRODUCT: EAGLE, FUSO

SEAFARER INTERNATIONAL
UNIT 2, THE PYRAMID CENTRE
AIRPORT SERVICE ROAD
PORTSMOUTH, HANTS PO3 5SH
0705 651001 FAX: 0705 651005

SG BROWN
TEWIN ROAD
WELWYN GARDEN CITY
HERTS AL7 1LR
0707 331299 FAX: 0707 334429

PRODUCT: GYRO COMPASS

SHIPMATE MARINE ELECTRONICS
5 ELM COURT
CRYSTAL DRIVE, SANDWELL BUSINESS PARK
SMETHWICK
WEST MIDLANDS B66 1RB
021 5521718 FAX: 021 5445488

DISTRIBUTES: ANRITSU, PANASONIC

SILVA (UK) LTD
UNIT 10
SKY BUSINESS PARK, EVERSLEY WAY
EGHAM, SURREY TW20 8RF
0784 471721 FAX: 0784 471097

SIMPSON LAWRENCE
218-228 EDMISTON DRIVE
GLASGOW, GLASGOW G51 2YT
041 4275331 FAX: 041 4275419

DISTRIBUTES: LOWRANCE

SOUTH MIDLAND COMMUNICATION
SCHOOL CLOSE
CHANDLERS FORD IND. EST.
EASTLEIGH, HANTS SO5 3BY
0703 255111 FAX: 0703 263507

PRODUCT: SMC

SOWESTER
STINSFORD ROAD
NUFFIELD INDUSTRIAL ESTATE, POOLE
DORSET BH17 7SW
0202 667700 FAX: 0202 668585

PRODUCT: MERCURY OUTBOARDS

THOMAS WALKER
INTERNATIONAL HOUSE
37-41 BISSELL STREET
BIRMINGHAM B5 7HR
021 6224475 FAX: 021 6224478

TRIMBLE NAVIGATION LTD
TRIMBLE HOUSE
MERIDIAN OFFICE PARK, OSBORN WAY
HOOK, HANTS RG27 9HX
0256 760150 FAX: 0256 760148

PRODUCT: LORAN

VDO INSTRUMENTS
SPECIAL PRODUCTS DIVISION
HOLFORD DRIVE, HOLFORD
BIRMINGHAM B6 7UG
021 3442000 FAX: 021 3442072

VETUS DEN OUDEN
38 SOUTH HANTS INDUSTRIAL PARK
TOTTON, SOUTHAMPTON
HANTS SO4 3SA
0703 861033 FAX: 0703 663142

YEOMAN MARINE
THE SHIPYARD
BATH ROAD, LYMINGTON
HANTS SO41 9YL
0590 679777 FAX: 0590 671717

INFORMATION TECHNOLOGY

AQUALOGIC
18 SWANMEAD
HIGHTOWN, RINGWOOD
HANTS BH24 3RD
0425 470001 FAX: 0425 470001

PRODUCT: MARINE PC HARDWARE

ISLAND COMPUTERS
41 HORSEBRIDGE HILL
PARKHURST, ISLE OF WIGHT PO30 5TJ
0983 821717 FAX: 0983 521608

PRODUCT: MARINE PC SOFTWARE

MARITEK
1-D7 TEMPLETON CENTRE
GLASGOW G40 1DA
041 5542492 FAX: 041 6391910

PRODUCT: NAV PROGRAM FOR PSION

PC MARITIME
BAIN CLARKSON HOUSE
BRUNSWICK ROAD, PLYMOUTH
DEVON PL4 0NP
0752 254205 FAX: 0752 253599

PRODUCT: MARINE PC SOFTWARE

SPECIALIST

HENSHAW INFLATABLES LTD
BENNETTS FIELD TRADING ESTATE
WINCANTON, SOMERSET BA9 9DT
0963 33237 FAX: 0963 34578

PRODUCT: RIB TUBES

KELVIN HUGHES
145 MINORIES
LONDON, LONDON EC3N 1NH
071 7099076 FAX: 071 4811298

PRODUCT: ADMIRALTY CHARTS

MATTHEW DAVIES PRECISION ENG.
PLANAR BUILDING
110 WINDMILL ROAD
SUNBURY ON THAMES
MIDDLESEX TW16 7HD
0932 770370 FAX: 0932 781151

PRODUCT: A FRAMES, DRY BOXES

PINTA PILOTS
UNIT 1
8 JOHN STREET, SHOREHAM BY SEA SUSSEX
BN3 1AR
0273 441051

PRODUCT: PINTA PILOT REPAIRS

RAMPATCH LTD
HALLOM HOUSE
20 MARBOROUGH RISE, CAMBERLEY
SURREY GU15 2ED
0276 675044 FAX: 0276 675003

PRODUCT: INSTANT TUBE REPAIRS

4WD VEHICLES

FORD MOTOR CO. LTD
BRENTWOOD, ESSEX CM13 3BW
0277 253000

ISUZU CARS (GB) LTD
RYDER STREET
WEST BROMWICH
WEST MIDLANDS B70 0EJ
021 522 2000

LADA CARS LTD
CARNABY INDUSTRIAL ESTATE
NR. BRIDLINGTON, YORKSHIRE YO15 3QX
0262 678011

LAND ROVER LTD
LODE LANE
SOLIHULL, WEST MIDLANDS B92 8NW
021 722 2424

MERCEDES BENZ CENTRE
TONGWELL
MILTON KEYNES, BUCKS MK15 8BA
0908 233133

MITSUBISHI
THE COLT CAR CO LTD
WATERMOOR, CIRENCESTER
GLOUCESTERSHIRE GL7 1LF
0285 655777

NISSAN GB LTD
RIVERS OFFICE PARK
DENHAM WAY, MAPLE CROSS
RICKMANSWORTH, HERTS WD3 2YS
0923 899999

SUZUKI GB CARS LTD
46-62 GATWICK ROAD
CRAWLEY, WEST SUSSEX RH10 2XF
0293 518000

TOYOTA GB LTD
THE QUADRANGLE
REDHILL, SURREY RH1 1PX
0737 768585

VAUXHALL MOTORS LTD
GRIFFIN HOUSE
OSBORNE ROAD, LUTON
BEDFORDSHIRE LU1 3YT
0582 21122

TRAILERS

INDESPENSION LTD
BELMONT ROAD
BOLTON, LANCS BL1 7AQ
0204 309797 FAX: 0204 309148

LEW-WAYS LTD
NORTHGATE
ALDRIDGE, WEST MIDLANDS WS9 8TY
0922 743131 FAX: 0922 743075

RM TRAILERS LTD
NEW FARM ROAD
ALRESFORD, HANTS
096273 2560 FAX: 096273 4027

Dahlia anemone - Urticina felina

Retailers

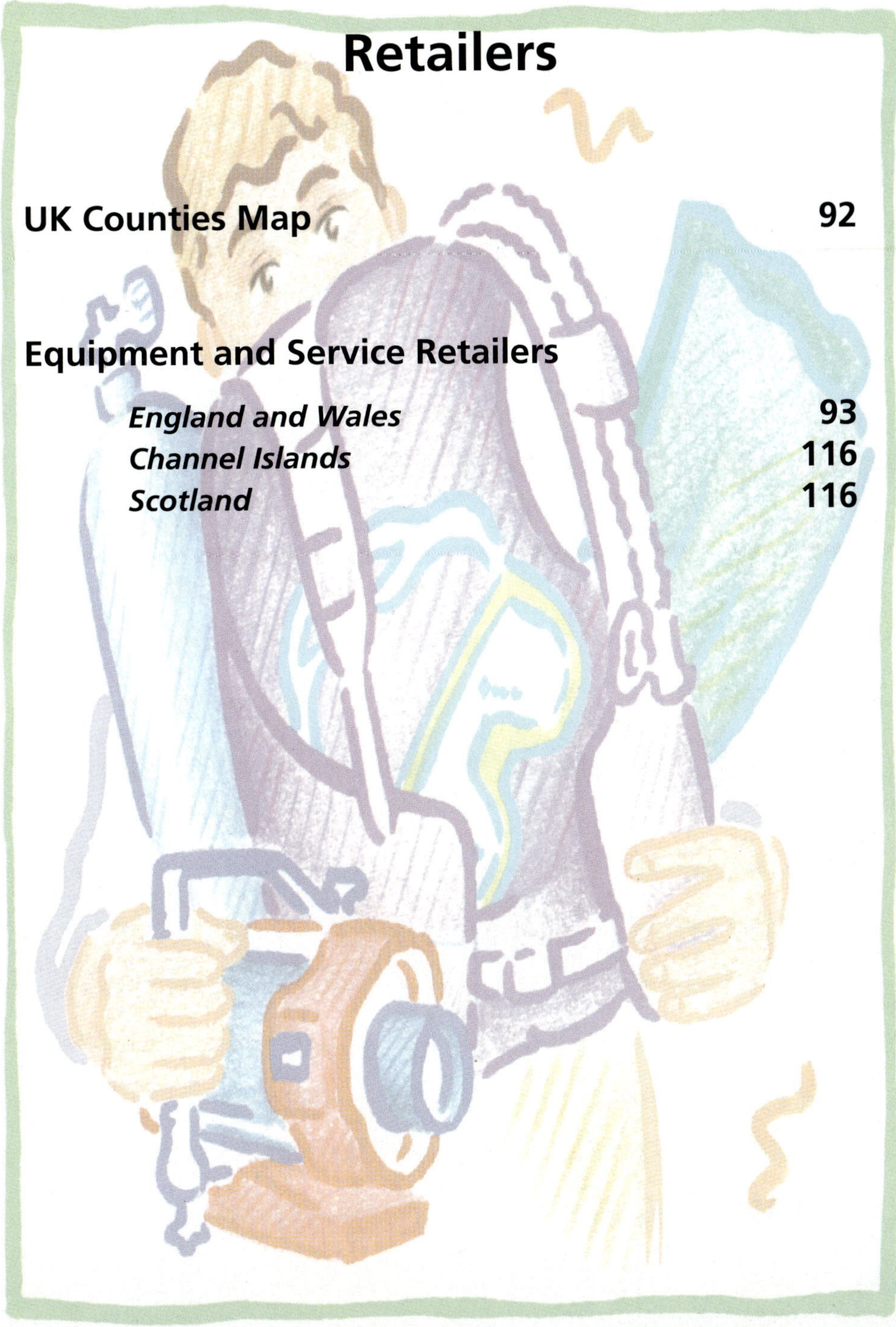

COUNTIES

Conical Orthomorphic Projection

For product key codes see reference page 347

Equipment and Service Retailers

AVON

BRISTOL DIVING CENTRE
52 OLD MARKET STREET
BRISTOL, AVON BS2 0ER
0272 299544 FAX: 0272 258571

TRAINING : PADI, BSAC
EQUPT : BAS, CTH, CAM, SFY, BKS
HIRE : BAS, CTH
REPAIRS : BAS, CTH, CAM
TANKS : TST, IDEST, FILL TO 300BAR
CHARTER : YES, ON BOARD OXYGEN
TRAVEL : HOLIDAYS
OPEN : MON-SAT 0900-1730
OPEN LATE : THU 0900-2000

CAMERAS UNDERWATER
10 KELLAWAY AVENUE
BRISTOL, AVON BS6 7XR
0272 445443

EQUPT : CAM
REPAIRS : CAM

CURRENT STATE DIVING
8 KELLAWAY AVENUE
REDLAND, BRISTOL
AVON BS6 7XR
0272 247030 FAX: 0272 245009

TRAINING : PADI, BSAC, NAUI
EQUPT : BAS, CTH, SFY, BKS
HIRE : BAS, CTH
REPAIRS : BAS, CTH
TANKS : TST, IDEST, FILL TO 300BAR
TRAVEL : HOLIDAYS
OPEN : MON-SAT 0900-1800

TRIDENT DIVING
361 FISHPONDS ROAD
EASTVILLE, BRISTOL, AVON BS5 6RD
0272 586620

TRAINING : PADI, BSAC
EQUPT : BAS, CTH, BKS
HIRE : BAS, CTH
REPAIRS : BAS, CTH
TANKS : TST, IDEST, FILL TO 240BAR
OPEN : MON-FRI 0830-1900, SAT 0830-1800

BEDFORDSHIRE

DEEP DIVE DIVING SERVICES
1 ARCHWAY PARADE
MARSH ROAD, LEAGRAVE
LUTON, BEDFORDSHIRE LU3 2RW
0582 572123 FAX: 0582 562688

TRAINING : PADI, BSAC
EQUPT : BAS, CTH, CAM, SFY, BKS
HIRE : BAS, CTH
REPAIRS : BAS, CTH
TANKS : TST, IDEST, FILL TO 255BAR
CHARTER : YES, ON BOARD OXYGEN
TRAVEL : HOLIDAYS
OPEN : MON-SAT 0900-1800

DIVE IN BEDFORD
28A AMPTHILL ROAD
BEDFORD, BEDFORDSHIRE MK42 9HG
0234 273058 FAX: 0234 273058

TRAINING : PADI
EQUPT : BAS, CTH, CAM, SFY, BKS
REPAIRS : BAS
TANKS : TST, FILL TO 232BAR
TRAVEL : HOLIDAYS
OPEN : TUE-SAT 0900-1800
OPEN LATE : TUE-THU 0900-2000

KEMPSTON DINGHY & LEISURE
100 HIGH STREET
KEMPSTON, BEDFORD,
BEDFORDSHIRE MK42 7AR
0234 854831 FAX: 0234 853980

TRAINING : PADI
EQUPT : BAS, CTH, CAM, SFY, BKS, BTS
HIRE : BAS
REPAIRS : BAS, CTH, BTS
TANKS : TST, FILL TO 232BAR
CHARTER : YES, ON BOARD OXYGEN
TRAVEL : HOLIDAYS
OPEN : MON,WED-FRI 1130-1745. SAT 0900-1700

BERKSHIRE

READING DIVE SHOP
17 SILVERDALE ROAD
EARLY, READING, BERKSHIRE RG6 2NZ
0734 264814 FAX: 0734 264814

TRAINING : PADI
EQUPT : BAS, CTH, CAM, SFY, BKS
HIRE : BAS, CTH
REPAIRS : BAS, CTH
TANKS : FILL TO 300BAR
OPEN : MON-SAT 0830-1730

CAMBRIDGESHIRE

DIVE IN GILDENBURGH
GILDENBURGH WATER
EASTREA ROAD, WHITTLESEY
PETERBOROUGH, CAMBRIDGESHIRE PE7 2AR
0733 351288 FAX: 0733 351299

TRAINING : PADI
EQUPT : BAS, CTH, SFY, BKS
HIRE : BAS, CTH, CAM
REPAIRS : BAS, CTH
TANKS : TST, IDEST, FILL TO 345BAR
TRAVEL : HOLIDAYS
OPEN : TUE-WED,FRI-SAT 0900-2200. SUN 0800-1730

TYRELLS MARINE LTD
23 BERMUDA ROAD
CAMBRIDGE
CAMBRIDGESHIRE CB4 3JX
0223 352847 FAX: 0223 62448

EQUPT : BAS, CTH, CAM, SFY, BKS, BTS
REPAIRS : BTS
TANKS : FILL TO 217BAR
OPEN : MON-SAT 0900-1730

AQUANAUT DIVERS INTERNATIONAL
GRAEME LA MAISTRE SPORTS
17 BATH STREET
ST HELIER
JERSEY, CHANNEL ISLANDS
0534 31001

CHESHIRE

CHESTER SCHOOL OF DIVING
(DEE SPORTS)
67 BROOK STREET, CHESTER
CHESHIRE CH1 3DZ
0244 314204

TRAINING : PADI
EQUPT : BAS, CTH, CAM, BKS
HIRE : BAS
REPAIRS : BAS, CTH
TANKS : TST, IDEST, FILL TO 238BAR
CHARTER : YES, ON BOARD OXYGEN
TRAVEL : HOLIDAYS
OPEN : MON-SAT 0900-1800

DIVERS JUST DIVERS
UNIT 7, DAIRY WORKSHOPS
HENRY STREET, CREWE
CHESHIRE CW1 4BH
0270 250317-582312 FAX: 0270 250317

TRAINING : BSAC
EQUPT : BAS, CTH, CAM, SFY, BKS
HIRE : BAS, CTH
REPAIRS : BAS, CTH
TANKS : TST, IDEST, FILL TO 272BAR
TRAVEL : HOLIDAYS
OPEN : MON-SAT 0900-1730

WATERWAYS DIVING CENTRE
SOUTH PIER WATERWAYS
ELLESMERE PORT
SOUTH WIRRAL
CHESHIRE L6S 4FY
051 3565550

TRAINING : PADI, BSAC
EQUPT : BAS, CTH, BKS
REPAIRS : BAS, CTH
TANKS : TST, IDEST, FILL TO 232BAR
CHARTER : YES, ON BOARD OXYGEN
OPEN : MON-SAT 0900-1730, SUN 1000-1600
THU 0900-1730

CLEVELAND

ATLANTIS UNDERWATER CENTRE
BON LEA TRADING ESTATE
THORNABY, CLEVELAND TS1 7AQ
0642 671399 FAX: 0642 671399

EQUPT : BAS, CTH, BKS, BTS
REPAIRS : BAS, CTH, BTS
TANKS : FILL TO 272BAR
OPEN : MON-SAT 0900-1800

REDCAR UNDERWATER CENTRE
DENNY DIVING
THE ESPLANADE, REDCAR
CLEVELAND TS10 3AQ
0642 483507 FAX: 0642 483507

EQUPT : BAS, CTH, CAM, SFY, BKS, BTS
REPAIRS : BAS, CAM, BTS
TANKS : TST, FILL TO 272BAR
CHARTER : YES
OPEN : MON-SAT 0900-1800. SUN 0900-1200
OPEN LATE : TUE-THU 0900-2000

CLWYD

DIVERS AIR
THE POPLARS
ROSSETT ROAD, HOLT, CLWYD LL13 9SY
0829 270985

TRAINING : PADI, BSAC, SAA
EQUPT : BAS, CTH, CAM, SFY, BKS, BTS
HIRE : BAS, CTH
REPAIRS : BAS, CTH, CAM, BTS
TANKS : TST, IDEST, FILL TO 374BAR
OPEN : MON-SUN 0800-2000

CORNWALL

ATLANTIC AQUA SPORTS
ALBERT STREET
PENZANCE, CORNWALL TR18 2LR
0736 65757 FAX: 0736 51626

EQUPT : BAS, CTH, BKS
REPAIRS : BAS
TANKS : FILL TO 272BAR
CHARTER : YES, ON BOARD OXYGEN
OPEN : MON-SAT 0830-1730.
SUN 1000-1300 (SUMMER ONLY)

CORNISH DIVING AND WATERSPORTS
BAR ROAD
FALMOUTH, CORNWALL TR11 4BN
0326 311265 FAX: 0326 311265

TRAINING : PADI
EQUPT : BAS, CTH, CAM, SFY, BKS, BTS
HIRE : BAS, CTH, CAM
REPAIRS : BAS, CTH, BTS
TANKS : TST, FILL TO 285BAR
CHARTER : YES, ON BOARD OXYGEN
TRAVEL : HOLIDAYS
OPEN : MON-SUN 0900-1730

R. S. PUBLICATION MARKETING

6 London Road, Stroud, Glos. GL5 2AA.
Tel. 0285 641953. Fax: 0453 752916

MODEL MAKERS & MANUFACTURERS OF PEWTER/METAL OBJET D'ART PRODUCTS – MAIL ORDER MANUFACTURING (TRADE ENQUIRIES WELCOME)

presents

"THE DIVING COLLECTION"

Treasure of the Deep

Limited Edition

REF I

Beautifully handcrafted bronzed objet d'art masterpiece

Size approx:
6" wide x $4^1/_2$" high

Priced at only
£69.95 inc p & p

order yours now

Ref A Solid Pewter Diver(s) dressed in CDBA
11cm high **£28.95** each

Ref B Solid Pewter Diver(s) dressed in SCUBA
11cm high **£28.95** each

Ref C Solid Pewter Diver(s) dressed in standard
11cm high **£28.95** each

Ref D 9ct Solid Gold Scuba Diver
2.5 cm length **£29.95** each

Ref E Sterling Silver Scuba Diver
2.5 cm length **£12.95** each

Ref F Pewter Divers Fin Keyring
£3.50 each

Ref G Pewter Divers Standard Helmet Keyring
£3.50 each

Ref H Pewter & Enamelled Diving Flag Alpha Keyring
£3.50 each

ORDER DIRECT FROM: R.S. PUBLICATION MARKETING, 6 LONDON ROAD, STROUD, GLOS. GL5 2AA.

Name ______________________

Address ______________________

____

______________________ Postcode ______________________

Telephone ______________________

Ref No. of Order(s)	A	B	C	D	E	F	G	H	REF I
Quantity									

TOTAL ENCLOSED £

CHEQUES OR POSTAL ORDERS PAYABLE TO: R.S. PUBLICATION MARKETING

POSTAGE IS FREE • DELIVERY WITHIN 14/21 DAYS

FALMOUTH UNDERWATER CENTRE
MAENPORTH BEACH
NR FALMOUTH, CORNWALL TR11 5HN
0326 250852 FAX: 0326 250852

TRAINING : **PADI, BSAC, HSA**
EQUPT : **BAS, CTH, SFY, BKS**
HIRE : **BAS, CTH**
REPAIRS : **BAS, CTH**
TANKS : **TST, FILL TO 272BAR**
CHARTER : **YES, ON BOARD OXYGEN**
TRAVEL : **HOLIDAYS**
OPEN : **MON-SUN 0900-1830.**
IN WINTER - OPEN WEEKENDS ONLY

FOWEY MARINE SERVICES
21-27 STATION RD, FOWEY, NR. ST AUSTELL
CORNWALL PL23 1DF
0726 833236

TRAINING : SAA
EQUPT : BAS, CTH, CAM, SFY, BKS, BTS
HIRE : BAS, CTH
REPAIRS : BAS, CTH, BTS
TANKS : TST, FILL TO 260BAR
CHARTER : YES, ON BOARD OXYGEN
OPEN : MON-SUN 0900-1900

MOUNTSBAY DIVING
MONROVIA
17 HAYLE TERRACE, HAYLE
CORNWALL TR27 4BU
0736 752135

TANKS : FILL TO 232BAR
CHARTER : YES
OPEN : MON-SUN BY APPOINTMENT

NEWQUAY DIVING SUPPLIES
WESLEY COURT
NEWQUAY, CORNWALL CR10 08J
0637 873697 FAX: 0637 873697

EQUPT : BAS, CTH, SFY, BKS
HIRE : BAS, CTH
REPAIRS : BAS, CTH
TANKS : FILL TO 272BAR
CHARTER : YES
TRAVEL : HOLIDAYS
OPEN : MON-SAT 0900-1730

OCEAN SPORTS
PENTEWAN VILLAGE
NR. ST AUSTELL, CORNWALL PL26 6BX
0726 842817-843781 FAX: 0726 842817

TRAINING : **PADI, BSAC, SAA**
EQUPT : **BAS, CTH, CAM, SFY, BKS, BTS**
HIRE : **BAS, CTH**
REPAIRS : **BAS, CTH, CAM, BTS**
TANKS : **TST, FILL TO 400BAR**
CHARTER : **YES, ON BOARD OXYGEN**
TRAVEL : **HOLIDAYS**
OPEN : **MON-SUN 0900-1800**

SEAWAYS DIVING CENTRE
INC. SEAQUEST CHARTERS
TIDAL HOUSE, COMMERCIAL ROAD
PENRYN, CORNWALL TR10 8AG
0326 375544 FAX: 0326 375401

EQUPT : **BAS, CTH, SFY, BKS**
HIRE : **BAS, CTH**
REPAIRS : **BAS, CTH**
TANKS : **TST, IDEST, FILL TO 310BAR**
CHARTER : **YES, ON BOARD OXYGEN**
OPEN : **MON-SAT 0900-1730 SUN 1530-1800**

UNDERSEA ADVENTURES
ST. IVES SCUBA DIVING
HARLEQUINS, THE BELYARDS
ST. IVES, CORNWALL TR26 2DB
0736 793353 FAX: 0736 793353

TRAINING : **PADI**
EQUPT : **BAS, CTH, CAM, SFY, BKS**
HIRE : **BAS, CTH**
REPAIRS : **BAS, CTH**
CHARTER : **YES, ON BOARD OXYGEN**
TRAVEL : **HOLIDAYS**
OPEN : **MON-SUN 0900-LATE.**

DERBYSHIRE

MERCIA DIVERS
36 HIGH STREET
REPTON, DERBYSHIRE DE5 8GD
0283 702246

EQUPT : BAS, CTH, SFY, BKS
REPAIRS : BAS, CTH
TANKS : TST, FILL TO 232BAR
TRAVEL : HOLIDAYS
OPEN : MON-TUE, THU-FRI 0900-1200/1400-1800.
SAT 0900-1300

SCUBA MARINE (CHESTERFIELD)
RINGWOOD ROAD
BRIMINGTON, CHESTERFIELD
DERBYSHIRE S43 1DB
0246 232369

TRAINING : PADI
EQUPT : BAS, CTH, CAM, SFY, BKS, BTS
HIRE : BAS
REPAIRS : BAS, CTH, CAM

TANKS : TST, FILL TO 232BAR
CHARTER : YES
TRAVEL : HOLIDAYS
OPEN : MON-SAT 0900-1730

DEVON

AQUANAUT
17 CLIFTON ROAD
EXETER
DEVON EX1 2BR
0392 218825 FAX: 0392 218825

TRAINING : BSAC
EQUPT : BAS, CTH, CAM, BKS, BTS
HIRE : BAS, CTH, CAM
REPAIRS : BAS, CTH, CAM
TANKS : TST, FILL TO 272BAR
CHARTER : YES, ON BOARD OXYGEN
OPEN : MON-TUE 0900-1700. WED 0900-1300.
OPEN LATE : THU-SAT 0900-1730

DIVE SHOP & UNDERWATER CENTRE
FORT BOVISAND
PLYMOUTH
DEVON PL9 0AB
0752 406646-408021 FAX: 0752 481843

TRAINING : PADI, BSAC
EQUPT : BAS, CTH, CAM, SFY, BKS
REPAIRS : BAS, CTH
TANKS : TST, IDEST, FILL TO 260BAR
OPEN : WED-MON 0900-1700
OPEN LATE : SAT 0830-1730

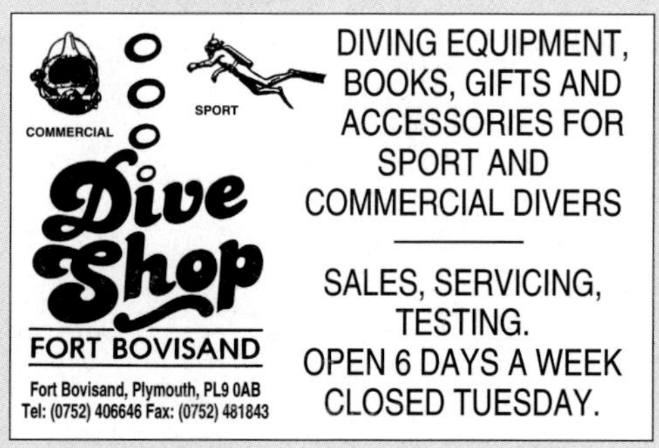

DIVER TRAINING SCHOOL
THO OLD BAKERY
5 CAMPERDOWN TERRACE
EXMOUTH
DEVON EX8 1ES
0395 266300
FAX: 0395 276341

TRAINING : PADI, BSAC, SAA
HIRE : BAS
REPAIRS : BAS
TANKS : TST, FILL TO 270BAR
CHARTER : YES, ON BOARD OXYGEN
OPEN : MON-FRI 0900-1700

HALLSAND HOTEL
NORTH HALLSAND
KINGSBRIDGE
DEVON TQ7 2EY
054 851264

TANKS : FILL TO 272BAR
CHARTER : YES, ON BOARD OXYGEN
OPEN : VARIES. PLEASE PHONE

INTERDIVE
THE DIVER TRAINING CENTRE
WEST HOE ROAD
PLYMOUTH
DEVON PL1 3BH
0752 255665 FAX: 0752 255344

TRAINING : HSA
EQUPT : BAS, CTH, CAM, SFY
HIRE : BAS, CTH, CAM
REPAIRS : BAS, CTH, CAM
TANKS : TST, FILL TO 350BAR
CHARTER : YES, ON BOARD OXYGEN
OPEN : MON-FRI 0830-1700

KINGSBRIDGE WATERSPORTS
39 FORE STREET
KINGSBRIDGE
DEVON TQ7 1PG
0548 852934

EQUPT : BAS, BKS
HIRE : BAS
TANKS : FILL TO 250BAR
CHARTER : YES, ON BOARD OXYGEN
TRAVEL : HOLIDAYS
OPEN : MON-SAT 0930-1700

NAUTIQUE
SOUTH QUAY
THE HARBOUR, PAIGNTON, DEVON TQ4 6DT
0803 550278 FAX: 0803 550278

EQUPT : BAS, CTH, CAM, SFY, BKS, BTS
HIRE : BAS
REPAIRS : BAS, CTH, CAM
TANKS : FILL TO 360BAR
CHARTER : YES, ON BOARD OXYGEN
OPEN : MON-SUN. 0900-LATE

SALCOMBE BOAT CO
& WATERSPORT CENTRE
NO1 ISLAND SQUARE, ISLAND STREET
SALCOMBE, DEVON TQ8 8DP
0548 844224 FAX: 0548 844224

EQUPT : BAS, CTH, BKS, BTS
HIRE : BAS, CTH
REPAIRS : BAS, CTH, BTS
TANKS : FILL TO 204BAR
CHARTER : YES, ON BOARD OXYGEN
TRAVEL : HOLIDAYS
OPEN : MON-SAT 0900-1800
OPEN LATE : BY APPOINTMENT

SANDFORD AND DOWN
24 PIER STREET
WEST HOE, PLYMOUTH, DEVON PL1 3BP
0752 266248 FAX: 0752 226131

EQUPT : BAS, CTH, CAM, SFY, BKS
REPAIRS : BAS
TANKS : TST, FILL TO 326BAR
OPEN : TUE-SAT 0900-1800

SCUBA WORLD DIVE CENTRE
LANGLANDS BUSINESS PARK
UFFCULME, DEVON, DEVON EX15 3DA
0884 840001 FAX: 0884 841770

TRAINING : PADI, BSAC, SSI
EQUPT : BAS, CTH, CAM, SFY, BKS
HIRE : BAS, CTH, CAM
REPAIRS : BAS, CTH, CAM
TANKS : TST, IDEST, FILL TO 340BAR
CHARTER : YES, ON BOARD OXYGEN
TRAVEL : HOLIDAYS
OPEN : MON-SAT 0900-1800 FRI 0900-2000
SUN 0900-1300

SEATON MARINE
THE HARBOUR
AXMOUTH, SEATON, DEVON EX12 4AA
0297 23344 FAX: 0297 23344

TRAINING : PADI
EQUPT : BAS, CTH, CAM, SFY, BKS, BTS
HIRE : BAS, CTH, CAM
REPAIRS : BAS, CTH, CAM, BTS
TANKS : TST, FILL TO 272BAR
CHARTER : YES, ON BOARD OXYGEN
OPEN : MON-SUN 0900-1700

SOUND DIVING
QUEEN ANNE'S BATTERY
COXSIDE, PLYMOUTH
DEVON PL4 OLP
0752 670674 FAX: 0752 670674

TRAINING : BSAC
EQUPT : BAS, CTH, CAM, BKS
HIRE : BAS, CTH, CAM
REPAIRS : BAS, CTH, CAM
TANKS : TST, FILL TO 250BAR
CHARTER : YES, ON BOARD OXYGEN
OPEN : APR-SEP MON-FRI 0900-1800 SAT 0830-1900
SUN 0830-1300
OPEN LATE : OCT-MAR MON-FRI 1300-1730
SAT 0900-1700 SUN 0930-1130

VENTURE SPORTS
371 TORQUAY ROAD
PRESTON, PAIGNTON
DEVON TQ3 2BT
0803 523023 FAX: 0803 523023

TRAINING : BSAC
EQUPT : BAS, CTH, SFY, BKS
HIRE : BAS, CTH
REPAIRS : BAS
TANKS : FILL TO 272BAR
OPEN : MON-SAT 0900-1730. SUN 0900-1200 (SUMMER)

DORSET

BRIDPORT DIVING SUPPLIES
71-73 EAST STREET
BRIDPORT, DORSET DT6 3LB
0308 56348 FAX: 0308 56348

TRAINING : SAA
EQUPT : BAS, CTH
HIRE : BAS
TANKS : TST, FILL TO 350BAR
CHARTER : YES
OPEN : MON-SUN 0900-1800

DIVERS DOWN (SWANAGE) LTD
THE PIER
HIGH STREET, SWANAGE
DORSET BH19 2AN
0929 423565

TRAINING : PADI, BSAC
EQUPT : BAS, CTH, CAM, SFY, BKS, BTS
HIRE : BAS, CTH, CAM
REPAIRS : BAS, CTH, CAM, BTS
TANKS : FILL TO 270BAR
CHARTER : YES, ON BOARD OXYGEN
TRAVEL : HOLIDAYS
OPEN : MON-SUN 0900-1700
OPEN LATE : SAT-SUN 0800-2000

DIVING LEISURE LTD
ROCKLEY PARK
NAPIER ROAD, HAMWORTHY
POOLE, DORSET BH15 4LZ
0202 680898 FAX: 0202 665322

TRAINING : PADI
EQUPT : BAS, CTH, BKS
HIRE : BAS, CTH
REPAIRS : BAS
TANKS : TST, FILL TO 232BAR
TRAVEL : HOLIDAYS
OPEN : PLEASE RING

DORSET DIVING SERVICES
UNIT 7, WEST HOWE INDUSTRIAL ESTATE
ELLIOT ROAD
BOURNEMOUTH, DORSET BH11 8JX
0202 580065 FAX: 0202 593529

TRAINING : BSAC
EQUPT : BAS, CTH, CAM, SFY, BKS
HIRE : BAS, CTH
REPAIRS : BAS, CTH
TANKS : TST, FILL TO 340BAR
CHARTER : YES, ON BOARD OXYGEN
TRAVEL : HOLIDAYS
OPEN : MON-SAT 0900-1830. SUN 0900-1230

OLD HARBOUR DIVE CENTRE & SCHOOL
11 NOTHE PARADE
WEYMOUTH, DORSET DT4 8TX
0305 760888-761666
FAX: 0305 760888-761666

TRAINING : PADI, BSAC
EQUPT : BAS, CTH, SFY, BKS
HIRE : BAS, CTH
REPAIRS : BAS, CTH
TANKS : FILL TO 272BAR
CHARTER : YES, ON BOARD OXYGEN
OPEN : MON-FRI 0900-1800, SAT-SUN 0800-LATE

PARRY'S DIVE SHOP
(SUB AQUATICS DIVING SUPPLIES)
VICTORIA SQUARE, PORTLAND
DORSET DT5 1AD
0305 821261

TRAINING : PADI
EQUPT : BAS, CTH, CAM, SFY, BKS
HIRE : BAS, CTH, CAM
REPAIRS : BAS, CTH, CAM
TANKS : TST, IDEST, FILL TO 232BAR
CHARTER : YES, ON BOARD OXYGEN
TRAVEL : HOLIDAYS
OPEN : MON-SUN 0900-1800(SUMMER)
MON-SUN 0900-1730(WINTER)

POOLE DIVE CENTRE
QUAY WEST MARINA
THE MARINER COMPLEX, POOLE
DORSET BH15 1HX
0202 677427 FAX: 0202 682744

TRAINING : BSAC
EQUPT : BAS, CTH, SFY, BKS
HIRE : BAS, CTH
REPAIRS : BAS, CTH
TANKS : TST, FILL TO 232BAR
CHARTER : YES, ON BOARD OXYGEN
OPEN : MON-SUN 0900-1800

WEST BAY WATER SPORTS
THE OLD TIMBER YARD
GEORGE STREET, WEST BAY
BRIDPORT, DORSET DT6 4EY
0308 421800 FAX: 0308 421800

TRAINING : PADI
EQUPT : BAS, CTH, CAM, SFY, BKS, BTS
HIRE : BAS, CTH, CAM
REPAIRS : BAS, CTH, CAM, BTS
TANKS : TST, FILL TO 250BAR
CHARTER : YES, ON BOARD OXYGEN
TRAVEL : HOLIDAYS
OPEN : MON-FRI 0800-1930, SAT-SUN 0730-1800

WEYMOUTH SCUBA CENTRE
43 WALPOLE STREET
WEYMOUTH, DORSET DT4 7HQ
03057 74652 FAX: 03057 74652

EQUPT : BAS, CTH, SFY, BKS
HIRE : BAS, CTH
REPAIRS : BAS, CTH
TANKS : TST, FILL TO 272BAR
CHARTER : YES, ON BOARD OXYGEN
TRAVEL : HOLIDAYS
OPEN : THU-MON 0800-1300/1400-1800
OPEN LATE : SAT-SUN 0800-2000

DYFED

ST DAVIDS DIVE CENTRE
GLAN-Y-MOR, CAERFAI ROAD
ST DAVIDS, DYFED SA64 6QT
0437 721788 FAX: 0437 721342

TRAINING : PADI
EQUPT : BAS, CTH, CAM, SFY, BKS
HIRE : BAS, CTH, CAM
REPAIRS : BAS, CTH, CAM
TANKS : FILL TO 272BAR
CHARTER : YES, ON BOARD OXYGEN
TRAVEL : HOLIDAYS
OPEN : MON-SUN 0900-1800

WEST WALES DIVING CENTRE
HASQUARD CROSS
HAVERFORD WEST, DYFED SA62 3SJ
0437 781457 FAX: 0437 781093

TRAINING : PADI, BSAC
EQUPT : BAS, CTH, SFY, BKS, BTS
HIRE : BAS, CTH
REPAIRS : BAS, CTH, BTS
TANKS : TST, FILL TO 272BAR
CHARTER : YES, ON BOARD OXYGEN
TRAVEL : HOLIDAYS
OPEN : MON-SUN 0830-1900

ESSEX

ADVENTURE DIVERS
WALTHAM ABBEY SWIMMING POOL
ROUNDHILLS, WALTHAM ABBEY
ESSEX EN9 1UP
0992 650674 FAX: 0992 650747

TRAINING : PADI
EQUPT : BAS, CTH, CAM, BKS
HIRE : BAS, CTH, CAM
REPAIRS : BAS, CTH
TANKS : TST, FILL TO 250BAR
CHARTER : YES, ON BOARD OXYGEN
TRAVEL : HOLIDAYS
OPEN : MON-SAT 1000-1900
OPEN LATE : WED 1000-2200

ADVENTURES IN DIVING
RAWLINGS FARM
MAIN ROAD, RETTENDON COMMON
CHELMSFORD, ESSEX EN9 1UP
0245 401225

TRAINING : PADI, BSAC
EQUPT : BAS, CTH, CAM, SFY, BKS
HIRE : BAS, CTH, CAM
REPAIRS : BAS, CTH, CAM
TANKS : TST, FILL TO 300BAR
TRAVEL : HOLIDAYS
OPEN : MON-SAT 0900-1800. SUN 1000-1230
OPEN LATE : FRI 0900-2000

BEL AIR SUB AQUA SUPPLIES
82 FAIRFAX DRIVE
WESTCLIFFE ON SEA, ESSEX SS0 9AF
0702 353205 FAX: 0702 353205

EQUPT : BAS, CTH, CAM, SFY, BKS
REPAIRS : BAS, CTH
TANKS : TST, FILL TO 340BAR
OPEN : MON-SAT 0900-1800

DIVERS 2000
394 GREEN LANE
SEVEN KINGS, ILFORD, ESSEX IG3 9JX
081 5979690 FAX: 081 5979690

TRAINING : PADI
EQUPT : BAS, CTH, CAM, SFY, BKS
HIRE : BAS, CTH, CAM
REPAIRS : BAS, CTH, CAM
TANKS : TST, IDEST, FILL TO 280BAR
CHARTER : YES, ON BOARD OXYGEN
OPEN : MON-SAT 0900-1800. SUN 1000-1400
OPEN LATE : THU 0900-2000

LAKESIDE DIVING CENTRE
ALEXANDRA LAKE
WEST THURROCK, GRAYS
ESSEX RM16 12N
0708 865745 FAX: 0708 863911

TRAINING : PADI, BSAC
EQUPT : BAS, CTH, CAM, SFY, BKS, BTS
HIRE : BAS, CTH
REPAIRS : BAS, CTH
TANKS : TST, FILL TO 285BAR
CHARTER : YES, ON BOARD OXYGEN
TRAVEL : HOLIDAYS
OPEN : MON-FRI 1000-1900. SAT-SUN 0730-1900.
WED 1000-2100

PUFF IN AIR SERVICES
UNIT 7 BARDWELL YARD
LATCHINGTON ROAD
COLD NORTON
ESSEX CM3 6UB
0621 828008 FAX: 0621 828008

TRAINING : PADI
EQUPT : BAS, CTH, CAM, SFY, BKS
HIRE : BAS, CTH, CAM
REPAIRS : BAS, CTH, CAM
TANKS : TST, IDEST, FILL TO 272BAR
TRAVEL : HOLIDAYS
OPEN : TUE-FRI 1100-1900. SAT 1000-1800

GLAMORGAN - MID

REMAR DIVING SERVICES
POPLAR ROAD
CAERPHILLY
GLAMORGAN-MID CF8 1LF
0222 860416 FAX: 0222 889194

TRAINING : PADI
EQUPT : BAS, CTH, CAM, SFY, BKS
HIRE : BAS, CTH
REPAIRS : BAS, CTH
TANKS : TST, IDEST, FILL TO 340BAR
OPEN : MON-FRI 0800-1730, SAT 0930-1230

GLAMORGAN-SOUTH

CARDIFF SPORTSGEAR
79 WHITCHURCH ROAD
CARDIFF
GLAMORGAN-SOUTH CF4 3JP
0222 621757 FAX: 0222 619343

EQUPT : BAS, CTH
TANKS : FILL TO 238BAR
OPEN : MON-SAT 0900-1800

GLAMORGAN-WEST

LEWIS AQUA SPORTS
64 COMMERCIAL ROAD
PORT TALBOT
GLAMORGAN-WEST SA13 1LG
0639 882312 FAX: 0639 882312

TRAINING : PADI
EQUPT : BAS, CTH, CAM, BKS
REPAIRS : BAS, CTH, CAM
TANKS : TST, FILL TO 285BAR
TRAVEL : HOLIDAYS
OPEN : MON-SAT 0900-1730
OPEN LATE : FRI 0900-2000

TREASURE ISLAND DIVING SERVICES
THE PROMENADE
ABERAVON
PORT TALBOT
GLAMORGAN-WEST SA12 6QR
0639 884108 FAX: 0639 884108

TRAINING : BSAC
EQUPT : BAS, CTH, CAM, SFY, BKS
REPAIRS : CTH, CAM
TANKS : TST, FILL TO 300BAR
CHARTER : YES, ON BOARD OXYGEN
TRAVEL : HOLIDAYS
OPEN : MON-SUN 0900-1730

GLOUCESTERSHIRE

DIVE 90
UNIT 24
KINGSBRIDGE BUSINESS CENTRE
CHELTENHAM
GLOUCESTERSHIRE GR1 9TA
0242 680003 FAX: 0242 68003

TRAINING : PADI, SAA
EQUPT : BAS, CTH, CAM, SFY, BKS
HIRE : BAS, CTH, CAM
REPAIRS : BAS, CTH
TANKS : TST, FILL TO 272BAR
CHARTER : YES, ON BOARD OXYGEN
TRAVEL : HOLIDAYS
OPEN : MON-SAT 1000-1800

GWENT

AQUASUB INTERNATIONAL
90 CHEPSTOW ROAD
NEWPORT, GWENT NP9 8EE
0633 223089 FAX: 0633 223089

TRAINING : PADI
EQUPT : BAS, CTH, CAM, SFY, BKS
HIRE : BAS, CTH, CAM
REPAIRS : BAS, CTH, CAM
TANKS : TST, FILL TO 232BAR
TRAVEL : HOLIDAYS
OPEN : MON-SAT 0900-1730
OPEN LATE : WED 0900-1900

GWYNEDD

DIVER TRAINING COLLEGE
PORT DAFARCH ROAD
HOLYHEAD, ANGLESEY
GWYNEDD LL65 2LP
0407 764545 FAX: 0407 763636

TRAINING : BSAC, SAA
EQUPT : BAS, CTH, SFY, BKS
HIRE : BAS, CTH
REPAIRS : BAS, CTH
TANKS : TST, FILL TO 240BAR
CHARTER : YES, ON BOARD OXYGEN
TRAVEL : HOLIDAYS
OPEN : MON-SUN 0900-1800

DIVING SERVICES
HEATHERCLIFF
RAVENSPORT ROAD
TREADDUR BAY
HOLYHEAD
GWYNEDD LL65 2AQ
0407 860318

TRAINING : PADI, BSAC
EQUPT : BAS, CTH, CAM, SFY, BKS
HIRE : BAS, CTH
REPAIRS : BAS, CTH
TANKS : IDEST, FILL TO 340BAR
OPEN : MON-SUN 0900-1800

HAMPSHIRE

ANDARK DIVING
256 BRIDGE ROAD
LOWER SWANWICK
SOUTHAMPTON, HANTS SO3 7FL
0489 581755 FAX: 0489 575223

TRAINING : PADI, BSAC
EQUPT : BAS, CTH, CAM, SFY, BKS, BTS
HIRE : BAS, CTH, CAM
REPAIRS : BAS, CTH, CAM, BTS
TANKS : TST, IDEST, FILL TO 275BAR
CHARTER : YES, ON BOARD OXYGEN
OPEN : MON-FRI 0930-1730. SAT 0930-1700. SUN 1000-1700

ATLANTIC DIVING
37 ANNSHILL ROAD
GOSPORT, HANTS PO12 3JX
0705 602442 FAX: 0705 602442

TRAINING : PADI, BSAC
EQUPT : BAS, CTH, CAM, BKS, BTS
HIRE : BAS, CTH
REPAIRS : BAS, CTH, BTS
TANKS : FILL TO 300BAR
CHARTER : YES, ON BOARD OXYGEN
TRAVEL : HOLIDAYS
OPEN : MON-SAT 0900-1730
OPEN LATE : WED-THU 0900-2100

PETER ANDERSON SPORTS LTD
48-50 ELM GROVE
SOUTH SEA, PORTSMOUTH, HANTS PO5 1JG
0705 820611

EQUPT : BAS, CTH
HIRE : BAS
TANKS : TST, FILL TO 204BAR
OPEN : MON-SAT 0900-1800

SOLENT DIVERS
122-128 LAKE ROAD
PORTSMOUTH, HANTS PO1 4HH
0705 814924 FAX: 0705 291538

EQUPT : BAS, CTH, CAM, BKS
REPAIRS : BAS, CTH, CAM
TANKS : TST, IDEST, FILL TO 300BAR
OPEN : MON-FRI 0830-1730 SAT 0800-1700

SOUTHERN CYLINDER SERVICES
UNIT 18
FORT FAREHAM INDUSTRIAL ESTATE
NEWGATE LANE
FAREHAM, HANTS PO14 1AH
0329 221125

TANKS : TST, IDEST, FILL TO 300BAR

SUB AQUA PRODUCTS
63-65 TWYFORD ROAD
EASTLEIGH, HANTS SO5 4ZG
0703 612144 FAX: 0703 611634

EQUPT : BAS, CTH, CAM, SFY, BKS
REPAIRS : BAS, CTH
TANKS : TST, IDEST, FILL TO 238BAR
OPEN : TUE-FRI 0900-1300/1400-1730, SAT 0900-1630

SUNSET DIVERS
145 THE HIGH STREET
ALDERSHOT, HANTS GU11 1TT
0252 319541 FAX: 0252 330198

TRAINING : PADI
EQUPT : BAS, CTH, CAM, SFY, BKS
HIRE : BAS, CAM
REPAIRS : BAS, CTH
TANKS : TST, FILL TO 300BAR
CHARTER : YES, ON BOARD OXYGEN
TRAVEL : HOLIDAYS
OPEN : MON-SAT 0900-1800
OPEN LATE : MON 0900-2100

HERTFORDSHIRE

BUDDIES DIVING CENTRE
1 HITCHIN STREET
BALDOCK
HERTS SG7 6AL
0462 491911 FAX: 0462 491911

TRAINING : PADI
EQUPT : BAS, CTH, CAM, SFY, BKS, BTS
HIRE : BAS, CTH, CAM
REPAIRS : BAS, CTH, CAM
TANKS : TST, IDEST, FILL TO 275BAR
CHARTER : YES, ON BOARD OXYGEN
TRAVEL : HOLIDAYS
OPEN : MON-SAT 0930-1800
OPEN LATE : THU-FRI 0930-2100

CROXLEY DIVERS
125 NEW ROAD
CROXLEY GREEN
HERTS WD3 3EN
0923 777700 FAX: 0923 896299

EQUPT : BAS, CTH, BKS
REPAIRS : BAS, CTH
TANKS : TST, IDEST, FILL TO 350BAR
TRAVEL : HOLIDAYS
OPEN : MON-SAT 0900-1800
OPEN LATE : THU 0900-1930

SHIERS DIVING
28 MILLARS LANE
STANSTEAD ABBOTTS, HERTS WD3 3EN
0920 871151

EQUPT : BAS, CTH
TANKS : TST, FILL TO 306BAR
OPEN : MON-SAT 0900-1730

HUMBERSIDE

YORKSHIRE DIVE & WATERSPORTS
9-11 HESSLE ROAD
CLIVE SULLIVAN WAY, HULL
HUMBERSIDE HU3 2AA
0482 29218 FAX: 0482 29218

TRAINING : BSAC
EQUPT : BAS, CTH, CAM, SFY, BKS
REPAIRS : BAS, CTH, CAM
TANKS : FILL TO 400BAR
OPEN : MON-SAT 0930-1730
OPEN LATE : BY APPOINTMENT

ISLE OF MAN

DIVING AIR SERVICES
THE OLD BOAT HOUSE
SOUTH QUAY, DOUGLAS, ISLE OF MAN
0624 628123 FAX: 0624 662370

EQUPT : BAS, CTH, CAM, SFY, BKS, BTS
HIRE : BAS
REPAIRS : BAS, CTH, BTS
TANKS : TST, FILL TO 231BAR
OPEN : MON-FRI 0830-1730. SAT 0900-1300

ISLE OF WIGHT

SCUBA TECHNIQUES I.O.W. LTD
ELMSWORTH LANE
PORCHFIELD
ISLE OF WIGHT PO30 4LR
0983 529023

TRAINING : PADI, BSAC
EQUPT : BAS, CTH, CAM, SFY, BKS
REPAIRS : BAS, CTH, CAM
TANKS : FILL TO 232BAR
TRAVEL : HOLIDAYS
OPEN : MON-SAT 0800-1800. SUN BY APPOINTMENT

KENT

AIR SERVICES
BEACONSFIELD ROAD
MAIDSTONE, KENT ME16 6RV
0622 758005

EQUPT : BAS, CTH, SFY, BKS
REPAIRS : BAS, CTH
TANKS : TST, IDEST, FILL TO 250BAR
OPEN : MON-SAT 0830-1730

AIR TESTING SERVICES LTD
UNIT 14
WEALDEN CLOSE,
BRADBOURNE VALE ROAD
SEVENOAKS, KENT
0732 451170

TANKS : TST, IDEST

AIR TESTING SERVICES LTD
74 HIGH STREET
GREEN STREET, GREEN
FARNBOROUGH, KENT
0689 858395

TANKS : TST, IDEST

C SPORTS LTD.
115 MAIN ROAD
SUTTON-AT-HONE
DARTFORD
KENT DA4 9HQ
0322 866261 FAX: 0322 868962

TRAINING : BSAC
EQUPT : BAS, CTH, BKS
HIRE : BAS, CTH
REPAIRS : BAS
TANKS : TST, IDEST, FILL TO 275BAR
OPEN : WED-SAT,MON 1000-1800
OPEN LATE : WED 1000-2000

KENT DIVING
7 OASTHOUSE WAY
ORPINGTON, KENT BR5 3PT
0689 875521 FAX: 0689 877246

EQUPT : BAS, CTH, CAM, BKS
REPAIRS : BAS, CTH
TANKS : TST, IDEST, FILL TO 238BAR
OPEN : MON-SAT 0900-1700

SOUTH EAST DIVING CENTRE
140 RICHMOND ROAD
GILLINGHAM
KENT ME7 1LS
0634 579624

TRAINING : PADI, BSAC, SSI
EQUPT : BAS, CTH, CAM, SFY, BKS
HIRE : BAS, CTH, CAM
REPAIRS : BAS, CTH, CAM
TANKS : TST, IDEST, FILL TO 306BAR
TRAVEL : HOLIDAYS
OPEN : MON-SAT 0900-1800
OPEN LATE : FRI 0900-2000

THE FOLKSTONE SUB AQUA CENTRE
(FORMERLY THE BOSUN'S LOCKER)
ARCH 5, TRAM ROAD
FOLKESTONE, KENT CT20 1QD
0303 255752

TRAINING : PADI, BSAC, SAA
EQUPT : BAS, CTH, CAM, SFY, BKS, BTS
HIRE : BAS, CAM
REPAIRS : BAS, CTH, BTS
TANKS : TST, FILL TO 250BAR
CHARTER : YES, ON BOARD OXYGEN
OPEN : TUE-SAT 0900-1700 SUN 0900-1200

LANCASHIRE

AQUAMARINE SCUBA
LEYTON HOUSE
80 NEW STREET, MAWDESLEY
NR. ORMSKIRK, LANCASHIRE L40 2QW
0704 822765 FAX: 0704 822903

TRAINING : PADI
EQUPT : BAS, CTH, CAM, SFY, BKS
HIRE : BAS, CTH, CAM
REPAIRS : BAS, CTH, CAM
TANKS : TST, FILL TO 232BAR
TRAVEL : HOLIDAYS
OPEN : MON-SUN BY APPOINTMENT

AQUARIUS SPORTS
24 BROWNLOW SHOPPING CENTRE
BROWNLOW WAY, BOLTON
LANCASHIRE BL1 3UR
0204 365120 FAX: 0204 365120

BLACKPOOL AREA DIVING CENTRE
32 BEECHWOOD DRIVE
THORNTON CLEVELEYS, NR BLACKPOOL,
LANCASHIRE FY5 5EJ
0253 869188 FAX: 0253 869188

TRAINING : PADI
EQUPT : BAS, CTH, CAM, SFY, BKS
HIRE : BAS, CTH
REPAIRS : BAS, CAM
TANKS : TST, IDEST, FILL TO 310BAR
CHARTER : YES, ON BOARD OXYGEN
TRAVEL : HOLIDAYS
OPEN : TUE-SAT 0930-1800

DIVER SERVICES
VERECROFT
PARSONAGE ROAD, BLACKBURN
LANCASHIRE BB1 4AG
0254 248009 FAX: 0254 245466

TRAINING : PADI, BSAC
EQUPT : BAS, CTH, CAM, SFY, BKS, BTS
REPAIRS : BAS, CTH, CAM, BTS
TANKS : TST, IDEST, FILL TO 250BAR
OPEN : MON-SAT 0900-2000

HYDROMAC
32 BOTANY LANE
ASHTON UNDER LYNE
LANCASHIRE OL6 9PG
061 3304574

REPAIRS : BAS
OPEN : MON-SUN 0900-1800

MANTA DIVER TRAINING CENTRE
4 LEEFIELDS CLOSE
UPPERMILL, OLDHAM
LANCASHIRE OL3 6LA
0457 873272

NORTHERN DIVER
THE STANDISH CENTRE
CROSS STREET, STANDISH
WIGAN
LANCASHIRE WN6 OHQ
0257 421330-424123 FAX: 0257 427409

EQUPT : BAS, CTH, CAM, SFY, BKS, BTS
HIRE : BAS, CTH
REPAIRS : BAS, CTH, BTS
TANKS : TST, FILL TO 250BAR
CHARTER : YES
OPEN : MON-FRI 0900-1800 SAT 0900-1600

PROBE DIVING SERVICES
183 LEES ROAD
OLDHAM
LANCASHIRE OL4 1JP
061 6330966 FAX: 061 6330966

EQUPT : BAS, CTH, CAM, SFY, BKS, BTS
HIRE : BAS, CTH, CAM
REPAIRS : BAS, CTH
TANKS : TST, FILL TO 350BAR
CHARTER : YES, ON BOARD OXYGEN
TRAVEL : HOLIDAYS
OPEN : MON-SAT 0930-1800

SCUBA TECH DIVE CENTRE
8 OWEN ROAD
SKERTON, LANCASTER
LANCASHIRE LA1 2AR
0524 381831 FAX: 0524 381381

TRAINING : PADI, BSAC
EQUPT : BAS, CTH, CAM, SFY, BKS, BTS
HIRE : BAS, CTH
REPAIRS : BAS, CTH, CAM
TANKS : TST, IDEST, FILL TO 290BAR
TRAVEL : HOLIDAYS
OPEN : TUE-THU 0930-1700. FRI 0930-1930. SAT 0930-1730

SLATER'S AQUA SPORTS
THE DOCKS DIVING CENTRE
WATERY LANE, ASHTON
PRESTON, LANCASHIRE PR2 1QJ
0772 732078

TRAINING : BSAC
EQUPT : BAS, CTH, SFY, BKS
REPAIRS : BAS, CTH
TANKS : TST, FILL TO 232BAR
OPEN : TUE-FRI 0930-1800 SAT 0930-1700

LEICESTERSHIRE

MIDLAND DIVING EQUIPMENT LTD
57 SPARKENHOE STREET
LEICESTER, LEICESTERSHIRE LE2 0TD
0533 624262 FAX: 0533 512227

EQUPT : BAS, CTH, CAM, BKS
REPAIRS : BAS, CTH
TANKS : TST, FILL TO 272BAR
OPEN : TUE-SAT 0900-1730

STONEY COVE MARINE TRIALS LTD
STONEY COVE
SAPCOTE ROAD, STONEY STANTON
LEICESTERSHIRE LE9 6DW
0455 273089 FAX: 0455 274646

TRAINING : PADI, BSAC
EQUPT : BAS, CTH, CAM, SFY, BKS
HIRE : BAS, CTH, CAM
REPAIRS : BAS, CTH, CAM
TANKS : TST, IDEST, FILL TO 245BAR
TRAVEL : HOLIDAYS
OPEN : MON-FRI 0830-1700 SAT-SUN 0700-1500

LONDON

AMPHIBIAN SPORTS
44A CHAPEL ROAD
WEST NORWOOD, LONDON SE27 0UR
081 7612458 FAX: 081 7619602

TRAINING : PADI, BSAC, SAA, HSA
EQUPT : BAS, CTH, CAM, BKS
HIRE : BAS, CAM
REPAIRS : BAS, CTH
TANKS : TST, IDEST, FILL TO 204BAR
OPEN : TUE-SAT 1000-1800
OPEN LATE : THU 1000-2000

BIG BLUE DIVING CO
291 RYE LANE, LONDON SE15 4UA
071 6355540 FAX: 071 6356510

TRAINING : PADI, BSAC
EQUPT : BAS, CTH, CAM, SFY, BKS, BTS
HIRE : BAS, CTH
REPAIRS : BAS, CTH, CAM
TANKS : TST, IDEST, FILL TO 300BAR
CHARTER : YES, ON BOARD OXYGEN
TRAVEL : HOLIDAYS
OPEN : TUE-FRI 1000-1900. SAT 0900-1800

BUBBLES DIVING CENTRE
207 HIGH ROAD
WILLESDEN, LONDON NW10 2SB
081 4594598 FAX: 081 4594598

TRAINING : SAA
EQUPT : BAS, CTH, SFY, BKS
HIRE : BAS, CTH
REPAIRS : BAS, CTH
TANKS : TST, IDEST, FILL TO 300BAR
TRAVEL : HOLIDAYS
OPEN : MON-SAT. VARIES PLEASE PHONE

DEEPSEA, G&H DIVING SERVICES
(REAR OF) 69-71 HARLINGTON ROAD EAST
FELTAM, LONDON TW13 5BX
081 7513771 FAX: 081 7512591

EQUPT	: BAS, CTH, SFY, BKS
HIRE	: BAS, CTH
REPAIRS	: BAS, CTH
TANKS	: TST, IDEST, FILL TO 300BAR
OPEN	: MON-SAT 0900-1800
OPEN LATE	: BY APPOINTMENT

DIVE FORCE MARINE
10-10A CHEAPSIDE
NORTH CIRCULAR ROAD, PALMERS GREEN
LONDON N13 5ED
081 8030241 FAX: 081 8840801

TRAINING	: PADI, BSAC, SAA
EQUPT	: BAS, CTH, CAM, SFY, BKS
HIRE	: BAS, CTH, CAM
REPAIRS	: BAS, CTH, CAM
TANKS	: TST, IDEST, FILL TO 350BAR
CHARTER	: YES, ON BOARD OXYGEN
TRAVEL	: HOLIDAYS
OPEN	: MON-SAT 1000-1800
OPEN LATE	: TUE 1000-LATE

DIVING LOCKER (UK) LTD
NEPTUNE HOUSE
201 CHISWICK HIGH ROAD
LONDON W4 2DR
081 7421696 FAX: 081 7471811

TRAINING	**: PADI, BSAC**
EQUPT	**: BAS, CTH, CAM, SFY, BKS, BTS**
HIRE	**: BAS, CTH**
REPAIRS	**: BAS, CTH, CAM**
TANKS	**: TST, IDEST, FILL TO 300BAR**
TRAVEL	**: HOLIDAYS**
OPEN	**: MON-SAT 0930-1800**

LONDON DIVING CENTRE
SOS LTD
240 WATFORD WAY, HENDON
LONDON NW4 4UB
081 2035744 FAX: 081 9597971

TRAINING	: PADI, BSAC
EQUPT	: BAS, CTH, CAM, SFY, BKS
HIRE	: BAS, CTH, CAM
REPAIRS	: BAS, CTH, CAM

WHEN YOUR LIFE DEPENDS ON DIVING EQUIPMENT WHO DO YOU TRUST TO CARE?

NAUTILUS

All your Best Quality Diving Equipment from One Source – Tried & Tested by Us

We at NAUTILUS pride ourselves in our high standards of diving equipment, servicing and advice. With our long experience we know what goes down well (and comes back up) – and we pass this on to your. You'll find no cheap gimmicky products in our store, only good quality diving gear tried and tested by ourselves. We don't cut corners to save a few pence – that can cost lives. Nautilus – There's a good deal behind the name.

<u>STOCKISTS OF:</u> * APEKS MARINE * AP BUDDY * AQUALUNG * AQUION * JW AUTOMARINE * AVON * BEAVER * BLANDFORD SUB AQUA * BS–AC * CRESSI * DACOR * DMS * DUI * HAMWORTHY * HYDROTECH * MARES * MDE * NAMRON * NORTHERN DIVERS * OCEANIC * POLAR BEARS * POSEIDON * SCUBAPRO * SEA + SEA * SIEBE GORMAN * SOLENT * SPIRO * TECHNISUB * TYPHOON * US DIVERS * VIKING * WENOKA etc or you tell us and well get it for you.

A large comprehensive selection of spare parts for regulators, drysuits, compressors and filters is also available. We operate a fast efficient mail order service so if you cannot call, send a large SAE for our catalogue and lists. Access/Barclaycard accepted. Datapost available if required.

NAUTILUS

IN DEPTH EXPERIENCE

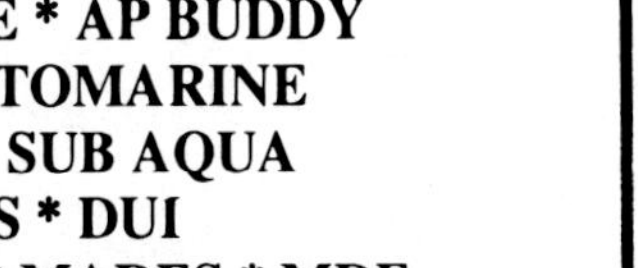

COLLINS & CHAMBERS LTD.
197-199 MARE STREET, LONDON, E8 3QF
Tel: 081-985 0752. Fax: 081-985 3123
Open Mon-Fri 9am to 6pm. Sats 9am to 5pm.

Nautilus is a registered trade mark of Collins & Chambers Ltd. Diving, Marine & Industrial Safety Equipment.

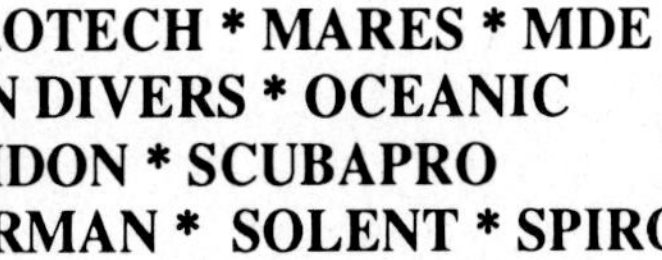

MAIL ORDER
HOT LINE
RING NOW FOR PRICES
081-985 0752

TANKS : TST, IDEST, FILL TO 250BAR
OPEN : MON-SAT 0930-1800

MIKES' WATERFRONT WAREHOUSE
RICHMOND SLIPWAYS
1 DUCK'S WALK, TWICKENHAM
LONDON TW1 2DD
081 744 9144 FAX: 081 744 1077

TRAINING : PADI, BSAC
EQUPT : BAS, CTH, CAM, SFY, BKS
HIRE : BAS, CTH
REPAIRS : BAS, CTH, CAM
TANKS : TST, IDEST, FILL TO 300BAR
TRAVEL : HOLIDAYS
OPEN : MON-SAT 1000-1800

NAUTILUS
197 - 199 MARE STREET
LONDON E8 3QF
081 9850752 FAX: 081 9853123

TRAINING : BSAC
EQUPT : BAS, CTH, CAM, SFY, BKS, BTS
HIRE : BAS
REPAIRS : BAS, CTH, CAM, BTS
TANKS : TST, IDEST, FILL TO 300BAR
CHARTER : YES, ON BOARD OXYGEN
OPEN : MON-FRI 0900-1800

OCEAN LEISURE LTD
11-14 NORTHUMBERLAND AVENUE
LONDON WC2N 5AQ
071 930 5050 FAX: 071 930 3032

TRAINING : PADI
EQUPT : BAS, CTH, CAM, SFY, BKS, BTS
REPAIRS : BAS, CTH, CAM, BTS
TANKS : TST, IDEST, FILL TO 240BAR
CHARTER : YES, ON BOARD OXYGEN
OPEN : MON-FRI 0930-1800. SAT 0930-1730
OPEN LATE : THU 0930-1900

OCEAN OPTICS
11-14 NORTHUMBERLAND AVENUE
LONDON WC2N 5AQ
071 9308408 FAX: 071 9303032

EQUPT : CAM, BKS
REPAIRS : CAM
OPEN : MON-FRI 0930-1800. SAT 0930-1730
OPEN LATE : THU 0930-1900

SCUBA TRAINING LTD
59 VICARAGE ROAD
LONDON SW14 8RY
081 7428531 FAX: 081 8765132

TRAINING : PADI, BSAC
EQUPT : BAS, CTH, CAM, SFY, BKS
HIRE : BAS, CTH, CAM
REPAIRS : BAS, CTH, CAM
TANKS : TST, IDEST, FILL TO 300BAR
CHARTER : YES, ON BOARD OXYGEN
TRAVEL : HOLIDAYS
OPEN : MON-SAT 1000-1800

THE DIVE SHOP LTD
UNIVERSAL HOUSE
UPLANDS TRADING ESTATE
BLACKHORES LANE
LONDON E17 5QJ
081 5235900 FAX: 081 5033222

TRAINING : PADI, BSAC
EQUPT : BAS, CTH, CAM, SFY, BKS
REPAIRS : BAS
TANKS : TST, FILL TO 300BAR
CHARTER : YES, ON BOARD OXYGEN
TRAVEL : HOLIDAYS
OPEN : MON-SAT 0930-1800 SUN 0930-1330

WIMBLEDON DIVING CENTRE
WHITE HORSES (AQUASPORTS)
574 KINGSTON ROAD, RAYNES PARK
LONDON SW20 8DR
081 543 4576 FAX: 081 543 3830

TRAINING : PADI
EQUPT : BAS, CTH, CAM, SFY, BKS
HIRE : BAS, CTH
REPAIRS : BAS, CTH, CAM
TANKS : TST, IDEST, FILL TO 250BAR
TRAVEL : HOLIDAYS
OPEN : MON-SAT 1000-1800
OPEN LATE : FRI 1000-2000

MANCHESTER

DIVE AIR
53 CHURCH STREET
RADCLIFFE, MANCHESTER M26 9SP
061 7233157

EQUPT : BAS, CTH, CAM, SFY, BKS
REPAIRS : BAS
TANKS : TST, FILL TO 280BAR
TRAVEL : HOLIDAYS
OPEN : MON-SAT 0900-1730
OPEN LATE : THU 0900-2000

DIVING & MARINE SERVICES
246 CHURCH ROAD
URMSTON, MANCHESTER M31 3HD
061 7481025 FAX: 061 7481025

TRAINING : PADI, BSAC
EQUPT : BAS, CTH, CAM, SFY, BKS, BTS
REPAIRS : BAS, CTH, CAM
TANKS : TST, FILL TO 300BAR
CHARTER : YES, ON BOARD OXYGEN
OPEN : MON-SAT 0900-1730
OPEN LATE : THU 0900-1930

MERSEYSIDE

WIRRAL SPORTS AND LEISURE
164-190 CLEVELAND STREET
BIRKENHEAD, MERSEYSIDE L64 3QQ
051 6475131 FAX: 051 6662631

EQUPT : BAS, CTH, CAM, SFY, BKS
REPAIRS : BAS, CTH, CAM
TANKS : TST, IDEST, FILL TO 350BAR
CHARTER : YES, ON BOARD OXYGEN
OPEN : MON-FRI 0900-1730, SAT 0900-1700

NORFOLK

AQUA MARINE DIVING SUPPLIES LTD
1 STEAM MILL LANE
GREAT YARMOUTH
NORFOLK NR21 0HP
0493 650996

EQUPT : BAS, CTH, BKS
REPAIRS : BAS, CTH
TANKS : FILL TO 232BAR
OPEN : MON-FRI 0900-1730

AR BUCKLAND GUN & DIVING SUPPLY
THE BLUE BARN
MILL ROAD
STOKE HOLY CROSS
NORWICH
NORFOLK NR14 8PA
0508 493177 FAX: 0508 492053

TRAINING : SAA
EQUPT : BAS, CTH, CAM, SFY, BKS
HIRE : BAS, CTH, CAM
REPAIRS : BAS, CTH
TANKS : TST, FILL TO 272BAR
OPEN : TUE-SAT 1000-1300/1400-1800

NORDIVE DIVER TRAINING
4 BRICK KILN ROAD
THURSFORD
NORFOLK NR21 0BQ
0328 878925 FAX: 0328 878925

TRAINING : PADI
EQUPT : BAS, CTH, CAM, SFY, BKS
HIRE : BAS, CTH, CAM
REPAIRS : BAS, CTH
TANKS : FILL TO 300BAR
OPEN : MON-SUN 0900-1730

NORTHAMPTONSHIRE

NORTHAMPTON SUB-AQUA SUPPLIES
43B ABBEY ROAD
FAR COTTON, NORTHAMPTON
NORTHAMPTONSHIRE NN4 9EY
0604 768623 FAX: 0604 768623

TRAINING : PADI
EQUPT : BAS, CTH, CAM, SFY, BKS, BTS
HIRE : BAS, CTH
REPAIRS : BAS, CTH, CAM
TANKS : TST, IDEST, FILL TO 250BAR
CHARTER : YES, ON BOARD OXYGEN
TRAVEL : HOLIDAYS
OPEN : MON-FRI 1200-1800. SAT 1000-1700. SUN BY APPOINTMENT

NORTHUMBERLAND

THE LODGE
146 MAIN STREET
SEAHOUSES
NORTHUMBERLAND
0665 720158

TANKS : FILL TO 306BAR
OPEN : VARIES. PLEASE PHONE

NOTTINGHAMSHIRE

BARRACUDA DIVE SHOP & SCHOOL
16 MAIN STREET
KIMBERLAND
NOTTINGHAM
NOTTINGHAMSHIRE NG16 2LL
0602 459303
FAX: 0602 459303

TRAINING : BSAC
EQUPT : BAS, CTH, CAM, SFY, BKS, BTS
HIRE : BAS, CTH
REPAIRS : BAS, CTH
TANKS : TST, IDEST, FILL TO 300BAR
CHARTER : YES, ON BOARD OXYGEN
TRAVEL : HOLIDAYS
OPEN : MON-SAT 0900-1730

NOTTINGHAM SCUBA CENTRE
59 TRENT BOULEVARD
WEST BRIDGEFORD
NOTTINGHAM
NOTTINGHAMSHIRE NG2 5BB
0602 822525
FAX: 0602 822525

TRAINING : PADI, BSAC, SAA
EQUPT : BAS, CTH, CAM, SFY, BKS, BTS
HIRE : BAS, CTH, CAM
REPAIRS : BAS, CTH, CAM
TANKS : TST, FILL TO 340BAR
TRAVEL : HOLIDAYS
OPEN : MON 1600-1900. TUE-SAT 0900-1900

OXFORDSHIRE

AQUARIUS DIVING
80-82 BROADWAY
DIDCOT
OXFORDSHIRE OX11 8AE
0235 512056 FAX: 0235 815352

TRAINING : PADI, BSAC
EQUPT : BAS, CTH, CAM, SFY, BKS
HIRE : BAS, CTH
REPAIRS : BAS
TANKS : TST, IDEST, FILL TO 300BAR
CHARTER : YES, ON BOARD OXYGEN
TRAVEL : HOLIDAYS
OPEN : MON-SAT 0930-1730
OPEN LATE : THU 0930-1930

SOMERSET

AIR TOO
UNIT 3
THE APPLE BUSINESS CENTRE
FROBISHER WAY
TAUNTON
SOMERSET TA2 6BB
0823 326577

EQUPT	: BAS, CTH, CAM
REPAIRS	: BAS, CTH
TANKS	: TST, FILL TO 400BAR
CHARTER	: YES, ON BOARD OXYGEN
TRAVEL	: HOLIDAYS
OPEN	: MON-FRI 1730-2000
OPEN LATE	: SAT 0930-1730

DORSET ADVENTURE SPORTS
THE GREEN
STOFORD, NR. YEOVIL
SOMERSET BA22 9UD
0935 77585

TRAINING	: PADI, SAA
EQUPT	: BAS, CTH, CAM, SFY, BKS, BTS
HIRE	: BAS, CTH
REPAIRS	: BAS, CTH
TANKS	: TST, FILL TO 400BAR
TRAVEL	: HOLIDAYS
OPEN	: MON-TUE, THU-SAT 0900-1800

STAFFORDSHIRE

DIVE IN DOSTHILL
DOSTHILL QUARRY
CHURCH ROAD, DOSTHILL
TAMWORTH, STAFFORDSHIRE B77 1LL
0827 281304

OUTDOOR PROFESSIONAL DIVE SHOP
24 RADFORD STREET
STONE
STAFFORDSHIRE ST15 8PA
0785 817658 FAX: 0785 817658

TRAINING	: BSAC
EQUPT	: BAS, CTH, CAM, SFY, BKS, BTS
HIRE	: BAS, CTH
REPAIRS	: BAS, CTH, BTS
TANKS	: TST, FILL TO 280BAR
TRAVEL	: HOLIDAYS
OPEN	: TUE-SAT 0900-1730

SUFFOLK

DIVELINE
ST. JOHNS WORKS
ST JOHNS ROAD, IPSWICH
SUFFOLK IP4 5DQ
0473 715533 FAX: 0473 271815

TRAINING : PADI
EQUPT : BAS, CTH, CAM, SFY, BKS
HIRE : BAS, CTH, CAM
REPAIRS : BAS, CTH
TANKS : IDEST, FILL TO 272BAR
OPEN : MON-TUE, THU-SAT 0830-1700

KINGS WATERSPORT
16 THE STREET
BLUNDESTON, SUFFOLK NR32 5AQ
0502 730182 FAX: 0502 731633

EQUPT : BAS, CTH
REPAIRS : BAS
OPEN : MON-SUN 0900-1800

NEWMARKET WATERSPORTS CENTRE
UNIT 3, VICTORIA WAY
NEWMARKET
SUFFOLK CB8 7SH
0638 661336

EQUPT : BAS, CTH, CAM, SFY, BKS
HIRE : BAS
REPAIRS : CAM
TANKS : TST, FILL TO 272BAR
OPEN : WED-THU 0900-1630, SAT 0900-1800
OPEN LATE : FRI 0900-1900

SURREY

69 DIVING & SPORTS WORLD
57 - 61 HIGH STREET
EWELL, SURREY KT17 1RX
081 7867821 FAX: 081 7867823

TRAINING : PADI
EQUPT : BAS, CTH, BKS
HIRE : BAS, CTH
REPAIRS : BAS, CTH
TANKS : TST, IDEST, FILL TO 340BAR
CHARTER : YES, ON BOARD OXYGEN
TRAVEL : HOLIDAYS
OPEN : MON-SAT 1000-1800
OPEN LATE : THU 1000-2030

CHALLENGER 10 LTD
129 WORSLEY ROAD
FRIMLEY, CAMBERLEY
SURREY GU16 5BB
0252 837499 FAX: 0252 837891

TRAINING : PADI
EQUPT : BAS, CTH, CAM, SFY, BKS
HIRE : BAS
REPAIRS : BAS, CAM
TRAVEL : HOLIDAYS
OPEN : MON-SAT 0930-1930

NEW DAWN DIVE CENTRE
148 SEND ROAD
SEND, WOKING
SURREY GU23 7EZ
0483 211103 FAX: 0483 211103

TRAINING : PADI
EQUPT : BAS, CTH, CAM, SFY, BKS
HIRE : BAS, CTH
REPAIRS : BAS, CTH
TANKS : TST, FILL TO 232BAR
CHARTER : YES
TRAVEL : HOLIDAYS
OPEN : MON-SAT 0900-1800
OPEN LATE : FRI 0900-2000

RUNNYMEDE DIVE
UNIT 11, EVERSLEY WAY
THORPE INDUSTRIAL ESTATE
EGHAM
SURREY TW20 8RG
0784 436909 FAX: 0784 436909

TRAINING : PADI
EQUPT : BAS, CTH, CAM, SFY, BKS
HIRE : BAS, CTH
REPAIRS : BAS, CTH
TANKS : TST, IDEST, FILL TO 300BAR
OPEN : MON-SAT 0800-1800

THE CATERHAM DIVE CENTRE
COULSDON PLACE
CATERHAM, SURREY CR3 5NL
0883 344202

EQUPT : CTH
OPEN : MON-SAT 0900-1730

SUSSEX

BLACK ROCK DIVING
4 THE BROADWAY
WHITEHAWK ROAD
BRIGHTON
SUSSEX-EAST BN2 5NF
0273 571402 FAX: 0273 602870

TRAINING : PADI
EQUPT : BAS, CTH, CAM, SFY, BKS, BTS
HIRE : BAS, CTH, CAM
REPAIRS : BAS, CTH, CAM
TANKS : TST, IDEST, FILL TO 250BAR
CHARTER : YES, ON BOARD OXYGEN
TRAVEL : HOLIDAYS
OPEN : MON-SUN 0800-1800

BRITANNIA WATERSPORTS
FISHERMAN'S QUAY
LITTLEHAMPTON
SUSSEX-WEST BN17 5BL
0903 722222 FAX: 0903 722222

EQUPT	: BAS, CTH, CAM, SFY, BKS, BTS
REPAIRS	: BAS, CTH, BTS
TANKS	: TST, IDEST, FILL TO 272BAR
CHARTER	: YES, ON BOARD OXYGEN
OPEN	: TUE-SAT 0900-1300/1400-1800. SUN 0900-1300

**CRAWLEY DIVE CENTRE
185 LONDON ROAD
COUNTY OAK, CRAWLEY
SUSSEX-WEST RH10 2TA
0293 529192 FAX: 0293 529992**

TRAINING	**: PADI, BSAC, SAA**
EQUPT	**: BAS, CTH, SFY, BKS**
HIRE	**: BAS, CTH**
REPAIRS	**: BAS, CTH**
TANKS	**: IDEST, FILL TO 300BAR**
CHARTER	**: YES, ON BOARD OXYGEN**
OPEN	**: TUE-SAT 1000-1900**

IDW / SHOREHAM WATERSPORTS
(INTN'L DIVING & WATERSPORT)
1 NEW ROAD, SHOREHAM BY SEA,
SUSSEX-WEST BN43 6RA
0273 455892 FAX: 0273 465149

TRAINING	: PADI
EQUPT	: BAS, CTH, SFY, BKS
REPAIRS	: BAS, CTH
TANKS	: TST, FILL TO 300BAR
TRAVEL	: HOLIDAYS
OPEN	: MON-SAT 0900-1300/1400-1730

LIFE SUPPORT ENGINEERING LTD
ROBELL WAY
STORRINGTON
SUSSEX-WEST RH20 3DN
0903 742322
FAX: 0903 745923

TANKS	: TST, IDEST, FILL TO 204BAR

ROCK BOTTOM DIVERS
RBD HOUSE
QUEENS STREET
ARUNDEL,
SUSSEX-WEST BN18 9JG
0903 884567
FAX: 0903 883776

TRAINING	: PADI
EQUPT	: BAS, CTH, CAM, SFY, BKS, BTS
HIRE	: BAS, CTH
REPAIRS	: BAS, CTH, BTS
TANKS	: TST, FILL TO 320BAR
CHARTER	: YES, ON BOARD OXYGEN
TRAVEL	: HOLIDAYS
OPEN	: MON-SUN 0800-1830

WITTERING DIVERS at SCUBA WORKS
THE ESPLANADE
GLOUCESTER ROAD
BOGNOR REGIS
SUSSEX-WEST PO21 1NU
0243 842402 FAX: 0243 842402

TRAINING	**: PADI, BSAC**
EQUPT	**: BAS, CTH, CAM, SFY, BKS**
HIRE	**: BAS, CTH**
REPAIRS	**: BAS, CTH, CAM**
TANKS	**: TST, IDEST, FILL TO 280BAR**
CHARTER	**: YES, ON BOARD OXYGEN**
TRAVEL	**: HOLIDAYS**
OPEN	**: MON-FRI 0900-1800, SAT-SUN 0900-LATE**

TYNE & WEAR

AQUANORTH
17A COAST ROAD
HEATON
NEWCASTLE UPON TYNE
TYNE & WEAR NE7 7RN
091 2666626 FAX: 091 2666626

TRAINING	**: PADI**
EQUPT	**: BAS, CTH, CAM, BKS**
HIRE	**: BAS, CTH**
REPAIRS	**: BAS, CTH**
TANKS	**: IDEST, FILL TO 250BAR**
TRAVEL	**: HOLIDAYS**
OPEN	**: MON-SAT 0930-1730**

DIVING CENTRE LTD
TRAILER BOAT LTD
ATLANTIS HOUSE, 159 WESTGATE ROAD
NEWCASTLE, TYNE & WEAR NE1 4AN
091 2327983 FAX: 091 2614948

TRAINING	: PADI
EQUPT	: BAS, CTH, CAM, SFY, BKS, BTS
HIRE	: BAS, CTH
TANKS	: FILL TO 238BAR
CHARTER	: YES
TRAVEL	: HOLIDAYS
OPEN	: MON-SAT 0930-1700
OPEN LATE	: THU 0930-1900

KENMORE TECHNICAL SERVICES
UNIT G3, NARVIC WAY, TYNE TUNNEL
TRADING ESTATE
NORTH SHIELDS, TYNE & WEAR NE29 7XJ
091 2596644 FAX: 091 2586363

TANKS	: TST, IDEST, FILL TO 300BAR

MARSDEN DIVE CENTRE
6 FALLOWS ROAD
MARSDEN, SOUTH SHIELDS
TYNE & WEAR NE34 7AQ
091 4277820

TRAINING	: BSAC
EQUPT	: BAS, CTH, CAM, BKS
REPAIRS	: BAS, CTH
TANKS	: FILL TO 340BAR
OPEN	: MON-SUN 1000-1800

WGP MARINE LTD DIVING CENTRE
165 WHITLEY ROAD
WHITLEY BAY, TYNE & WEAR NE26 2DN
091 2510388 FAX: 091 2963243

TRAINING	: PADI
EQUPT	: BAS, CTH, BKS
HIRE	: BAS, CTH
REPAIRS	: BAS, CTH
TANKS	: TST, IDEST, FILL TO 300BAR
TRAVEL	: HOLIDAYS
OPEN	: MON-SAT 0900-1700, SUN 0800-1000

WARWICKSHIRE

WARWICKSHIRE SCUBA CENTRE
5 CAMPION TERRACE
LEAMINGTON SPA
WARWICKSHIRE CV23 4SU
0926 313681 FAX: 0926 313681

TRAINING	**: PADI**
EQUPT	**: BAS, CTH, CAM, SFY, BKS**
HIRE	**: BAS, CTH, CAM**
REPAIRS	**: BAS, CTH, CAM**
TANKS	**: TST, FILL TO 275BAR**
CHARTER	**: YES, ON BOARD OXYGEN**
TRAVEL	**: HOLIDAYS**
OPEN	**: TUE-SAT 1000-1200/1300-1800**

WEST MIDLANDS

AQUASPORT INTERNATIONAL
80 ALCESTER ROAD
MOSELEY, BIRMINGHAM
WEST MIDLANDS B13 8BB
021 4494148 FAX: 021 449148

TRAINING : PADI, BSAC
EQUPT : BAS, CTH, CAM, BKS
HIRE : BAS, CTH, CAM
REPAIRS : BAS, CTH, CAM
TANKS : TST, FILL TO 250BAR
TRAVEL : HOLIDAYS
OPEN : MON-SAT 0900-1800

COMDEAN LTD
DIVING AND WATERSPORTS
90 WATERFALL LANE, OLD HILL
WARLEY, WEST MIDLANDS B64 6RJ
021 5593659-8659 FAX: 021 5614128

TRAINING : PADI, BSAC
EQUPT : BAS, CTH, CAM, SFY, BKS
HIRE : BAS, CTH, CAM
REPAIRS : BAS, CTH, CAM
TANKS : TST, FILL TO 272BAR
TRAVEL : HOLIDAYS
OPEN : MON-SAT 0900-1730
OPEN LATE : THU 0900-1930

COMDEAN LTD
DIVING AND WATERSPORTS
68 STRATFORD ROAD, SHIRLEY
SOLIHULL, WEST MIDLANDS B90 3LP
021 7441526

TRAINING : PADI, BSAC
EQUPT : BAS, CTH, CAM, SFY, BKS
HIRE : BAS, CTH, CAM
REPAIRS : BAS, CTH, CAM
TANKS : TST, FILL TO 272BAR
TRAVEL : HOLIDAYS
OPEN : TUE-SAT 0900-1730
OPEN LATE : THU 0900-1930

MIDLAND AQUA SUPPLIES
100 HAWTHORN ROAD
KINGSTANDING, BIRMINGHAM
WEST MIDLANDS B44 8QP
021 3824923 FAX: 021 3824923

EQUPT : BAS, CTH, CAM, SFY, BKS
HIRE : BAS, CTH
REPAIRS : BAS, CTH
TANKS : TST, IDEST, FILL TO 272BAR
CHARTER : YES, ON BOARD OXYGEN
OPEN : MON-TUE, THU-SAT 0930-1730

ROCKY COVE EQUIPPED FOR ADVENTURE
78 OLDBURY ROAD
BLACKHEATH, ROWLEY REGIS
WARLEY, WEST MIDLANDS B64 0JS
021 5590701 FAX: 021 5590701

TRAINING : PADI, BSAC
EQUPT : BAS, CTH, CAM, SFY, BKS
HIRE : BAS, CTH, CAM
REPAIRS : BAS, CTH, CAM
TANKS : TST, FILL TO 250BAR
OPEN : MON-WED 0900-1700 FRI-SAT 0900-1730
OPEN LATE :THU 0900-1930

THE DIVING INITIATIVE
143 HOSPITAL STREET
NEWTOWN, BIRMINGHAM
WEST MIDLANDS B19 3XA
021 3334312 FAX: 021 3596043

TRAINING : PADI
EQUPT : BAS, CTH, CAM, BKS
HIRE : BAS, CTH, CAM
REPAIRS : BAS, CTH
TANKS : TST, FILL TO 300BAR
TRAVEL : HOLIDAYS
OPEN : MON-FRI 0900-1730,
SAT 0900-1300 (WINTERS ONLY)

THE SCUBA SCHOOL
1171 BRISTOL ROAD SOUTH
NORTHFIELD, BIRMINGHAM
WEST MIDLANDS B31 2SL
021 4757082

TRAINING : PADI
EQUPT : BAS, CTH, CAM, SFY, BKS
HIRE : BAS, CTH
REPAIRS : BAS, CTH
TANKS : TST, FILL TO 300BAR
CHARTER : YES, ON BOARD OXYGEN
OPEN : TUE-THU,SAT 0900-1830 SUN 1000-1230
OPEN LATE : MON,FRI 0900-2030

WALSALL DIVING SERVICES
137-138 STAFFORD STREET
WALSALL
WEST MIDLANDS WS2 8EA
0922 614787 FAX: 0922 30766

EQUPT : BAS, CTH, CAM, SFY, BKS, BTS
HIRE : BAS, CAM
REPAIRS : BAS, CTH
TANKS : TST, FILL TO 348BAR
TRAVEL : HOLIDAYS
OPEN : MON-SAT 0900-1800

WILTSHIRE

AQUALEISURE SPECIALIST SPORTS
2 MARKET PLACE
MELKSHAM, WILTSHIRE SN12 6EX
0225 706604 FAX: 0225 790341

TRAINING : PADI
EQUPT : BAS, CTH, CAM, SFY, BKS, BTS
HIRE : BAS, CTH
REPAIRS : BAS, CTH, BTS
TANKS : TST, FILL TO 300BAR
TRAVEL : HOLIDAYS
OPEN : MON-SAT 0900-1730
OPEN LATE : FRI 0900-2000

OK DIVING SERVICES SWINDON
63 FARLEIGH CRESCENT
SWINDON, WILTSHIRE SN3 1JY
0793 695479 FAX: 0793 695479

TRAINING : PADI, HSA
EQUPT : BAS, CTH, CAM, SFY, BKS
HIRE : BAS, CTH, CAM
REPAIRS : BAS, CTH, CAM
TANKS : TST, IDEST, FILL TO 300BAR
OPEN : MON-SAT 0900-2100
OPEN LATE : BY APPOINTMENTS

WHITE HORSE SCHOOL OF DIVING
UFFCOT FARM
BROAD HINTON
NR SWINDON,
WILTSHIRE SN4 9NB
0793 731843

TRAINING : PADI
EQUPT : BAS, CTH, CAM, SFY, BKS, BTS
HIRE : BAS, CTH, CAM
REPAIRS : BAS, CTH, CAM
TANKS : TST, FILL TO 272BAR
CHARTER : YES, ON BOARD OXYGEN
TRAVEL : HOLIDAYS
OPEN : MON-SUN 0900-1800

WORCESTERSHIRE

SEASTYLE
UNIT 21
THREE SPRINGS TRADING ESTATE
VINCENT ROAD
WORCESTER
WORCESTERSHIRE WR5 1BW
0905 351528 FAX: 0905 351528

TRAINING : PADI
EQUPT : BAS, CTH, CAM, SFY, BKS
HIRE : BAS, CTH, CAM
REPAIRS : BAS, CTH, CAM
TANKS : TST, FILL TO 300BAR
OPEN : TUE,THU-FRI 1000-1800 SAT 1000-1600
OPEN LATE : WED 1000-1900

YORKSHIRE

AMK DIVING
90-92 CLIFTON
(REAR OF CROSS OF YORK)
YORK
YORKSHIRE-NORTH YO3 6BA
0904 643795 FAX: 0904 630365

TRAINING : PADI
EQUPT : BAS, CTH, CAM, BKS, BTS
HIRE : BAS
REPAIRS : BAS, CTH, CAM, BTS
TANKS : TST, FILL TO 272BAR
CHARTER : YES
TRAVEL : HOLIDAYS
OPEN : MON-SAT. TIME VARIES. PLEASE CALL

DIVE ACTION WATERSPORTS
19 HELREDALE ROAD
WHITBY
YORKSHIRE-NORTH YO22 4JG
0947 820616
FAX: 0947 820616

TRAINING : PADI, BSAC
EQUPT : BAS, CTH, CAM, SFY, BKS, BTS
HIRE : BAS, CTH, CAM
REPAIRS : BAS, CTH, CAM, BTS
TANKS : TST, FILL TO 300BAR
CHARTER : YES, ON BOARD OXYGEN
TRAVEL : HOLIDAYS
OPEN : TUE-SAT 0930-1730

THE DIVER TRAINING COLLEGE
ASHLEY HOUSE
MALT KILN LANE
APPLETON, ROEBUCK
YORK
YORKSHIRE-NORTH YO5 7DT
0904 744424
FAX: 0904 744724

TRAINING : PADI, BSAC
EQUPT : BAS, CTH, SFY, BKS
HIRE : BAS, CTH
REPAIRS : BAS, CTH
TANKS : TST, FILL TO 280BAR
CHARTER : YES, ON BOARD OXYGEN
TRAVEL : HOLIDAYS
OPEN : MON-TUE, THU-SAT 0930-1700
OPEN LATE : THU 0930-2000

NAMRON DIVING CENTRE
CANKLOW MEADOW INDUSTRIAL EST
WEST BAWTRY ROAD
ROTHERHAM
YORKSHIRE-SOUTH S6O 2XL
0709 838382
FAX: 0709 367295

TRAINING : PADI
EQUPT : BAS, CTH, SFY, BKS
HIRE : BAS, CTH
REPAIRS : BAS, CTH
TANKS : TST, IDEST, FILL TO 272BAR
OPEN : MON-SAT 0900-1715

SCUBA MARINE (SHEFFIELD)
122 HANDSWORTH ROAD
SHEFFIELD
YORKSHIRE-SOUTH
0742 560060

TRAINING : PADI
EQUPT : BAS, CTH, CAM, SFY, BKS, BTS
HIRE : BAS
REPAIRS : BAS, CTH, CAM
TANKS : TST, FILL TO 232BAR
CHARTER : YES
TRAVEL : HOLIDAYS
OPEN : MON-SAT 0900-1730

SDS WATERSPORTS
66-70 STATION ROAD
HALFWAY, SHEFFIELD
YORKSHIRE-SOUTH S19 5GW
0742 488688 FAX: 0742 488689

TRAINING : BSAC
EQUPT : BAS, CTH, CAM, SFY, BKS, BTS
HIRE : BAS
REPAIRS : BAS, CTH, CAM, BTS
TANKS : TST, IDEST, FILL TO 270BAR
TRAVEL : HOLIDAYS
OPEN : MON-SAT 0930-1800. SAT 0900-1700. SUN 1100-1600. THU 0930-2000

UPPERFIELD MARINE/DIVING SUPPLY
18 GREASBOROUGH ROAD
PARKGATE, ROTHERHAM
YORKSHIRE-SOUTH S62 6HN
0709 525480

TRAINING : PADI, BSAC
EQUPT : BAS, CTH, CAM, SFY, BKS
HIRE : BAS, CTH
REPAIRS : BAS, CTH
TANKS : IDEST, FILL TO 340BAR
OPEN : TUE-FRI 1200-2000. SAT 0900-1700

MIDWAY WATERSPORTS
GRANARY WHARF
NEVILLE STREET, LEEDS
YORKSHIRE-WEST LS1 4BR
0532 444315 FAX: 0532 444316

TRAINING : PADI
EQUPT : BAS, CTH, CAM, SFY, BKS
HIRE : BAS, CTH
REPAIRS : BAS, CTH, CAM
TANKS : TST, IDEST, FILL TO 272BAR
TRAVEL : HOLIDAYS
OPEN : MON-SAT 0930-1730
OPEN LATE : THU 0930-1900

ROBIN HOOD WATERSPORTS
152 LEEDS ROAD
HECKMONDWIKE
YORKSHIRE-WEST WF16 9BJ
0924 443843 FAX: 0924 474529

TRAINING : BSAC
EQUPT : BAS, CTH, CAM, SFY, BKS
HIRE : BAS, CTH, CAM
REPAIRS : BAS, CTH, CAM
TANKS : TST, IDEST, FILL TO 272BAR
CHARTER : YES, ON BOARD OXYGEN
TRAVEL : HOLIDAYS
OPEN : MON-SAT 0915-1800
OPEN LATE : THU 0915-2000

THE DIVERS WAREHOUSE
29 WALKER TERRACE
WAKEFIELD ROAD, BRADFORD
YORKSHIRE-WEST BD4 7HP
0274 307555-727252 FAX: 0274 307555

EQUPT : BAS, CTH, CAM, SFY, BKS
HIRE : BAS, CTH
REPAIRS : BAS, CTH
TANKS : TST, FILL TO 255BAR
OPEN : MON-SAT 0930-1730
OPEN LATE : THU 0930-2000

TOTAL DIVING
7 FLINT STREET
FARTOWN
HUDDERSFIELD
YORKSHIRE-WEST HD1 6LG
0484 456419

EQUPT : BAS, CTH, CAM, SFY, BKS
REPAIRS : CTH
TANKS : FILL TO 272BAR
CHARTER : YES, ON BOARD OXYGEN
TRAVEL : HOLIDAYS
OPEN : MON-SAT 0900-1800
OPEN LATE : THU 0900-2000

CHANNEL ISLANDS

DIVE & SKI SPORTS
13 COLOMBERE
ST HELIER
JERSEY
CHANNEL ISLANDS JE2 4QB
0534 36209 FAX: 0534 68989

TRAINING : PADI, BSAC
EQUPT : BAS, CTH, CAM, SFY, BKS, BTS
HIRE : BAS, CTH, CAM
REPAIRS : BAS, CTH, BTS
TANKS : TST, FILL TO 272BAR
CHARTER : YES, ON BOARD OXYGEN
OPEN : MON-SAT 0900-1730

WATERSPORTS DIVING CENTRE &
JERSEY UNDERWATER CENTRE
FIRST TOWER
ST HELIER
JERSEY, CHANNEL ISLANDS
0534 32813-61817 FAX: 0534 32813

TRAINING : PADI, BSAC
EQUPT : BAS, CTH, CAM, SFY, BKS
HIRE : BAS, CTH, CAM
REPAIRS : BAS, CTH, CAM
TANKS : TST, FILL TO 232BAR
CHARTER : YES, ON BOARD OXYGEN
TRAVEL : HOLIDAYS
OPEN : MON-SUN 0800-2100

SCOTLAND

BORDERS

BAREFOOT DIVE CENTRE
NORTHBURN HOLIDAY HOME PARK
EYEMOUTH, BORDERS T44 5ER
08907 51050 FAX: 08907 51462

TRAINING : PADI, BSAC
EQUPT : BAS, CTH, CAM, BKS
HIRE : BAS, CAM
REPAIRS : CTH
TANKS : FILL TO 306BAR
CHARTER : YES, ON BOARD OXYGEN
TRAVEL : HOLIDAYS
OPEN : BY APPOINTMENT

SCOUTSCROFT DIVING CENTRE
ST. ABBS ROAD
COLDINGHAM, BORDERS TD14 5NB
08907 71338 FAX: 08907 71746

EQUPT : BAS, CTH, CAM, SFY, BKS
TANKS : FILL TO 232BAR
OPEN : MON-SUN 0900-1800

ST ABBS AIR CENTRE
ROCK HOUSE, ST ABBS, EYEMOUTH
BORDERS TD14 5PW
08907 71288

TANKS : FILL TO 270BAR
OPEN : VARIES. PLEASE PHONE

DUMFRIES & GALLOWAY

SCOTTISH DIVING SUPPLIES
3 CASTLEDYKES ROAD, KIRKCUDBRIGHT
DUMFRIES & GALLOWAY DG6 4AN
0557 30301 FAX: 0557 30301

EQUPT : BAS, CTH, CAM, SFY, BKS, BTS
REPAIRS : BAS
TANKS : FILL TO 232BAR
OPEN : MON-SAT 0800-1800

THE DECOMPRESSION STOP
5 HANOVER LANE
STRANRAER
DUMFRIES & GALLOWAY DG9 7RW
0776 7170-6260

TRAINING : PADI
EQUPT : BAS, CTH, CAM, SFY, BKS, BTS
HIRE : BAS, CAM
REPAIRS : BAS, CTH, CAM, BTS
TANKS : TST, FILL TO 270BAR
CHARTER : YES, ON BOARD OXYGEN
TRAVEL : HOLIDAYS
OPEN : MON-SAT 0930-1200/1300-1700. SUN 0900-1300

GRAMPIANS

ABERDEEN WATERSPORTS & LEISURE
79 WATERLOO QUAY
ABERDEEN
GRAMPIANS AB2 1DE
0224 581313
FAX: 0224 581313

TRAINING : BSAC
EQUPT : BAS, CTH, CAM, BKS
REPAIRS : BAS, CTH
TANKS : TST, FILL TO 300BAR
TRAVEL : HOLIDAYS
OPEN : MON-SAT 1000-1730

OCEAN WATERSPORTS
76 ROSEMOUNT VIADUCT
ABERDEEN
GRAMPIANS AB1 1NU
0224 638588
FAX: 0224 638588

TRAINING : PADI
EQUPT : BAS, CTH, CAM, SFY, BKS
HIRE : BAS, CTH, CAM
REPAIRS : BAS, CTH, CAM
TANKS : TST, FILL TO 250BAR
TRAVEL : HOLIDAYS
OPEN : TUE-WED,FRI 0900-1730,SAT 0900-1700
OPEN LATE : THU 0900-1930

HIGHLANDS

LOCHALINE DIVE CENTRE
LOCHALINE
HIGHLANDS PA34 5XT
0967 421662
FAX: 0967 421662

TANKS : FILL TO 272BAR
TRAVEL : HOLIDAYS

LOTHIAN

CROMWELL MARINE LTD
CROMWELL HARBOUR
SHORE STREET, DUNBAR
LOTHIAN EH42 1HN
0368 63354 FAX: 0368 65463

TANKS : FILL TO 272BAR
OPEN : MON-SUN 0900-1230/1400-2100

EDINBURGH DIVING CENTRE
1 WATSON CRESCENT
EDINBURGH, LOTHIAN EH11 1HD
031 2294838 FAX: 031 2296306

TRAINING : PADI, BSAC
EQUPT : BAS, CTH, CAM, BKS
HIRE : BAS
REPAIRS : BAS, CTH
TANKS : TST, IDEST, FILL TO 272BAR
CHARTER : YES, ON BOARD OXYGEN
OPEN : MON-SAT 0930-1730

HUNTER DIVING & WATERSPORTS
44 BROUGHTON STREET
EDINBURH, LOTHIAN EH1 3SA
031 5565366 FAX: 031 5565366

EQUPT : BAS, CTH, SFY, BKS
HIRE : BAS, CTH
REPAIRS : BAS, CTH
TANKS : TST, FILL TO 230BAR
OPEN : MON-SAT 0930-1730

ORKNEY ISLANDS

DIVING CELLAR
4 VICTORIA STREET
SCAPA FLOW, STROMNESS, ORKNEY
ISLANDS KW16 3BY
0856 850395-850055

TRAINING : PADI
EQUPT : BAS, CTH, SFY, BKS, BTS
HIRE : BAS, CTH
REPAIRS : BAS
CHARTER : YES, ON BOARD OXYGEN
TRAVEL : HOLIDAYS
OPEN : MON-SAT. VARIES PLEASE PHONE

SHETLAND ISLANDS

SKOLLA DIVING CENTRE
GULBERWICK, SHETLAND ISLANDS ZE2 9JX
0595 4175

EQUPT : BAS, CTH, CAM, BKS
HIRE : BAS, CAM
REPAIRS : BAS
TANKS : TST, FILL TO 340BAR
CHARTER : YES
TRAVEL : HOLIDAYS
OPEN : VARIES. PLEASE CALL

STRATHCLYDE

AQUATRON MARINE LTD
30 STANLEY STREET
GLASGOW, STRATHCLYDE G41 1JB
041 4295902 FAX: 041 4295364

TRAINING : PADI
EQUPT : BAS, CTH, SFY, BKS, BTS
HIRE : BAS, CTH
REPAIRS : BAS, CTH
TANKS : TST, FILL TO 300BAR
CHARTER : YES, ON BOARD OXYGEN
TRAVEL : HOLIDAYS
OPEN : MON-FRI 1000-1800. SAT 0900-1700
OPEN LATE : THU 1000-1900

C&C MARINE LEISURE
LARGS YACHT HAVEN
IRVINE ROAD, LARGS
STRATHCLYDE KA30 8EZ
0475 687180 FAX: 0475 687388

EQUPT : BAS, CTH, SFY, BKS, BTS
REPAIRS : BAS, CTH, BTS
TANKS : TST, FILL TO 300BAR
CHARTER : YES, ON BOARD OXYGEN
OPEN : MON-SUN 0900-1800

KIP WATERSPORTS
KIP MARINE
INVERKIP, GREENOCK
STRATHCLYDE PA16 0AS
0475 521281 FAX: 0475 521821

TRAINING : PADI
EQUPT : BAS, CTH, CAM, SFY, BKS
HIRE : BAS, CTH
REPAIRS : BAS, CTH
TANKS : TST, FILL TO 272BAR
CHARTER : YES, ON BOARD OXYGEN
OPEN : MON-SUN 0900-1800

PUFFIN DIVE CENTRE & OBAN DIVERS
LAGGAN, GLENSHELLACH, OBAN
STRATHCLYDE PA34 4QJ
0631 64142-62755 FAX: 0631 64142

TRAINING : PADI
EQUPT : BAS, CTH, BKS
HIRE : BAS, CTH
REPAIRS : BAS, CTH
TANKS : TST, FILL TO 250BAR
CHARTER : YES, ON BOARD OXYGEN
OPEN : MON-SUN 0900-1800
OPEN LATE : BY APPOINTMENT

SEA & SKI SPORTS LIMITED
3 COLVILLES ROAD
KELVIN INDUSTRIAL ESTATE
EAST KILBRIDE
GLASGOW G75 0RS
03552 21514
FAX: 03552 41241

SPLASH SPORTS SERVICES
UNIT 5
8 MEADOW ROAD, PARTICK
GLASGOW
STRATHCLYDE G11 6HX
041 3372828 FAX: 041 3397788

TRAINING : BSAC, SAA
EQUPT : BAS, CTH, CAM, SFY, BKS, BTS
HIRE : BAS, CTH
REPAIRS : BAS, CTH, CAM
TANKS : TST, FILL TO 300BAR
CHARTER : YES, ON BOARD OXYGEN
TRAVEL : HOLIDAYS
OPEN : MON-SAT 0900-1730

SPORTS LIMITED
3 COLVILES ROAD
KELVIN INDUSTRIAL ESTATE
EAST KILBRIDE
STRATHCLYDE G75 0RS
03552 21514 FAX: 03552 41241

TRAINING : PADI
EQUPT : BAS, CTH, CAM, SFY, BKS
HIRE : BAS, CTH, CAM
REPAIRS : BAS, CTH, CAM
TANKS : TST, FILL TO 350BAR
CHARTER : YES
TRAVEL : HOLIDAYS
OPEN : TUE-WED 0900-1800. FRI-SAT 0900-1700
OPEN LATE : THU 0900-2000

WEST COAST DIVER TRAINING
OLD CUSTOMS HOUSE
BOWLING HARBOUR, BOWLING
STRATHCLYDE
0389 75267

TRAINING : BSAC, SAA
EQUPT : BAS, CTH, SFY, BKS, BTS
REPAIRS : CTH
OPEN : MON-SAT 0900-1700

TAYSIDE

SPLASH SPORT SERVICES
UNIT 8
MARKET MEWS, MARKET STREET
DUNDEE, TAYSIDE DD1 3LA
0382 452828 FAX: 041 3397788

EQUPT : BAS, CTH, CAM, SFY, BKS, BTS
HIRE : BAS, CTH
REPAIRS : BAS, CTH, CAM
TANKS : TST, FILL TO 245BAR
CHARTER : YES, ON BOARD OXYGEN
TRAVEL : HOLIDAYS
OPEN : MON-SAT 1000-1730

WESTERN ISLES

UIST OUTDOOR CENTRE
LOCHMADDY
OUTER HEBRIDES, WESTERN ISLES PA82 5AE
08763 480

TANKS : FILL TO 242BAR
CHARTER : YES
TRAVEL : HOLIDAYS
OPEN : MON-SUN BY APPOINTMENT

For a listing in the next issue of UK Divers' Source contact the publishers at the address on page 1.

Sea slug - Janolus cristatus

UK Diving

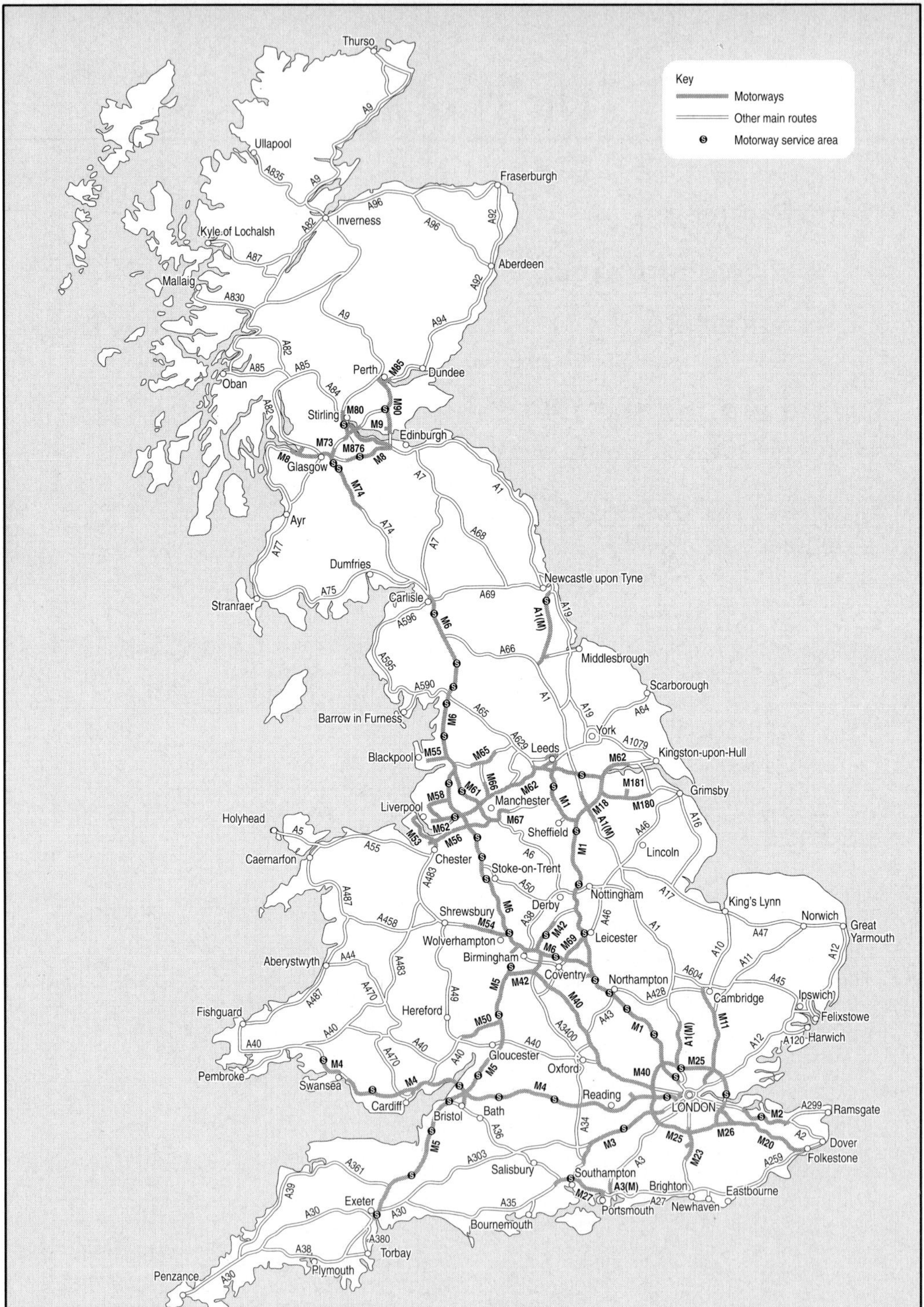
Key
Motorways
Other main routes
Motorway service area
Thurso
A9
Ullapool
A835
Fraserburgh
A96
Inverness
A82
A92
Kyle of Lochalsh
A87
Aberdeen
Mallaig
A830
A94
A85
Perth
M85
Dundee
Oban
A84
M90
Stirling
M80
M9
Edinburgh
M73
M876
M8
Glasgow
M74
A7
A1
Ayr
A77
A74
A68
Dumfries
Newcastle upon Tyne
A75
Carlisle
A69
Stranraer
A596
M6
A1(M)
A19
A66
Middlesbrough
A595
A590
Scarborough
A65
Barrow in Furness
A64
York
A629
Leeds
A1079
Blackpool
M55
M65
M62
Kingston-upon-Hull
M66
M61
M58
M181
M1
M18
M180
Grimsby
Manchester
Liverpool
Holyhead
A5
M67
M62
M53
M56
Sheffield
A46
A16
Lincoln
A55
Caernarfon
Chester
A6
A483
Stoke-on-Trent
A50
Nottingham
A17
King's Lynn
A487
Derby
Shrewsbury
A458
M54
A38
M42
Leicester
Norwich
Great Yarmouth
Wolverhampton
M69
A47
Birmingham
Aberystwyth
A44
Coventry
A604
A10
A11
A12
Northampton
A428
A45
A470
A49
M5
M42
M40
A43
Cambridge
Ipswich
Fishguard
Hereford
Felixstowe
M50
A3400
M1
A1(M)
M11
Harwich
A120
A40
Gloucester
Oxford
M25
Pembroke
M4
Swansea
M40
Reading
Cardiff
Bristol
LONDON
A299
Ramsgate
M2
Bath
A36
A34
M3
M25
M26
M20
Dover
Folkestone
A2
A259
A361
A303
M23
Salisbury
Southampton
A39
A3(M)
Brighton
Eastbourne
M27
Exeter
A35
Portsmouth
A27
Newhaven
Bournemouth
A380
Torbay
A38
Plymouth
Penzance
(20x9 HL3)

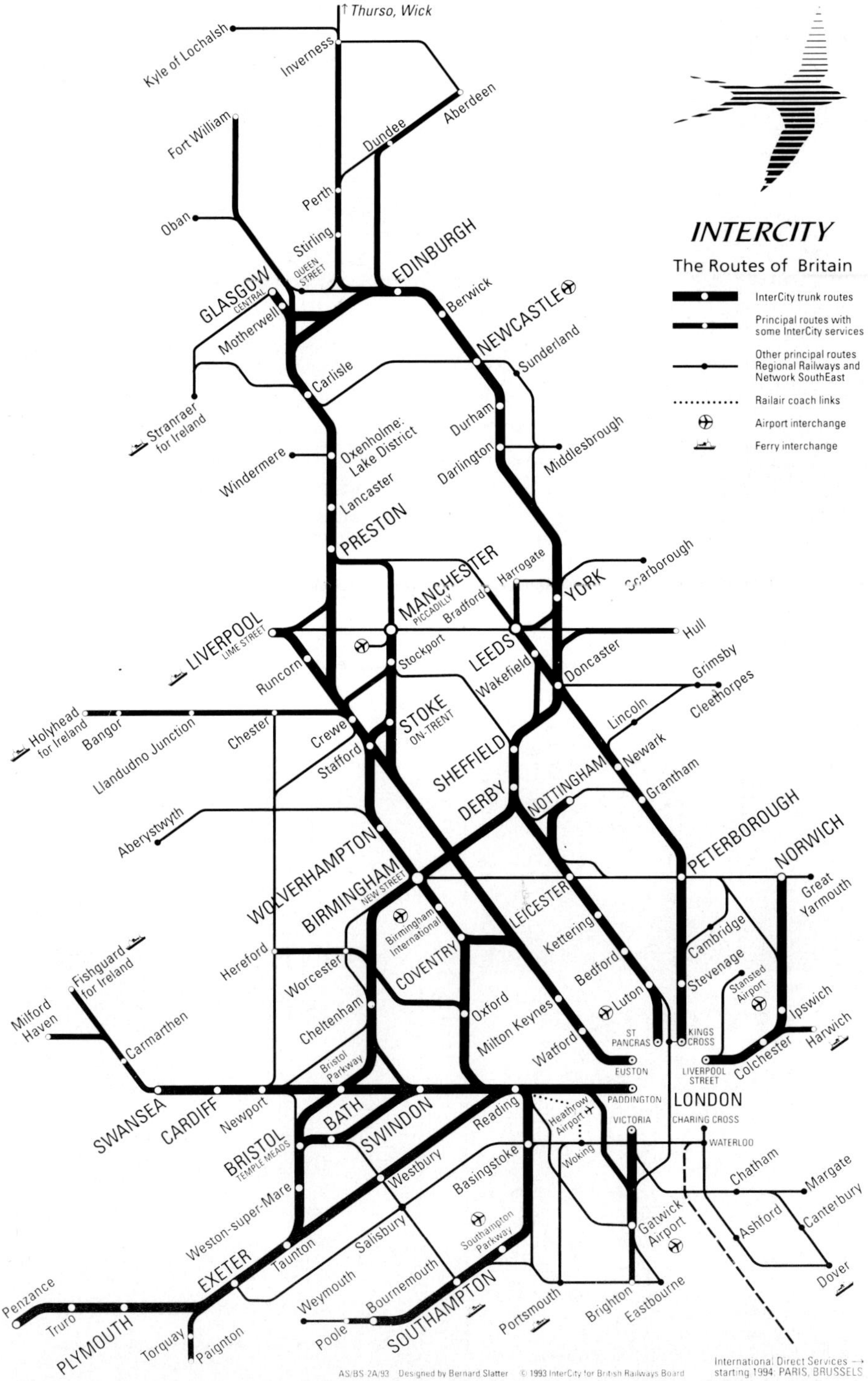
INTERCITY
The Routes of Britain
InterCity trunk routes
Principal routes with some InterCity services
Other principal routes Regional Railways and Network SouthEast
Railair coach links
Airport interchange
Ferry interchange
↑ Thurso, Wick
Kyle of Lochalsh
Inverness
Aberdeen
Dundee
Fort William
Perth
Oban
Stirling
GLASGOW CENTRAL
QUEEN STREET
EDINBURGH
Berwick
NEWCASTLE
Sunderland
Motherwell
Stranraer for Ireland
Carlisle
Durham
Darlington
Middlesbrough
Windermere
Oxenholme: Lake District
Lancaster
PRESTON
MANCHESTER PICCADILLY
Harrogate
YORK
Scarborough
Bradford
LIVERPOOL LIME STREET
LEEDS
Hull
Stockport
Runcorn
Wakefield
Doncaster
Grimsby
Cleethorpes
Holyhead for Ireland
Bangor
Llandudno Junction
Chester
Crewe
STOKE ON-TRENT
Lincoln
Stafford
SHEFFIELD
Newark
DERBY
NOTTINGHAM
Grantham
Aberystwyth
WOLVERHAMPTON
PETERBOROUGH
NORWICH
BIRMINGHAM NEW STREET
LEICESTER
Great Yarmouth
Birmingham International
Kettering
Cambridge
Fishguard for Ireland
Hereford
COVENTRY
Bedford
Stevenage
Milford Haven
Worcester
Stansted Airport
Carmarthen
Cheltenham
Oxford
Luton
Ipswich
Milton Keynes
ST PANCRAS
KINGS CROSS
Harwich
Bristol Parkway
Watford
Colchester
EUSTON
LIVERPOOL STREET
SWANSEA
CARDIFF
Newport
BATH
SWINDON
Reading
PADDINGTON
LONDON
Heathrow Airport
VICTORIA
CHARING CROSS
BRISTOL TEMPLE MEADS
WATERLOO
Woking
Westbury
Basingstoke
Chatham
Margate
Weston-super-Mare
Southampton Parkway
Gatwick Airport
Ashford
Canterbury
Salisbury
EXETER
Taunton
Dover
Penzance
Weymouth
Bournemouth
SOUTHAMPTON
Truro
Portsmouth
Brighton
Eastbourne
PLYMOUTH
Torquay
Paignton
Poole
AS/BS-2A/93 Designed by Bernard Slatter © 1993 InterCity for British Railways Board
International Direct Services → starting 1994: PARIS, BRUSSELS

Diving around the UK

by Richard Bull

Richard Bull entered the diving business in 1979, after 14 years as a professional musician, as a staff instructor with Oslo Froskemannsskole, Norway's oldest and largest diving school. He worked for Norwegian diving schools and taught rescue in the North Seas for the Norwegian Government for several years. Following a brief spell in the UK he spent two years as a resort instructor in the Mediterranean returning to Britain in 1985 to found Current State Diving in Bristol. After many years diving with mixed gas Richard, along with Rob Palmer, became one of the founders of the European Association of Technical Divers - later to become the International Association of Nitrox and Technical Divers - UK. Throughout his diving career Richard has contributed to books, magazines and technical publications. He is currently writing about equipment performance for technical divers.

Every diving area in the world has its own special quality , something unique that makes it worth a visit. Sometimes this characteristic is obvious - such as the crystal clear majestic depths of the Egyptian Red Sea. Sometimes you have to look twice. What is special about the waters of the British Isles? What have we got here?

Most obviously we enjoy an abundant and unrivalled variety of wreck dives. Quite simply we've got the best wreck diving in the world. Strong words? Not at all. Many in the UK dive purely for the wrecks. Think of the amount of shipping in the English Channel and of the accidents that are bound to have occurred over the centuries. Consider the turbulent history of Europe and the numerous naval battles that have been fought around our coasts. A diver could spend a lifetime researching and diving just the victims of U-boat attack (now there's a thought for a book!) or it could be the submarines themselves that inspire the recreational diver. Submarines always look "right" when you dive them - I suppose it's because they are meant to be there - underwater I mean. Sometimes its as though they are not wrecks at all, merely vessels resting between missions.

The *M-2* is a submarine at the bottom in 36m just off Portland, and is a site frequented at weekends by clubs from all over the south of England. The first time that I dived it I approached the day with a degree of indifference because so many others had described their dives here that mine just couldn't be anything special. It was just another run of the mill club dive, I was wrong! As I sat on the conning tower and gazed through the clear water towards the bows it was the marine growth that reminded me that the vessel had been here since 1932. I needed reminding because the *M-2* is intact and sits upright on the bottom - more resting than wrecked.

I think that the *M-2* illustrates an important aspect of British wreck diving - lots of very good and exciting wrecks are easily accessible to the average diver. It is no more than our familiarity with the quantity and quality of wrecks on our doorstep that obscures our good fortune in this direction.

One and a half miles off Swanage, the *"Kyarra"* lies in 30m. Many hundreds of divers remember this ship as their first 30m dive. It is huge, easily accessible, largely intact and there are lots of things to find on it. If it wasn't one of hundreds of such wrecks it would probably be considered quite special.

Such great wreck diving in the UK may obscure some of the other attractions of underwater Britain. Scenic shore diving is plentiful around most of the coastline. Making the most of this involves some knowledge of what you are looking at. Do some homework, take a long shallow linger, and behold, diving comes to life. In one dive this summer I saw cuttlefish, pipefish, a John Dory, dogfish, edible crabs, spider crabs, a lobster, mating sea hares, pollock, scallops, wrasse and lots more - all in 7m of water. A short distance away the beach was crowded with holidays makers unaware that Torquay had anything more to offer in the way of fish than the kind supplied in batter and served with chips.

Lets have a look around the UK and see what the various areas have to offer. I'd like to give a general impression of each of the areas and also offer some personal opinions on particular sites.

Wales

I will restrict myself to three areas in particular - Anglesey, Pembrokeshire and the Gower Peninsular.

Anglesey has a great deal to offer the diver. For a start, you can always find lee-shore which is good news for the diver as the area is quite a trek from most parts of the UK (unless of course you live in North Wales) and the guaranteed diving makes the long trip more acceptable. Visibility here is variable but improves greatly a short distance offshore. There are plenty of shore diving sites and even more inshore locations that can be reached with the aid of a small inflatable boat. In fact, because of the rocky shores, a small boat puts you in touch with many interesting inshore sites, the area around Trearddur Bay for example. Here you can dive in a few metres from the shore along gradually sloping sandy beaches or launch a small boat for the short journey to inshore sites where the rocks descend vertically into the water to depths up 20m.

Holyhead harbour and the small bay just outside it must be considered when talking about shore sites in Anglesea. The water is easily accessible from many points around the harbour and entry by the Coast Guard station provides an interesting shallow dive with plenty of marine life. Entering from the harbour wall you encounter more depth but a somewhat ordinary muddy seabed though the occasional octopus lurks in small kelp patches.

The small bay immediately to the north of the harbour is very interesting. Here lies the flint wreck. Well, there is little evidence of the wreck itself but the cargo of musket flints remains. This site is easily approached from the shore, its depth is about 10-15m and, with a little diligent searching musket flints can usually be found. Wreck diving proper in Anglesey abounds. There is a great variety from near-shore wrecks such as the *"Lady Meath"* which sits in about 20m of water and is only just outside the harbour, to more adventurous offshore sites like the *"Castilian"* which is sited out on the Skerries and is different proposition altogether. It's an adventurous dive for experienced divers.

Pembrokeshire

Pembrokeshire and west Wales provide excellent diving whatever your interests - but beware of treacherous tidal streams in many areas especially around the islands of Skomer and Skokholm. The wreck of the *"Lucy"* is popular with more experienced divers.

Martins Haven is approached via a steep track from the carpark and is best known as a launch site. However, do not ignore it as shore site as it's a magnificent marine reserve. I don't know how far the bottom slopes down but I've been to about 25m and it was still going down. The beauty of the site is that you can choose to dive at any depth that you want.

The variety and abundance of marine life is spectacular. Lobsters and edible crabs stroll past with a confidence that only comes from living in a marine reserve! Parts of the sea bed are carpeted with brittle stars and there is always the chance of an inquisitive seal taking an interest. Visibility is usually good.

The Gower Peninsular

While Gower Peninsular doesn't offer the variety or quantity of diving found in west Wales or Anglesey, it does have the advantage of being far more accessible from the rest of the world!

Oxwich Bay is typical of the Gower. It's shallow with a relatively uninteresting seabed although there is a wreck which is visible at low tide, on the right hand side of the bay.

On the other side of the peninsular is Worms Head. This is supposed to be the site of a wrecked Spanish Galleon. No wreck has been located but periodic finds of coins spark off frenzied bouts of hunting.

Scotland

Many books have been written about the diving in Scotland. In fact many volumes have been dedicated to individual sites. In short Scotland not only has an incredible variety of spectacular diving, it has some of the most famous dives sites in the world. Were we to work our way around Scotland from the southwest we would find that each area provided sufficient interesting dives to be well known in its own right.

The extreme southwest of the Scottish coast from Dumfries to Irvine is a region which is missing from the "sites" list of most divers. This is probably because it is often geographically lumped in with the rest of the country where environments tend to be impressive and majestic.

While the area lacks the impressive scenery usually associated with Scottish diving, there are numerous shipwrecks - at least 650 of them! Further up the coast is an area which seems somewhat taken for granted by the locals but which, as a foreigner, I rate very highly - the Clyde and Firth of Clyde.

The best of Clyde diving is not for the inexperienced or those preferring an easy life underwater. The wreck of *"SS Wallachia"*, only 259 feet long, is one of the attractions. There are many artifacts here and she is small enough to be explored in a single dive. She lies in about 34m but she has hazards common to most of the Clyde wrecks; poor visibility, difficult tides, and the additional problem of lost fishing nets draped over the wreck. The *Wallachia* is a good site - but is for the experienced wreck diver only.

Although deep, dark, wrecks are characteristic of Clyde diving they are not the whole story. Go to Largs, launch your RIB and head out to Little Cumbrae. Here you will find good visibility, lots of crustaceans and you will almost certainly dive in the company of seals. This is the other face of the Clyde!

Divers heading north from England frequently bypass southwestern Scotland and the Firth of Clyde with barely a thought. Their minds are set on Oban and the diving opportunities afforded by this beautiful west coast Port.

Oban enjoys excellent visibility and shore dives abound among the islands and inlets. Although there are many wrecks in the immediate area, the best known is to be found a little further north - the *"Breda"* in Ardmucknish Bay.

In contrast to the Clyde wrecks this is a safe, popular dive and visibility is usually good. The *Breda* was a 130m long convoy vessel that came to grief in 1942. She rests in an upright position in about 30m of water, her highest point coming to within about 15m of the surface. An excellent wreck for the tourist diver and photographer as well as the wrecker.

It is difficult to pass any location in northern, northwestern or northeastern Scotland but the attraction of the country's most famous dive site tempts many to do just that. Scapa Flow in Orkney is surely one of the best known sites it the world.

The surrender of the German High Seas Fleet in 1918 led to its internment in Scapa Flow. The commander of the Fleet, Vice Admiral Ludwig Von Reuter decided that, at all costs, this fleet should not fall into allied hands and on June 21 1919 he gave the order for it to be scuttled. Although it is this fleet that has made Scapa Flow famous there are many more wrecks in the area - a total of 92 have been logged and many more unidentified wreck sites are known.

However, it is the massive German warships resting on the bottom at Scapa Flow that have made this site a magnet for divers from all over the world.

Talk to anyone who has dived the *"Kron Prinze Wilhelm"*, for instance, and a common thread seems to run thorough all the tales and stories - SIZE. No wonder! This was a 25,000 tonne battleship, 177m long, with massive 30cm guns. It would be spectacular enough to find this ship on its own, but it's not!

There are a further two battleships, four light cruisers and five destroyers from the German High Seas Fleet, a WWII German Destroyer, two German submarines, 32 blockships, two British Battleships and a lot more.

So dive Scapa Flow - it's not expensive and there are a good number of charter boats working out of Stromness. Is it the best wreck diving site in the world? I don't know, but I would find it hard to argue with anyone who said it was.

The extreme southeast of Scotland offers quite different diving to that of Scapa Flow. Although there are wrecks in the area, St Abbs is noted as a Marine Nature Reserve with shallow waters, good visibility and an abundance of marine life. It is an area where the camera rules - not the crowbar.

The Northeastern coast and Yorkshire

With the exception of the Farne Islands, the northeastern coast of England and the Yorkshire coast do not attract the visiting diver which is a shame as there is some superb diving in these areas. I think that a major reason for this rejection by the travelling diver is that if the wind happens to be from the wrong direction you just can't dive!

Its not that you can't dive your planned site, you just can't dive. If you travel to virtually any south coast or west country dive venue you can usually tuck in under a lee shore somewhere. Cornwall has its north and south coasts and the opposite sides of the Lizard. In Oban and there is always the lee shore of an Island somewhere. However, on the northeastern or Yorkshire coast if a strong wind blows on shore - that's it - no diving.

Maybe the local divers don't look upon this as a big drawback as they can decide to dive at short notice, when conditions are just right - and they don't have hoards of visiting divers to compete with.

The coastline from Yorkshire down through Lincolnshire, Norfolk, Suffolk, Essex and Kent is not noted for its excellent diving as it offers even less to the visiting diver. However, a bit of creative thinking goes a long way. Let me give you an example. For some years I was a member of a diving club in Colchester, Essex.

Weekend after weekend we would trail our boats down to the south coast and spend hours sitting in our cars in traffic jams. None of us questioned this ritual until eventually one member determined to dive the Essex coast. He reasoned that if you picked the right day and went far enough offshore you could find some good diving.

Above all he felt that it was better to spend three hours sitting in a boat than three hours sitting in a car. That, at least, was hard to dispute.

He did pick the right days, and he did spend a long time sitting in boats but he lead the club to some superb dives on undived wrecks. Nevertheless diving along the English east coast is the province of enthusiastic and resilient local divers.

Things start to change on the Sussex coast. There may be no books on diving Essex and Kent but Sussex boasts a couple of good texts. Visibility is variable but acceptable and I have certainly had many enjoyable dives from hard boats based in Littlehampton.

Drift diving here can be excellent and the amount of ground covered in this way more than makes up for the lack of reefs, rocky walls, and drop offs. Plaice, sole, skate and other flatfish are plentiful. Once again though it is the wrecks that make the area known among the diving community. One big wreck for the adventurous to be found off the Sussex coast is the *"Moldavia"*. With a gross tonnage of 9,500 she is a big ship and lies in 48m of water, with a depth at the top of the wreck of 37m.

This is a memorable dive for the experienced diver - there is good visibility and portholes to be had - but it needs careful planning. As a result of the depth Low Water slack is really the only time to dive her and the weather must be almost perfect as no one looks forward to a three to four hour trip on small charter boat in bad weather conditions.

Charter boat skippers well acquainted with the *Moldavia* can be contacted in Littlehampton.

The South Coast

The south coast - Hampshire, Dorset and Devon - benefits from a reasonably warm climate and because of the indented coastline, there is usually somewhere to dive, whatever the wind directions. The prevailing winds are, in fact, south-westerly, and if these winds are at all strong sites must be chosen carefully.

Chesil Cove, at the Portland end of Chesil Beach, is a delightful shore diving site. There is good visibility, the seabed slopes quickly to a depth of about 14m, there is some interesting wreckage from a Greek freighter, the *"Preveza"*, and even an eighteenth century cannon. The only trouble is that Chesil Cove faces to the west and even a force three or four makes entry and exit from the water very difficult. However, along the south coast it is not hard to find somewhere sheltered. One well dived site - Brixham Breakwater Beach - even faces north!

There are many well know offshore wreck sites along this part of the coast and I have already described two of them - the *M2* and the *Kyarra*.

Cornwall

In many ways diving Cornwall is the epitome of British diving - and it sees thousands of visiting divers each year. The water is clear, the coastline rocky and if any area is synonymous with ship wrecks it is this county.

Cornwall is about 75 miles long and although much of its deeply indented coastline has steep cliffs going straight down into the sea, there are plenty of sandy beaches. The underwater scenery is beautiful and can be enjoyed from many places along the shore. One small area around PorthKerris, Porthoustock, and the Manacles reef has a wide variety of diving that can be experienced in the immediate vicinity.

There is a good shore dive at Porthkerris. Turn left as you enter Porthkerris beach and you will see a large outcrop of rock that divides the main beach from the smaller northern area. Park near the MOD building and you will find easy access over a rocky shore into about 18m of water. This also makes an excellent night dive.

Just offshore here, and a very popular boat dive, is the wreck of the *"Volnay"*. If you are first on to it the visibility is good, but there is quite a lot of silt and at peak times this quickly takes its toll. There are plenty of things to be wary of on this wreck, live ammunition and phosphorus for instance but there are also plenty of small relics that can be retrieved such as thousands of lead balls from anti personnel shells and if you are really lucky you might find a timing cone. These make beautiful trophies when they are cleaned up but they are few and far between these days.

Just down the coast lies Porthhoustock, the principal launch site for those wishing to dive the Manacles Reef. This sunken headland provides impressive diving for the experienced diver with peaks and reefs that come within a few metres of the surface and drop away to great depths. Diving the Vase Rock for instance is like flying down an Alpine Peak covered with a carpet of anemones. Needless to say, these reefs and pinnacles have claimed their fair share of shipping over the years.

The *"Mohegan"*, is one of many. She was a 7000 tonne passenger vessel that went down in 1898 and now lies about 26m of water with her boilers and bows coming to within about 17m of the surface. A warning - its not only ships that have come to grief on the Manacles - divers have too!

Diving the Manacles is not to be underestimated. Strong tides and deceptive depths make them a site to be avoided by beginners and the inexperienced.

One easy dive just off Porthoustock Beach is the remains of the fully rigged steel ship the *"Andola"*. Although there is not much left here, she lies in only 8m of water and there is always the chance of a trophy. An excellent grovel dive. Porthoustock and Porthkerris - a little bit of Cornwall with a lot to offer!

I meet a lot of people who say that they only dive abroad and can't be bothered to dive in the UK. As far as I am concerned they are rejecting some of the best diving in the world - and it's only a matter of time before the rest of the world realises it so let's make the most of it while we have it to ourselves.

Marine life in UK waters

by Dr Paul Naylor

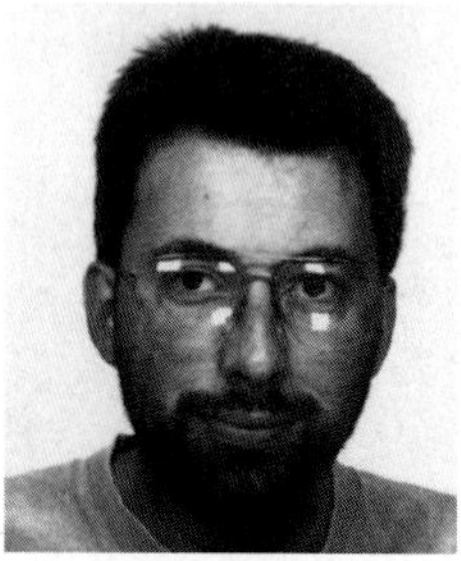

Paul Naylor has a background of biological research and a doctorate in marine biology. He took up diving in 1984 in order to watch and photograph marine animals in their natural habitat. Despite several overseas trips, he believes that the UK fauna holds a unique fascination for divers, and attempts to put this across by writing regularly for diving magazines.

An impressive and sometimes bewildering array of marine life awaits the diver in our home waters. Spectacular and varied animals are more usually associated with exotic locations such as The Great Barrier Reef and the Red Sea but representatives of virtually every animal group, apart from the reef-building hard corals, can be found off our coasts.

It is this great variety that can bewilder the observer, coupled with the fact that many sea creatures belong to groups not represented on land at all.

Fish are vertebrate animals like reptiles or mammals, crabs and lobsters can be viewed as marine insects, but where are the terrestrial starfish?

To further confuse the issue, animals with very different evolutionary backgrounds can be strikingly similar because they have been exposed to the same set of environmental conditions and come up with the same answer, a process known as convergent evolution.

In this article I aim to describe some of the important features of the major animal groups and some common representatives of each group that are frequently seen while diving round the UK.

Sponges

Of the animals made up from many cells, rather than just a single one like the Protozoans, sponges are the simplest. Being sessile and attached to the sea-bed, they were once thought to be plants. In essence, a sponge is a large animated filter, and this is indeed how it feeds. A sponge has many tiny openings through which water is drawn by the current in its body cavity created by the tiny whip-like extensions (flagella) of special cells. Any tiny organisms or particles of food are extracted from this current of water which then leaves the sponge by way of a single large opening. The richness of the sea is amply demonstrated by the fact that animals as diverse as the humble sponge and the mighty blue whale can make a living from simply straining large volumes of its waters.

There are many different types of sponge in British waters and their form varies considerably. In exposed sites encrusting forms, which lie flat with the sea-bed, are usually found while in more sheltered waters, species with more delicate branched structures can be common. One of the most noticeable sponges is the boring sponge, *Cliona celata*, which sometimes bores down into soft rock, hence the name. Yellow in colour and sometimes more than a metre across, it is common in areas where strong currents flow.

Sponges are often found in association with other animals; the sea-orange, *Suberites domuncula*, sometimes forms a globular mass around the whelk-shell home of a hermit crab.

The stinging cell animals - sea anemones, soft corals and jellyfish

If a group of animals were nominated for their outstanding contribution to the underwater scenery around Britain it would have to be the sea anemones and soft corals. Whether it be a dive on wrecks such as the Lucy (Pembrokeshire) or the Hispania (Sound of Mull) encrusted with thousands of plumose anemones, a fast drift across a sea-bed covered entirely with dead man's fingers or a shallow shore dive down gullies coated in multicoloured dahlia anemones, these animals create a wonderful seascape.

The anemones, corals and jellyfish (the latter are, in essence, floating sea anemones) are simple animals, which posses a central mouth, that also serves as an anus, surrounded by tentacles. These tentacles are heavily armed with thread capsules, or stinging cells (Cnida) that are the distinguishing feature of this group of animals and give rise to their name, the *Cnidarians*.

The stinging cells are masterpieces of engineering in miniature and each contains a coiled hollow thread. When a cell is triggered, by a small fish brushing against a tentacle for example, the thread is turned inside-out by an increase in pressure and shoots out to entrap the unfortunate victim. The minute threads are often armed with barbs and can inject toxin into the prey.

Metridium senile - Plumose anemone
Picture: Dr P Naylor

Particularly powerful cells like those of the lion's mane jellyfish, *Cyanea capillata*, can inflict painful stings on humans. Plumose (*Metridium senile*) and dahlia (*Urticina felina*) anemones and dead mans' fingers (*Alcyonium digitatum*) have already been mentioned. Dead man's fingers are colonial soft corals; each "finger" representing a colony of tiny anemone-like animals whose flexible skeletons are merged into a single mass. The only hard coral commonly found in British waters, the Devonshire cup coral, *Caryophyllia smithii*, is a solitary animal unlike its reef-building relatives found in tropical waters.

Worms

Few animal groups demonstrate how different their aquatic and terrestrial members can appear as clearly as the worms. From the appearance of earthworms, one would hardly expect the beauty of some of the marine worms.

The most attractive worms are those that build a tube that sits proud of the substrate.

Aphrodite aculeata - Sea mouse *Picture: Dr P Naylor*

From this home, they extend feathery, flower-like, gills which are used to entrap passing food and which can be withdrawn incredibly rapidly when a potential predator (or an underwater camera!) is detected. Two good examples of these creatures are the peacock worm, *Sabella pavonina*, and the fan worm, *Bispira volutacornis*. An interesting animal that doesn't even look like a worm is the sea-mouse, *Aphrodite aculeata*. Its oval, muddy-brown, body is fringed by coarse iridescent hairs.

Crabs, lobsters and prawns

Crustacean shellfish such as crabs, lobsters and prawns are related to the insects as they are part of the giant animal group known as Arthropods, which literally means animals with "jointed limbs". A predominant feature of these animals is their hard skeleton or casing which is worn outside the body, rather than forming an internal framework like that of ours or the fish. The casing provides excellent protection against most predators but, unlike an internal skeleton, must be shed periodically to allow growth.

Many of the "dead" crabs washed up on beaches are simply the exoskeletons of crabs that have outgrown them. A careful examination of these cast-offs will reveal the slit at the back and sides of the shell which opens up to allow the top part to hinge forward so the crab can climb out. The new leathery coat starts to harden up as soon as the animal has moulted, but until this process is completed, the Crustacean is very vulnerable.

The moulting cycle affects the life-styles of these animals in many ways. When newly hardened they have large appetites and are constantly looking for food to, in effect, fill the new shell but when about to moult they will stop eating and become listless. Furthermore, the female of most crab species can only mate when soft. This is why a male crab is often seen carrying a smaller female tucked underneath him; he is making sure that when she moults, he will be immediately available. Crabs are some of the most distinctive animals in UK waters. The edible crab, *Cancer pagurus*, with its characteristic "pie-crust" shell is very common but the velvet swimming crab, *Liocarcinus puber*, with its superb red eyes and dark blue lines on its limbs is possibly the species most often seen. This may be partly because, when approached, velvet swimming crabs will often take on an aggressive posture with claws spread wide, rather than shrinking back into a crevice as one might expect.

Munida rugoso - Long clawed squat lobster
Picture: Dr P Naylor

The lobster, *Homarus gammarus*, with its rich blue coloration and massive claws is an impressive, but all too rare, sight as is the orange-brown crawfish, *Palinurus elephas*, with its heavily armoured antennae but no large claws.

Prawns and shrimps are the small cousins of the crabs and lobsters and have a very similar body plan. The exoskeleton of hermit crabs only covers their front-end and their soft hindparts are hidden in "borrowed" whelk shells or the like.

Some distinctive relatives of the hermit crabs are the squat lobsters; the spiny squat lobster, *Galathea strigosa*, is beautifully coloured with blue banding on its brilliant red shell but is normally hidden in the tightest rock cracks. The long-clawed squat lobster, *Munida rugosa*, appears to be much bolder. It is surprising that barnacles are also crustaceans, and not molluscs as one might suspect.

Molluscs

When one thinks of the marine molluscs it tends to be the varieties with obvious hard shells that spring to mind, whether they have one shell like the limpets and whelks or two like the mussels, cockles, clams and scallops.

However, two groups of molluscs that lack this obvious feature must rank among the most fascinating marine animals. The Nudibranchs are sea slugs and have no shell at all; in fact the term Nudibranch means "naked gills" since these animals also lack the mantle cavity that houses the gills in most molluscs. Without a shell, these animals must rely on other forms of defence and some are superbly camouflaged while others produce poisonous substances in their tissues. Like other noxious animals, many sea slugs are brightly coloured in order to teach predators to avoid them. Some sea slugs can eat stinging-cell animals such as sea anemones and incorporate the undischarged thread capsules into their own tissues where they are used in defence.

The second group of "surprise molluscs" to which I referred are the Cephalopods; an even more unusual group which includes the octopus, cuttlefish and squid. The Cephalopod most frequently seen by British divers is the fascinating cuttlefish, *Sepia officinalis*. The cuttlefish has a shell, but it is situated internally and comprises a stack of thin-walled chambers largely filled with gas. This structure gives the cuttlefish superb buoyancy control and, when approached, they will often rise slowly from the sea-bed where they have been resting and float almost motionless in front of you.

Sepia officinalis - Cuttlefish Picture: Dr P Naylor

If they are slowly followed, their amazing capacity for colour change can be observed; over kelp-covered rock they will take on a dark brown colour, but over pale sand, they can instantly turn almost completely white. Even when stationary, different patterns of stripes will play along the back of the animal. If pursued too vigorously, a cuttlefish will emit a cloud of ink and use water jetted from the funnel on its underside to shoot rapidly backwards in a series of bursts.

Starfish and their relatives

Some of the most unusual and colourful animals around our coasts are the starfish. They belong to the group known as Echinoderms, or "spiny-skinned" animals and, even by the standard of marine invertebrates, are very unusual creatures. The body is in the form of a central disk from which a series of arms radiate outwards. With no head, the animal can move equally well in any direction which it does using a unique system of hydraulics. Interconnecting canals drive hundreds of small tentacles, called tube-feet, positioned on the underside of the arms. Perhaps surprisingly, starfish are very effective predators as typified by two frequently seen British species; the common starfish, *Asterias rubens*, and the spiny starfish, *Marthasterias glacialis*. The fact that these animals move slowly is no problem as their usual prey are bivalve molluscs, such as mussels, which hardly move at all.

The problem with the molluscs is the tightly shut shell which the starfish overcome very elegantly. Using many of the suckered tube-feet in unison, a starfish exerts a continuous pull on its prey which can resist for a time but eventually tires. The starfish only needs to create a tiny gap because it then everts its stomach into the body cavity of the mollusc and digests it where it is.

Species such as the two mentioned above usually have five arms, the normal number for starfish, but two of the most attractive members of this animal group have many more. The superbly coloured common sunstar, *Crossaster papposus*, and the purple sunstar, *Solaster endeca*, have between about seven and 13 arms. Other Echinoderms include the sea-urchins, brittle-stars, feather-stars and sea-cucumbers which all have the same basic body plan as the starfish.

Sea squirts

Though appearing to be rather like sponges, and in fact having a similar life-style in terms of extracting food from the sea water pumped through their bodies, these animals are classified as Chordates (animals with a dorsal nerve cord) like us, the fish and other vertebrates. The false impression created by sea squirts is because only their tadpole-like larvae posses the cord. The adult stage is sessile and the body tends to represent a leathery tunic surrounding a U-shaped tube, the two ends of which form the inhalant and exhalant siphons; often very noticeable features of these animals.

Typical British sea squirts are the cream coloured common sea squirt, *Ciona intestinalis*, and the smaller dome-shaped gooseberry sea-squirt, *Dendrodoa grossularia*, coloured red or orange. Both species can occur in dense aggregations but are not truly colonial unlike the star squirt, *Botryllus schlosseri* which forms tiny but distinctive star-shaped groups within a colony.

Fish

From the tiny goby to the gigantic basking shark and from the flattened plaice to the cylindrical eel, a staggering variety of fish are to be found in British waters. Part of their fascination seems to be that it is so easy to see how many of the different forms are adapted to their environment.

Flatfish such as plaice, sole, dab, flounders, turbot and brill are superbly adapted for living on flat sand or mud. They are actually compressed from side to side but lie on either their right or left side, with both eyes on the upward facing side. They are coloured to blend in with the sea-bed and many species can change colour to match their immediate surroundings. By using their fins to flick a thin covering of sand over themselves, they become almost invisible both to predators and presumably also to prey animals who swim by without due concern.

Another fish obviously adapted to its habitat is the conger eel, *Conger conger*, which is the perfect shape for hiding away in deep cracks and crevices and so is often found on wrecks. It is usually only the head that is seen because they emerge to feed mainly at night and when you are lucky enough to find one out of its lair, the size of its huge body is often quite a shock.

Labrus mixtus - Cuckoo wrasse
Picture: Dr P Naylor

Apart from conger eels, wrecks are superb places for watching fish, so that the wishes of both marine life enthusiasts and wreck ferrets can sometimes be satisfied in a single location. Not only does a wreck provide plentiful cover for fish that hide away, it provides a good hunting ground for free-swimming fish such as pollack, *Pollachius pollachius*. The wrasse are among the fish most commonly seen by British divers and there are five common species native to our waters. The cuckoo wrasse, *Labrus mixtus*, is a beautiful animal and large males, with their fabulous deep blue and orange coloration will sometimes follow you throughout an entire dive. Oddly, all cuckoo wrasse start out as females and some of these turn into males part way through their life. Other wrasse have similarly interesting habits. The smaller, but colourfully striped male corkwing wrasse, *Crenilabrus melops*, can be seen building a nest from seaweed fragments, which it will try to defend against all comers, including divers, except a gravid female which it will endeavour to entice into the nest where she will lay her eggs. Paternal care of the young is in fact very common among shallow-water fish. Another small wrasse, the rock cook, *Centrolabrus exoletus*, acts as a cleaner on larger fish, yet another aspect of marine life behaviour not confined to tropical waters.

No summary of British fish could ignore the tompot blenny, *Parablennius gattorugine*. Despite usually living in rock crevices, this delightful fish will sometimes emerge from its hiding place to observe the passing diver and some will even allow themselves to be gently stroked.

Where to find Britain's marine animals

The British Isles are fairly small and many of the common marine animals can be found anywhere round our coasts, making the variation in fauna between locations quite subtle. Of more importance than geographic location is the type of habitat being dived on; both the type of sea-bed (hard or soft) and the degree of exposure (sheltered or swept by currents or swell) are influential. For example, the absence of many species from the southern North Sea is probably merely due to the lack of rocky substrate in that area.

Many sponges and sea anemones are found anywhere there is suitable hard substrate, wrecks all around our coasts providing an ideal anchoring point for species such as the plumose anemone and an advantageous elevation into food-bearing currents. Confusingly, the Devonshire cup coral is found on most coasts.

Of the worms mentioned, the fan worm, Bispira, seems much more common in the south-west while the scale worm and peacock worm are found more often off Scottish coasts.

Most of the common Crustaceans are very widely distributed but the crawfish, *Palinurus elephas*, is confined to western coasts and the long-clawed squat lobster, *Munida rugoso*, seems mainly restricted to the north-west. The cuttlefish, *Sepia officinalis*, is seen much more often in the south.

The common starfish, as the name suggests, is very widespread while the spiny starfish is a south-western species and the beautiful sunstars are common in the north.

Of the fish mentioned, the flatfishes and conger eel can be seen in their favoured habitats anywhere. This also goes for most of the wrasse but the rock cook seems to be absent from the North Sea as does the tompot blenny. While the pollack is very widespread, its close relative the saithe is relatively more common in the north.

From my personal experience I find that fish life is more prolific in the south and the rich variety of invertebrates is more impressive in the north-west. There are no hard and fast rules however, and this view might simply be biased by the places where I dive.

The influence of warm currents sweeping up from the south-west, generally cleaner water and more varied habitats produce a greater variety of life on western shores though it is sometimes difficult to believe this when you are swimming down a rock gully off St Abbs! If one thing is certain, it is that you should find plenty of interest wherever you dive, and I haven't even mentioned the seaweeds!

Chartering Boats

by John Elliss

John Elliss began snorkelling in the 1960's and was involved in SCUBA by the early 70's. Within a few years he had decided to commit his time to diving and chartering. John is a BSAC 2nd class diver, Advanced Instructor, O_2 Instructor, Lifesaver Examiner and a BSAC/RYA Boat Handling Instructor and holds HSE Part IV and First Aid Certificates as well as Local Authority and DoT Boatmans Licenses. He is involved with, Seaways Diving who run the *Seaquest of Mylor*, a 35ft Lochin, which holds £1 million Third Party and Public Liability insurance cover, as well as both local authority and, DoT licenses. Having dived all over the world he maintains that Cornwall takes some beating!

Every year sports diving clubs and/or groups scour the classified sections of the diving press, searching for that perfect advertisement. The one which describes the boat they are to enjoy (or endure) during the next year's diving trip to their chosen corner of the British Isles.

Without knowing the area, the vessel or the skipper (usually and annoyingly referred to as Skip, although we answer to various other names - mine is John), the HDG (Holiday Diving Group) are able to refer to little more than the ad before, after much discussion and gallons of liquid beverage, they make their final decision and book a boat from the selection available for charter.

Arrival on the quay at 08.30hrs on a calm and sunny Saturday morning may herald feelings of joyous elation as the group sets eyes upon the floating palace which is to transport them on the trip of the year - the voyage of a lifetime; or it may give rise to sheer horror at the sight of the untidy, stinking thing that strains at its mooring ropes, surrounded by the blackened remnants of ancient car tyres, that beckons the eager divers.

The competent skipper

Almost all reputable boats and skippers operate under the control of either their Local Authority or the DoT (Department of Transport).

Through these offices sea worthy vessels that comply with certain regulations are granted an area, or areas of operation for the conveyance of passengers.

Such vessels will be equipped with ALL the essential safety equipment required by the relevant authority ie;

Life jackets for all persons on board
Life buoys
Life floats and/or life rafts
Flares
Fire extinguishers
Bilge pumps
First aid Box, and of course
The ever essential radio.

All vessels operating under these licenses will carry Third Party and Public Liability insurance cover, in some cases up to £1 million.

However, no insurance company will extend cover to those Lemming-like passengers who choose to throw themselves overboard whether they are wearing diving equipment or not.

It is up to these individuals to ensure they have adequate personal insurance cover in force. Skippers operating these vessels will also hold either a Local Authority Boatman's License and/or a DoT Boatman's License, ensuring that they are competent to operate a passenger carrying vessel for hire or reward.

Beware the cowboy

How many times have you heard the tale "Old so and so will take you out for a few quid" from divers who have put their trust in someone who is neither certificated nor insured.

Remember, it is YOUR life you are playing with. It's all too easy to get out of the boat and INTO the water, but it's a different kettle of fish when it comes to climbing back in.

How many times have you seen a diver struggling up the side of a boat with only car tyre fenders to help him climb from the water. All too often the cowboys do not have even the basic equipment required by divers or other passengers.

Lives are at stake and in these days of litigation only a fool would offer a service and take money without bothering to go to the expense of equipping a vessel properly. Be wary.

Wheelhouse equipment is another important consideration when it comes to chartering Hard Boats for diving, as on site location is paramount.

A radio is an essential item and the better vessels carry two: one fixed, the other portable. Radar can be fitted along with two sounders, one being a paper recorder, the other colour.

Two navigators are useful, one Decca the other GPS which is interfaced with a plotter unit.

It is essential that the minimum amount of time is spent looking for sites and a magnetometer can be carried to ensure elusive wreck location.

Diver recovery from the water can be aided by a vertical spineladder.

The Professional Boatman's Association

Late in 1991 the Professional Boatman's Association was formed. In order to enter into discussions with the DoT, along with 11 other interested bodies, in response to a proposed Code of Practice for charter vessels that is being introduced by the Government.

The original draft copy of the Code of Practice made horrendous reading. In our case it looked as though we either sold our 33ft boat and packed it in, or transformed it into a large cargo carrier to accommodate all the proposed bits and pieces, to say nothing of conforming with the proposed manning requirements.

However, after many meetings with the DoT, a final copy of the Code of Practice for all vessels up to 24m in length is expected to be issued soon

This code, when fully implemented, will ensure that vessels for charter will conform to a set standard.

So the next time you are thinking of chartering, take heed and give thanks to all those who have worked so hard to keep the charter fleet afloat and working, whether it be for diving, sea angling, bird watching or yachting.

Enjoy your diving.

LIFE BELOW 1 ATM

by B. Hugo

Dive assured

by Bob Archell

Bob Archell has over 16 years experience in the insurance industry field and has dealt with claims and investigations as far afield as Canada, Nigeria, Angola, Italy and many other countries. A keen diver and under-water swimmer, Bob has been associated with many difficult insurance salvage situations around the world. As Managing Director of Dive Master Insurance Consultants Ltd he has written or co-written many innovative policies.

As divers we all have to learn some basic laws of physics and physiology in order that we may dive safely.

Diving requires a greater degree of physical fitness and intelligence than some other pastime sports. It seems incredible therefore that after qualifying as a sports diver, some people should put their minds into neutral when selecting what could be the most important purchase of their lives - diving insurance.

In common with most aspects of this sport there are some simple rules to apply which will assist you in selecting the most appropriate insurance cover for your diving requirements.

The golden rule is to always read the insurance policy wording and if it does not appear to cover your specific requirements ask the insurance company or intermediary to explain why.

Never be afraid to ask the Insurer questions or to ask for a full written reply on any point you cannot understand. Many Insurers use traditional wordings in policies which can be confusing. Some Insurers however use plain language policies which state the extent of cover exactly in an understandable fashion.

The structure of any policy will be broken down into conditions which specify the area of cover. Warranties are obligations you must comply with to make the policy operative, and Exclusions exclude certain risks.

The Excess is the amount you have to pay before the insurance company has an interest in a claim. Some policies do not have an Excess.

Read all sections of the policy carefully and if it does not cover your exact requirements ask if your particular risk can be covered by extension or endorsement. The answer from the Insurer may be no, but at least you will have addressed yourself to that area of concern before you buy the product.

The second golden rule is to always fill in the proposal or application for insurance truthfully. If you state something that is untrue or misleading on your proposal form this may be considered as a breach of upmost goodfaith and the insurers may have the right to void the policy from the outset.

Special attention should be given to completing marine insurance proposal forms for craft or vessels as these policies are subject to the 1906 Marine Insurance Act and there is a great deal of case law which allows Insurers to void or reject cover where they have been given misleading or false information at the proposal stage.

Seek the advice of a specialist marine broker or intermediary when insuring your boat.

As a diver there are certain key areas of insurance cover that you should be specifically interested in. These are:

- **Equipment Insurance**
- **Medical/Accident Insurance**
- **Travel Insurance**
- **Life Cover**
- **Boat Insurance**
- **Liability**

Make sure your current life, pensions and investment policies cover your diving risk. Once again check the wording carefully to make sure these existing policies are not prejudiced by your sports diving activities.

Diving equipment represents a considerable investment, and we estimate that a novice diver will spend on average £1,500 in the first year of training. Check to see if your existing insurance policies, such as house contents or any other specific policy covering your sporting activities covers your diving equipment.

The areas to specifically clarify with your insurers are transit, storage and cover during use and emergency jettison.

Certain contingencies will not be covered under these equipment policies, and these will include wear and tear and gradual deterioration due to operating causes. In simple terms this means Insurers are not prepared to pick up the cost of wear and tear or servicing of diving equipment which should be borne by the diver as part of the overall annual maintenance cost.

Insurers will insure against a fortuity such as an unforeseen set of circumstances leading to the loss or damage of a piece of diving equipment.

Generally speaking you will also be covered for your own negligence, so long as the degree of negligence does not constitute a lack of due diligence.

This is the most misunderstood category in current insurance claims, and many divers believe that they are not covered for their own negligence. Generally speaking you are, however if you sustain loss, damage or injury as a result of your own actions and it was perfectly clear at the outset that these circumstances would lead to loss, damage or personal injury then your Insurers may take the view that you did not act with due diligence and therefore the consequence of your actions resulted in an inevitable loss, damage or injury.

Under these circumstances Insurers can refuse payment.

The principle is to act as if you are uninsured at all times and act in your own best interests. Then if something happens to you which is unavoidable your Insurers will be satisfied that you have acted in a diligent fashion.

Should a dispute arise between you and your insurer you should pursue the matter in writing with the company who sold you the policy in the first instance.

If you do not receive satisfaction from them you can write to the manager of the insurance company, and if that does not lead to satisfaction being given you can refer the matter to the Insurance Ombudsman Bureau at 31 Southampton Row, London WCIB 5HJ.

The Insurance Ombudsman is the independent watchdog for the Insurance Industry and will deal with complaints on policies issued to individuals. If you have an insurance policy issued to your company or corporation you should write to: The Association of British Insurers, Aldermary House, 10/15 Queen Street, London EC4N 5HJ.

The ABI will act in the same fashion as the ombudsman but for corporate insurance policies.

Travelling abroad

Special consideration should be given to your life and medical cover when travelling abroad.

Emergency services in the UK are amongst the best in the world and generally speaking the diver will not have to pay for any action or treatment given.

Additionally there are reciprocal agreements within the EEC and you should consult your travel agent before travelling to find out if these apply.

In some parts of the world a sick or injured diver will be expected to pay for treatment and possibly parts of the emergency services response.

You should make sure that you are fully protected against these contingencies. When you are buying a diving holiday from a travel agent or dive tour operator make sure that the insurance policy that is sold to you covers your sports diving contingencies.

We are aware of too many cases where divers are sold policies that do not cover the risk adequately or in some situations exclude the sports diving risk completely.

Try to use a specialist broker or intermediary and explain the type of cover you require, and check with your qualifying association or club to see if certain contingencies of your sports diving risk are covered under a block cover or premium that has been paid by your association.

Never be afraid to ask to see the full policy wording of these block covers as sometimes they exclude certain areas of your private diving activities.

During your sports diving training you will have learned the axiom 'Plan the Dive - Dive the Plan' - we in the insurance industry would add one further axiom: 'Plan the Dive - Dive Assured'.

This small craft capsized in a river near Sandwich, Kent. The owner had parked her over an outfall pipe and when the tide went out, over she went. It was a half hour job to right her and motor back to the boatyard.
Picture: Bob Archell

Diving Boat Charter

CORNWALL

BRUCE VICCORS
FLUSHING COVE
GILLAM, CORNWALL GR12 6HQ
0326 231244

NAME : RUM TUNA, PASS 8, DL, DKS, FD
EQUPT : ES, GPS\DECCA, VHF
SAFETY : EMG, AID

CHALICE DIVING
ARWENACK BARTON
GROVE PLACE, FALMOUTH,
CORNWALL TR11 4AU
0326 319124

NAME : CHALICE, PASS 12, DL, CREW, AIR TO 245BAR, DKS, FD
EQUPT : ES, RDR, GPS\DECCA, VHF
SAFETY : EMG, AID

DOUGIE WRIGHT
3 TRESKILLARD FIELDS, TRESKILLARD,
REDRUTH, CORNWALL 0209 716970

NAME : BALEINE, PASS 12, DL, DKS
EQUPT : ES, RDR, GPS\DECCA, VHF
SAFETY : EMG, AID, OXY

KEN & SANDY DUNSTAN
AUTUMN MOON
MYLOR YACHT HARBOUR
FALMOUTH
CORNWALL TR11 5UF
0326 374897
EMERGENCY: 0872 862080

NAME : AUTUMN MOON, PASS 12, DL, CREW, AIR TO 340BAR, DKS, FD
EQUPT : ES, RDR, GPS\DECCA, VHF
SAFETY : EMG, AID, OXY

McGREGOR CRUISES
RIVERVIEW
BEECH TERRACE, WEST LOOE
CORNWALL PL13 2AQ
0503 263584
EMERGENCY: 0374 148399

NAME : McGREGOR, PASS 12, DL, CREW, AIR TO 300BAR, DKS, FD
EQUPT : ES, RDR, GPS\DECCA, VHF
SAFETY : EMG, AID, OXY

MIKE TUFFREY
6 HILLSIDE ROAD
FALMOUTH, CORNWALL TR11 4HE
0326 313265

NAME : PATRICE II, PASS 12, DL, CREW, DKS, FD
EQUPT : ES, RDR, GPS\DECCA, VHF
SAFETY : EMG, AID, OXY

SEAQUEST
TIDAL HOUSE
COMMERCIAL ROAD, PENRYN
CORNWALL TR10 8AG
0326 375544
EMERGENCY: 0831 684009
FAX: 0326 375401

NAME : SEAQUEST, PASS 12, DL, CREW, DKS
EQUPT : ES, RDR, GPS\DECCA, VHF
SAFETY : EMG, AID, OXY

COUNTY ANTRIM

TONY CECIL
RATHIN DIVE
RATHIN ISLAND, BALLYCASTLE,
COUNTY ANTRIM BT54 6RT
0265 763915

DEVON

DOUGLAS POOLEY
12 STANDBURY AVENUE
CROWN HILL, PLYMOTH, DEVON PL6 5AT
0752 776059

NAME : C-CHEETAH, PASS 12, DKS, FD
EQUPT : ES, RDR, GPS\DECCA, VHF
SAFETY : EMG, AID

JOHN HOLMAN
254 AUSTIN CRESCENT
CROWN HILL, PLYMOUTH, DEVON PL6 5QT
0752 790605 EMERGENCY: 0850 672862

NAME : BEATRICE, PASS 12, DL, DKS, FD
EQUPT : ES, RDR, GPS\DECCA, VHF
SAFETY : EMG, AID, OXY

JOHN WALKER
BOLSHAYNE FARM
SOUTHLEIGH ROAD, COLYTON,
DEVON EX13 6RX
0297 552160

NAME : MISS PATTIE, PASS 12, DL, AIR TO 280BAR, DKS
EQUPT : ES, RDR, GPS\DECCA, VHF
SAFETY : EMG, AID, OXY

MAURICE WOODGER
11 BROAD STREET
ILFRACOMBE, DEVON EX34 9EE
0271 863849

NAME : OUR UNITY, PASS 12, CREW, DKS
EQUPT : ES, RDR, GPS\DECCA, VHF
SAFETY : EMG, AID

MIKE & PENNY ROWLEY
PO BOX 9
DARTMOUTH, DEVON TQ6 9TZ
0602 655033
EMERGENCY: 0860 571012

NAME : MAUREEN 0F DART, PASS 12, DL, CREW, AIR TO 50BAR, DKS, FD
EQUPT : ES, RDR, GPS\DECCA, VHF
SAFETY : EMG, AID, OXY

PETER PHILLIPS
CDF CHARTERS
23 QUARRY PARK ROAD, HEADTREE
EXETER, DEVON EX2 5PH
0392 431841
EMERGENCY: 0831 672993

NAME : CHALUTIER, PASS 12, DL, CREW, AIR TO 200BAR, DKS, FD
EQUPT : ES, RDR, GPS\DECCA, VHF
SAFETY : EMG, AID, OXY

RICHARD KINGS
20 WOODLAND TERRACE
GREEN BANK, PLYMOUTH, DEVON PL4 8NL
0752 663247 FAX: 0752 125536

NAME : CEE KING, PASS 10, DL, DKS, FD
EQUPT : ES, RDR, GPS\DECCA, VHF
SAFETY : EMG, AID

RICHARD LINFORD
WEMBURY DIVERS
121 CHURCH STREET, WEMBURY
DEVON PL9 0LB
0752 862488
EMERGENCY: 0860 463233

NAME : UK NATIONAL, PASS 12, DL, CREW, AIR TO 272BAR, DKS, FD
EQUPT : ES, RDR, GPS\DECCA, VHF
SAFETY : EMG, AID, OXY

ROD DAVIES
68 MEWSTONE AVENUE
WEMBURY
DEVON PL9 0HT
0752 862165

NAME	: STORM, PASS 10, CREW, DKS, FD
EQUPT	: ES, RDR, GPS\DECCA, VHF
SAFETY	: EMG, AID

DORSET

BRIAN CHARLES
15 OLD COASTGUARD COTTAGES
PORTLAND BILL
PORTLAND
DORSET DT5 2JT
0305 822846

NAME	: J.V.C., PASS 12, DL, CREW, DKS, FD
EQUPT	: ES, RDR, GPS\DECCA, VHF
SAFETY	: EMG, AID, OXY

CHRIS CAINES
22 KILLICKS HILL
PORTLAND
DORSET DT5 1JW
0305 821177 FAX: 0305 821177

NAME	: TIGER LILY, PASS 12, DL, CREW, DKS, FD
EQUPT	: ES, RDR, GPS\DECCA, VHF
SAFETY	: EMG, AID, OXY

CURRENT SPEED CHARTERS
SEA REST VIEWS
29 ST JOHN STREET, POOLE
DORSET DH15 7BW
0202 659721

NAME	: JOANNA, PASS 12, DL, CREW, DKS, FD
EQUPT	: ES, RDR, GPS\DECCA, VHF
SAFETY	: EMG, AID, OXY

D SAYWELL
12 WATERFORD CLOSE
PARK STONE, POOLE, DORSET BH14 8FA
0202 749122

NAME	: JAMES ALEXANDER, PASS 12, DL, DKS, FD
EQUPT	: ES, RDR, GPS\DECCA, VHF
SAFETY	: EMG, AID, OXY

DAVE FAIRCLOUGH
58 MUSCLIFFE ROAD
WINTON, BOURNEMOUTH
DORSET BH9 INW
0202 518673 EMERGENCY: 0850 596695

NAME	: POOLE ANGLER, PASS 12, DL, CREW
EQUPT	: ES, RDR, GPS\DECCA, VHF
SAFETY	: EMG, AID, OXY

ERIC "BUDGIE" BURGESS
BREAKWATER DIVING CENTRE
CASTLETOWN, PORTLAND
DORSET DT5 1BD
0305 860269

NAME	**: BREAKWATER DIVER, PASS 12, DL, CREW, AIR TO 300BAR**
EQUPT	**: ES, GPS\DECCA, VHF**
SAFETY	**: EMG, AID, OXY**

GORDON McGRAIL
GRAILSDON
21 RECTORY ROAD, OAKDALE
POOLE, DORSET BH15 3BH
0202 686454

NAME	: SEA RANGER, PASS 12, DL, DKS, FD
EQUPT	: ES, RDR, GPS\DECCA, VHF
SAFETY	: EMG, AID, OXY

GRAHAME KNOTT
38 GROVE AVENUE
WEYMOUTH, DORSET DT4 7RJ
0305 771371 EMERGENCY: 0831 467621

NAME	: WEY CHIEFTAIN, PASS 12, DL, CREW, DKS, FD
EQUPT	: ES, RDR, GPS\DECCA, VHF
SAFETY	: EMG, AID, OXY

IAN BALL
33 DERBY STREE
WEYMOUTH, DORSET DT4 7HX
0305 760009

NAME	: R PHYLLIS, PASS 12, DL, CREW, DKS, FD
EQUPT	: ES, RDR, GPS\DECCA, VHF
SAFETY	: EMG, AID

JAN CORNWELL
ASANTI
WEST CLIFF, WEST BAY, DORSET DT6 4HR
0308 23706 EMERGENCY: 0308 24380

NAME	: LINDY LOU, PASS 12, DL, CREW, DKS
EQUPT	: ES, RDR, GPS\DECCA, VHF
SAFETY	: EMG, AID, OXY

JIM SCOTT
8 SEABANK CLOSE
UPTON, POOLE
DORSET DH16 5LW
0202 621868

NAME : DORAYDO, PASS 10, DL, CREW, DKS, FD
EQUPT : ES, RDR, GPS\DECCA, VHF
SAFETY : EMG, AID, OXY

JON AYLING
J & B DIVING
3 LOWER ST EDMONDS STREET
WEYMOUTH, DORSET DT4 8AJ
0305 789492 FAX: 0305 760065

NAME : WHITE HORSE, PASS 12, DL, CREW, AIR TO 272BAR, DKS, FD
EQUPT : ES, RDR, GPS\DECCA, VHF
SAFETY : EMG, AID, OXY

MIKE O'SHEA
30 GROVE AVENUE
LODMOOR, WEYMOUTH
DORSET DT4 7RA
0305 781732 EMERGENCY: 0860 433137

NAME : HURRICANE, PASS 12, DL, CREW, DKS, FD
EQUPT : ES, RDR, GPS\DECCA, VHF
SAFETY : EMG, AID, OXY

PAT CARLIN
23 SOUTHDOWN ROAD
RODWELL, WEYMOUTH
DORSET DT4 9LJ
0305 787155 EMERGENCY: 0831 559176
FAX: 0305 787155

NAME : CHANNEL CHIEFTAIN, PASS 12, DL, CREW, DKS
EQUPT : ES, RDR, GPS\DECCA, VHF
SAFETY : EMG, AID, OXY

PAUL PIKE
33 ST LEONARDS ROAD
WEYMOUTH
DORSET DT4 8LD
0373 467107 EMERGENCY: 0836 619148
FAX: 0373 467107

NAME : DIVE TIME, PASS 12, DL, CREW, DKS, FD
EQUPT : ES, RDR, GPS\DECCA, VHF
SAFETY : EMG, AID, OXY

RICHARD TITCHENER
21 ELLIS ROAD
BOVINGTON CAMP
WAREHAM, DORSET BH20 6JW
0929 405178

NAME : SIDEWINDER, PASS 12, DL, CREW, DKS
EQUPT : ES, RDR, GPS\DECCA, VHF
SAFETY : EMG, AID, OXY

ROGER WAGSTAFF
SEACOURT HOTEL
6 TAUNTON ROAD
SWANAGE
DORSET BH19 2BZ
0929 424731

NAME : KYARRA II, PASS 12, DL, AIR TO 232BAR
EQUPT : ES, RDR, GPS\DECCA, VHF
SAFETY : EMG, AID, OXY

BRIAN WATERS
29 KINGS QUAY STREET
HARWICH, ESSEX CO12 3ES
0255 502354

NAME : BECKFORD, PASS 12, DL, CREW, AIR TO 230BAR, DKS, FD
EQUPT : ES, RDR, GPS\DECCA, VHF
SAFETY : EMG, AID

ESSEX

JOHN NEGUS
72 BURNHAM ROAD
HULL BRIDGE, ESSEX SS5 6PQ
0702 231664

NAME : SWEET SURRENDER, PASS 5, DL, AIR TO 272BAR
EQUPT : ES, RDR, GPS\DECCA, VHF
SAFETY : EMG, AID, OXY

HAMPSHIRE

BUTCH HUNDSON
19 CARRINGTON LANE
MILFORD ON SEA, LYMINGTON
HANTS S041 0RA
0590 644225

NAME : BOY SCOUT, PASS 12, DL, CREW, DKS, FD
EQUPT : ES, RDR, GPS\DECCA, VHF
SAFETY : EMG, AID

DAVID FAITHFULL
302 QUEENS ROAD
COPNOR, PORTSMOUTH, HANTS PO2 7NQ
0705 672886

NAME : WOODPECKER, PASS 12, DL, CREW, DKS
EQUPT : ES, RDR, GPS\DECCA, VHF
SAFETY : EMG, AID

STEVE COLLETT
96 TICHBORNE WAY
ROWNER, GOSPORT, HANTS PO13 0BN
0329 220461 EMERGENCY: 0850 215676

NAME : HERO, PASS 10, DL, DKS, FD
EQUPT : ES, RDR, GPS\DECCA, VHF
SAFETY : EMG, AID, OXY

HUMBERSIDE

CLEAN AIR
11 STATION COURT
STATION ROAD, BRIDLINGTON
YORKSHIRE YO16 4LZ
0262 400325 EMERGENCY: 0850 912315

NAME : VOLANTE, PASS 12, CREW, DKS, FD
EQUPT : ES, RDR, GPS\DECCA, VHF
SAFETY : EMG, AID, OXY

MIDDLESEX

JOHN ARMSTRONG
THANECRAFT LTD
CREST HOUSE, 102-104 CHURCH ROAD
TEDDINGTON, MIDDLESEX TW11 8PY
081 9771105

NORTHUMBERLAND

STAN HALL
FARNE DIVING SERVICES
ST EBBAS HOUSE, BEADWELL
NORTHUMBERLAND NE67 5AP
0665 720615

NAME : ST EBBASS III, PASS 12, DL, AIR TO 272BAR
EQUPT : ES, RDR, GPS\DECCA, VHF
SAFETY : EMG, AID

SURREY

DAVE COLES (Charters in Dorset)
2 ORCHARD COURT
WICKHAM ROAD, SHIRLEY
CROYDON, SURREY CR0 8EA
0836 757218 EMERGENCY: 0831 246347

NAME : DAWN LOUISE, PASS 12, DL, CREW, AIR TO 232BAR, DKS, FD
EQUPT : ES, RDR, GPS\DECCA, VHF
SAFETY : EMG, AID, OXY

SUSSEX

ALAN YOUNG
AQUARIUS CHARTERS
3 DOWER CLOSE, OVINGDEAN
BRIGHTON, SUSSEX BN2 7BW
0273 300388

NAME : AQUARIUS, PASS 12, DL, DKS
EQUPT : ES, RDR, GPS\DECCA, VHF
SAFETY : EMG, AID

ALEX COSTA
VALERIE BOAT CHARTER
LITTLEHAMPTON MARINA, LITTLEHAMPTON
SUSSEX BN17 5DS
081 8574551

NAME : VALERIA, PASS 8, DL, DKS
EQUPT : ES, RDR, VHF
SAFETY : EMG, AID

COLIN JOHNSTON
CHANNEL DIVING
66 LANGDALE GARDENS, HOVE
SUSSEX BN3 4HH
0273 770979 EMERGENCY: 0831 663274

NAME : MANLY, PASS 12, DL, CREW, AIR TO 232BAR, DKS, FD
EQUPT : ES, RDR, GPS\DECCA, VHF
SAFETY : EMG, AID, OXY

DEREK DALMON
MARTYNS
HENFIELD ROAD, SMALL DOLE
SUSSEX BN5 9XJ
0903 814461 EMERGENCY: 0850 724159

NAME : RIPTIDE, PASS 12, DL, CREW, DKS
EQUPT : ES, RDR, GPS\DECCA, VHF
SAFETY : EMG, AID

IVAN WARREN
PHELTON HOUSE
CROSS BUSH, ARUNDEL
SUSSEX BN18 9PQ
0903 884892 EMERGENCY: 0850 503812

NAME : MICHELLE MARY, PASS 12, DL, AIR, DKS, FD
EQUPT : ES, RDR, GPS\DECCA, VHF
SAFETY : EMG, AID

TIM BENNETTO
INDIGO CHARTERS
35 CISSBURY AVENUE
PEACEHAVEN
SUSSEX BN10 8TN
0273 586445

NAME : CIRRUS, PASS 12, DL, CREW, DKS
EQUPT : ES, RDR, GPS\DECCA, VHF
SAFETY : EMG, AID, OXY

CHANNEL ISLANDS

ANDREW LEAMAN
LE GRAND FORT FARM
SARK, CHANNEL ISLANDS 0481 83207
EMERGENCY: 0481 832396
FAX: 0481 832565

NAME : LUCY, PASS 12, DL, CREW
EQUPT : ES, RDR, GPS\DECCA, VHF
SAFETY : EMG, AID, OXY

GUERNSEY SCHOOL OF DIVING
LES QUARTES VENTS
RUE DES MONTS, DELANCEY
ST SAMPSONS, GUERNSEY GU2 4HT
0481 47664-49524

NAME : HARVEST QUEEN, PASS 12, DL, CREW, AIR, DKS, FD
EQUPT : ES, RDR, GPS\DECCA, VHF
SAFETY : EMG, AID, OXY

SCILLIE ISLES

TIM ALLSOP
HIGHERTOWN
ST MARTINS, ISLE OF SCILLIE TR5 OQL
0720 22848

NAME : MORVOREN, PASS 12, DL, AIR, DKS, FD
EQUPT : ES, RDR, GPS\DECCA, VHF
SAFETY : EMG, AID, OXY

SCOTLAND

BORDERS

ALASTAIRE CROWE
12 BRIERY DEAN
ST ABBS, BERWICKSHIRE TD14 5PQ
08907 71412

NAME : AQUA VISTA, PASS 16, DL, CREW, DKS
EQUPT : ES, RDR, GPS\DECCA, VHF
SAFETY : EMG, AID

HIGHLANDS

AMELIA DALTON (Charters in Highlands)
POINTDRAKE LTD
MANOR FSRM, CHAIGLEY
CLITHEROE, LANCS BB7 3LS
0254 826591
EMERGENCY: 0831 121156
FAX: 061 8320467

NAME : MONACO, PASS 12, DL, CREW, AIR TO 207BAR, DKS, FD
EQUPT : ES, RDR, GPS\DECCA, VHF
SAFETY : EMG, AID

ANDY HOLBROW
ATLANTIC DIVING SERVICES
PORT COTTAGE, TANERA MHOR
ACHILTIBUIE
ULLAPOOL, HIGHLANDS IV26 2YN
0854 82261 FAX: 0854 82401

NAME : HERON, PASS 12, DL, CREW, AIR TO 240BAR, DKS, FD
EQUPT : ES, RDR, GPS\DECCA, VHF
SAFETY : EMG, AID, OXY

GEORGE WILSON
3 ADMORE
WATERNISH, ISLE OF SKYE
HIGHLANDS IV55 8GW
047 083324

NAME : LINDEN, PASS 6, DL, CREW, AIR TO 310BAR, DKS, FD
EQUPT : ES, VHF
SAFETY : EMG, AID

JOHN MACAULAY
12 PICT AVENUE
INVERNESS, HIGHLANDS IV3 6LX
0463 225398

NAME : AN IASGAIR, PASS 12, DL, CREW, AIR TO 272BAR, DKS, FD
EQUPT : ES, RDR, GPS\DECCA, VHF
SAFETY : EMG, AID, OXY

MARY ROBINSON
DOUNE MARINE
DOUNE, KNOYDART
MALLIAG, HIGHLANDS PH41 4PV
0687 2667 FAX: 0687 2667

NAME : MARY DOUNE, PASS 12, DL, CREW, AIR TO 272BAR, DKS, FD
EQUPT : ES, RDR, GPS\DECCA, VHF
SAFETY : EMG, AID

LOTHIAN

LYNNE GREER
7 GLENBURN GARDENS
WHITBURN
WEST LOTHIAN EH47 8NL
0501 7742514 FAX: 031 4454686

NAME : JEAN DE LA LUNE, PASS 12, DL, CREW, AIR TO 300BAR, DKS, FD
EQUPT : ES, RDR, GPS\DECCA, VHF
SAFETY : EMG, AID, OXY

ORKNEY ISLANDS

ANDY CUTHBERTSON
FLAT 2
34 VICTORIA STREET, STROMNESS, ORKNEY
ISLANDS KW16 3AD
0856 850879 FAX: 0856 850879

NAME : JENNIFER, PASS 12, DL, AIR TO 232BAR, DKS, FD
EQUPT : ES, RDR, VHF
SAFETY : EMG, AID, OXY

ANTONY DUNCAN
SCAPA FLOW DIVING CENTRE
BURRAY, ORKNEY ISLANDS KW17 2SS
0856 73225-253-266

NAME : SHALDER, PASS 12, DL, AIR TO 232BAR, DKS, FD
EQUPT : ES, RDR, VHF
SAFETY : EMG, AID, OXY

DAVID & INGRID COSBY
NORTH ISLE DIVING
QUARRYBRAE, HILLSIDE ROAD
STROMNESS, ORKNEY ISLANDS KW16 3HR
0856 850832 FAX: 0856 850832

NAME : RADIANT QUEEN, PASS 12, DL,
AIR TO 242BAR, DKS, FD
EQUPT : ES, RDR, VHF
SAFETY : EMG, AID, OXY

DAVIE SCOTT
24 NICHOLSON STREET
KIRKWALL, ORKNEY ISLANDS KW15 1BD
0856 875047

NAME : CROMBIE, PASS 12, DL, AIR TO 340BAR, DKS, FD
EQUPT : ES, RDR, GPS\DECCA, VHF
SAFETY : EMG, AID

ERLAND JEFFREY
8 DUNDAS STREET
STROMNESS, ORKNEY ISLANDS KW16 3BZ
0856 850489

NAME : SHARON ROSE, PASS 12, CREW,
AIR TO 240BAR, DKS
EQUPT : ES, RDR, VHF
SAFETY : EMG, AID, OXY

FLOW CHARTERS
SEA PEACE COTTAGE
KIRKWALL, ORKNEY ISLANDS KW16 1AQ
0856 877113

NAME : MERRY ROVER, PASS 12, DL, CREW,
AIR TO 242BAR, DKS
EQUPT : ES, RDR, GPS\DECCA, VHF
SAFETY : EMG, AID, OXY

GEORGE LITTS
SCAPA FLOW DIVING & LEISURE
BRAEHEAD COTTAGE
STROMNESS, ORKNEY ISLANDS 0856
850434 FAX: 0856 851350

NAME : MARA, PASS 12, DL, CREW, AIR TO 270BAR
EQUPT : ES, RDR, GPS\DECCA, VHF
SAFETY : EMG, AID, OXY

JOHN THORNTON
POLRUDDEN HOUSE
KIRKWALL, ORKNEY ISLANDS KW15 1RK
0856 874761 FAX: 0856 874761

NAME : SCAPA COURIER, PASS 12, DL, CREW,
AIR TO 300BAR, DKS, FD
EQUPT : ES, RDR, GPS\DECCA, VHF
SAFETY : EMG, AID, OXY

MURRAY & RUTH DRYLEY
THE FLOWDIVE
TURNPIKE
TOAB
ORKNEY ISLANDS KW17 2QG
0856 86249

NAME : EVENING STAR, PASS 12, DL,
AIR TO 232BAR, DKS, FD
EQUPT : ES, RDR, GPS\DECCA, VHF
SAFETY : EMG, AID, OXY

STEPHEN ROBERTS
HOUTON DIVING
HEATHERLEA, HOUTON
ORPHIR
ORKNEY ISLANDS KW17 2RE
0856 81251 FAX: 0856 81251

NAME : DEMDYKE, PASS 6, DL, DKS, FD
EQUPT : ES, RDR, GPS\DECCA, VHF
SAFETY : EMG, AID, OXY

STEVE MOWAT
BARKLAND
CAIRSTON ROAD
STROMNESS
ORKNEY ISLANDS KW16 3JT
0856 850624 FAX: 0856 850624

NAME : KRITON, PASS 12, CREW,
AIR TO 232BAR, DKS, FD
EQUPT : ES, RDR, GPS\DECCA, VHF
SAFETY : EMG, AID, OXY

SUNRISE CHARTERS
KRUANA
CAIRSTON ROAD
STROMNESS
ORKNEY ISLANDS KW16 3JU
0856 851242
EMERGENCY: 0836 343334

NAME : SUNRISE, PASS 12, DL, CREW,
AIR TO 230BAR, DKS, FD
EQUPT : ES, RDR, GPS\DECCA, VHF
SAFETY : EMG, AID, OXY

TERRY TODD
LINDISFARNE
BUAN JUNCTION, STROMNESS, ORKNEY
ISLANDS KW16 3LL
0856 850828 EMERGENCY: 0831 637606

NAME : GIRMINA, PASS 12, DL, AIR TO 306BAR, DKS, FD
EQUPT : ES, RDR, GPS\DECCA, VHF
SAFETY : EMG, AID, OXY

STRATHCLYDE

ALAN CAMPBELL
NERVOUS WRECK
GANVAN SANDS, OBAN
STRATHCLYDE PA34 5NR
0631 66000-66126 FAX: 0631 66000

NAME : NERVOUS WRECK, PASS 5, DL, DKS, FD
EQUPT : ES, VHF
SAFETY : EMG, AID, OXY

AQUATRON CHARTERS
30 STANLEY STREET
GLASGOW G41 1JB
041 4295902 FAX: 041 4295364

NAME : AQUATRON, PASS 12, DL, CREW, AIR TO 340BAR, DKS, FD
EQUPT : ES, GPS\DECCA, VHF
SAFETY : EMG, AID, OXY

BOB JONES
KIRK BRAE
LOCHALINE, MORVERN
OBAN, STRATHCLYDE PA34 5XW
0967 421654

NAME : GAELIC ROSE, PASS 12, DL, CREW, AIR TO 204BAR, DKS, FD
EQUPT : ES, RDR, GPS\DECCA, VHF
SAFETY : EMG, AID

CHARLIE LAVERTY
BALISCATE HOUSE
TOBERMORY, ISLE OF MULL PA75 6QA
0688 2048

NAME : AMIDAS, PASS 12, DL, CREW, DKS, FD
EQUPT : ES, GPS\DECCA, VHF
SAFETY : EMG, AID

DAVID & JANE AINSLEY
DENAVERTY
CLACHAN SEL, BY OBAN
STRATHCLYDE PA34 4TC
08523 203 EMERGENCY: 0836 555901

NAME : PORPOISE, PASS 12, DL, DKS, FD
EQUPT : ES, RDR, GPS\DECCA, VHF
SAFETY : EMG, AID, OXY

DAVID SHELLOCK
TRALEE BAY HOLIDAY PARK
TRALEE BAY, BENDERNOCH
NR OBAN, STRATHCLYDE PA37 1QR
063172 255-217 FAX: 063172 545

NAME : TRALEE DIVER, PASS 6, DL, DKS, FD
EQUPT : ES, VHF
SAFETY : EMG, AID

ERIC & JANE REID
STRATHCLYDE BOAT CRUISES
C\O PIER MASTER, NORTH PIER
OBAN, STRATHCLYDE PA34 5NZ
0831 628200

NAME : JANE R, PASS 12, AIR TO 240BAR, DKS, FD
EQUPT : ES, RDR, GPS\DECCA, VHF
SAFETY : EMG, AID

JIM LAVERTY
10 CREGAN PARK
TOBERMONY, ISLE OF MULL
STRATHCLYDE PA75 6PT
0688 2083

NAME : SHEARWATER, PASS 12, DL, DKS, FD
EQUPT : ES, VHF
SAFETY : EMG, AID

MIKE STEWART
CRINAN BOATS
CRINAN, STRATHCLYDE PA31 8SP
054683 232-282 FAX: 054683 231

NAME : NORTH WIND, PASS 6, DL, CREW, DKS, FD
EQUPT : ES, VHF
SAFETY : EMG, AID

TONY RATCLIFFE
THORNLIEBANK
STRATHCLYDE TERRACE, TOBERMORY
ISLE OF MULL, STRATHCLYDE
0688 2303-2515
EMERGENCY: 0831 511940

NAME : MARIE LOUISE, PASS 12, DL, DKS, FD
EQUPT : ES, RDR, GPS\DECCA, VHF
SAFETY : EMG, AID, OXY

TONY WASS
22 TEMPLAND ROAD
DALRY, STRATHCLYDE KA24 5EV
0294 833724

NAME : RACHAEL CLAIRE, PASS 12, CREW, DKS, FD
EQUPT : ES, RDR, GPS\DECCA, VHF
SAFETY : EMG, AID, OXY

WESTERN ISLES

CHARLES ENGEBRETSEN
HEBRIDEAN HOLIDAYS LTD
SANDWICK, SANDWICK ROAD
STORNAWAY, ISLE OF LEWIS PA86 0BQ
0851 702304 FAX: 0851 704010

NAME : RIBS, PASS 5, DL, CREW, DKS, FD
EQUPT : ES, VHF
SAFETY : EMG, AID, OXY

Boats may also be chartered through some dive retailers. ***See page 93.***

Port and Harbour Authorities

AVON

BRISTOL CITY COUNCIL
BRUNEL LOCK CUMBERLAND BASIN
AVON, BS1 6XL
0272 273633

THE BRISTOL PORT COMPANY
ST. ANDREWS RD, AVONMOUTH, BRISTOL
AVON, BS11 9DQ
0272 820000

CAMBRIDGESHIRE

FENLAND DISTRICT COUNCIL
PORT OF WISBECH NENE PARADE
CAMBRIDGESHIRE, PE13 3BY
0945 582125

CLEVELAND

TEES AND HARTLEPOOL PORT AUTHORITY LTD
QUEENS SQUARE, CLEVELAND, TS2 1AH
0642 241121

COUNTY DURHAM

SEAHAM HARBOUR DOCK CO
SEAHAM HOUSE
NORTH TERRACE, SEAHAM HARBOUR
CO DURHAM, SR7 7EU
091 581 3877

CORNWALL

CARRICK DISTRICT COUNCIL
HARBOUR MASTERS OFFICE
EXCHEQUER QUAY
CORNWALL, TR10 8LS
0326 373352

CARRICK DISTRICT COUNCIL
HARBOUR OFFICE
TOWN QUAY, CORNWALL, TR1 2HJ
0872 72130

FALMOUTH HARBOUR COMMISSIONERS
44 ARWENACK ST
CORNWALL, TR11 3JH
0326 312285

FOWEY HARBOUR COMMISSIONERS
SLIPWAY
POLRUAN, FOWEY, CORNWALL, PL23 1PA
0726 870348

HARBOUR COMMISSIONERS
HARBOUR OFFICE
CORNWALL, PL13 1DX
0503 262839

MEVAGISSEY HARBOUR TRUSTEES
HARBOUR OFFICE
THE QUAY, MEVAGISSEY, ST. AUSTELL
CORNWALL, PL26 6QU
0726 843305

NEWLYN PIER & HARBOUR COMMISSIONERS
HARBOUR OFFICES
NORTH PIER
NEWLYN, PENZANCE
CORNWALL, TR18 5JB
0736 62523

NEWQUAY HARBOURMASTER
SOUTH QUAY
THE HARBOUR
CORNWALL, TR7 1HR
0637 872809

PADSTOW HARBOUR COMMISSIONERS
WEST QUAY, CORNWALL, PL28 8AQ
0841 532239

PENZANCE HARBOUR
WHARF RD, CORNWALL, TR18 4AB
0736 66113

CUMBRIA

PORT OF WORKINGTON
PRINCE OF WALES DOCK
CUMBRIA, CA14 1BN
0900 602301

WHITEHAVEN HARBOUR COMMISSIONERS
PEARS HOUSE
1 DUKE ST, CUMBRIA, CA28 7HW
0946 692435

DEVON

BRIXHAM HARBOUR
NEW FISH QUAY, DEVON, TQ5 8AJ
0803 853321

CATTEWATER HARBOUR COMMISSIONERS
2 THE BARBICAN, DEVON, PL1 2LR
0752 665934

PAIGNTON HARBOUR
SOUTH QUAY
THE HARBOUR, DEVON, TQ4 6DT
0803 557812

SALCOMBE HARBOUR
HARBOUR OFFICE
WHITESTRAND FORE ST
DEVON, TQ8 8BU
0548 843791

SUTTON HARBOUR CO
HARBOUR OFFICE
SUTTON HARBOUR
DEVON, PL4 0ES
0752 664186

TEIGNMOUTH HARBOUR MASTER
HARBOUR MASTERS OFFICE
NEWQUAY ST, DEVON, TQ14 8DA
0626 773165

TORQUAY HARBOUR
BEACON QUAY
DEVON, TQ1 2BG
0803 292429

DORSET

HARBOUR MASTER
LYME REGIS HARBOUR THE COBB
DORSET, DT7 3JJ
0297 442137

POOLE HARBOUR COMMISSIONERS
HARBOUR OFFICE
THE QUAY, DORSET
BH15 1HG
0202 685261

SWANAGE PIER
PIER APPROACH, DORSET, BH19 2AW
0929 427058

WEYMOUTH & PORTLAND
BOROUGH COUNCIL
HARBOUR MASTERS OFFICE
20 CUSTOM HOUSE, QUAY
DORSET, DT4 8BE
0305 206421

EAST SUSSEX

SHOREHAM PORT AUTHORITY
ALBION ST, EAST SUSSEX, BN42 4ED
0273 592613

ESSEX

BRIGHTLINGSEA HARBOUR COMMISIONERS
4 COPPERAS RD
BRIGHTLINGSEA
COLCHESTER
ESSEX, CO7 0AP
0206 302200

CROUCH HARBOUR AUTHORITY
THE QUAY, ESSEX, CM0 8AS
0621 783602

HARWICH HAVEN AUTHORITY
HARBOUR HOUSE
THE QUAY, ESSEX, CO12 3HH
0255 243030

HAMPSHIRE

LANGSTONE HARBOUR OFFICE
FERRY RD
HAMPSHIRE, PO11 0DG
0705 463419

LYMINGTON HARBOUR COMMISSIONERS
HARBOURMASTERS OFFICE
BATH RD, HAMPSHIRE, SO41 9SE
0590 672014

ISLE OF WIGHT

COWES HARBOUR COMMISSIONERS
HARBOUR OFFICE
TOWN QUAY, ISLE OF WIGHT, PO31 7AS
0983 293952

YARMOUTH HARBOUR COMMISSIONERS
HARBOUR MASTERS OFFICE
THE QUAY, ISLE OF WIGHT, PO41 0NT
0983 760321

KENT

CANTERBURY CITY COUNCIL
WHITSTABLE HARBOUR
HARBOUR ST, KENT, CT5 1AB
0227 274086

DOVER HARBOUR BOARD
HARBOUR HOUSE
MARINE PARADE
KENT, CT17 9BU
0304 240400

MARGATE PIER & HARBOUR CO
THE PIER
KENT, CT9 1HA
0843 221960

PORT OF BALTIMORE
34 WILLOW PARK
OTFORD, SEVENOAKS
KENT, TN14 5NE
0959 525055

RAMSGATE HARBOUR AUTHORITY
MILITARY RD, KENT, CT11 9LQ
0843 592277

MERSEYSIDE

MERSEY DOCKS & HARBOUR CO
PORT OF LIVERPOOL BUILDING
PIER HEAD
MERSEYSIDE, L3 1BZ
051 200 2020

NORFOLK

CARROW BRIDGE
CARROW RD
NORFOLK, NR1 2BT
0603 625091

GREAT YARMOUTH PORT AUTHORITY
20/21 SOUTH QUAY
NORFOLK, NR30 2RG
0493 855151

WELLS HARBOUR COMMISSIONERS
HARBOUR OFFICE
OLD LIFEBOAT HOUSE
WEST QUAY
NORFOLK, NR23 1AT
0328 711646

NORTH HUMBERSIDE

HARBOUR COMMISSIONERS
HARBOUR OFFS NORTH PIER
NORTH HUMBERSIDE, YO15 2NR
0262 670148

NORTH YORKSHIRE

SCARBOROUGH BOROUGH COUNCIL
HARBOUR OFFICE
PIER RD, NORTH YORKSHIRE, YO21 3PU
0947 602354

NORTHUMBERLAND

BERWICK HARBOUR COMMISSIONERS
27 MAIN ST
TWEEDMOUTH
BERWICK UPON TWEED
NORTHUMBERLAND, TD15 2AA
0289 307404

WARKWORTH HARBOUR COMMISSIONERS
QUAYSIDE
AMBLE, MORPETH
NORTHUMBERLAND, NE65 0AP
0665 710306

SOMERSET

WEST SOMERSET DISTRICT COUNCIL
HARBOURMASTERS OFFICE
ESPLANADE
SOMERSET, TA23 0AJ
0984 631264

SUFFOLK

HARBOUR MASTER
SOUTHWOLD HARBOUR OFFICE
BLACKSHORE, SOUTHWOLD
SUFFOLK, IP18 6TA
0502 724712

IPSWICH PORT AUTHORITY
OLD CUSTOM HOUSE COMMON QUAY
KEY ST, SUFFOLK, IP4 1BY
0473 231010

TYNE AND WEAR

PORT OF SUNDERLAND AUTHORITY
BARRACK ST, TYNE AND WEAR, SR1 2BU
091 514 0411

PORT OF TYNE AUTHORITY
BEWICK ST
NEWCASTLE, NEWCASTLE UPON TYNE
TYNE AND WEAR, NE1 5EF
091 232 5541

WEST SUSSEX

CHICHESTER HARBOUR CONSERVANCY
HARBOUR MASTERS OFFICE
THE STREET, ITCHENOR, CHICHESTER
WEST SUSSEX, PO20 7AW
0243 512301

HARBOUR MASTER LITTLEHAMPTON
HARBOUR BOARD
PAINES WHARF, PIER RD
WEST SUSSEX, BN17 5LR
0903 721215

IRELAND

COUNTY ANTRIM

BELFAST HARBOUR COMMISSIONERS
CORPORATION SQUARE
CO ANTRIM, BT1 3AL
0232 234422

HARBOURMASTER'S OFFICE
WEST PIER THE HARBOUR
CO ANTRIM, BT38 7BQ
096 03 51292

LARNE HARBOUR LTD
9 OLDERFLEET RD
CO ANTRIM, BT40 1AS
0574 279221

PORTRUSH HARBOUR CO
HARBOUR RD, CO ANTRIM, BT56 8DF
0265 822307

COUNTY DOWN

CARLINGFORD LOUGH COMMISSION
42 GREENCASTLE ST
KILKEEL, NEWRY, CO DOWN, BT34 4BH
069 37 64606

DONAGHADEE HARBOUR OFFICE
HARBOUR HOUSE
THE PARADE, CO DOWN, BT21 0HE
0247 882377

COUNTY LONDONDERRY

HARBOUR COMMISSIONERS
THE HARBOUR, CO LONDONDERRY, BT52 1BJ
0265 42012

WALES

DYFED

FISHGUARD PORT HEALTH OFFICE
FISHGUARD HARBOUR
FISHGUARD, GOODWICK, DYFED, SA64 0BU
0348 873412

LLANELLI BOROUGH COUNCIL
THE HARBOUR, DYFED, SA16 0ER
0554 834315

SAUNDERSFOOT HARBOUR
COMMISSIONERS
THE HARBOUR, DYFED, SA69 9HE
0834 812094

THE HARBOURMASTER
TOWN QUAY
DYFED, SY23 1BJ
0970 611433

GWENT

HARBOUR COMMISSIONERS
DOCK ST LOWER
GWENT, NP9 1EG
0633 265702

GWYNEDD

CAERNARVON HARBOUR TRUST
HARBOUR OFFICE
SLATE QUAY
GWYNEDD, LL55 2PB
0286 672118

CYNGOR DOSBARTH DWYFOR
HARBOUR MASTERS OFFICE
GWYNEDD, LL49 9LU
0766 512927

CYNGOR DOSBARTH DWYFOR
HARBOUR MASTERS OFFICE
GWYNEDD, LL53 5AY
0758 614728

HARBOUR MASTER
THE WHARF
SEA VIEW TERRACE
GWYNEDD, LL35 0EF
0654 767626

YNYS MON BOROUGH COUNCIL
FISH DOCK
TURKEY SHORE RD
GWYNEDD, LL65 2DE
0407 760139

GLAMORGAN

PORTHCAWL HARBOUR
EASTERN PROMENADE
MID GLAMORGAN, CF36 3BN
0656 782756

SCOTLAND

BORDERS

EYEMOUTH HARBOUR TRUST
THE HARBOUR MASTERS OFFICE
1 MARINE PARADE
BERWICKSHIRE, TD14 5HR
089 07 50223

CENTRAL

FORTH PORTS PLC
DOCK OFFICE
STIRLINGSHIRE, FK3 8UE
0324 482591

FIFE

ANSTRUTHER HARBOUR
SHORE ST
FIFE, KY10 3AQ
0333 310836

HARBOURS
HARBOUR OFFICE
KINCARDINESHIRE, AB3 2GN
0569 62741

GRAMPIAN

ABERDEEN HARBOUR BOARD
16 REGENT QUAY
ABERDEENSHIRE, AB9 1SS
0224 592571

BUCKIE HARBOUR AUTHORITY
28B COMMERCIAL RD
BANFFSHIRE, AB56 1UN
0542 31700

BURGHEAD HARBOUR MASTER
THE HARBOUR
GRANARY ST
BURGHEAD, ELGIN
MORAYSHIRE, IV30 2UA
0343 835337

FRASERBURGH HARBOUR COMMISSIONERS
HARBOUR OFFICE
SHORE ST
ABERDEENSHIRE, AB43 5BR
0346 25858

LOSSIEMOUTH HARBOUR OFFICE
HARBOUR MASTER
PITGAVENY ST
MORAYSHIRE, IV31 6NT
0343 813066

MACDUFF HARBOUR
32 SHORE ST
ABERDEENSHIRE, AB44 1TX
0261 32236

MORAY DISTRICT COUNCIL
FISH MARKET
THE HARBOUR, BANFFSHIRE, AB56 1UN
0542 34141

PETERHEAD BAY AUTHORITY
BATH HOUSE
BATH ST, ABERDEENSHIRE, AB42 6DX
0779 74020

HIGHLANDS

CROMARTY FIRTH PORT AUTHORITY
PORT OFFICE
SHORE RD, ROSS-SHIRE, IV18 0HD
0349 852308

INVERNESS HARBOUR TRUSTEES
HARBOUR OFFICE
LONGMAN DRIVE, INVERNESS-SHIRE, IV1 1SU
0463 715715

MALLAIG HARBOUR AUTHORITY
HARBOUR BUILDINGS
THE PIER, INVERNESS-SHIRE, PH41 4PX
0687 2154

PORT OFFICER
ULLAPOOL HARBOUR, ROSS-SHIRE, IV26 2UE
0854 612724

SCRABSTER HARBOUR TRUST
SCRABSTER HARBOUR
CAITHNESS, KW14 7UJ
0847 62779

ULLAPOOL HARBOUR OFFICE
PIER, ROSS-SHIRE, IV26 2UH
0854 612091

WICK HARBOUR TRUST
HARBOUR TERRACE
CAITHNESS, KW1 5HB
0955 2030

LOTHIAN

EAST LOTHIAN DISTRICT COUNCIL
HARBOUR MASTER HARBOUR TERRACE
EAST LOTHIAN, EH39 4JW
0620 3333

FORTH PORTS AUTHORITY
1 PRINCE OF WALES DOCK
LEITH DOCKS
EDINBURGH
MID LOTHIAN, EH6 7DX
031 554 4343

ORKNEY ISLANDS

DEPT OF HARBOURS
HARBOUR AUTHORITIES BUILDINGS
SCAPA ST.OLA, KIRKWALL
ISLE OF ORKNEY, KW15 1SD
0856 873636

HARBOUR MASTER
HARBOUR HOUSE
SANDAY, ORKNEY
ISLE OF ORKNEY, KW17 2BJ
085 75 227

HARBOUR MASTER
HARBOUR ST
ISLE OF ORKNEY, KW15 1LE
0856 872292

SHETLAND ISLANDS

LERWICK HARBOUR TRUST
ALBERT BUILDINGS
ESPLANADE
ISLE OF SHETLAND, ZE1 0LL
0595 2991

STRATHCLYDE

ARDROSSAN HARBOUR CO
DOCK RD
AYRSHIRE, KA22 8DB
0294 63972

CLYDE PORT LTD
ESTUARY CONTROL TOWER
CAMPBELL ST
RENFREWSHIRE, PA16 8AW
0475 26221

IRVINE HARBOUR CO
THE HARBOUR, AYRSHIRE, KA12 8PZ
0294 78132

ROTHESAY HARBOUR
HARBOUR MASTERS OFFICE
THE PIER ROTHESAY HARBOUR
ISLE OF BUTE, PA20 9AQ
0700 503842

TARBERT HARBOUR AUTHORITY
HARBOUR MASTERS OFFICE
HARBOUR ST
ARGYLL, PA29 6UD
0880 820344

TAYSIDE

DUNDEE PORT AUTHORITY
HARBOUR CHMBS
DOCK ST, ANGUS, DD1 3HW
0382 24121

MONTROSE PORT AUTHORITY
SOUTH QUAY
FERRYDEN, MONTROSE, ANGUS, DD10 9SL
0674 72302

WESTERN ISLES

STORNOWAY HARBOUR
SLIPWAY
GOAT ISLAND, STORNOWAY
ISLE OF LEWIS, PA87 2RS
0851 703143

STORNOWAY PIER AND HARBOUR
COMMISSION
AMITY HOUSE, ESPLANADE QUAY
ISLE OF LEWIS, PA87 2XS
0851 702688

Ferry Services

AVON

BRISTOL FERRY BOAT CO
THE BARGE TEMPORA WELSHBACK
AVON, BS1 4SB
0272 273416

CORNWALL

C TOMS & SON
SLIPWAY
BODINNICK, FOWEY
CORNWALL, PL23 1LX
0726 870453

KING HARRY STEAM FERRY CO.LTD
BOSCAWEN HOUSE
CHAPEL HILL
CORNWALL, TR1 3BN
0872 72463

POLRUAN FERRY CO
1A TOWER PARK
CORNWALL, PL23 1JD
0726 832626

TORPOINT FERRY
2 FERRY ST, CORNWALL, PL11 2AX
0752 812233

DEVON

KINGSWEAR LOWER FERRY
LOWER FERRY OFFICE
KINGSWEAR, DARTMOUTH
DEVON, TQ6 0AA
0803 752342

THE SALCOMBE FERRY OPERATING CO.LTD.
BOATHOUSE
FORE ST, DEVON, TQ8 8JG
0548 842061

DORSET

BOURNEMOUTH SWANAGE MOTOR ROAD
& FERRY CO
FERRY RD
STUDLAND, SWANAGE
DORSET, BH19 3BA
092 944 203

CONDOR WEYMOUTH LTD
THE QUAY
DORSET, DT4 8DX
0305 761551

HAMPSHIRE

HURST CASTLE FERRY & CRUISES
19 EVERTON RD
HORDLE
LYMINGTON
HAMPSHIRE, SO41 0FF
0425 610784

HYTHE FERRY & PIER
TOWN QUAY
HAMPSHIRE, SO1 0AQ
0703 333584

THE HAYLING FERRY
87 OAKLANDS RD
HAMPSHIRE, PO9 2RL
0705 482868

WIGHTLINK ISLE OF WIGHT FERRIES
GUNWHARF RD
HAMPSHIRE, PO1 2LA
0705 812011

ISLE OF WIGHT

COWES FLOATING BRIDGE
MEDINA RD
ISLE OF WIGHT, PO31 7BX
0983 293041

HOVERTRAVEL LTD
QUAY RD
ISLE OF WIGHT, PO33 2HB
0983 811000

RED FUNNEL I.O.W FERRIES
FOUNTAIN PIER
ISLE OF WIGHT, PO31 7AR
0983 292101

KENT

WHITE HORSE FERRIES LTD
FERRY TERMINAL
WEST ST
KENT, DA11 0BL
0474 566220

MERSEYSIDE

MERSEY FERRIES
VICTORIA PLACE, MERSEYSIDE, L44 6QY
051 630 1030

NORTHUMBERLAND

KIELDER WATER CRUISES
TOWER KNOWGH INFORMATION CENTRE
KIELDER WATER, HEXHAM
NORTHUMBERLAND, NE48 1BX
0434 240436

NORMAN MACKAY
7 SEAFIELD RD
NORTHUMBERLAND, NE68 7SL
0665 720155

STAFFORDSHIRE

DINGLE FERRY COMPANY
FERRY COTTAGE
THE DINGLE, STAFFORDSHIRE, DE15 9HF
0283 35278

ISLE OF MAN

ISLE OF MAN STEAM PACKET CO
IMPERIAL BUILDINGS
ISLE OF MAN, IM
0624 661661

SCOTLAND

STRATHCLYDE

CALEDONIAN MACBRAYNE LTD
FERRY TERMINAL
ARGYLL, PA22 3AP
070 084 235

CALEDONIAN MACBRAYNE LTD
FERRY TERMINAL
KENNACRAIG, TARBERT
ARGYLL, PA29 6YF
088 073 253

CALEDONIAN MACBRAYNE LTD
FERRY TERMINAL
RAILWAY PIER
ARGYLL, PA34 4LW
0631 62285

WESTERN FERRIES LTD
MARINE PARADE, HUNTER'S QUAY
ARGYLL, PA23 8HN
0369 4452

CALEDONIAN MACBRAYNE LTD
ARRAN BERTH THE HARBOUR
AYRSHIRE, KA22 8ED
0294 603226

CALEDONIAN MACBRAYNE LTD
FERRY TERMINAL
AYRSHIRE, KA22 8EW
0294 63470

CALEDONIAN MACBRAYNE LTD
FERRY TERMINAL
AYRSHIRE, KA30 8BG
0475 674134

CALEDONIAN MACBRAYNE LTD
FERRY TERMINAL
ISLE OF ARRAN, KA27 8AU
0770 2166

CALEDONIAN MACBRAYNE LTD
FERRY TERMINAL
ISLE OF BUTE, PA20 9AQ
0700 502707

CALEDONIAN MACBRAYNE LTD
FERRY TERMINAL
ISLE OF GIGHA, PA42 7DW
0496 2209

CALEDONIAN MACBRAYNE LTD
FERRY TERMINAL
TOBERMORY, ISLE OF MULL, PA75 6NU
0688 2017

WESTERN FERRIES LTD
16 WOODSIDE CRESCENT
LANARKSHIRE, G3 7UL
041 332 9766

CALEDONIAN MACBRAYNE LTD
FERRY TERMINAL
RENFREWSHIRE, PA18 6AA
0475 520521

CALEDONIAN MACBRAYNE LTD
THE FERRY TERMINAL
RENFREWSHIRE, PA19 1QP
0475 33755

ORKNEY ISLANDS

ORKNEY ISLANDS SHIPPING CO LTD
4 AYRE RD, ISLE OF ORKNEY, KW15 1QX
0856 872044

HIGHLANDS

A NICOLSON
THE AVENUE
ISLE OF RAASAY, KYLE
ROSS-SHIRE, IV40 8PB
047 862 226

CALEDONIAN MACBRAYNE LTD
FERRY TERMINAL
INVERNESS-SHIRE, PH41 4QB
0687 2403

CALEDONIAN MACBRAYNE LTD
FERRY TERMINAL, ISLE OF SKYE, IV41 8PL
0599 4482

CALEDONIAN MACBRAYNE LTD
FERRY TERMINAL
PARK RD, ISLE OF SKYE, IV51 9EP
0478 2075

CALEDONIAN MACBRAYNE LTD
ARMADALE, ARDVASAR,
ISLE OF SKYE, IV45 8RS
047 14 248

CALEDONIAN MACBRAYNE LTD
FERRY TERMINAL
UIG, PORTREE, ISLE OF SKYE, IV51 9XX
047 042 219

CALEDONIAN MACBRAYNE LTD
FERRY TERMINAL
ROSS-SHIRE, IV26 2UR
0854 612358

CORRAN FERRY
ARDGOUR
INVERNESS-SHIRE, PH33 7AA
085 55 243

GLENELG KYLERHEA CAR FERRY
CORRIEHALLIE
INVERINATE, PORTREE
ISLE OF SKYE, IV51 9HD
059 981 302

JOHN O'GROATS FERRY
ORKNEY FERRY PIER
CAITHNESS, KW1 4YR
095 581 353

N MACSWEEN
3 STROMEVIEW
ISLE OF SCALPAY, PA84 3XU
085 984 220

WESTERN ISLES

CALEDONIAN MACBRAYNE LTD
FERRY TERMINAL
TARBERT, HARRIS
ISLE OF HARRIS, PA85 3DG
0859 2444

CALEDONIAN MACBRAYNE LTD
MARITIME BUILDING, KING EDWARD WHARF
ISLE OF LEWIS, PA87 2XU
0851 702361

CALEDONIAN MACBRAYNE LTD
FERRY TERMINAL
ISLE OF NORTH UIST, PA82 5AA
087 63 337

CALEDONIAN MACBRAYNE LTD
FERRY TERMINAL
ISLE OF SOUTH UIST, PA81 5TH
087 84 288

DONALD.A MACASKILL
6 BORVE, BERNERAY, LOCHMADDY
ISLE OF NORTH UIST, PA82 5BJ
087 67 230

DONALD CAMPBELL
AN ATAIREACHD BHUAN LUDAIG
EAST KILBRIDE, LOCHBOISDALE
ISLE OF SOUTH UIST, PA81 5TS
087 84 216

BS▾AC
SCHOOLS
Complete Diver Training
BS▾AC
SCHOOLS
The complete diver training package is available from all BSAC Schools for new and experienced divers alike. BS AC Schools are recognised as centres of excellence with a commitment to learning and safety.

Scorpion spider-crab - Inachus dorsettensis

Special Interest

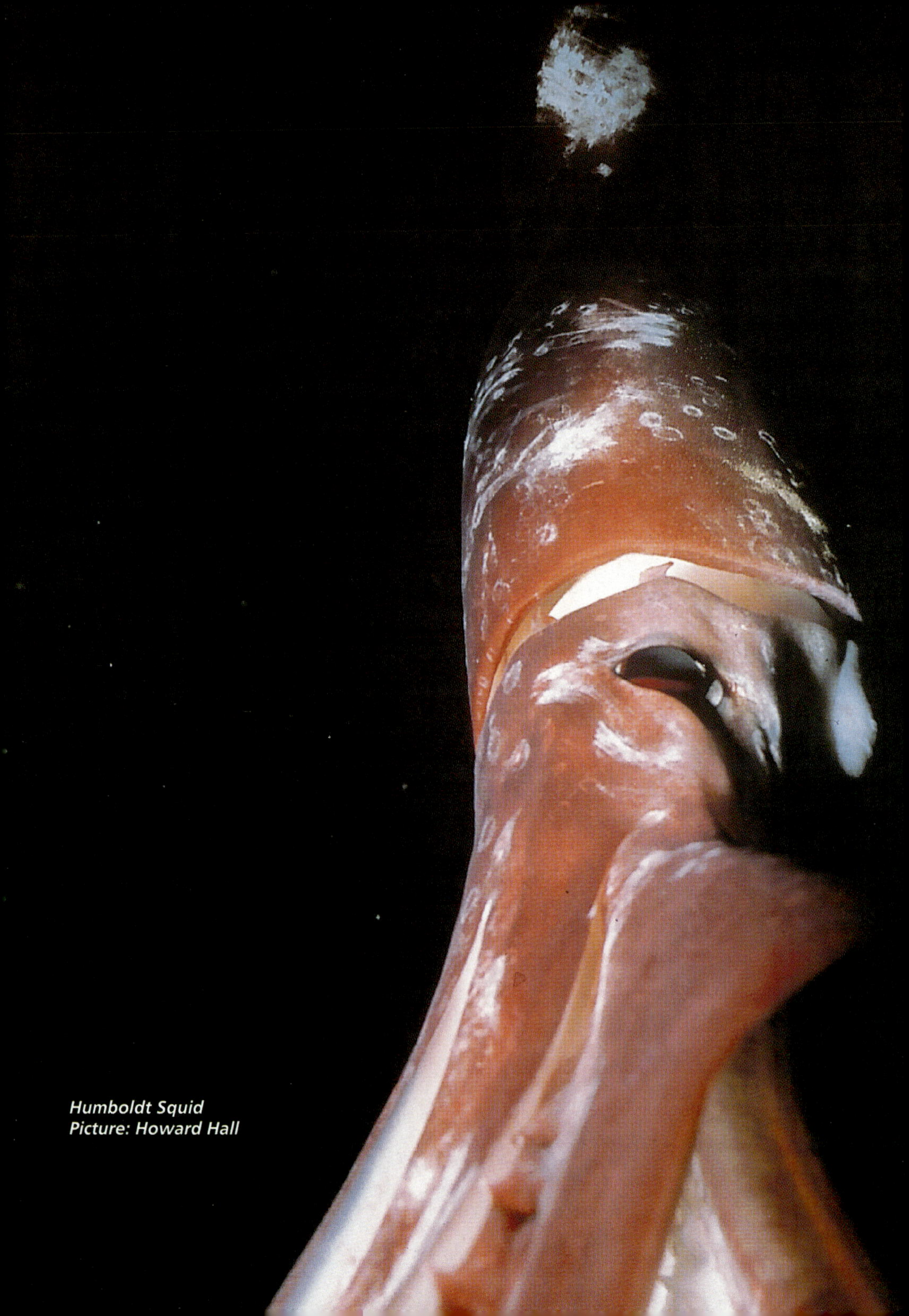

Humboldt Squid
Picture: Howard Hall

Mugged by a Squid

by Howard Hall

Howard Hall spent almost two years diving and filming in the Sea of Cortez to complete a documentary on the wildlife in the area entitled *Shadows in a desert sea*. *Shadows* was aired by the BBC in the UK and by PBS Nature in the US. This is an account of one of the many experiences of Hall and his film crew.

Perhaps you were driving home one New Year's Eve and a guy in the opposite lane woke up just before crossing the double yellow line. You may have been that close. On the very edge of the abyss. And you never knew it.

Was I on the very edge or was I completely safe? The question drifted through my mind as I turned the 1300 watt movie lights aside and looked straight down the monofilament line as it descended into the darkness.

The lights were so bright that the glare actually hindered vision. But the power was necessary for filming big animals underwater at night. I was hoping for big animals. And I hoped I was being imaginative and not stupid. In the natural history film business, the difference between being imaginative and being recklessly stupid can simply be whether or not things go your way.

Aboard the *Ambar III*, my Dad was doubled over a big game fishing pole in cheerful agony. His back was near failure and he occasionally passed the pole off to Bob Cranston when his muscles began to spasm. I'd brought my Mom and Dad along on the Sea of Cortez expedition to work as production assistants. Simple nepotism. They know nothing about natural history film production.

I had no idea what Dad had on the other end of the line. But Mike McGettigan, owner of the *Ambar III*, had explained that if you caught something big, at night, in deep water, giant squid would sometimes follow it to the surface.

Some Mexican fishermen had seen some big squid in this area. When we asked, "How big?", they spread their arms as wide as possible and said "grande!". One fishermen noticed our diving gear and asked if we intended to swim with the squid. When we said yes, he shook his head solemnly and said, "Not a good idea".

My eyes played tricks on me as I hung suspended in oppressive darkness staring down the fishing line. Startling shapes would begin to materialise and then suddenly vanish. Imagination.

I wondered about what the fishermen had said. Maybe this wasn't such a good idea. I looked up toward the surface and could see the three skipjack tuna hanging over the side of the *Ambar III* for the squid to feast upon should they come up.

I didn't know if the squid were dangerous or not. I'd never seen a Humboldt squid. But I knew of other things that hunted in deep, dark waters that are attracted to bleeding tuna. I'd forgotten my anti-shark suit. Left it at home in San Diego. Not a good idea at all.

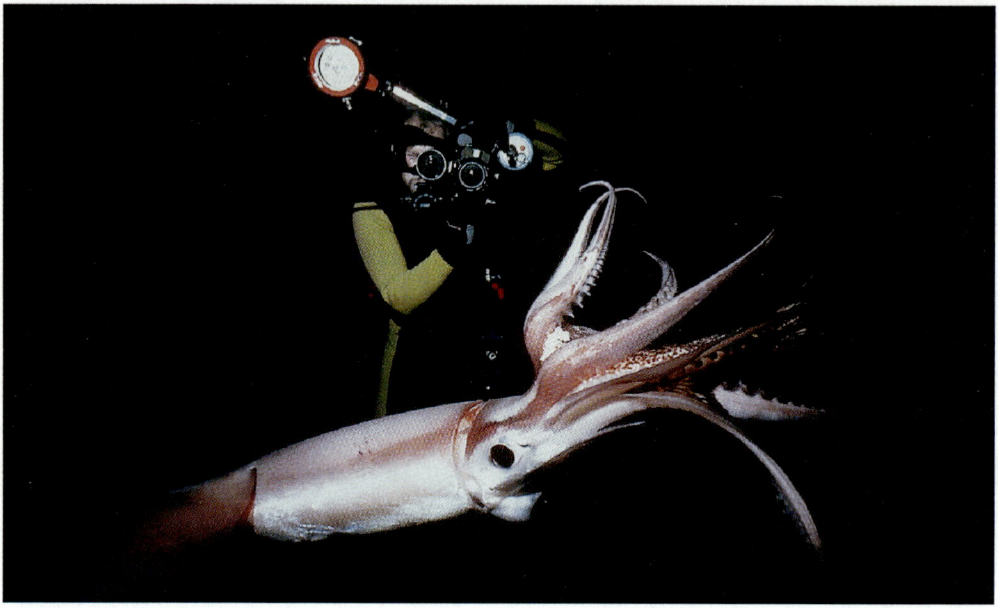

"Every time I turned toward the squid with the lights they descended and vanished." Picture: Howard Hall

A large shape materialised in the dark water below. In an instant I knew this one was real. After almost two hours of fighting, Dad was about to reel in a 14ft bigeye thresher shark. The lure had snagged the shark in the tail. I surfaced and tried to make myself heard over the whooping and hollering. "Let it go. I'll try to get a shot of it as it swims away", I yelled. Then I dropped back down to 30ft and waited for the shark to be set free.

Alex Kerstitch jumped in with his still camera and grabbed a few shots of the shark before he began working to free the lure. While he was working, instinct induced me to look down.

Flashing! There were objects far below and they were flashing as if someone down there had a rapid fire strobe going off about five times a second! As the shapes ascended I could see they were squid. The largest squid I'd ever seen.

A squid rushed past me and attacked the head of the thresher shark. The squid was about 5ft long. A small one as this species of squid go. Humboldt squid reach 13ft and 300lb! As it grasped the face of the shark, it began flashing from bright red to ivory white. It almost hurt my eyes. After a moment it let go of the shark and descended like a failing bomb.

Another, much larger, squid rocketed past me. It grabbed a 4ft needle fish that was swimming just below the surface. The squid was more than 5ft long and probably close to 70lb. As it descended with the needle fish it began tearing it apart leaving a cloud of blood and scales in its wake.

Alex unhooked the shark and it dropped past me. I made a half conscious effort of filming it and botched the shot.

Alex then swam out toward a squid that was ripping apart one of the skipjacks we had set out as bait. Squid were rushing past me. Most were in the 40 or 50lb class. Some may have approached 6ft and 100lb or more.

Something grabbed me from behind and for a moment I could feel water rushing by as I was pulled back and down. I twisted around and saw the squid that had grabbed me rush away.

I'd been pulled down about 10ft. I swam back up to 30ft and neutralised my buoyancy. I didn't take the time to consider what might have happened if the squid hadn't let go, or if more than one squid had grabbed me, or if a really big one had...

Everything seemed to be happening too fast. I still hadn't captured a single good shot. Every time I turned toward the squid with the movie lights, they descended and vanished. I suddenly realised it was the lights. They didn't like the lights! That was going to make filming them very difficult.

I wanted to film a squid attacking a free swimming fish. But noticing how they avoided the glare of the movie lights, I decided to film one of the squid that was feeding on a skipjack bait.

An enormous 6ft squid had engulfed one of the bait fish and was tearing it apart. I swam over and began shooting. The squid fed so aggressively that it refused to leave its prey even when the lights were inches away. Blood and scales flew from the cluster of arms as they ripped at the fish.

I shot a variety of close-ups and then decided to get better acquainted. I reached out to touch the animal and was startled as a large fleshy arm shot out and grabbed my hand. I jerked away and winced. Blood beaded on the back of my hand. This was not like handling an octopus! Alex had warned us that the big squid had sharp hooks that surround each powerful sucker disk. Not only does the sucker grab, but it also digs into the flesh. I was not curious enough to try it again.

Alex was behind me in the darkness with no movie lights to ward off the squid. A group ascended from the depths below, frenzied by the smell of blood in the water.

Three large squid grabbed Alex at the same time. Suddenly he felt himself rushing backward and down. A tentacle reached around his neck and ripped off his pre-Columbian gold pendant and chain, tearing the skin on his neck. Another ripped his decompression computer off his pressure gauge. Tentacles tore his dive light from his wrist and his collection bag off his waist. Then as suddenly as they had grabbed him, the squid were gone.

By the time I'd climbed back on board, Alex had already retired to bed. He hadn't mentioned anything about the incident to the rest of the crew and I hadn't seen it happen. So we continued to dive throughout the night. We thought it strange that Alex had quit so early, though. He loved to night dive.

The squid mugging hadn't really terrified Alex while it was happening. He was too busy to be afraid. But when he'd got back on board he began to wonder what if... ? What if they held on just a little longer? In moments they might have dragged him down into abyssal depths. What if they ripped out his regulator? And his worst fear, what if that beak (much larger than the largest parrot's beak) had grabbed his neck and ripped out a 2lb hunk of flesh? As he thought about it, his knees became progressively weaker. He decided he needed some rest.

Bob Cranston, Mark Conlin, and I continued to dive through the night without incident. I was frustrated because the squid consistently avoided my lights.

About 3.00am I gave up. Bob decided to make one last dive to shoot stills of a large squid that had snagged itself on the fishing lure that still dangled over the side of the boat.

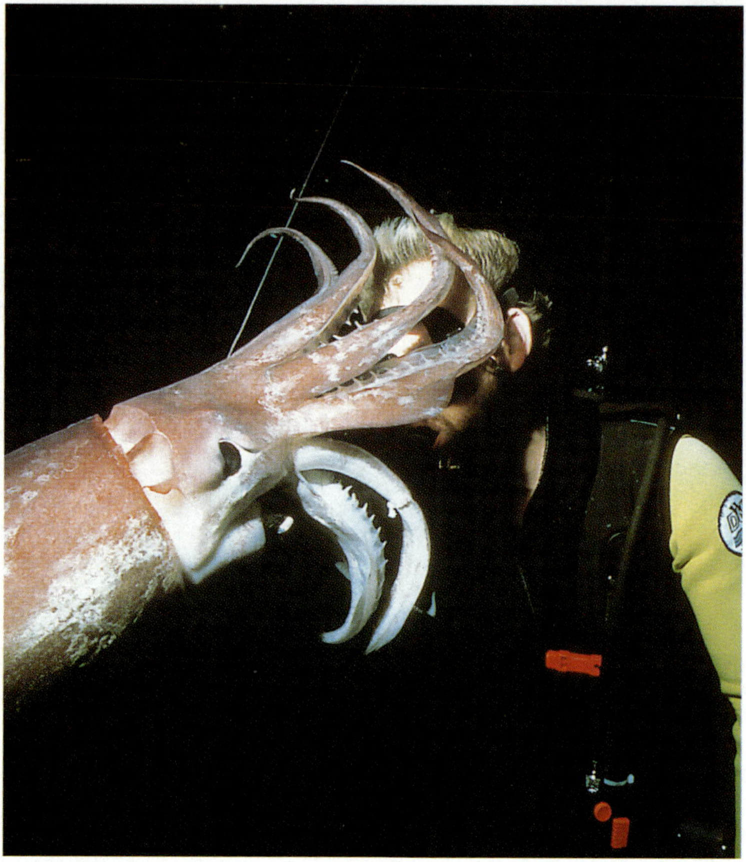

Mugged by a squid. Picture: Howard Hall

Just as Bob pulled his mask down over his face, the line on the reel began spooling out as fast as if a two ton marlin had taken the bait! I dropped my tank on the deck and rushed over to put on the drag.

The spooling didn't stop. I increased the drag as much as possible. Still the line rushed out. This was the fishing gear that had landed that 14ft thresher!

There was nothing I could do. The line continued to spool out. I looked over to Bob who was ready to jump in, his regulator in his mouth and camera in hand. He stared at the spooling reel for a long moment. "Going diving?" I asked. Bob continued to watch the spooling reel.

"Better hurry. What ever it is looks like it's going to get away," I said. Bob watched the spooling reel.

"But then again, it seems hungry. Maybe it'll come right back." Bob set his camera down then dropped his tank on the deck. "Maybe not," he said.

"Good idea!" said Mark.

I reached into the cooler and pulled out three beers. Bob, Mark, and I took long pulls and watched the rest of the line spin off the reel.

Picture this

by Martin Edge

Martin Edge is one of Britain's top underwater photographers. His work has won several major underwater photography competitions. Articles in recent diving magazines have brought a new dimension to underwater photographic instruction and he now extends this to his popular courses on underwater photography both in the UK and abroad. These courses have received glowing testimonials and former students are gaining all kinds of awards. His book - The Underwater Photographer - is due out later this year.

Most divers after their first few years seem to experience the sub-aqua menopause. It happened to me and to many of my friends. I am convinced that the prime reason for the tremendous turn-over of divers in the UK is one of 'purpose'.

After the initial excitement of getting wet has worn off, 'even under the shower on pool night' we look for a purpose. Some find their own, others do not.

We have all seen the type: keen as mustard one year but stagnation sets in and they disappear from the scene. Be it wrecking, marine biology, archaeology or underwater photography it matters not, you need a purpose that develops, gains momentum and motivates you.

Wrecking appeals to numerous divers throughout the country. Hammer and chisel in hand they search for treasures of shinning brass and bronze. Flatly, lobster and crab 'bashing' was a popular pastime of the early 80s. I have had my fair share in the past but lately I have noticed a decline.

An awareness of marine conservation has come to the fore and there is little doubt that the popularity of the new and decline of the old are somewhat intertwined.

Why underwater photography?

By now almost everyone has had some experience of the "inner space" beneath the world's seas. Glimpses of the ocean realm are brought to people in the form of pictures - some moving, others still.

Trying to describe a sea anemone to a non-diving friend is near-on impossible. Underwater photography is the tool that we use to capture the amazing things seen whilst diving. In this way divers are able to share the excitement of the ocean realms with non-divers, family and friends. We are also able to remember the excitement and beauty of a particular dive long after it is over.

Underwater photography can lead to personal satisfaction. You must understand a few basic rules and learn to apply them to obtain the desired result. In this way you should be able to take good underwater photographs from the start.

'Pipe reflections': A recent picture taken under Swanage Pier in June 1993. I have been attempting to photograph the simple subject in a completely different way. Many attempts go into the bin but once in a while an image appears which makes it all worth the effort. Picture: Martin Edge.

The problems

I have had quite a few problems over the years and I understand the frustration that creeps in with many newcomers to photography. In the early days they hit the water with great expectations, all too often however, the circumstances in which they dive in order to take the photographs defy all the odds.

If you are diving on a drift, with an SMB and perhaps a novice in tow, then take a camera with you by all means, but learn to appreciate the results you achieved in light of the conditions that prevailed.

The first time that I took a camera underwater was on a dive around the Medas Islands of Spain in 1979. I missed everything. Absolutely everything! Octopus, grouper and several other fish I would have loved to have seen. Over the next five years I became increasingly selective and decided before diving when I was likely to get any kind of results and when it was best to leave the camera on dry land and just enjoy the dive.

These days I dive purely to take underwater photographs. Diving is just a means to an end. If I could use waders and a waterproof coat in order to achieve a particular shot, then that's what I would do.

Around the UK there are numerous divers who pursue underwater photography. Each is unique in terms of commitment, and each approach differs as a result of their priorities. At one end of the scale is the committed underwater photographer who dives solely for that purpose. At the other is the diver who owns a camera system but has many other responsibilities: trainer, cox, dive marshall. This diver may take a camera with him in order to record what he sees during his dive and is often frustrated if he fails to produce the same quality pictures as the person who dives for images alone.

Whatever your ambitions in underwater photography and no matter where you stand between the two extremes, there is camera equipment to suit your own individual needs.

Cameras for snorkelling

Both Kodak and Fuji have cheap single use camera's that work well down to 2m in clear, well-lit waters. EWA Marine produce flexible housings for both compact land cameras and SLR cameras that are effective to a maximum depth of 10m.

A little deeper

If you require a system that you can take to any reasonable depth, check out the Sea and Sea Explora. This has a flash unit which will restore the colours filtered out by absorbtion.

Red disappears at about 10m and at 20m you are just left with a blue/grey colour or a green shade in and around the UK.

The Explora and flash costs around £350 and a supplementary 20mm adapter is about £130. The 20mm allows you to reduce the water column between the lens and the subject. The result, is a colourful and vibrant image.

Professional system

The Sea and Sea Motor Marine II with various accessories will allow you to develop your skills as an underwater photographer in almost any environment. It can focus between 20in and infinity. A TTL flash-gun can be detached from the camera to reduce the effects of backscatter (particles in the water that are illuminated by the flash and reflect back into the lens like snow).

The Sea and Sea Motor Marine has both wide-angle and closeup adaptors. For an overall price of about £800 it's good value for money.

The Nikonos system

There is nothing that I can write about this system that has not been written before. The Nikonos V remains the most widely used underwater camera in the world with a wide range of accessories and the finest optics available.

The wreck of the Cedar Pride *in Aquaba, Jordan, lies on its port side in 30m of water. This shot was taken with a 16mm fish-eye lens on a Nikon F2 in an Oceanic Hydro housing. Picture: Martin Edge*

The Nikonos is rugged and reliable. In fact if it's just snaps you're after then the accurate TTL flash-gun makes it almost a point and shoot camera.

If you intend to develop and work at your images the system will provide you with ultimate in quality. It's not cheap. In fact it is a financial commitment to most people. Shop around, you can find bargains both new and second-hand.

Nikonos RS

Nikon have recently launched the RS - a break-through in underwater camera design in that it is the first underwater single lens reflex camera with auto-focus. At over £5,000 for the whole system, it is aimed solely at the professional or the enthusiast come millionaire.

Conclusion

Underwater photography is infectious and to me the most rewarding of pastimes.

If your diving has become that little bit mundane then beg steal or borrow a system and give it a go! Be fair and give yourself the best possible chance to obtain pictures that you can be proud of.

Try a shallow dive from the shore with a buddy who knows your purpose and is happy to support your efforts. Diving shallow allows you the time to begin to develop your skills and minimises the preoccupations associated with depth, time and decompression.

Shore diving minimises the hassle of boats, sea-sickness, anchor-lines etc. Learn to subjectively evaluate your pictures, this avoids disappointment when you consider your results taken at 40m over a period of five minutes, with a similar specimen taken at 5m over a period of one hour. Rarely will they compare.

The importance of the role that underwater photography plays in diving cannot be overestimated.

Go on, get in and give it a bash.

The International Association of Nitrox & Technical Divers (UK)

by Rob Palmer

Rob Palmer is at the leading edge of technical diving with IANTD (UK) which can be contacted on 0749-840685

In early 1992, the European Association of Technical Divers was formed in the UK to promote Nitrox and other training standards in Europe, and to develop technical diving as a concept on the eastern side of the Atlantic.

The formation of EATD was a direct response to the recent upsurge of interest in what the American diving world terms 'technical diving' - where an increasing number of divers are exploring beyond the limits suggested by the various national and international training organisations.

In January 1993, EATD and its co-affiliate in the US, IAND (the International Association of Nitrox Divers), officially merged to become IANTD, the International Association of Nitrox and Technical Divers. This created a truly international body to represent technical diving in the international diving forum.

It must be emphasised, however, that technical diving is neither an excuse for outrageous diving practises, nor does it promote them. It is the application of new or advanced diving techniques in the safest and most legitimate way to advanced sport diving.

Technical diving is neither normal recreational diving (though some of the techniques filter down, and make recreational diving safer - like Nitrox) nor is it commercial diving.

It is about accepting the future of diving as well as its past, and developing training standards to make what divers actually do at the sharper end of sport diving as safe as possible.

IANTD (UK) has, or is currently developing, qualification and experience-based courses to cover the use of Nitrox, deep diving, trimix, overhead environment diving and closed-circuit rebreather diving.

Of these techniques, perhaps that arousing the most interest in recent months has been the use of Nitrox, or, more properly, Enriched Air Nitrox (EANx).

Nitrox

Nitrox has several distinct advantages over ordinary compressed air. Enriched air Nitrox is air with an increased oxygen content, and mixtures containing up to 40% oxygen can safely be used with ordinary scuba gear without special preparation or cleaning, though IANTD (UK) recommends divers follow manufacturer's advice when it comes to specific equipment compatibility.

The most common mixtures contain either 32% or 36% oxygen. The latter, Nitrox 36, can be used safely to 30m with a maximum operating depth (MOD) of 34m, and Nitrox 32 can be used to 35m, with a MOD of 40m.

Beyond these depths, the partial pressure of oxygen in the mixture becomes too great (over 1.6 bar) and oxygen toxicity can pose a problem. (Air, by the way, reaches a PPO_2 of 1.6 at 66m).

The safe operating depth (SOD) uses a partial pressure of approximately 1.4 bar, where oxygen toxicity is extremely unlikely to pose a problem even on working dives.

Reducing the amount of nitrogen in the mix also reduces the narcotic effect of the mix and its decompression obligation. Bottom time is safely increased, no-stop time on the Buhlmann tables at 21m on Nitrox 36 being 75 minutes, compared with 35 minutes on air.

The potential for decompression sickness is reduced accordingly, and if decompression limits are exceeded, decompression time is comparatively shorter for the same depth/time increments.

There is less residual nitrogen in the tissues on surfacing, and thus less sub-clinical DCS.

Through Technical Diving Ltd, Nitrox courses began being taught in September '92, and several hundred students have completed the Nitrox Diver courses. A number of British diving shops have installed Nitrox supply systems, and other training centres are springing up.

IANTD-qualified Nitrox divers heading to the USA and Caribbean, will find their cards allow them to purchase and use Nitrox mixtures (where use of the gas has really taken off, especially in Florida and the Keys). This is also the case in Australia and in an increasing number of resorts where operators are quickly coming to realise the safety advantages of Nitrox for regular resort diving.

IANTD plans not only to develop training courses and standards, but to act as a medium

20 METRES COMPARATIVE NO-DECOMPRESSION TIME

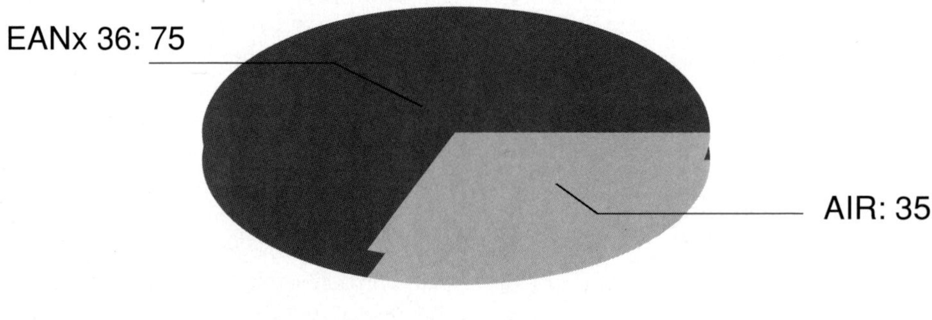

Time in minutes

for Nitrox and technical divers to exchange news, run special diving meets and promote safe techniques for advanced diving practices.

It will have its own newsletters on a quarterly basis, available not only in printed form but also by computer mail. It will soon be possible for members to plug into a computerised 'chat-line' to exchange views and information with other technical divers in the UK and abroad.

What of the others?

The other major sport training organisations are all considering the use of Nitrox and gas mixtures other than air, and are well aware that this is the way ahead.

So far NAUI, SSI and the US-YMCA have openly accepted the use of Nitrox in the USA, ratifying the IANTD training programmes in the States, and insuring appropriately qualified instructors to both use and teach Nitrox.

Closer to home, both the Sub Aqua Association and Scottish Sub-Aqua Club have endorsed the use of Nitrox for their members, SAA recognising the IANTD syllabus and qualification, and awarding members who have completed an IANTD course a logbook endorsement, while SSAC are developing their own internal Nitrox course.

The BS-AC is looking closely at the development of Nitrox diving over here, though it has announced it has no plans to train divers in Nitrox use and that its insurance will not cover them.

PADI has noted developments and recognised that there are benefits offered by Nitrox, but has not at the time of writing made any public statement on training standards, other than to say that it has no plans to train divers through its own programme, though its instructors are covered to dive with divers using Nitrox.

The Health and Safety Executive have publicly stated they believe that Nitrox, trimix and rebreathers are here to stay, and that all they wish for is to see an accepted and responsible training programme in place.

The HSE were convinced by the 15,000 or so incident-free commercial dives made in the southern sector of the North Sea on Nitrox.

However long it takes for Nitrox use to become commonplace in the recreational community, there is no denying that it is a diving gas that, with proper training and standards, is safer at recreational depths than air, and that it is here to stay.

Given the rash of accidents in British diving in the summer of '92, perhaps it is no bad thing to have a mixture in your cylinder that is less narcotic and carries less of a comparative decompression obligation than air.

Dr Morgan Wells of NOAA, the early Nitrox pioneer, made the increasingly-quoted statement that really sums it all up: "Mother Nature provided the planet Earth with a Nitrox atmosphere known as air. She never said that air was the best breathing medium for divers."

Archaeological Diving

by Mensun Bound

Mensun Bound is Director of Archaeology at Oxford University MARE and Visiting Research Fellow in Maritime Archaeology at the University of Wales at Bangor.

One would have to be made of stone not to be excited by the thought of a shipwreck on the ocean floor. Mention the word to most people and it will conjure up visions of stately structures with fish darting in and out of the rigging, the skeleton of the skipper still lashed to the helm and maybe even the odd treasure chest half opened and spilling its opulence on to the deck. It is an image that helped to lure most of us into donning fins for the first time.

But, of course, as all divers soon find out, wrecks are never like this. Mauled by time and tide and savaged by wood-consuming marine organisms, within a few years most wrecks are reduced to an apparently unintelligible spread of non-perishable and semi-perishable artifacts, frequently cemented together by corrosion products and partially obscured by weed and marine deposits. In high energy areas the surviving material is likely to be broken, ground down by abrasion and spread over a wide area.

Excavating, recording, decoding, piecing-together, conserving and interpreting such sites is a painstaking and costly process that, if done properly, is likely to take years. So why bother? What is so special about shipwrecks?

In a word - information. Field archaeology, whether on land or under water is, in broad terms, about the acquisition and dissemination of new information, particularly that which relates to the origin, development and behaviour patterns of man. At another level it is also about understanding and preserving our heritage. In all cases, however, it is mainly concerned with artefacts, and the most informative artefact of all must be the ship and all it contains.

The ship (it can be argued) was the most important vehicle in the ascent and spread of civilization. Not only did it carry products, ideas and emigrants and fight battles upon which the course of history has pivoted, but it was also the finest expression of the technology of its society and times.

Furthermore, a ship on the sea-bed is usually there as the result of a sudden catastrophe, and thus represents a little squirt of time, a discreet moment in history, a section of life which, if properly investigated, can give a valuable insight into society that is different, and potentially fuller, from that obtainable from most land based sites.

The maritime archaeologist is, therefore, not only interested in the cargo that a vessel was carrying, but also in the people, lifestyle and social stratification on board; how the ship was built, equipped and navigated, and how all these factors together reflect the society, economy and civilization in which the crew lived and its vessel operated.

It is difficult to say exactly when maritime archaeology began. The Roman barges in Lake Nemi, south of Rome, were being investigated as far back as the Renaissance; there was some smash-and-grab type work being conducted on historic wrecks by hard-hat divers during the 1800's, and, during the first decade of this century, there were some spectacular recoveries of ancient artworks from wrecks off Greece and Tunisia.

But this was salvage rather than archaeology. The turning point came in the 1950's when two eminent land archaeologists, Nino Lamboglia in Italy and Fernand Benoit in France, became involved in major underwater excavations. Benoit was in fact the archaeologist for the first major French underwater excavation, that of a Roman amphora wreck off Grand Congloué near Marseilles.

This project, which was directed by none other than Jacques Cousteau, made some major errors, but these were pioneering days and, whatever the faults, Benoit succeeded in producing the first book length report on an underwater excavation. An achievement which, sadly, few have emulated since.

If qualified direction and controlled technique, followed by scientific publication, is the measure of a proper underwater archaeological project, then we in Britain can claim to have been amongst the first. In the mid 1950's a British team carried out harbour work in Greece, that involved archaeologists getting wet and precise mapping of the finds (using grids). Furthermore, there was prompt, scholarly publication of the results in a highly esteemed academic journal. However, because of the uncharismatic nature of the project and the innate reserve of those involved, this work has been ignored by commentators both in Britain and abroad.

In the second half of the 50's, we see a conscious striving for scientific improvement in underwater archaeology. Nino Lamboglia (now rightly heroized in Italy) was making impressive strides and although, like Benoit, not a diver himself, he was a first rate archaeologist. While the work of Lamboglia was dominating headlines in Italy, divers in Denmark were carrying out preliminary underwater studies on a series of important Medieval boat finds in the Roskilde Fjord at Skuldelev, and in Turkey a Hemmingwayesque adventurer by the name of Peter Throckmorton was working with the sponge divers and listing their wreck finds.

It was thanks to Throckmorton's efforts that, in 1960, the American George Bass began the excavation of a Bronze Age wreck off Cape Gelidonya that was to set new standards in underwater archaeological technique and procedure.

The outstanding importance of this site was impossible to ignore and the world of humane studies began grudgingly to admit that perhaps there was more to maritime archaeology than just fun-in-the-sun. Today Gelidonya is widely recognised as the beginning of scientific underwater archaeology, but I think of it as the end of the beginning; the culmination of a series of trends and improvements that were going on in the second half of the fifties which were openly discussed by the major practitioners at the first underwater archaeological congresses that were held at the time. After Gelidonya there could be no going back; phase two in the history of maritime archaeology had begun.

The work at Gelidonya, the raising of the *Wasa* near Stockholm in 1961 and the excavation of the Roskilde ships (from within coffer damns) the year after, were certainly a source of inspiration to British divers; but underwater archaeology in Britain did not get off to an auspicious start. Despite good intentions, work on such important wrecks as the *Association* in the Scillies, soon became (for reasons that were beyond the control of the excavators) something of a free-for-all and much of the material was eventually sold on the market. Other sites had similar experiences but, as a result of all this despoliation, it became evident that something had to be done and in 1973 the Protection of Wrecks Act was passed.

Greek pot painted with two combatting warriors c.600 BC. Excavated by Oxford Univ. MARE on wreck off island of Giglio in the Tuscan Archipelago. Drawing: Mensun Bound.

Throughout the second half of the sixties and into seventies teams were active on a number of British sites. Then, as now, almost all the work concentrated on the post-1500 period.

One of the first historic wrecks to be identified was the Dutch East Indiaman *De Liefde* (1711) in the Shetlands. Others that followed included the *Lastdrager* (1652) and *Kennermerland* (1664) also in the Shetlands, the *Adelaar* (1728) off the Outer Hebrides, the *Dartmouth* (1690) off Mull, the *Hollandia* (1742) in the Scillies, and of course, there were the now well known Spanish Armada ships of 1588: *El Gran Griffon* off Fair Isle, the *Trinidad Valencera* off County Donegal and the *Girona* off County Antrim. The work on these sites was carried out by such pioneers as Colin Martin and Robert Stenuit.

The latter part of the 1970's was, of course, dominated by Margaret Rule's excavation of Henry VIII's *Mary Rose* (1545), the most complicated and ambitious underwater project of its kind ever attempted, and which culminated in a spectacular feat of engineering with the raising of what was still surviving of the vessel's hull.

Some of the best underwater archaeology carried out by British practitioners has been done abroad: Honor Frost was at work during the seventies on a Punic ship near Marsala, while Toby Parker of Bristol University carried out a series of exemplary small-scale projects off Southern Sicily. In the first half of the 1980's I directed Oxford University's excavation of an Etruscan or Greek wreck (c. 600 BC) off the Tuscan island of Giglio. This was certainly the largest of the post-*Mary Rose* projects involving as it did, in one season alone, over 120 people.

The Giglio project was so successful that, in 1984, the governing body of the University voted to establish a maritime archaeological unit for itself which was christened Oxford University MARE (Maritime Archaeological Research and Excavation).

In the latter part of the 1980's the MARE team went on to conduct work on a Roman wreck off the Island of Montecristo, a Hellenistic wreck off Giglio, a 4th century BC wreck beside Dattilo at Panarea in the Aeolian Islands, and a number of smaller projects. Currently MARE is involved on sites off the prison island of Gorgona, Tuscany, the Island of Zakynthos in Greece, the Turks and Caicos Islands in the West Indies, Alderney in the Channel Islands, Bound Skerry in the Shetlands, the Falkland Islands, Uruguay and Gibraltar (much of the recent work - such as that at Alderney and Gibraltar - being in collaboration with the University of Wales at Bangor).

Excavating shipwrecks is a slow, painstaking process that not only costs a fortune but, because of conservation, research and publication, is likely to take years. As a result of this and other more complex reasons, excavation is not something to be entered into lightly.

Most of the projects so far highlighted represent archaeology on the grand scale, of what may be called *haute* archaeology; most of the projects currently taking place are less ambitious, involving mainly reconnaissance work, survey and small-scale, or partial, excavation. At present there are only two major projects taking place in British waters: a 17th century wreck off Duarte Point in Scotland, which is being excavated by divers from St Andrews University under Colin Martin; and an Elizabethan wreck off Alderney, on which work is being directed by archaeologists from Oxford University MARE and Bangor University.

Drawing a Roman anchor stock raised from the sea off the Italian prison island of Gorgona. Picture: G. Ristich, Oxford Univ. MARE.

Whatever the nature of a project, detailed recording is at its heart. As archaeologists, both ambient and underwater, never tire of telling us, "excavation is destruction" - in other words, you must get it right the first time. Mess it up and it can be like trying to unscramble eggs. To help avoid this you must document every detail, so that everything can be re-evaluated and every step of the way recreated. Even things you do not understand may become clear later on paper.

One example of this is the site plan. On an early wreck I excavated we spent two years mapping every single find, every tiny fragment, however apparently insignificant, onto a plan view of the site. For all that time these little specks appeared to have no useful or logical pattern, but then, within a period of days, the gaps began to fill; suddenly everything imploded into a rational whole and we found ourselves looking at a line of artefacts that mapped out the trajectory of the sinking ship. We ran a rope along the line

Oxford Univ. MARE at work on Dattilo wreck of Panarea in the Aeolian Islands. Drawing: C. Caldwell

and, by extending it at each end, we not only found the point at which the vessel had impacted on the reef but also, at the other end, the ship's keel.

But maritime archaeology is not, as many think, just the recovery and identification of artefacts for the delectation of the public. If that were so, ours would be a limited and very petty discipline. It would be a bit like knowing the names of the actors in a play without understanding the script.

These days most of us are seeking wider connections and deeper layers of meaning in our work, and as a result of this we are making increasing demands of science (a subject which I will return to presently). For my part, I have become very interested in those aspects that go beyond the palpable; why, for instance, is something missing?

Why, in one wreck we surveyed, was there a gap in the amphora stack? Maybe nothing had been there, or maybe there was a 'ghost' cargo that washed away or dissolved in the sea when the vessel sank. For abstract questions like these, I have coined the word 'metafact'. In short, good thought must now go hand in hand with good technique - which is one of the reasons why maritime archaeologists deplore the activities of treasure hunters who usually have neither.

Treasure hunters are motivated by either greed, adventure or notoriety - certainly not archaeology, otherwise they would not be involved in the destruction of our maritime heritage. To see them at work is like watching hogs grubbing for truffles, and on those occassions when they do have sophisticated hi-tech equipment (which these days is increasingly often) it is usually used a way that is crude and anti-archaeological.

MARE diver with metal detector off the island of Montecristo. Picture: G. Sacco, Oxford Univ. MARE.

Proper excavation is a slow forensic process involving many specialists all of whom work together in an integrated fashion to tease forth the information, detail by detail, pursuing every nuance. The treasure hunter by contrast will bludgeon the site to pieces; with crushing time and financial imperatives, he cannot afford the meticulous, measured pace of scientific excavation; nor, of course, can he afford the post-excavation process which can involve years of work. For the treasure hunter, bills have to be paid, profits made and backers satisfied; once the 'goodies' have been filmed for the documentary and photographed for the popular book, they must be rushed to auction, where whole artefact assemblages are then dispersed and lost forever, to become curios on people's mantelshelves.

Treasure hunters will claim the rights of free enterprise and say they earn what they receive because of the risks they take. However, archaeologists take the same risks,

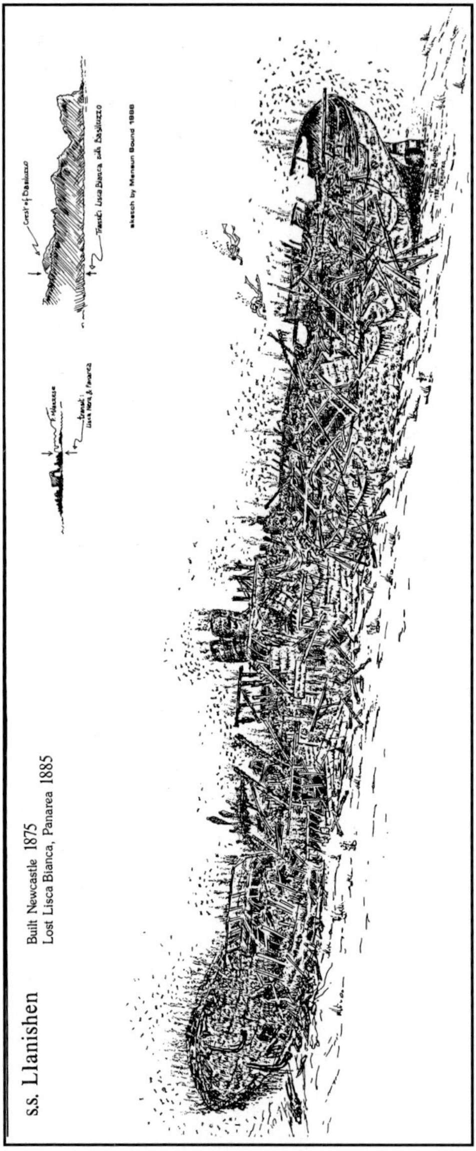

19th century wreck surveyed by MARE in Aeolien Islands. Drawing: Mensun Bound.

but what they do is for the enrichment of all. Historic wrecks are a valuable cultural resource, but they are finite in number and once gone they are lost forever. If they are to be dismembered then it must be done in a way that is archaeological.

Small wonder that in wreck diving in recent years (particularly abroad) there has been no issue more divisive or acrimonious than treasure hunting. In Britain, perhaps because of our less passionate temperaments and long traditions of tolerance, there is less open hostility between the camps. Nevertheless, maritime archaeologists here do seem to divide more or less evenly between those who are happy to work with the treasure hunters, and those who will not be satisfied with anything short of a public lynching.

For my part, I believe that the mindset and methods of the treasure hunter make it impossible for us to work together. But I do believe in dialogue. I have found over the years that both penitent and prodigal can make excellent archaeologists and, after all, we do all share a common denominator in our fascination with wrecks, and this can be used to build better and more productive relationships.

And what of the average recreational diver, who could never be called a treasure hunter, but simply likes to spend his weekends, happy as a clam in mud, up to his elbows in a wreck? If the truth be known that is probably how most of my generation first became involved in maritime archaeology. Many of us discovered however that it was much more rewarding to work as part of an archaeological team, to understand the vessel we were digging, and to see our finds become things of lasting value instead of crumbling to dust in some small corner of a basement museum. In fact, amateur divers have been the backbone of British maritime archaeology, and despite some worrying trains of thought coming from the more doctrinaire corners of our discipline, will, I hope, remain so for many years to come. The Mary Rose, of course, was the triumph of the amateur volunteer diver; and over the years many hundreds have also worked for me in the field. The debt of the maritime archaeologist to the sports diver is enormous.

Ironically, the worst destroyers of the maritime heritage have not been treasure hunters, but rather the maritime archaeologists! By failing to publish, or by not publishing in a rational, clinical and scholarly manner, we have destroyed these sites just as surely as if we had gone in with siege howitzers. Of all the hundreds of wrecks ever excavated world-wide less than a dozen have been fully published and documented- that is how bad things are!

But maritime, or underwater archaeology (or even 'hydro' archaeology - a term we have just adopted in this country without caring to acknowledge that it has been used abroad for many years) is not just about ships in salt water settings. It also involves river and lake craft; submerged settlement sites; the sacrificial cenotes of the Yucatan; the sinkholes of Florida; inundated sites such as the Aswan High Dam and the reservoirs of Wales; ancient harbours such as that of Caesarea in Israel; sunken cities such as Port Royal in Jamaica or Dunwich off East Anglia; the submerged land-bridges between the continents; and even the drains, cisterns and sewers under modern day ancient cities. Indeed, one of my colleagues has been active in the water-filled tunnels under the Colosseum in Rome recovering the bones of animals that had been slaugtered in the amphitheatre above.

Also, the sea-bed has been the repository for some of the world's most renowned works of art. From the waters off Tuscany, Italy, came one of the finest treasures in the Louvre: the Piombino Boy. From Cape Artemisium in Greece came the famous Zeus, or Poseidon, with arms outstretched in the act of throwing a thunderbolt or trident. From the Bay of Marathon, also in Greece, came the famous Marathon Boy. In more recent years the world was riveted by the spectacular discovery of the famous Bronzes of Riace, two large male nudes from shallow waters off Calabria - in a few short years more ink has been spilt on these latter pieces than on any similar work of art. In the normal run of events such sublime creations do not survive - bronzes like those of Riace make excellent gun metal, and marbles, such as those from the famous Antikythera and Mahdia wrecks which have filled rooms in the National Museum of Athens, and the Bardo in Tunis, make high grade lime which is ideal for construction work. But on the sea-bed such works survive because, until recent times they have been safe from man.

Such isolated discoveries do not have to be grand and glamorous and hail from the Classical era to have archaeological significance. Weighty books have been written on isolated archaeological finds of a more mundane nature that have come from single rivers. The Tiber, Rhine, Rhône and Danube have been particularly rich in finds, but to illustrate my point, let me stay closer to home: the Thames.

The range of finds from the Thames covers everything from weaponry, tools, household implements and trinkets to ships themselves. From the pre-Roman and Roman periods, for instance, have come a remarkable series of swords, daggers, axeheads and spearheads. Most famous of all is a First Century BC shield found off Battersea and now housed in the British Museum. The reasons for these items being there are just as varied; ritual deposition, battles, fire, accidental loss, shipping casualties and so forth. However, the majority of these objects were deliberately discarded for, until more ecologically conscious times, the Thames was

MARE diver with amphora coming up from a Roman wreck in the Aeolian Islands.

seen and used by many as a communal rubbish dump. For early Thames-side residents in particular, the favoured refuse tip, if not the nearest window, was certainly the river. When one looks at the finds from the Thames one is struck by their excellent state of preservation, which brings me to my next point: water, sand and silts can be wonderful preserves, and deep, cold water with a soft bottom is best of all. The cold retards the processes of natural deterioration, and deep silts and sands are fundamentally oxygen free, the latter being the principle ingredient that agents of both micro and macro biological decay need to survive.

Nowhere is the preservative capability of water and mud better illustrated than in lake archaeology, an activity in which many hundreds of amateur divers are involved throughout Europe. These are sites which because of land subsidence, rising water levels, or both, have been submerged. Large numbers of such sites are known, and many have been investigated by divers; for instance, one site on Lake Neuchâtel covering 7,200 square metres, has been completely excavated, and even larger excavations are currently in progress. In terms of our origins and the understanding of human behaviour, such sites can be far more informative than wrecks or habitation sites of similar period on land.

In its fundamentals, archaeology is the scientific recovery and study of artefacts that have been abandoned, lost or discarded by succeeding generations of man in his long climb to the present era. As a rule, on an ambient, or dry-land site, these artefacts represent only a tiny fraction of man's myriad activities, and give but a small insight into the general working of society, the way of life and the manner in which all this effected the environment. Mechanical erosion, chemical degradation and the agents of biological decay, usually ensure the absence of textiles, wood and food remains. Thus it is that, on land, we have been left with an extremely deficient, or worse still, deceptive document on which to base our conclusions.

During my journeyman days on land I spent months scraping dirt in search of fugitive patches of discoloured soil that might, or might not, have been post holes. Divining from these the layout of individual buildings and enclosures, and isolating them from adjacent and overlapping patterns of construction, or reconstruction, and then synchronizing them all, one to the other and group to group, was enough to defeat even the most experienced practitioner. Underwater, however, at such submerged habitation sites as Fiave in Italy, or some of the sites in Lake Zurich or Neuchâtel in Switzerland, the architectural components

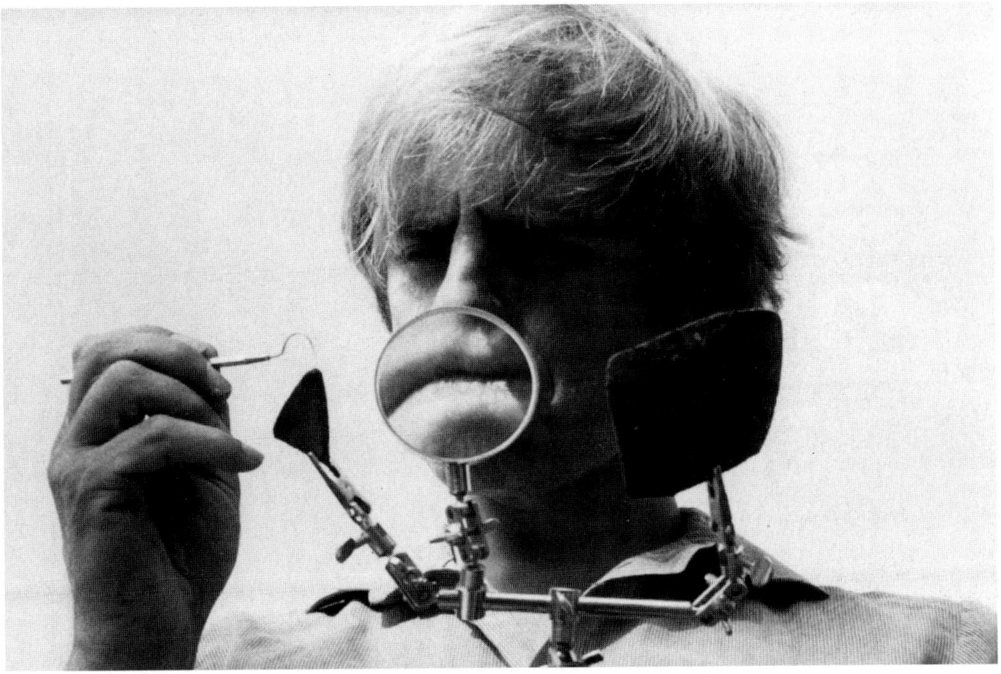

The author, examining pottery fragments from a wreck. Picture: M. Gotlieb, Oxford Univ. MARE.

themselves (posts, joists, beams and planks) still survive in excellent states of preservation, while clustered around them are numerous, equally well preserved, tools and implements. Thanks to dendrochronology, sorting them out and placing them in time and space can be a relatively straight forward procedure; if indeed enough sapwood survives, the very season (as well as the year) in which the tree was felled can be determined.

In addition to preserving artefacts, the sediments also retain a record of climatic alterations and water level changes, as well as a profile of the evolutionary trends in neighbouring vegetation. With the careful application of science this valuable information can be coaxed forth.

Most of the plant remains on a typical submerged freshwater site are of anthropogenic origin and when identified help build up a picture of vegetation in the near and more distant vicinity. More particularly, they give valuable information on man's eating habits and food gathering activities, as well as his ability to exploit (and thus transform) the natural environment. Insights can also be gleaned on food management. Fruits and berries of a highly perishable nature would have been consumed shortly after picking, whereas certain other fruits and nuts (hazelnuts, acorns, walnuts, beech-nuts and wild apples, etc) would have been storable, and thus would certainly have been a key factor in the survival of a settlement during the barren months.

If there was crop cultivation then evidence of this will also survive in the sediments. Wheat, barley and emmer are found on most submerged European sites from Neolithic

Working with amphora from a site off Marsala, Sicily.

times onwards, and sometimes evidence of secondary crop cultivation (e.g. flax, peas) has been found. Chaff is an extremely common find on most submerged prehistoric sites, proof that cereal processing (the removal of the grains from their glumes and rachides) was taking place within the community. The remains of weed flora sometimes point to the season in which the crops were sewn or harvested. Charred strata alternating with strata rich in cereal pollens can be taken to indicate the practices of slash-and-burn agriculture. Timber chippings, hearth fuel remains, wooden artifacts and the structural remains themselves, give further evidence of the community's links with, and exploitation of the forest, its understanding of the mechanical and physical properties of the various species, and its technological capability to fashion timber into those forms necessary to serve its purpose. Objects recovered during Alpine lake excavations have shown that a hard wood, like box, was frequently used for pins, combs and other such delicate utensils; a flexible wood, like yew, was more often than not, used for bows; a hard shock-resistant wood such as ash or maple was usually employed for axe handles, while the flexibility of lime fibres made them ideal for basketry and ropework.

Analyses of the timber species used in hut construction can be most helpful in unravelling a complicated submerged settlement. The drowned neolithic site at Charavines 'Les Baigneurs' beneath Lake Paladru in France was particularly interesting. This was a habitation area which, according to dendrochronological determinations supported by stratigraphic evidence, had experienced two occupational phases with a 30-40 year gap separating them. During the first phase the great majority of the posts were of silver fir, but, during the second phase, ash, alder and elm were the main trees to be employed. Presumably the forest which had been opened to light during the first phase, had replenished itself during the interim with a different balance of the species.

Pollen analyses is also a critical factor in our understanding and interpretation of submerged freshwater sites. This is perhaps best illustrated by pursuing the example of Charavines 'Les Baigneurs'. Here, the pre-occupation levels gave tree pollen levels of 95 per cent, which dropped to 65 per cent during the occupational phase, reflecting the community's deforestation of its surroundings. The extensive use of fir noted above in the construction work of phase one, was reflected by a drop in the pollen level of the species to a meagre five per cent. During the second phase there was a significant drop in elm pollen, which again reflects its use in huts and other structures. A dramatic drop in beech pollen was more puzzling, as there was relatively little evidence for worked beech during this phase; the inference to be drawn is that beech was the favoured fuel of their fires.

Other scientific studies from this site gave the positions of the threshing areas, as well as important insights on animal husbandry, winter foddering, deforestation, grassland growth and the cultivation of open land. Regarding the latter, it was observed that garlic pollens were only found during the occupational phases, from which it can be deduced that garlic at this site was a cultivated plant.

The study of insect remains, excreta (both human and animal), bones and residues from cooking pots, as well as the study of artefacts themselves (weapons, tools, implements, fishing equipment, etc) gives a full and rounded picture, the like of which is rarely obtainable on terrestrial sites. In fact, when I think about it in these terms, I am perplexed as to why it is that our colleagues on land are being so slow to recognise the importance of underwater archaeology. Are they perhaps being just a touch disingenuous? Would it be churlish of me to suspect that they are perhaps the tiniest bit jealous? If so, who could blame them?

Further Reading

Throckmorton P., ed, 1987, History from the Sea; Shipwrecks and Archaeology, London.

Muckelroy, K., (ed), 1980, Archaeology. Underwater, An Atlas of the World's Submerged Sites, London.

Green, J., 1990, Maritime Archaeology, A technical handbook, Academic Press, London.

McGrail, S., 1987, Ancient Boats in North West Europe, Longman Group, U.K.

Dean, M., et alii (eds)., 1992, Archaeology Underwater; The NAS Guide to Principles and Practices, NAS and Archetype Publications, London.

Academic Journals

The International Journal of Nautical Archaeology, Academic Press; 24-28 Oval Rd, London NW1.

The Oxford Maritime Archaeology Series Nelson Ltd., P.O. Box 9, Oswestry, Shropshire SY11 1BY

Volume 1 (in press) The Archaeology of Ships of War

Volume 2 Medieval Ship Archaeology

Societies

The Nautical Archaeology Society. Membership includes a quarterly newsletter. The NAS also publishes The International Journal of Nautical Archaeology. NAS Membership Secretary: 206 Moorview Way, Skipton, North Yorkshire, BD23 2TN.

The Society for Nautical Research. Membership includes a quarterly newsletter and The Mariner's Mirror. SNR Membership Secretary, 5 Goodwood Close, Midhurst, Sussex GU29 9JG.

Training

The NAS runs weekend training courses in maritime archaeology. For information write: The NAS Training Officer, 19 College Rd, HM Naval Base, Portsmouth P01 3LJ.

Academic Study

A three year undergraduate degree programme in maritime archaeology is available at the University of Wales at Bangor. Study for a graduate degree in maritime archaeology is available at the University of St Andrews. Post-graduate study in maritime archaeology can be conducted at St Andrews and the University of Oxford. Enquiries should be addressed to the Admissions Office of the individual universities.

Maritime archaeological organizations that can provide consultancy services, or general advice and evaluations on sites or isolated finds include:

National Maritime Museum, Greenwich, London SE10 9NF.

Archaeological Diving Unit, St Andrews University, St Andrews, Fife (a government sponsored unit whose broad duty it is to monitor and report on 'licensed' sites to the appropriate government agency).

* Oxford University MARE, 4 Butts Rd, Horspath, Oxford OX33 1RH.

* Maritime Archaeological Group, Department of History and Maritime Archaeology, University of Wales at Bangor.

* Scottish Institute of Maritime Studies, University of St Andrews, St Andrews, Fife.

* Scottish Trust for Underwater, Archaeology, University of Edinburgh, Department of Archaeology, 16-20 George Square, Edinburgh.

The Mary Rose Trust, HM Naval Base, Portsmouth, Hants P01 3LX.

For Hampshire and Isle of Wight:

Hampshire and Wight Trust for Maritime Archaeology, University of Southampton, University Rd, Southampton, S09 5NH.

Those prefixed with an asterisk also have active field units specializing in excavation. N.B. Oxford University MARE is the only organization that, in addition to work in Britain, also specializes in work overseas.

Conferences

Oxford University MARE (usually in collaboration with Bangor University or the Nautical Archaeology Society), regularly holds international conferences on maritime archaeology. These are all open to the public and divers in particular are encouraged to attend. These conferences provide an excellent opportunity for divers to meet the archaeologists, find out what is happening and become involved. The next major conference is a four day international event on Freshwater Archaeology (i.e. Lakes and Rivers) and will be held at (and in collaboration with) Bangor University from 1 to July 4 1994. Other conferences in preparation include The Maritime Archaeology of Great Britain and the British Dependent Territories, The Archaeology of the Ancient Mediterranean, and Hulk Archaeology. For ticket information write, with two self-addressed stamped envelopes, to Oxford University MARE, 4 Butts Rd, Horspath, Oxford OX33 1RH. Information on other maritime history and archaeology conferences can be found in the newsletters of the NAS and SNR.

The NAS

by The Nautical Archaeological Society

We are fortunate in Britain that there has been a long tradition of amateur involvement in archaeological projects on land and this has continued in the last 20 years with their counterparts underwater. Most of the excavation on the well-known 'Mary Rose Project' was carried out by sport divers and the majority of underwater archaeological sites investigated in Britain to date have been discovered by amateur divers.

At present there is little funding available for excavations underwater but it is still important that we find out how much of our seafaring heritage remains preserved around our coasts. Search and survey programmes will form a vital part of this work and the Nautical Archaeology Society intends to co-ordinate a number of programmes through its membership. One initiative, started in 1993, is to help the Royal Commission on the Historic Monuments to create a record of our underwater heritage. Forms have been produced for recording details of sites seen by divers underwater and, by filling these in, any diver can help add to our knowledge of wrecks that have survived.

The Society also works with local organisations such as The Hampshire and Wight Trust for Maritime Archaeology, by assisting with their sea bed surveys and excavations. Divers who have enroled on the NAS Training Scheme, but do not have a project of their own, can thus practice their newly acquired skills.

How to learn more about maritime archaeology

Since 1985, The Nautical Archaeology Society has been running a training scheme for all those who would like to know more about subject. By the autumn of 1993, over 1200 divers had attended the introductory course that forms Part I of the scheme and many had continued to the higher levels. The scheme consists of Parts I to IV, a series of components at progressively advancing levels, all with a strong emphasis on practical work.

Part I is a two-day course, normally a weekend, entitled 'An Introduction to Archaeology Underwater'. It is a broad based introduction to the subject involving practical demonstrations and exercises as well as lectures introducing the theory and principles of archaeology. An important part of the course is the pool work where divers try out the surveying and recording techniques they have been shown. They often find it is harder to do underwater than they expect!

Part II builds on the theory, techniques and knowledge introduced in Part I, by more detailed lectures or demonstrations and a mandatory two days of conferences. The final and most important aspect of Part II is a project that the participants carry out and write up by themselves, although the staff and tutors from NAS Training can give advice and guidance where necessary. The project will often be a survey, but a wide range of alternatives within the scope of nautical archaeology are acceptable for consideration as Part II projects. Non-divers can participate by choosing a related nautical topic which is not based underwater.

Part III can either take the form of a full time field-school or of a series of modules on individual topics such as: Remote sensing; Site survey; Photography for Underwater Archaeology; Archaeological Science; Artefact Drawing etc. The main objective of the Part III course is to help develop a competent fieldworker who would be an asset to any project.

Part IV is the final element and provides a high level of certification for those who may not have studied archaeology at university but would like to supervise work on an archaeological site in conjunction with an archaeological director or advisor. This component requires experience on a number of archaeological sites and the completion of a dissertation, including a site report prepared to publication standard.

The NAS has also published a comprehensive Handbook on the subject entitled "Archaeology Underwater - The NAS Guide to Principles and Practice". It contains a wealth of information in 336 pages with 146 illustrations and covers topics from search and survey to excavation and recording. Other chapters outline the basic principles of archaeology, project planning and post-fieldwork recording, analysis and publication. It is the standard textbook for the NAS certification scheme.

How to become involved

An ideal starting point is to join the Nautical Archaeology Society. As a member, you will receive the "Newsletter", which gives details of all the training courses the Society organises, as well as details of conferences, lectures, projects, meetings and events. With

Surveying lead ingots on a scattered wreck site.
Picture: C. Dobbs

its wide international membership, the Society acts as a focal point for archaeologists and divers and aims to cater for all levels of interest or involvement. Keen members can also subscribe to the "International Journal of Nautical Archaeology" at a reduced rate. This publication is a quarterly journal with articles, papers and site reports, covering the whole range of the subject. Members can also buy the Handbook, discussed above, at a discount price.

For details of both NAS courses and membership, write to the NAS at the addresses listed at the back of this section.

Diving Expeditions

by Raleigh International

Raleigh International is a youth development charity which organises a series of conservation and community projects in the UK and around the world.

Over 1,000 young people aged 17 to 25, take part in ten week expeditions to countries such as Chile, Guyana, Malaysia, Mauritius and Zimbabwe every year. Diving projects are an integral part of many of the expeditions and they provide one of the most exciting challenges available to participants.

In Mauritius, teams of young people are currently carrying out seabed surveys. They are learning to identify the different corals and fishes, setting up transects and quadracts and making accurate recordings of the data, which will be used to measure future changes.

In the past, other Raleigh International diving projects have included: the eradication of the Crown of Thorns starfish, assessing the damage to corals from fish bombings, archaeological surveys on wrecks, collection of sponges to be used in cancer research and surveys into the health of the giant clam population.

Safety is of paramount importance on all expeditions. Project sites are supervised by professional and skilled staff and diving instructors must possess an instructor's qualification. They also need additional skills, such as the ability to maintain equipment including outboards, compressors and generators because sites are often in remote and inaccessible areas.

The participants must have a qualification equating to BSAC Novice Diver (any CMAS equivalent qualification is acceptable) with open water dives if they want to take part in the diving projects. All diving takes place under BSAC rules and recommendations and the young novices receive further training on the expedition and usually qualify as basic sports divers.

Raleigh International in Malaysia. Jacky Chapman © Raleigh International

Depending on the nature of the diving projects, a dive site usually consists of 16 to 20 young people, plus 12 staff. On some expeditions there are two dive sites, so obviously the equipment needed to sustain such numbers is substantial. Over three

SPECIAL INTEREST

months it will be subjected to the wear and tear equivalent to two or three years club diving. Any major malfunction will frustrate the work of the project. This puts tremendous pressures upon the staff members who have to maintain it.

As well as the more obvious living accommodation, each camp needs areas for compressing, equipment storage, outboard maintenance, fuel storages, water stores and boat moorings. Local supply lines need to be established for water, fuel and food.

Occasionally there are special requirements such as during the recent expedition to Malaysia, where the activities of pirates necessitated working closely with the local police.

After the camp is established (two or three days hard work) diving activities commence. This means initially completing the open water part of the novice divers training. But the concept of training an expedition is far more comprehensive than this. A further task for staff members is to help the young people acquire competence in a broad range of diving associated skills.

Whenever practicable, participants can expect to progress a stage further in diving qualifications. Moreover, each will be trained to be competent in compressor operating, boat handling, dive marshalling and dive planning.

Those who wish to will also learn about dive equipment, compressors, outboard and boat maintenance.

All this is in addition to acquiring the skills necessary to carry out the projects - remember, the diving is only the means by which the projects can be completed.

After the meal the days activities have to be de-briefed, some of the equipment repaired, dive logs updated, the scientific observations written up. During the day and in the evening there will be training lectures.

Living conditions on the diving sites are basic and the work hard, so it's no wonder that many find the other phases of their expedition much easier by comparison. They often find that building a bridge or a school is an easy option after the rigours of a Raleigh diving project.

So are all the physical and mental rigours worth it? How could you, the diver benefit from of a Raleigh International expedition? Well! If you join a Raleigh International expedition to a remote part of the world, you will learn to understand local people, their customs and the problems of every day life.

You will be part of a small, but self reliant team living in difficult conditions (no fresh water for washing, unless it rains). You will have the satisfaction of learning about yourself, as well as undertaking a series of worthwhile projects.

In addition you will learn more about all aspects of diving in a very short period of time under very intensive conditions. But a word of warning - because you can dive competently in tropical waters, don't believe you can tackle the north sea, it is very different!

As well as diving skills you will learn other underwater skills. Identifying corals, or fishes, recording data accurately and occasionally some underwater archaeology; make no mistake, many club divers spend years of diving without acquiring these skills, so you really will be privileged.

Into the blue

by Mark Stevens

Mark Stevens is one of the national organisers for British Divers Marine Life Rescue He has worked for the charity since the winter of 1988/89, is married with two children and is currently studying for a BEd (Hons) at the University of Greenwich. He is a member of Swale BSAC with 14 years diving experience, an Advanced Diver and Instructor and is the Training officer of his Branch.

When the North Sea's seal population was being decimated by the seal distemper virus of 1988/89, a diver from Corby, Ray Gravener, realised that all the existing rescue agencies such as the RSPCA were shore based. Ray felt that people needed to get out to the seal colonies and work on the problem from there.

Dive clubs were contacted and soon a small flotilla of RIBs were massed in the Wash. Animals were caught, treated and, when safe to do so, were released. Ray's reputation was such that he was made BSAC Diver of the Year and British Divers Marine Life Rescue was formed with two other directors: Mike Brett, from Lincoln and Alan Knight from Kent.

The organisation keeps a watching brief on the Wash and the seals living there. We are often called upon to release pups back in to the colonies by the RSPCA and other rehabilitation groups. We try to take interested people from outside the group on trips like this and feel it is especially important that children be made aware of such places.

Seal being released back into the wild at the Wash after rehabilitation by BDMLR volunteers. Picture: BDMLR

Volunteers with severed dolphin heads - evidence which led to the prosecution of Faroese fishermen. Picture: BDMLR

In 1990 a team was despatched to the Faroe islands to investigate the slaughter of pilot whales and dolphins. It is estimated that over 1,500 are killed per year. The team went there with an open mind - after all, if this was subsistence hunting then who were they to pass judgement? What they found was astounding: the Faroese have one of the highest standards of living in Europe.

The meat taken from the hunts is rarely eaten and a large amount of frozen whale meat is discarded either because nobody wants it or because there is no room in the freezer for fresh catches. While there the team heard of the killing of some 30 to 50 dolphins.

When this was investigated it was found to be true and, due to the nature of the kill, several locals were prosecuted and fined. This was the first time such a prosecution had been brought.

As the charity's fame spread we were called upon to perform other tasks. One, the *'Into The Blue'* project, was set up to fly three captive dolphins from Britain to the Turks and Caicos islands, rehabilitate them and return them to the wild.

British Divers Marine Life Rescue had the task of building transport crates for the animals, capturing the animals in the UK, supervising the shipment via Gatwick and preparing the centre in the Turks.

This was a very high profile project not so much from the point of view of the public, who knew little of BDMLR's involvement, but because the dolphinarium trade were watching events closely - they were, naturally, opposed to the whole project.

Thankfully *Into The Blue's* success is well documented. It resulted in a documentary about the work being televised by the BBC, who reported massive public response and requests for it to be repeated.

BDMLR has no paid employees - many people find it more satisfying to raise money for an organisation which, after covering administration costs, uses it's resources solely to fund projects.

A great deal of money was required when a call for help was received from the Turkish government who found themselves with a international incident on their hands. The problem became known as 'Brightness', a Beluga whale that had escaped from the Russians and had taken up residence of the coast of northern Turkey.

British Divers Marine Life Rescue arranged for a vet to treat the animal and for a feeding programme to be set up. Fortunately he had become such a media star that much of the project's funding came from TV companies who wanted to film him.

Despite preventative efforts he was eventually returned to the Russians. Negotiations involving several trips to the Kremlin were started to secure the whale's release. But by the time an agreement had been reached, he had taken the matter into his own hands and escaped again. Brightness returned to Sinop and, when last heard of, was happy with his adopted town where he is considered a national treasure.

More recently we have had to deal with problems associated with the opening of Dolphinariums in some of the poorer countries in Europe.

These countries see the large profits made by places like Sea World and try to copy the idea in their search for hard currency.

Into the Blue final vet checks prior to release. Picture: BDMLR

Ray Gravener with Brightness. Picture: BDMLR

Unfortunately they have neither the resources nor the experience to undertake such projects and inevitably the dolphins suffer. We find ourselves being called in to stabilise animals while we talk to the countries about the cruelty of the proposed dolphinarium. Some may see this as supporting the dolphin trade. Unfortunately, in many cases the animals are in immediate danger. It is only sensible to keep the animals alive whilst trying to negotiate their release.

The moral: Do not visit dolphinariums. If they don't pay they will close, which is the best option for both dolphin and man. People who wish to see dolphins can see them in the wild. Cardigan Bay has one of the largest groups of Bottle Nosed Dolphins in the UK. Of course there is also Fungi, a hermit dolphin that lives in Dingle Bay, County Kerry, so why not pay them a visit? Boat trips are arranged to watch these animals in their natural environment.

Those of you who prefer a touch of the sun with your whale can find a large resident pod of Long Finned Pilot Whales only too willing to pose for the cameras in Tennerife. Again, boat trips are available. One tip though: if you try to swim with them use a snorkel as the exhaust from a DV frightens them.

One current project is the monitoring of the use of drift nets. These can kill diving birds, seals and dolphins. There is no law against them and it is only a matter of time before a diver is drowned in one, so if you see them being used please report your sighting to us or the RSPB, our partners in the project. We are a UK registered charity No. 803438 and also run a 24-hour emergency line on (0634) 281680.

BRITISH DIVERS
MARINE LIFE RESCUE

Commercial Diving

by Peter Bernardes

So you would like to turn a hobby into a profession. How do you begin? It would be wise to consider initially that, whereas sports diving is an end in itself, commercial diving is a means to an end - in other words, commercial diving is a job of work in an underwater environment.

In the pressures and strictures of our industrial world the would be diver will ideally possess those skills that the profession demands, for example; civil engineering, construction, drilling, explosives, inspection or photography. He must then learn how to adapt these skills in order that they might be employed underwater.

So, as a professional on dry land, what is to stop you simply jumping into the water and starting work?

Well, there is the law for a start or more specifically, the Diving Operations at Work Regulations 1981, which state that anyone working for payment in UK waters or from a UK registered vessel worldwide, must hold a recognised Commercial Diving Certificate as approved by the Health and Safety Executive (HSE).

However, those who have little or no experience in the above areas need not despair as many of the skills required in the fields of commercial diving are taught as part of the courses leading to an HSE approved qualification.

There are four main grades of HSE certificate. They are:

- **Professional Scuba Diver - HSE part 4**
- **Inshore Air Diver - HSE part 3**
- **Offshore Air Diver - HSE part 1**
- **Mixed Gas Diver - HSE part 2**

These then are the four "tickets" to commercial diving - your passport to the professionals.

Which is the right qualification for you? It all depends on the nature of the work that you wish to undertake. The HSE 4, for example, is the ideal choice for the photographer, scientist, marine biologist, fishery technologist or paid instructor (should you wish to set up your own diving school). Typically, this course lasts for four weeks and includes examinations on practice and theory as well as continuous assessment. In other words, you must demonstrate that you can sustain the disciplined approach to your diving that is necessary in a working environment.

The next step up the ladder is the HSE 3. This course, incorporating some of the work undertaken in part four, also introduces the diver to surface air supply systems. You will learn to use and maintain the umbilicals and masks, compressors and communications systems as well as a range of tools including welding, cutting and lifting equipment that are necessary to work effectively underwater.

This qualification enables a diver to apply to those firms working in the inshore diving fields. These include water boards, fish farms, harbour authorities and civil engineering firms.

For divers wishing to work in the oil industry, either in the North Sea or anywhere in the world, the HSE 1 is the minimum qualification required. This is not a course for the faint hearted. It generally lasts for ten weeks and aims to teach many of the skills that trainees could be called upon to use in the commercial world. In addition to those tools introduced on the HSE 3 course you will become familiar with more appliances, bell diving, surface decompression and explosives.

All of these courses involve a substantial amount of theory covering the laws of physics, diving diseases, first aid, decompression tables and the theory of tools. Students will also be expected to understand the workings and safety procedures associated with all of the equipment that they use.

One of the most essential prerequisites of success in any of the HSE courses is the ability to work well within a team. The safety of the diver on the bottom depends to a large degree on the competence of those at the surface. The diver, often working alone in zero visibility and at great depth, has to trust the people giving instructions and controlling the dive. All students, when not diving, take turns in helping to kit-up other divers, checking equipment and operating the communication systems. A standby diver system is also in operation and, during training, the group's responses can be tested in simulated emergencies - good training but a little nerve wracking at the time!

So what type of person makes a good commercial diver? Superman springs readily to mind. Ideally you will not be afraid of hard work. Forget the glamour; diving can often be physically exhausting work in filthy conditions and freezing water which carries an element of risk (life insurance premiums are not cheap). You should be able to remain calm and think quickly; a sense of humour/ is an advantage as is an even temper. Some of your jobs will be as boring and repetitive as those more usually associated with a factory production line but without the teabreaks.

Still interested? Now you need to get yourself an HSE "ticket". The first step is to apply to one of the numerous commercial training schools in the UK. The school must be registered with the HSE and be regularly inspected to ensure that the level of training is up to the required standard and that safety measures are stringent. This training is not cheap. Typically, a Part 4 course will cost around £1000, a Part 3 £1800 and a Part 1 will not leave you with much change from £5000. Some schools operate an aptitude course where basic standards of English and Mathematics are assessed together with physical fitness and water confidence. English? I hear you ask. Well there are all of those theory examinations to sit and employers will expect written survey reports on underwater structures etc. Physical fitness is also assessed in a fairly stringent medical for which there is also a fee.

The HSE qualifications can be gained progressively. If you already hold a Part 4 qualification then a Part 3 can be obtained in only two weeks and a part one takes less time depending on the experience that you have acquired since completing Part 3.

Having gained your qualification you will now be looking for work. Unfortunately, the recession has effected job prospects in the diving industry just as it has elsewhere. As I explained earlier, if you already possess the right professional qualification the prospects of finding work are very much higher. The supply of basic underwater divers more than meets demand. However, if you are prepared to travel anywhere at a moments notice and persist in following up existing job opportunities the chances are there. With a little experience under your belt it is easier to get other jobs and build up your expertise. For those experienced and dedicated divers (members of the masochists club) there is then the opportunity to take up Saturation Diving training. The remuneration here is, or at least can be, very good. Remember, there is a limited amount of time that a diver can physically work under saturated conditions and he is therefore rewarded accordingly.

This then is the hitch-hiker's guide to becoming a commercial diver - to entering a universe that encompasses everything from photographing models in the Red Sea to living for weeks at a time in a pressure chamber with several other hairy divers; from checking a sewage outfall off the British coast to welding a fixture onto an oil rig platform; from monitoring the effects of pollution on whelks to inspecting the foundations of a bridge.

It is a rich and varied profession and is open only to those men and women determined enough to train hard, work hard, and reap the rewards.

Special Interest Organisations

PHOTOGRAPHIC

THE BRITISH SOCIETY OF UNDERWATER PHOTOGRAPHERS (BSOUP)
12 CONINGSBY ROAD
SOUTH CROYDON
SURREY CR2 6QP
081 6688168
FAX: 081 6688168

TECHNICAL

AMERICAN NITROX DIVERS INC (ANDI)
74 WOODCLEFT AVENUE
FREEPORT
NY 11520 USA
010 1 516 5462026
FAX: 010 1 516 5466010

AMERICAN NITROX DIVERS INC (ANDI) & AQUACORPS
PO BOX 498
LONDON,
081 7890961
FAX: 081 7802018

CAVE DIVING GROUP OF GREAT BRITAIN
ELM COTTAGE
PEAK FOREST, BUXTON
DERBYSHIRE SK17 8EN

INTERNATIONAL ASS. OF NITROX & TECHNICAL DIVERS (IANTD)
1545 NE 104 STREET
MIAMI SHORES
FL 33138 USA
010 1 305 7514873
FAX: 010 1 305 7514873

INTERNATIONAL ASSOC. OF NITROX AND TECHNICAL DIVERS (IANTD)
NEIGHBOURNE COTTAGE
NEIGHBOURNE
OAK HILL
SOMERSET BA3 5BQ
0749 840685
FAX: 0749 840685

NATIONAL ASSOCIATION OF CAVE DIVERS (NACD)
PO BOX 14492
GAINESVILLE
FL 32604 USA
010 1 904 8778196
FAX: 010 1 904 8779782

ARCHAEOLOGICAL

COMMITTEE OF HISTORIC WRECKS
MARINE DIRECTORATE
DEPARTMENT OF TRANSPORT
SPRING PLACE
105 COMMERCIAL ROAD
SOUTHAMPTON
HAMPSHIRE SO1 0ZD
0703 329100 FAX: 0703 322247

MARITIME ARCHAEOLOGICAL RESEARCH & EXCAVATION (MARE)
4 BUTTS ROAD
HORSPATH, OXFORD
OXON OX33 1RH
0865 872896 FAX: 0865 872896

NAUTICAL ARCHAEOLOGY SOCIETY (NAS)
NAS MEMBERSHIP SECRETARY
206 MOORVIEW
SKIPTON
NORTH YORKSHIRE BD23 2TN

NAUTICAL ARCHAEOLOGY SOCIETY (NAS)
NAS TRAINING
19 COLLEGE ROAD, HM NAVAL BASE
PORTSMOUTH, HANTS PO1 3LJY
0705 818419 FAX: 0705 818419

CONSERVATION

BRITISH DIVERS MARINE LIFE RESCUE (BDMLR)
MILL COTTAGE
WINDMILL HILL
BRENCHLEY, KENT TN12 7NR
0634 281680
FAX: 0634 281680

FRIENDS OF THE EARTH
26-28 UNDERWOOD STREET
LONDON N1 7JQ
071 4900881

GREENPEACE
CANONBURY VILLAS
LONDON N1 2PN
071 3545100 FAX: 071 6960012

MARINE CONSERVATION SOCIETY (MCS)
9 GLOUCESTER ROAD
ROSS ON WYE
HEREFORDSHIRE HR9 5BU
0989 66017
FAX: 0989 67815

NATIONAL INSTITUTE OF MARINE
EDUCATION & SCIENCE
47 OAKFIELDS
BRAODACRES
GUILDFORD
SURREY GU3 3AS
0483 31597

EXPEDITIONS

RALEIGH INTERNATIONAL
RALEIGH HOUSE
27 PARSONS GREEN LANE
LONDON, LONDON SW6 4HZ
071 3718585 FAX: 071 3715116

RESEARCH

CARMELLAN RESEARCH LTD
11 HILLSIDE CLOSE
ELLINGTON, HUNTINGDON,
CAMBRIDGESHIRE PE18 0AR
0480 890946 FAX: 0480 890946

CRANFIELD INSTITUE OF TECHNOLOGY
MARINE TECHNOLOGY CENTRE
CRANFIELD, BEDFORD
BEDFORDSHIRE MK43 OAL
0234 750111 FAX: 0234 750875

FOUNDATION FOR SPORTS AND ARTS
PO BOX 20
LIVERPOOL, LIVERPOOL L9 6EA
051 5240235 FAX: 051 5240285

SOCIETY FOR UNDERWATER TECHNOLOGY
76 MARK LANE
LONDON, LONDON EC3R 7JN
071 4810750 FAX: 071 4814001

BOATING

BRITISH INFLATABLE BOAT OWNERS
ASSOCIATION (BIBOA)
HATTON HOUSE
LEVEN, FIFE KY8 5QD
0333 320218 FAX: 0333 320218

PROFESSIONAL BOATMANS ASSOCIATION
(PBA)
LEATFIELD
459A TAVISTOCK ROAD
ROBOROUGH, PLYMOUTH PL6 7HE
0752 773496

ROYAL YATCHING ASSOCIATION (RYA)
RYA HOUSE
ROMNEY ROAD, EASTLEIGH
HANTS SO5 4YA
0703 629962 FAX: 0703 629924

Training for special interest may be found on page 238

by B. Hugo

Jewel anemone - Corynactis viridis

Education and Training

The 90's diver

by Steve Warren

Scuba diving has recently become a very accessible activity. All around the world recreational divers in their millions are taking to the water in pursuit of adventure and relaxation with friends and family. Improved equipment and better training programmes mean that almost anyone who is reasonably confident in water, in good health and meets the minimum age for scuba training (usually 12 to 14) can enjoy all that recreational scuba diving has to offer.

The tremendous popularity of scuba diving is easy to understand. In exchange for a little investment of time (it can take from five days to earn initial certification) and a financial outlay that often pleasantly surprises newcomers to the sport, you may join the ranks of divers currently exploring the underwater world.

Tuition from a professional diving instructor often costs significantly less than coaching for sports such as tennis or snow skiing. Amateur clubs frequently provide training for a nominal fee or even for free.

A full kit of quality scuba equipment costs about the same as a set of golf clubs or a camcorder. A full tank of air can easily last an hour and costs about the same as a pint of beer while a days diving from the beach or at a local inland site will be cheaper than a visit to a zoo (or an aquarium). Even a full day aboard a dive charter boat including two or more dives can cost less than a day out on a coach.

Beginners usually discover early on in their training that learning to dive is fun and easy. The necessary theory is taught using an effective and stimulating mix of self study books, audiovisual and live action video together with instructor elaboration.

Diving skills are mastered as small progressive steps in strictly controlled conditions, usually a swimming pool in the UK, though overseas instruction may take place in calm shallow water. A series of carefully controlled dives in open water, during which the student completes basic exercises, lead to final certification as an entry level diver.

Scuba diving incorporates a multitude of underwater activities. Bonded by a love of being underwater, today's divers pursue the sport at many different levels of commitment, in a variety of environments with a number different personal goals. Diving is non-competitive; there are no winners or losers. Divers are participants who experience their sport, rather than spectators who merely watch others doing something they may never experience. When a football fan watches the world cup, he probably knows with absolute certainty that he will never play for England. When a diver watches a Ron and Valerie Taylor special on television he knows that he too can dive there and experience a similar adventure himself.

The 1990s are exciting times for diving. On one hand we see the sport attracting participants who dive solely in the warm, clear, shallow waters of their annual holiday resorts who only a few years ago would have found the long trudge through military derived training programmes a discouraging factor; on the other we find the emerging Technical diving movement which is extending the diving envelope with the use of mixed gas breathing systems and other advanced techniques to explore a realm that was previously beyond our reach. In the centre are the recreational divers for whom diving represents a major part in their lives and who dive within well established sport diving parameters.

Regardless of which activities you pursue you are an individual and belong to a corp of ordinary people who are regularly enjoying extraordinary experiences. You are a diver.

In the next few pages we will meet some of the people who have joined the sport....

Mike Keeping, 44, has been a diver for 12 years. A Chartered Surveyor by profession, Mike describes the attraction of diving as "a massive dose of escapism and probably the best sport I have ever done".

Although a civilian, Mike learned to dive through the Army Sub Aqua Association while based in Gibraltar. Now living in Lewes and a member of Sussex Diving Club he holds a BSAC Advanced Diver qualification and is considering moving up to instructor level.

He would like to put something back into diving and is particularly keen to help disabled people to dive. Listing his first dive and swimming with seals as being personal favourites he asserts: "Every dive normally has something good in it".

A passionate wreck diver he has made the pilgrimage to Europe's wreck capital, Scapa Flow in Scotland. "To dive in the Orkneys is to dive into history. The land of Churchill's barriers, the sad story of the Royal Oak, the sinking of the Hampshire which claimed Lord Kitchener's life. . . The era is summed up in my first dive on the scuttled German wreck of the Brummer. As I gently finned along the barrel of a massive gun I imagined it firing in anger".

Not surprisingly Mike's 15-year-old son, Max, shares his fathers enthusiasm. Already a BSAC Diveleader, he began scuba diving in 1991 after many years of snorkelling with his father. Diving the Inverclyde off Brighton was especially significant for Max; "My Dad had talked about the Inverclyde so much that in my life it became the legendary Inverclyde and just to dive it with my Dad was so satisfying that I felt I had made a dream come true".

Recently he returned to Gibraltar to dive and was thrilled to join Mike exploring the interior of the wreck of the SS Excellent. He plans to dive Scapa and hopes to become an instructor and occupy his year off from college teaching in the Med.

Last year's non-swimmer, 30-year-old *Michelle Fitzpatrick*, is this years' qualified BSAC Novice Diver II and is planning to move up to Sports Diver. She trained with Nautilus Diving in Corfu, has also dived Cancun and hopes to dive the Caymans. The Glasgow based telephonist wasn't particularly attracted to diving and became involved more for "the challenge and because my husband always did the 'exciting ' things".

"Diving has positively changed my life!" states Michelle.

"It has given me confidence and made me learn to swim".

On safety Michelle comments: "With so much emphasis on safety and safe diving I have never felt so comfortable in a potentially dangerous environment".

Jay Butler agrees. The former Diving Officer for Sussex University (the club saw an increase in membership of 61% during her term) says: "Diving is only dangerous if you are badly taught".

Jay started diving in 1990 and is now a BSAC Club instructor and a PADI Assistant Instructor - she is working towards BSAC Advanced Instructor and PADI Open Water Instructor as she loves teaching. Jay is also addicted to observing marine life. So far she has only dived in the UK, but would most like to dive in the Red Sea. Jay is 32 and a full time PhD student.

PADI Rescue Diver *David Fenton,* 28, started diving independently in 1989, before joining a BSAC club, gaining his Sport Diver and subsequently transferring to PADI. Currently he is training to become a PADI Divemaster with Aquatron and intends to progress to instructor level.

"I became interested in diving," explains the ICI fitter.

"After meeting a diver at an outward bound course. Wreck diving is my particular interest as each wreck is like a time capsule. It is fascinating to explore them , not knowing what you may come across. In some areas with heavy bottom dredging, which is becoming common, they provide a haven for marine life. Diving has given me more satisfaction than any other adventure activity I have tried.

"The public perceive diving as being expensive, difficult and dangerous. Like most other adventure sports diving is as expensive as you make it. By starting out with a combination of secondhand, rented and new gear and by diving locally, costs can be kept pretty low. Helped along by a good instructor diving is not beyond the capabilities of most people and concerning the aspect of danger I feel safer in the water than I do on most roads travelling to the dive site!".

David, a Scot, has dived extensively in his home waters including the Firth of Clyde, Mull, Eyemouth, Oban and, inevitably, Scapa Flow. He departs for Tenerife for his first taste of overseas diving shortly and would love to dive the legendary Japanese Fleet in Truk Lagoon , Micronesia.

He will not be pressed to nominate a 'best dive'. "They all have different attractions," he states firmly.

Celebrating her 50th birthday this year is Brighton-based *Margarett Stally*. She has been diving for just three years, having taken a PADI Open Water course on a whim on holiday in Kenya.

Already she has notched up dives as far afield as Spain, Canada, the Far East, Gozo, Malta, Ireland and the Red Sea in addition to diving extensively around Britain's south coast. She has been fortunate to dive with dolphins and orcas (killer whales) in the wild.

A PADI Master Scuba Diver Trainer, Margarett is a professional instructor with Black Rock Diving. She also holds a BSAC Advanced Diver qualification. Margarett is pursuing the higher PADI professional levels and would also like to become a DAN instructor. Her prime interest lies in teaching others to dive which she likes to break up with a little underwater photography.

Duncan Law is 22 and has been diving for four years. He is a member of Kingston University branch and is a BSAC Club Instructor. He is a floor manager for a London watersports store and is training through them to become a PADI Divemaster.

Duncan intends to achieve both BSAC Advanced Instructor and PADI Open Water Instructor certification "to further my own knowledge and ability because one should never stop learning and improving. If you learn to dive in a club it can be very cheap, although it can be a long process. Learning to dive is very easy and painless".

Although he hasn't yet dived abroad he has found quite enough to interest him in British waters, exploring wrecks and taking photographs. One of his best dives to date took place under 12cm of ice. "With my drysuit and excessive amounts of underclothing I was actually too hot. The visibility was very good, 15m or so and playing with my bubbles under the ice sheet was incredible".

Australian *Jodie Corica* is 23 and is on a working holiday in the UK. She took up diving in 1989, joining a PADI Open Water course in Perth, Western Australia. Two years later she completed the Advanced Open Water course in Egypt and this year flew to Florida to become a Rescue Diver. She has dived Hawaii, Indonesia and the Greek Islands. Shortlisted for her next dive trip are Kenya, Belize or Antigua.

"Lots of diving activities interest me; conservation, deep diving and in particular underwater photography - primarily because it gives you something to take back with you," says Jodie, who would like to become an instructor so that she can work in the diving industry as she heads around the world.

Insurance underwriter *Rob Aston* is 23 and lives in Glasgow. In 1990 he trained as a Novice Diver with Comdean in Birmingham and completed his BSAC Sports Diver in Malta with Maltaqua. He intends to pursue Diveleader and Lifesaving Awards. He is also planning to dive Gibraltar. Rob does not consider diving to be dangerous, that is "not unless you're an airhead".

In 1987, aged 16, *Julian Smith* learned to dive at the Diver Training School in Exmouth. Over a three week period he trained intensively and achieved BSAC Advanced Diver status. "The course was fun. Diving gave me a greater self confidence, a greater respect for water and the sea in general and a qualification that made me feel different from the average person in the street".

Joining Brighton Polytechnic SAA he achieved Club Instructor at 18. Looking for a greater purpose in his diving he tried a new angle.

"I booked onto a Part 4 Commercial Diving Course to become a professional scuba diver, at the Diver Training School. The course was fantastic. The people I learnt with came from all walks of life, some were welders, others were builders there was even a body builder".

"The theory was no problem but the practical side was very physically demanding and I had to grow up fast. I returned home a really different person. I really felt I had changed".

Julian has since returned to gain the Part 3 Inshore Commercial Diver Certificate. He is reading marine biology and oceanography at Bangor University, has participated in the Coral Cay Conservation project in Belize and is currently involved in a marine biology project in Southern Ireland. "Anyone wishing to take up diving either as a sport or a career should do so without delay. It is a great sport that has something to offer everyone. It is a sport where you are learning all the time, both about diving and yourself".

Jack Morrison is a veteran of 30 years of diving and is an accomplished underwater photographer. Based in Glasgow where he owns a hairdressers he bought his first mask from Woolworths aged eight.

"I was always fascinated by the sea and what was in it," he recalls.

"In those days Porpoise and Basking Shark were not uncommon on the Clyde. At about this time Cousteau's film 'The Silent World' was on at our local cinema. I went every night it was on. On TV Robert Beatty presented a live broadcast from Cousteau's first excavation of a Roman wreck in the South of France.

"A night dive in your living room on a saturday night; a bit better than Beadles About. But the programme that was definitely the biggest influence on me was 'Diving to Adventure' with Hans and Lotte Hass. They sailed their research ship Xarifa through the Red Sea and the Indian Ocean diving what were then remote islands called the Maldives then up to the Nicobar Islands and the Andamans finishing up in Sava".

"I still remember individual programmes about sharks, octopus, coral reefs and the gorgeous Lotte but I had to wait until 1961 when a diving club opened up in my area before I could become a diver".

Making his first dive in 1962 Jack became a Third Class Diver with the Scottish Sub Aqua Club the following year. He is now a Second Class Diver and also holds PADI Advanced certification which at the time was more widely recognised abroad. Jack is happy with his present qualifications though he is interested in courses that would further his knowledge of underwater photography and marine archaeology.

Jack is widely experienced in Scottish waters where he has explored all along the West Coast and the islands of Islay and Mull. He has visited Lanzarote and Gozo and the Red Sea where he has dived both the North and Southern Sinai including Eilat, Namibia, Ras Mohammed and the Straits of Tiran. The Red Sea is an area he plans to revisit.

"I'm asking around to find out when and where the best place for big fish and sharks is. I enjoy fish watching on coral reefs and trying to take photographs of them. All photography is just a record and I enjoy making a record of what I see".

On the issue of safety Jack explains: "The secret of safe diving is good training and it should be emphasised to newcomers not to do anything or go anywhere if they do not feel completely happy about it. It has been my experience that diving is not as dangerous as it sounds.

"Dangerous divers are experienced divers who think they can go anywhere (70m plus), anytime (in a howling gale) and survive. They can't. Most people know their limitations and never exceed them".

"After three decades and over 1500 dives Jack Morrison is well qualified to state: "Diving is still as exciting and exhilarating to me as it was on my first dive. It has more than met my expectations and still does".

"I have never felt any dive to be routine. They have all been an adventure and always will be".

Childs Play

by Adam Parkes

Adam Parkes certified as a PADI Junior Open Water Diver, aged 12, in 1988, through Cydive in Cyprus. He celebrated his 15th birthday by qualifying as an Advanced Open Water Diver through Black Rock Diving of Brighton. Adam has made over 100 dives in the UK, Cypriot and Maltese waters. His invention of a Dive Equipment Cleaning device won him a B for his GCSE CDT Technology Award. Adam is currently a student.

When the conversation moves onto `adventure' sports, one invariably creates an image of a 6ft tall bronzed Californian hurling himself off a bridge with no more than a piece of elastic and his wrap-around shades between himself and oblivion. Most sports in this realm such as surfing, sky diving and wind-surfing carry the glamorous Baywatch image, with one noticeable exception - SCUBA diving.

Unfortunately diving, if it does create an image at all, conjures up a middle-aged bloke in a rubber suit waddling around in a none too attractive way. This obviously does not do the industry any favours, unless you particularly like rubber suits that is.

The lack of media exposure that surrounds diving seriously undermines its image as an adventure sport, especially amongst the young (under 25's) who represent a huge potential market.

Amongst young people, diving tends to be seen as something for amateur marine biologists or for people with a serious rubber fetish. Either way it doesn't seem to carry the same instant appeal as yelling, "Cowabunga" while "shootin a tube" or attempting to OD on concrete by lobbing oneself out of a perfectly sound aircraft.

This seems a bit of a shame really because on closer inspection, by either trying it for yourself or by talking to someone who already has, diving does generate quite an interest. It does seem to be one of those activities which people say they've always wanted to try, but never got round to doing.

OK, so it may be fairly low on the list of priorities if you feel you have but a short time to live, but why wait that long? Why not start young? Or if you're not young, start now because, although classed as an adventure sport, diving can be taken at virtually any pace by virtually anyone.

That is the beauty of the sport. It doesn't have to be done at breakneck speed or threaten serious risk to life and limb.

Diving can be therapeutic - who can forget the British Gas advert with the toddler paddling through the crystal clear waters off a coral reef and many successful divers are quite severely disabled but have found a release through the sport which would be impossible anywhere else.

There are a number of reasons why so few young people are attracted to the sport - most of which can be easily overcome. The first is difficulty. Many people in the industry believe that very young people, ten to 12 years-old, are quite simply physically and mentally unable to competently carry out all that is necessary to safely engage in the sport.

This is, in a word - wrong. I learned to dive at the age of 12 in sunny Cyprus.

The only physical limitation is whether or not the child can carry the cylinder, and as everyone knows, children tend to learn far quicker than adults who are less flexible when it comes to understanding concepts of dive theory.

The next argument echoing from the ranks of the disbelievers is that "it's all very well learning to dive somewhere like Cyprus, but British diving is real diving".

This usually comes from the entry-level diver who has no ambition to advance his skills and who ventures out to Stoney Cove once a month, but not if it's raining. (No offence to Stoney Cove, I've spent many a good week-end there myself).

The other argument regarding the exclusion of young people from the sport is expense. This is a little more difficult to disregard.

Expense is a major limiting factor in diving irrespective of age and the problem is very much a catch-22. Diving is a very small industry; an aqualung is not exactly an item found in every home, but then again neither was the TV 40 years ago.

Manufacturers will only be able to reduce prices enough to encourage the mass market rather than the hardy enthusiast when the sport gains mass appeal. Perhaps not to the extent that no sooner have all the polystyrene bits been meticulously picked-up off the carpet than a better and cheaper TV is on the market, but there is certainly room for improvement.

The only problem is generating the initial interest to enable manufacturers to produce better, cheaper kit without commiting financial suicide.

So, who can be easily influenced into making diving popular and fashionable? Well, if the young can believe that flares are back in fashion then I don't think it would be too difficult to get them involved in a sport which has such a great deal to offer.

Obviously support for the young diver is essential. I was lucky enough to have a father with a friendly checkbook and a mother happy to drive me to Newhaven at some ridiculous hours of the morning or evening.

But that is not all a young diver needs. A young diver needs to be treated the same as the rest of his group, and should expect to find encouragement as well as acceptance, because the young are the best tool this industry has to become something other than an interesting sport and a pub conversation.

Many more 17 year-olds should be able to say that, like myself, they've dived the Azure window and the blue hole in Gozo, Stoney cove in Leicester, wrecks in Cyprus or Newhaven ferryport at night, to name but a few.

What is needed is open encouragement and enthusiasm for all new and potential divers, rather than the stagnation that is evident in this exciting and addictive activity.

Precision Buoyancy Control

by Peter Wallingford

Peter Wallingford was born in 1951 and gained his BS (Business Administration) from Jacksonville University in 1974. He attended the PADI College in 1977, The Ocean Corporation (Commercial Diving School) in 1983 and the National Oceanic and Atmospheric Administration (NOAA) Dive Accident Management program in 1984. Since 1977 his primary focus has been Dive Center (multi-store) retail management and diver education. Peter is president and Chief Executive Officer of Buoyancy Training Systems Inc. (0101 206 241 2634) of Seattle, Washington.

Scuba Diving is one of the world's fastest growing activities. We have an increasing responsibility as an industry and as participants of this wondrous activity to dive safely and preserve the environment in which we dive.

To accomplish this without instituting restrictions or severe regulations, that could have negative, economic repercussions in various countries, I have designed a fun, market based environmental education program to razzle dazzle the dive industry.

This comprehensive Mid-watermanship development program has been designed because scuba divers can have a deleterious impact on the underwater environment, and today's scuba training programs do not (uniformly) deal adequately with this problem.

Without continued improvement, the sport diving industry may have a long term negative affect, in particular, on coral reefs, archaeological sites and shipwrecks.

A brief history of the program.

One of the first questions we asked before embarking on this immense project four years ago was: "How can we objectively determine if we have adequately taught and/or learned the diving skills we need?".

With thousands of diving schools and clubs that provide diver training internationally, it has been difficult, to say the least, to sort through the infinitely varied subjective skill evaluations and student centred learning procedures in order to discover which skills should be mandatorily taught and to what lengths we must go to ensure diver proficiency.

I determined that BTSI's prime objective would be to create an objective measurement by which we (the entire industry) could uniformly judge overall buoyancy skills (the most important element of diver ability).

Having first determined what basic buoyancy skills a diver must demonstrate to be labelled proficient, I then designed a training program to more directly focus on proper skill development by utilising the same tools. The National Oceanic and Atmospheric

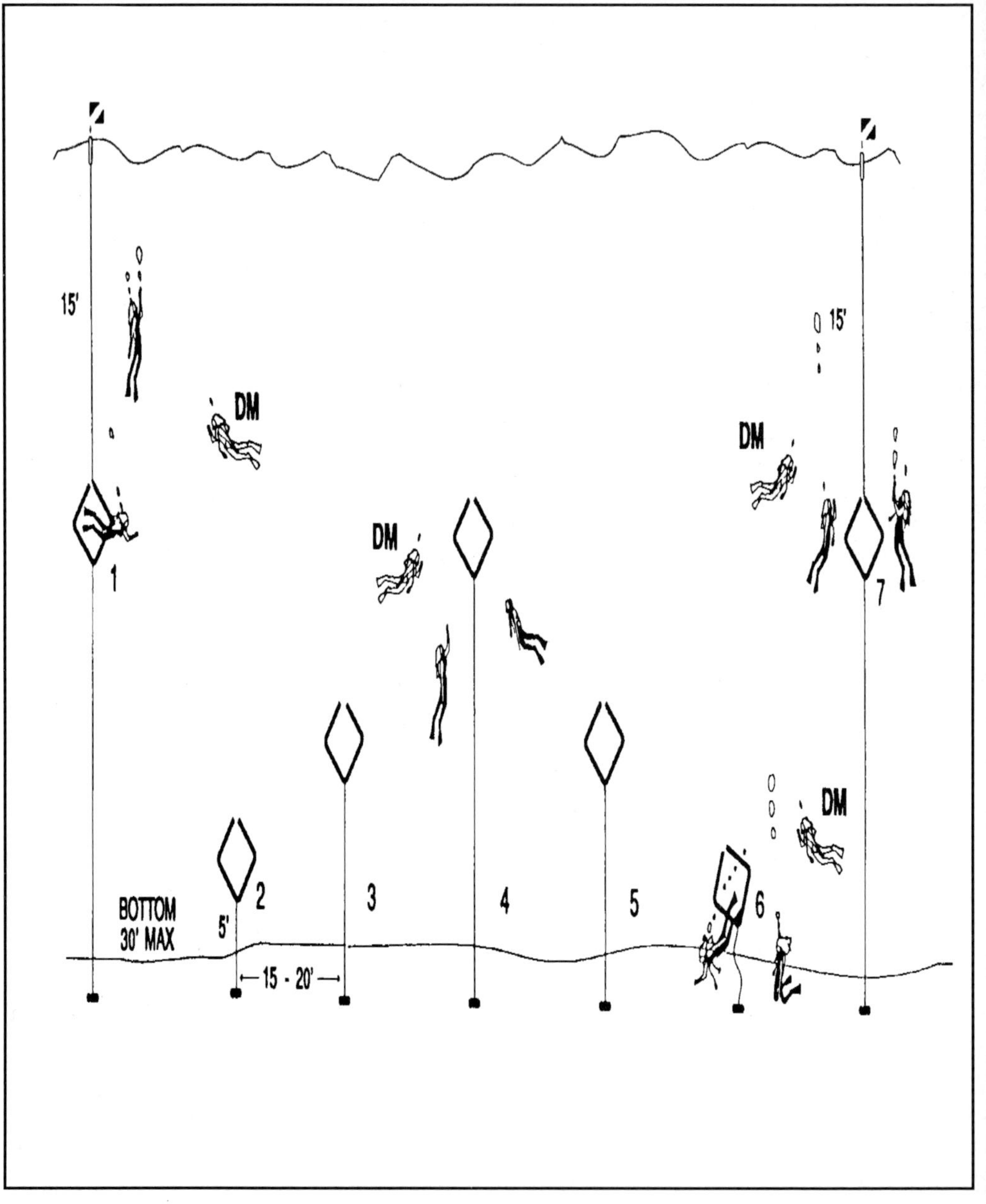

Figure 1: One of the many layouts that the Diamond Reef System offers. Each scientifically designed and sized Hover Station can be raised and lowered in the water column to simulate an infinite number of training sites in all dive training conditions (night or day). It has been proven that by making an acclimation dive on this artificial reef prior to diving sensitive and challenging dive sites that participants will have the opportunity to receive immediate tactile feedback as to their abilities which will enable them to make the necessary adjustments to remain safer and more environmentally conscientious.

Administration (NOAA), a branch of the US Government, was the first organisation to incorporate our training program. Since 1991 over 50,000 divers have experienced the Diamond Reef System in over 13 countries.

By additionally encouraging annual diver participation through tropical acclimation dives, fun events and competitions (The Diamond Reef Challenge) we have successfully transformed recertification and refresher courses into internationally respected and enjoyable programs. Making diver expertise more internationally "translatable", utilising an industry standard measuring device, will make that expertise a more visible goal that all divers can aim for.

An artificial reef to traln scuba divers

To address the above issues, the Diamond Reef System, a simulated artificial training reef was designed to give scuba divers, including underwater photographers, the opportunity to perfect their skills before diving around real reefs and challenging dive sites.

The development of the training system involved addressing three objectives; increasing diver awareness of how easily coral reefs can be damaged; teaching divers how to descend to a reef without touching the bottom and ascend safely to the surface; and augmenting the diver's confidence so that he/she does not need to make contact with the bottom to maintain control.

Improved buoyancy control is the basis for our objectives, and challenging divers to raise their proficiency with a fun test of skill provides the venue.

The modular training device and curriculum that makes up the patented Diamond Reef System embodies the ultimate in Mid-watermanship skill development with a comprehensive Non-destructive Manouvering Specialty program. This superior educational program is available to dive centres, clubs and instructors representing all certifying agencies worldwide.

During this combined training and practice program, divers are required to make their way through a series of buoyant obstacles tethered with line at different depths over a designated time frame.

The ultimate goal is to run the circuit course in slow motion without touching tile Diamonds and in so doing perfect hovering, breath control, simultaneous equipment handling techniques, proper weighting and buddy teamwork.

The Diamonds were specifically designed to offer immediate feedback to student and educator due to their innovative design. The design is such that upon contact both diver and educator are alerted through touch and sight to the error.

The brightly coloured line that links each Diamond to its anchor point and connects all anchor points together, provides a highly visible path for dive teams to follow.

Improved control over large groups in limited visibility and during night buoyancy training is an important feature of this program. As divers learn to hover for five seconds within each Diamond shaped frame, during instructor monitored practice sessions, they develop enhanced levels of somatosensory awareness.

This sixth sense is important in preventing the accidental damage to reefs etc., caused by fin kicks, dragging gauges, cylinders and improper handling.

Teaching ascent rate control and hover aptitude.

There is a lack of agreement in the scuba diving industry about the proper rate of ascent; however it seems widely accepted that a staged ascent with a hover or safety stop may help divers off-gas and prevent decompression sickness or arterial gas embolism (AGE). Most certification courses do not devote sufficient time to the practice of these staged ascents with and without the aid of a down line. Instructors who have used the Diamond Reef System over the past three years have testified that a better trained more confident diver is produced in less time. Furthermore, divers who can ACE. the test (Awareness and Control through Education) in the open water environment have proven that they are competent, safe divers.

The Industry's only mark of skill and competence

Currently, at no level of diver training are buoyancy skills taught to this level of precision. The Diamond Reef Challenge course invites divers to systematically practice overall buoyancy control skills (beginning in the pool and developing into controlled open water conditions) without the initial fears associated with adventurous semi-solo open water diving.

Very much like automobile driver training, the goal is to produce a technically proficient scuba diver so that future diving experiences may be safely enjoyed without damaging the environment. This course also provides the dive educator with specific guidelines for determining a diver's skill level, based on industry accepted standards, and upon completion, grants the diver the dive industry's first annual validation of qualification. As Divers successfully complete the annual International Diamond Reef Challenge, they earn the Diamond Reef logbook validation stamp.

This beautiful, scientifically illustrated marine conservation stamp symbolizes divers' awareness of responsibility for their own (and their buddy's) safety, and the recognition of the ease with which accidental damage can be caused to our fragile marine environment. Those who actually ACE the course additionally receive a mark of skill that compliments the stamp in the diver's logbook. Both stamp and seal expire one year from date of issue and further symbolize a regional validation of ability by stating the country and state where the test was taken. This international validation program readily encourages annual warm-ups, refreshers and updates.

When a diver displays the current Diamond Reef Stamp and BTSI's Diving ACE Seal in his/her logbook, there is no more objective written proof in the industry today, of the diver's skill in overall buoyancy control. The gold seal with the stamp attests to the diver's ability to ace the eight to ten minute test of skill, thereby providing the diving industry with the first objective mark of skill since the invention of scuba. This will provide new dive buddies and unfamiliar professionals with a clearer measurement of proficiency.

In the near future, participating resorts will offer special benefits to those divers who present their Diamond Reef and Diving ACE. validated logbooks. Through the sale of related philatelic products and future Diamond Reef Challenge events, BTSI will be able to donate needed funds for the management and development of marine sanctuaries throughout the world without taxing the diver. Diver safety combined with a new respect for fragile marine life is our primary concern. The Diamond Reef System clearly and concisely addresses these issues.

Fun from day one

The PADI open water dive course is divided into three parts: classroom, confined water (pool) and four actual open-water scuba dives with a qualified PADI instructor. Each part is fun and ensures that you learn what you need to enjoy diving to the full.

PROGRAMME

A complete programme of classroom, pool and open-water sessions will train you to dive safely and become comfortable entering the underwater world. The open-water diver course offers tremendous flexibility.

It also features state-of-the-art education: video integration with the PADI open-water diving manual allows the new diver the to prepare for classroom sessions in the comfort of their own home and to suit their own schedule.

Complete student crew-pack kit, course schedules and costs with everything needed to get started can be obtained by contacting your local PADI Dive Centre.

WORLD SUPPORT

PADI maintains local and service offices in the UK, USA, Japan, Sweden, Norway, Switzerland, Australia, Canada and New Zealand to provide support services, texts and other training materials in dozens of languages to PADI members.

All PADI members, regardless of language, have access to the same PADI system of diver training, ensuring educational consistency worldwide.

PADI's policy of offering a programme suited to today's customer, whether they wish to dive at home or abroad, has proved to be as popular in the UK as in the rest of the world.

There's no greater adventure than diving! Whether you're taking your first look at it, or whether you've been diving for 20 years there's always something new, fascinating or challenging about venturing into the underwater world.

Your mind may be mesmerised by clouds of colourful fish, your curiosity raised by the mysterious remains of sunken ships or your creativity awakened by the art of underwater photography.

SOMETHING FOR EVERYONE

Your diving interests may range from a casual pastime pursued on holiday, to a constant passion - even a career. The PADI education system offers something for every one.

PADI®

PADI Continuing Education Course Flow

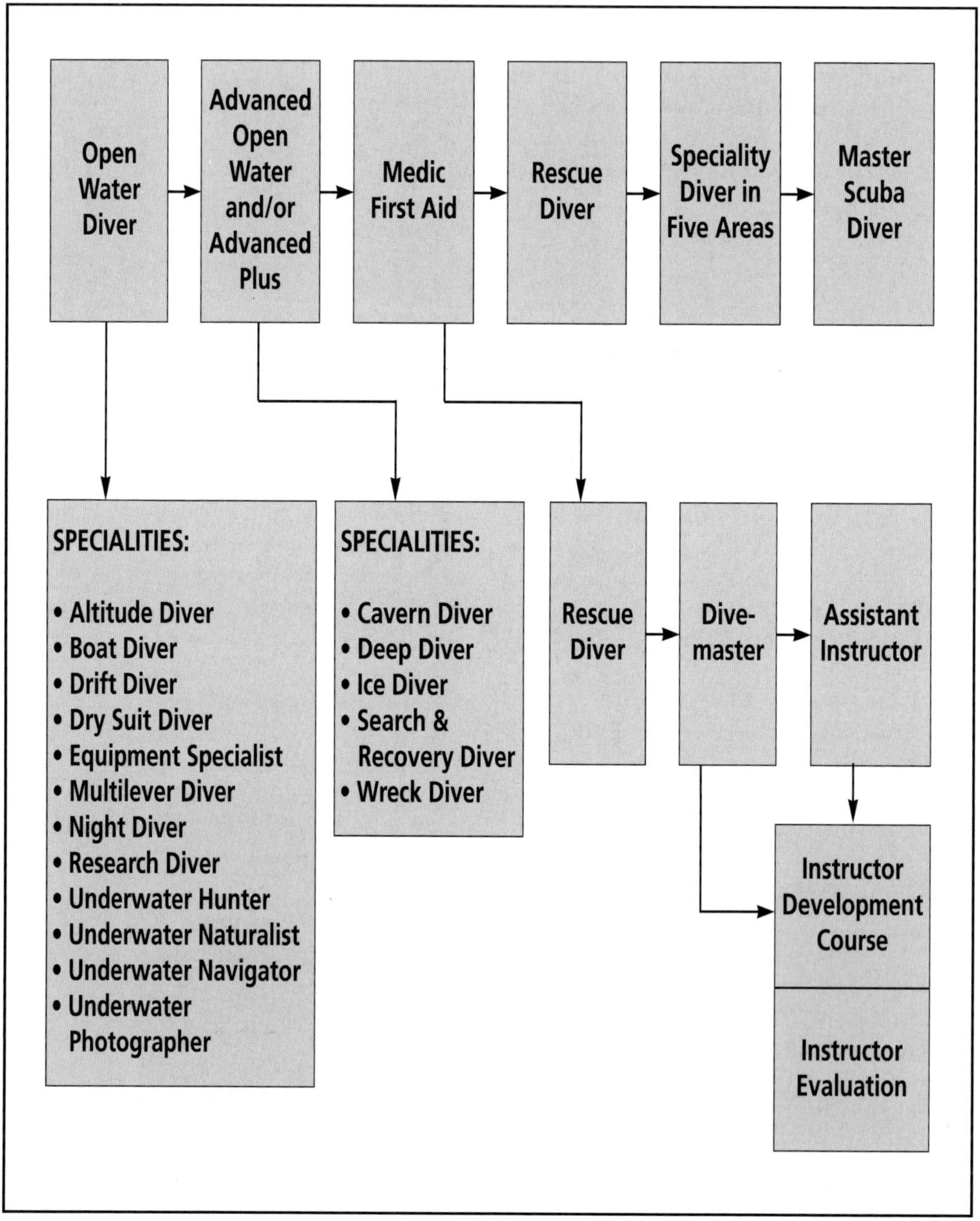

PADI IDC candidates attain NVQs

by Mark Caney

Candidates taking a PADI Instructor course in UK now have an exciting new option - to gain two prestigious awards at once!

Not only will they complete the PADI Instructor Development Course, entitling them to attend an Instructor Examination, they can also obtain a City and Guilds award in Training and Development. This award is the British National Vocational Qualification (NVQ) Level III.

Not only does this result in two highly respected qualifications instead of one, it usually costs no more than a simple IDC because the Government pays 25% of the fee if the course will lead to an NVQ.

CITY AND GUILDS

City and Guilds is the largest body issuing vocational qualifications in the UK. Their awards are specifically related to the needs of real-life working situations rather than being generalised academic qualifications.

For this reason the qualifications are highly valued by employers because they represent a measured quantity of relevant experience.

City and Guilds follow guide-lines established by the National Council for Vocational Qualifications (NCVQ).

This body has been appointed by the government to insure that all qualifications issued in industry are of a common standard. This means that a City and Guild qualification is also a National Vocational Qualification or NVQ. As a result it is recognised throughout the UK.

STANDARDISATION

The standardisation of NVQs is also essential to permit British qualifications to be understood by employers in other EEC member countries.

NVQs can be obtained in almost all sectors. They were conceived after extensive consultations with the various industries and as a result they accurately meet the need for an established system for measuring ability in the real working environment.

The fact that the sport diving industry can now issue NVQs to its members has considerably enhanced it's standing in the UK.

NVQ linked IDCs are now being offered by almost all British PADI Course Directors due to a special arrangement made by PADI and Training Through Diving, a British based organisation specialising in linking diving qualifications with NVQs.

VALUED

PADI Instructors who hold this rating have found that their credentials are much more highly valued outside of the diving industry, and that many new avenues of assistance from government sponsored organisations are open to them.

The BSAC Coaching Scheme

The BSAC coaching scheme provides a team of experienced divers, all of whom are BSAC qualified instructors, to help branches and members with instruction and advice on any aspect of diver training, as well as branch organisation and management matters. Important objectives of the scheme are to promote acceptable standards of instruction and performance, and to help branches achieve self-sufficiency in all their activities.

Coaches also play an important part in assisting with the formation of new BSAC branches within their region and act as a liaison link in the event of diving accidents and serious incidents. They also have responsibilities for promoting the club and representing the interests of all divers at meetings with regional sports councils and similar bodies.

The scheme operates principally in the British Isles where there are 14 coaching regions. Each is headed by a BSAC regional coach whose function is to co-ordinate coaching activities within that region.

Each regional coach can call upon the help of a team of assistant coaches who provide various services required by branches within their own immediate area. The regional coach will be involved anywhere in the region, where their wider experience may be advantageous. Every effort is made to find the best person to provide whatever coaching services are required.

Neither the regional coaches nor the assistant coaches are full time employees of the BSAC. All serve the membership in their own leisure time.

While new branches receive most attention from the coaching scheme, any branch may seek help from its regional coach as often as it wishes, and every effort will be made to meet requests. The provision of services to branches at their pool or dry meetings is free, except for any equipment hire charges which may apply.

Regional coaching teams are also responsible for running a range of weekend courses, most of which lead to Skill Development Course qualifications. The variety of courses available includes Boat Handling, Chartwork, Practical Rescue Management, Marine Radio, Marine Life Identification, Compressor Operation and Management, and many others. Weekend and day courses are not part of the free coaching service: a course fee is charged.

Regional coaching teams can call upon stocks of diving and support equipment from BSAC headquarters for use during branch visits and on courses. The coaching scheme may also be able to provide newly-formed branches with aqualung sets for initial training purposes, on a short term loan basis.

The equipment available to coaches includes basic equipment, aqualungs, air purity test kits, depth gauge test rigs, resuscitation manikins, instructional and promotional films.

Branches and members wishing to take advantage of coaching services should in the first instance contact the BSAC regional coach for their area.

Where there are significant groups of BSAC branches in countries outside the UK, the club will endeavour to appoint an overseas liaison officer.

The function of OLOs is different from that of coaches in that they serve as a liaison link between the branches in that country and club HQ.

They also have responsibility for co-ordinating instructor visits by senior BSAC instructors. Where possible and where geography permits, they may also set up and lead various skill development courses for the benefit of branches in the area.

BSAC SCHOOLS

The original concept of BSAC diver training was that instruction would be given to new members by branch instructors at weekly branch meetings. In recent years however, an increasing number of people wish to obtain diving qualifications in a shorter period of time and for them instruction at a BSAC school is likely to be more expedient.

BSAC Schools are commercially-run diving schools, often attached to diving equipment shops, which have been inspected and approved to teach diving to BSAC standards and award the appropriate qualifications. Many schools have BSAC branches attached to them so that trainees can take out club membership not only to gain BSAC qualifications but to remain together as a social group in order to continue with the sport.

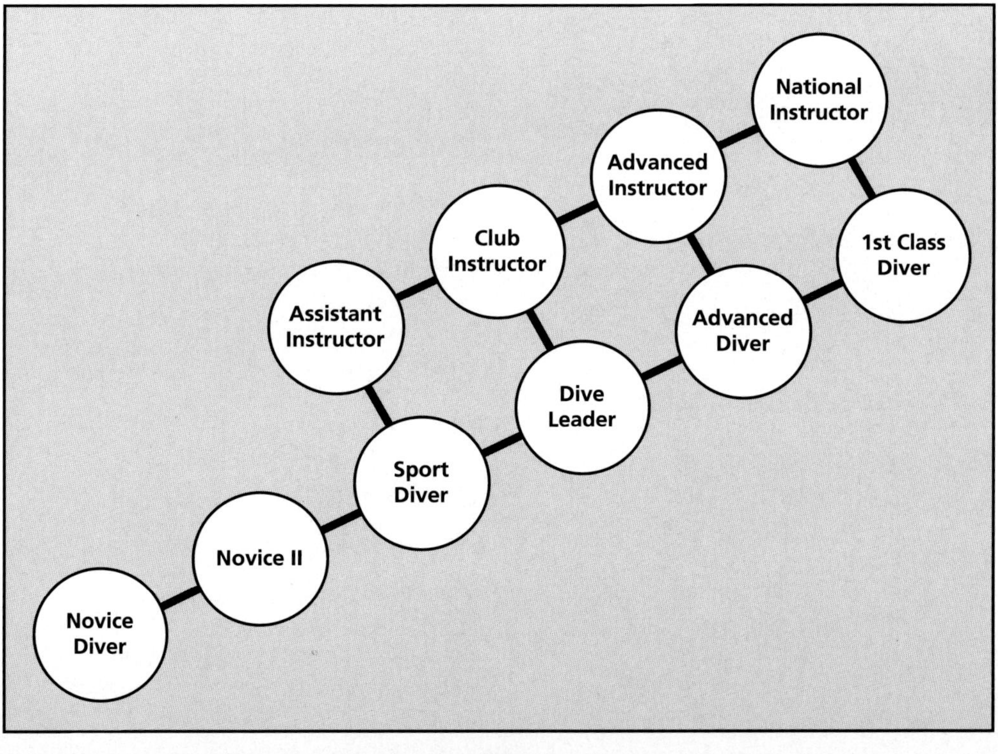

PADI Dive Centres

ENGLAND

AVON

BRISTOL DIVING CENTRE **(5*)**
52 OLD MARKET STREET
BRISTOL, AVON BS2 OER
(0272) 299544

CURRENT STATE DIVING
8 KELLAWAY AVENUE
REDLAND
BRISTOL, AVON BS6 7XR
(0272) 247030

TRIDENT DIVING
361 FISHPONDS ROAD
BRISTOL, AVON BS5 6RD
(0272) 586620

BEDFORDSHIRE

"DIVE IN" BEDFORD
289A AMPTHILL ROAD
BEDFORD, BEDFORDSHIRE MK42 9HG
(0234) 273058

KEMPSTON DINGHY & LEISURE
100 HIGH STREET, KEMPSTON
BEDFORD, BEDFORDSHIRE MK42 9HG
(0234) 854831

BIRMINGHAM/WEST MIDLANDS

AQUA SPORT INTERNATIONAL
80 ALCESTER ROAD
MOSELEY, BIRMINGHAM B13 8BB
(021) 449-4148

COMDEAN LTD. DIVING & WATERSPORTS
90 WATERFALL LANE, OLD HILL
WARLEY, WEST MIDLANDS B64 6RJ
(021) 559-3659

DIVE SITE SCUBA SERVICES
130 HURSTCROFT ROAD, LEA VILLAGE
BIRMINGHAM B33 9OU
(021) 789-7779

THE DIVING INITIATIVE **(5*)**
143 HOSPITAL STREET
NEWTOWN, BIRMINGHAM B19 3XA
(021) 333-4312

ROCKY COVE
78 OLDBURY ROAD
BLACKHEATH, BIRMINGHAM
(021) 559-0701

CAMBRIDGESHIRE

GILDENBURGH WATER **(5* IDC)**
EASTREA ROAD, WHITTLESEY
PETERBOROUGH, CAMBRIDGESHIRE PE7 2AR
(0733) 351288

CHESHIRE

DEE SPORTS
67 BROOK STREET
CHESTER, CHESHIRE CH1 3D2
(0244) 314204

WATERWAYS DIVING CENTRE
SOUTH PIER, WATERWAYS
ELLESMERE PORT, SOUTH WIRRAL,
CHESHIRE L65 4EF
(051) 356-4286

CORNWALL

CORNISH DIVING AND WATERSPORTS
BAR ROAD, FALMOUTH, CORNWALL TRLL 4BN
(0326) 311265

FALMOUTH UNDERWATER CENTRE
MAENPORTH BEACH, MAENPORTH
FALMOUTH, CORNWALL TRLL 5HN
(0326) 250852

UNDERSEA ADVENTURES
HARLEQUINS, THE BELYERS
ST IVES, CORNWALL TR26 2DB
(0736) 793353

DERBYSHIRE

SCUBA MARINE
RINGWOOD ROAD, BRIMINGTON
CHESTERFIELD, DERBYSHIRE S43 LDG
(0246) 232369

DEVON

FORT BOVISAND UNDERWATER CENTRE
FORT BOVISAND
PLYMOUTH, DEVON PL9 OAB
(0752) 408021

SCUBA WORLD WATERSPORTS CENTRE
LANGLAND BUSINESS PARK, UFFCULME
CULLOMPTON, DEVON EX15 3DA
(0884) 840001

SEATON MARINE SERVICES
THE HARBOUR
SEATON
EAST DEVON EX12 4AA
(0297) 23344

DORSET

DIVERS DOWN
THE PIER, HIGH STREET
SWANAGE
DORSET BH19 2AN
(0929) 423565

DIVING LEISURE LIMITED **(5* IDC)**
ROCKLEY PARK, HAMWORTHY
POOLE, DORSET BH15 4LZ
(0202) 680898

PARRY'S SUB AQUATICS
VICTORIA SQUARE
PORTLAND, DORSET DT5 1AL
(0305) 821261

WEST BAY WATERSPORTS
OLD TIMER YARD, GEORGE STREET
WEST BAY, DORSET DT6 4EY
(0308) 421-800

ESSEX

ADVENTURE DIVER TRAINING
RAWLINGS FARM BUILDNGS
MAIN ROAD (A-130)
RETTENDON COMMON
CHELMSFORD, ESSEX CM3 5NY
(0245) 401225

ADVENTURE DIVERS
WALTHAM ABBEY SWIMMING POOL
ROUNDHILLS, WALTHAM ABBEY
ESSEX EN9 1UP
(0992) 650674

DISCOVER SCUBA
7 CAPRICORN CENTRE
CRANES FARM ROAD
BASILDON, ESSEX SS14 3JJ
(0268) 272272

DIVERS 2000
394 GREEN LANES, SEVEN KINGS
ILFORD, ESSEX IG3 9JX
(081) 597-9690

PUFF-IN AIR SERVICES **(5* IDC)**
UNIT 7, BARDWELLS YARD
LATCHINGTON ROAD, COLD NORTON
ESSEX, CM3 6UB
(0621) 828008

GLOUCESTERSHIRE

DIVE 90/TWO THIRDS BLUE
KNIGHTSBRIDGE BUSINESS CENTRE
KNIGHTSBRIDGE
CHELTENHAM
GLOUCESTERSHIRE GL51 9FA
(0242) 680003

HAMPSHIRE

ANDARK DIVING
256 BRIDGE ROAD
LOWER SWANWICK
SOUTHAMPTON
HAMPSHIRE S03 7FL
(0489) 581755

SUNSET DIVERS
145 HIGH STREET
ALDERSHOT
HAMPSHIRE GU11 1TT
(0252) 319541

KENT

SOUTH EAST DIVING CENTRE
140 RICHMOND ROAD
GILLINGHAM
KENT ME7 1LS
(0634) 579624

LANCASHIRE

BLACKPOOL AREA DIVING CENTRE **(5*)**
32 BEECHWOOD DRIVE
THORNTON-CLEVELEYS, BLACKPOOL
LANCASHIRE FY5 5EJ
(0253) 869188

DIVER SERVICES
VERECROFT PARSONAGE ROAD
BLACKBURN, LANCASHIRE BB1 4AG
(0254) 248009

MANTA DIVER TRAINING CENTRE **(5*)**
4 LEEFIELDS CLOSE, UPPERMILL
OLDHAM, LANCASHIRE OL3 6LA
(0457) 873272

SCUBA-TECH
8 OWEN ROAD, SKERTON
LANCASTER, LANCASHIRE LA1 2AR
(0524) 381831

LEICESTERSHIRE

STONEY COVE **(5* IDC)**
STONEY COVE, STONEY STANTON
LEICESTERSHIRE LE9 6DW
(045) 527-2768

LONDON

AMPHIBIAN SPORTS /
OCEAN BLUE DIVE CENTRE **(5*)**
44A CHAPEL ROAD, WEST NORWOOD
LONDON SE27 0UR
(081) 984-7323

THE BIG BLUE DIVING CO. LTD
291 RYE LANE, LONDON SE15 4UA
(071) 635-5540

DIVE FORCE **(5*)**
10 CHEAPSIDE, NORTH CIRCULAR ROAD
LONDON N13 5ED
(081) 803-0241

THE DIVE SHOP LTD
UNIVERSAL HOUSE, UPLANDS TRADING EST
BLACK HORSE LANE, LONDON E17 5QJ
(081) 523-5900

DIVING LOCKER (UK) LTD
NEPTUNE HOUSE
201 CHISWICK HIGH ROAD
CHISWICK, LONDON W4 2DR
(081) 742-1696

LONDON DIVING CENTRE
240 WATFORD WAY
HENDON, LONDON NW4 4UB
(081) 203-5744

MIKE'S WATERFRONT WAREHOUSE
1 DUCK'S WALK ,TWICKENHAM
LONDON TWL 2DD
(081) 744-9144

OCEAN LEISURE LTD
EMBANKMENT PLACE
13/14 NORTHUMBERLAND AVENUE
LONDON WC2N 5AQ
(071) 930-5050

WIMBLEDON DIVE CENTRE **(5*)**
574 KINGSTON ROAD
RAYNES PARK
LONDON SW19 8DR
(081) 543-4576

NORTHAMPTONSHIRE

NORTHAMPTON SUB AQUA SUPPLIES
43B ABBEY ROAD
NORTHAMPTON
NORTHAMPTONSHIRE NN4 9EY
(0604) 768623

NORTHUMBERLAND

AQUANORTH (5* IDC)
17A COAST ROAD
HEATON
NEWCASTLE UPON TYNE,
NORTHUMBERLAND NE7 7RN
(091) 266-6626

TRAIL-A-BOAT LTD **(5* IDC)**
ATLANTIS HOUSE
159 WESTGATE ROAD
NEWCASTLE UPON TYNE
NORTHUMBERLAND NE1 4AN
(091) 232-7983

NOTTINGHAMSHIRE

NOTTINGHAM SCUBA CENTRE
59 TRENT BOULEVARD
WEST BRIDGEFORD
NOTTINGHAM
NOTTINGHAMSHIRE NG2 5BB
(0602) 822525

OXFORDSHIRE

AQUARIUS DIVING
82 ON THE BROADWAY, DIDCOT
OXFORDSHIRE OX11 8AE
(0235) 512056

SUFFOLK

DIVELINE LTD
ST. JOHNS WORKS
ST. JOHNS ROAD
IPSWICH, SUFFOLK IP4 5DQ
(0473) 715533

SURREY

CHALLENGER 10 LTD
129 WORSLEY ROAD, FRIMLEY
CAMBERLEY, SURREY GUL6 5BB
(0252) 837499

NEW DAWN DIVE CENTRE **(5*)**
148 SEND ROAD, SEND
WOKING, SURREY GU23 7EY
(0483) 211103

RUNNYMEDE DIVE SERVICE
UNIT 11, EVERSLEY WAY
THORPE INDUSTRIAL ESTATE
EGHAM, SURREY TW20 8RG
(0784) 436909

69 DIVING & SPORTSWORLD LTD
59-61 HIGH STREET
EWELL, SURREY KT17 1RX
(081) 786-7821

SUSSEX

BLACK ROCK DIVING **(5*)**
4 THE BROADWAY
WHITEHAWK ROAD
BRIGHTON, SUSSEX BN2 5NF
(0273) 571402

ROCK BOTTOM DIVERS
R.B.D. HOUSE, QUEEN STREET
ARUNDLE, WEST SUSSEX BN18 9JG
(0903) 884567

WITTERING DIVERS, AT SCUBAWORKS
THE ESPLANADE
GLOUCESTER ROAD
BOGNOR REGIS
WEST SUSSEX PO21 1NU
TEL/FAX: 0243 842402

TYNE & WEAR

W.G.P MARINE LTD
165 WHITLEY ROAD
WHITLEY BAY
TYNE & WEAR NE26 2DN
(091) 251-0388

WARWICKSHIRE

WARWICKSHIRE SCUBA CENTRE
5 CAMPION TERRACE
LEAMINGTON SPA
WARWICKSHIRE SC32 5EH
(0926) 313681

WILTSHIRE

OK DIVING SERVICES SWINDON
63 FARLEIGH CRESCENT
SWINDON, WILTSHIRE SN3 1JY
(0793) 695479

WHITE HORSE SCHOOL OF DIVING **(5*)**
UFFCOTT HOUSE, BROAD HINTON
NEAR SWINDON
WILTSHIRE SN4 9NB
(0793) 731843

NORTH YORKSHIRE

DIVE ACTION WATER SPORTS
19 HELREDALE ROAD
WHITBY
NORTH YORKSHIRE Y022 4JG
(0947) 820616

THE DIVER TRAINING COLLEGE **(5*)**
ASHLEY HOUSE, MALT KILN LANE
APPLETON ROEBUCK, YORK
NORTH YORKSHIRE Y05 7DT
(0904) 84424

SOUTH YORKSHIRE

NAMRON DIVING CENTRE **(5*)**
CANKLOW MEADOW LND. ESTATE,
WEST BAWTRY ROAD
ROTHERHAM, SOUTH YORKSHIRE S60 2XL
(0709) 838382

S.D.S. WATERSPORTS
66-77 STATION ROAD
SHEFFIELD
SOUTH YORKSHIRE S19 5GW
(0742) 488688

WEST YORKSHIRE

DIVE EASY LTD
29 NORTHGATE
WAKEFIELD, WEST YORKSHIRE
(0924) 200363

DIVERS WAREHOUSE
29 WALKER TERRACE
BRADFORD, WEST YORKSHIRE BD4 7HP
(0274) 307555

MIDWAY WATERSPORTS AND LEISURE **(5*)**
GRANARY WHARF
NEVILLE STREET
LEEDS, WEST YORKSHIRE LS1 4BE
(0532) 444315

WALES

ANGLESEY

DIVING SERVICES - ANGLESEY
HEATHERCLIFF RAVENSPOINT ROAD
TREARDDUR BAY, ANGLESEY LL65 2AQ
(0407) 860318

DYFED

DYFED DIVER TRAINING SCHOOL
SYNOD INN
LLANDYSUL, SA44 6SA
(0545) 580085

ST DAVIDS DIVE CENTRE
GLAN-Y-MOR, CAERFAI ROAD
ST DAVIDS, DYFED SA62 6QT
(0437) 721788

MID GLAMORGAN

REMAR DIVING SERVICES
POPLAR ROAD
CAERPHILLY
MID GLAMORGAN CF8 LLF
(0222) 860416

WEST GLAMORGAN

LEWIS SPORTS
64 COMMERCIAL ROAD
PORT TALBOT
WEST GLAMORGAN SA13 1LG
(0639) 882312

GWENT

AQUASUB INTERNATIONAL **(5*)**
90 CHEPSTOW ROAD
NEWPORT, GWENT NP9 8EE
(0633)223089

PEMBROKESHIRE

WEST WALES DIVING CENTRE
HASGUARD CROSS, NR HAVERFORD WEST
PEMBROKESHIRE SA62 3SJ
(0437) 781457

CHANNEL ISLANDS

JERSEY

AQUANAUT DIVERS INTERNATIONAL
GRAEME LE MAISTRE SPORTS
17 BATH STREET, ST HELIER, JERSEY
(0860) 740301

DIVE & SKI SPORTS
13 COLOMBERIE, ST HELIER, JERSEY
(0534) 36209

DIVING CENTRE JERSEY **(5*)**
1ST TOWER, ST HELIER, JERSEY
(0534) 32813

REPUBLIC OF IRELAND

CORK

KINSALE DIVE CENTRE
GUARDWELL, KINSALE, COUNTY CORK
(021) 772282

THE DIVE SHOP
30 ST FINBARRS ROAD, CORK
(353) 21-312510

DUBLIN

GREAT OUTDOORS
CHATHAM HOUSE
CHATHAM STREET, DUBLIN 2
(01) 679-4293

OCEANTEC LTD **(5* IDC)**
10-11 MARINE TERRACE
DUN LAOGHAIRE
COUNTY DUBLIN
(01) 280-1083

KERRY

WATERWORLD
UPPER ROCK STREET
TRALEE, COUNTY KERRY
(066) 25803

SCOTLAND

GRAMPIAN

SUB SEA SERVICES **(5*)**
631-633 GEORGE STREET
ABERDEEN AB2 3YE
(0224) 638588

LOTHIAN

BLUE DOLPHIN SCUBA CENTRE
32 MONTROSE TERRACE
EDINBURGH, LOTHIAN EH5 7DL
(031) 661-3321

STRATHCLYDE

AQUATRON DIVE LOCKER
30 STANLEY STREET, GLASGOW G41 1JB
(041) 429-5902

KIP WATERSPORTS
KIP MARINA, LNVERKIP
STRATHCLYDE PA16 0AS
(0475) 521281

PUFFIN DIVE SCHOOL, OBAN DIVERS **(5* IDC)**
LAGGAN, GLENSHELLACH
OBAN, ARGYLL PA34 4QJ
(0631) 64142

BS-AC Schools

UNITED KINGDOM

NORTH WEST

PREMIER SCHOOL
AQUATICUS DIVING SCHOOL
99 HUDDERSFIELD ROAD
OLDHAM, LANCS OLL 3NO
061 665-1370

PREMIER SCHOOL
SLATER'S AQUA SPORTS
WATERY LANE, ASHTON
PRESTON, LANCS PR2 10J
0772 732078

PREMIER SCHOOL
NATIONAL DIVER TRAINING
TELFORD'S QUAY
ELLESMERE PORT, CHESHIRE L65 4FY
051 356-5550 FAX: 051 357 2625

SCUBA-TECH DIVE CENTRE
8 OWEN ROAD, SKERTON
LANCASTER, LANCS LA1 2AR
TEL/FAX: 0524 381831

NORTH EAST

PREMIER SCHOOL
ROBIN HOOD DIVE SCHOOL
152 LEEDS ROAD
HECKMONDWIKE
WEST YORKSHIRE WF16 9BJ
0924 443843 FAX: 0924 474529

PREMIER SCHOOL
SDS WATERSPORTS
66-70 STATION ROAD, HALFWAY
SHEFFIELD
WEST YORKSHIRE S19 5GW
0742 488688 FAX: 0742 488689

MARSDEN DIVE SCHOOL
6 FALLOW ROAD
MARSDEN, SOUTH SHIELDS
TYNE AND WEAR NE32 8DY
091 427 7820

DIVE ACTION WATERSPORTS
19 HELREDALE ROAD
WHITBY, NORTH YORKSHIRE Y022 4JG
TEL/FAX: 0947 820616

THE DIVER TRAINING COLLEGE
MALT KILN LANE
APPLETON ROEBUCK
YORK Y05 7DT
0904 84424 FAX: 0904 84724

BRIDLINGTON DIVER TRAINING SCHOOL
11 STATION COURT
STATION ROAD, BRIDLINGTON
EAST YORKSHIRE Y016 4LZ
0262 400325

YORKSHIRE DIVE SCHOOL
9/11 HESSLE ROAD, HULL
NORTH HUMBERSIDE, HU3 2AA

MIDLANDS

PREMIER SCHOOL
DIVE BARRACUDA
16 MAIN STREET, KIMBERLEY
NOTTINGHAM, NOTTS NG23 5BE
TEL/FAX: 0602 459303

PREMIER SCHOOL
ROCKY COVE
78 OLDBURY ROAD, BLACKHEATH
WARLEY, WEST MIDLANDS B65 OJS
TEL/FAX: 021 559-0701

COMDEAN SCUBA TRAINING CENTRE
90 WATERFALL LANE, OLD HILL
WARLEY, WEST MIDLANDS B64 6RJ
021 559-3659 FAX: 021 559-8659

SCUBA TRAINING SERVICES
50 MICHAEL COURT, EDGBASTON
BIRMINGHAM B5 7TS
021 440-4499

DIVETRAIN SCUBA SCHOOL
70 TRINITY ROAD, LUTON, BEDS LU3 2LW
0582 585636

AQUARIUS DIVING
82 BROADWAY
DIDCOT, OXON OX11 8AE
0235 512056 FAX: 0235 815352

EASTERN

ADVENTURES IN DIVING
RAWLINGS FARM BUILDINGS
RETTENDON COMMON
CHELMSFORD, ESSEX CM3 8DY
0245 401225 FAX: 0245 570612

OCEAN BLUE
4/5 BRYSON BUSINESS CENTRE
131 CHURCH ELM LANE
DAGENHAM, ESSEX RM10 9RR
081 984-7323

HERTS & ESSEX DIVING SCHOOL
SIRIUS, STRETHALL ROAD
LITTLEBURY, ESSEX CBL 14TQ
0799 520605

LONDON

PREMIER SCHOOL
LONDON UNDERWATER CENTRE
13 GLENDOWER ROAD
LONDON SW14 8NY
081 876-0735 FAX: 081 959-7971

SCUBA DIVE INSTRUCTION
ADONIS COURT, NORTHFIELD AVENUE
EALING, LONDON W13 9RJ
081 840-7772 FAX: 081 567-6971

DIVE FORCE MARINE
10 CHEAPSIDE
NORTH CIRCULAR ROAD
LONDON N13 5ED
081 803-0241 FAX: 081 884-0801

SCUBA TRAINING LTD.
59 VICARAGE ROAD
LONDON SW14 8RY
081 876-5132

SCUBA TRAINING LTD.
AT THE DIVING LOCKER
201 CHISWICK HIGH ROAD
LONDON W4 2DR
081 742-1696 FAX: 081 747-1811

THE BIG BLUE DIVING SCHOOL
291 RYE LANE, PECKHAM
LONDON SE15 4UA
071 635-5540 FAX: 071 639-9267

SUB ACTION
90 HARBUT ROAD, LONDON SW11 2RE
071 585-2589

RICHMOND DIVING SCHOOL
MIKE'S WATERFRONT WAREHOUSE
1 DUCKS WALK, TWICKENHAM
MIDDLESEX TWL 2DD
081 744-9144 FAX: 081 744-1077

SOUTH EAST

PREMIER SCHOOL
SOUTH EAST DIVING CENTRE
140 RICHMOND ROAD
GILLINGHAM, KENT ME7 1LS
0634 579624

PREMIER SCHOOL
C-SPORTS SCUBA CENTRE
115 MAIN ROAD, SUTTON AT HONE
DARTFORD, KENT DA4 9HO
0322 866261 FAX: 0322 868962

PREMIER SCHOOL
'CHALLENGER 10' LTD.
129 WORSLEY ROAD, FRIMLEY
CAMBERLEY
SURREY GU16 5BB
0252 837499 FAX: 0252 837891

FATHOMS AND LEAGUES UNDERWATER SCHOOL
60 BANSTEAD ROAD
CARSHALTON BEECHES
SURREY SM5 3NL
TEL/FAX: 081 642-6159

GLOBAL DIVING
20 SHEEPHOUSE GREEN
WOTTON, DORKING
SURREY RH5 6QW
0306 888261

SOUTH

PREMIER SCHOOL
ANDARK DIVING
256 BRIDGE ROAD, LOWER SWANWICK
SOUTHAMPTON, HANTS S03 7FL
0489 581755 FAX: 0489 575223

PREMIER SCHOOL
THE POOLE DIVE CENTRE
THE MALL - THE MARINERS COMPLEX
QUAY WEST MARINA, WEST QUAY ROAD
POOLE, DORSET BHL5 1HY
0202 677427 FAX: 0202 682744

PREMIER SCHOOL
OLD HARBOUR DIVE SCHOOL
1 1 NOTHE PARADE
WEYMOUTH, DORSET DT4 8TX
TEL/FAX: 0305 761666

DORSET DIVING SCHOOL
THE NEW HOUSE, EAST STOKE
WAREHAM, DORSET SH20 6AN
0929 463732 FAX: 0202 593529

DIVERS DOWN
THE PIER, HIGH STREET
SWANAGE, DORSET BH19 2AN
0929 423565

WITTERING DIVERS, AT SCUBAWORKS
THE ESPLANADE, GLOUCESTER ROAD
BOGNOR REGIS, WEST SUSSEX PO21 1NU
TEL/FAX: 0243 842402

SOUTH WEST

PREMIER SCHOOL
TRURO DIVING SERVICES
SEAWAY HOUSE, COMMERCIAL ROAD
PENRYN, CORNWALL TR10 8AG
0326 375893

PREMIER SCHOOL
FORT BOVISAND UNDERWATER CENTRE
PLYMOUTH, DEVON PL9 OAB
0752 408021 FAX: 0752 481952

PREMIER SCHOOL
DIVER TRAINING SCHOOL
5 CAMPERDOWN TERRACE
EXMOUTH, DEVON EX8 1EJ
0395 266300 FAX: 0395 276341

PREMIER SCHOOL
SCUBA WORLD DIVE CENTRE
LANGLANDS BUSINESS PARK, UFFCULME
CULLOMPTON, DEVON EX15 3DA
0884 840001 FAX: 0884 841770

SOUND DIVING INSTRUCTION
QUEEN ANNE'S BATTERY MARINA
COXSIDE
PLYMOUTH, DEVON PL4 8DX
TEL/FAX: 0752 670674

FALMOUTH UNDERWATER CENTRE
MAENPORTH BEACH
FALMOUTH
CORNWALL TR11 5HN
TEL/FAX: 0326 250852

FASTRAK DIVER TRAINING /
VENTURE SPORTS
371 TORQUAY ROAD, PRESTON
PAIGNTON, DEVON TQ3 2BT
TEL/FAX: 0803 523023

AQUANAUT
17 CLIFTON ROAD
EXETER, DEVON EX1 2BR
TEL/FAX: 0392 218825

BRISTOL DIVING SCHOOL
6B EASTFIELD, HENLEAZE
BRISTOL BS9 4BQ
TEL/FAX: 0272 624428

TRIDENT DIVING
361 FISHPONDS ROAD, EASTVILLE
BRISTOL BS5 6RD
0272 586620

CURRENT STATE DIVING
8 KELLAWAY AVENUE
REDLANDS
BRISTOL BS6 7XR
0272 247030 FAX: 0272 245009

SCOTLAND

PREMIER SCHOOL
EDINBURGH DIVING SCHOOL
1 WATSON CRESCENT
EDINBURGH EH11 1HD
031 229-4838 FAX: 031 229-6306

RGIT DIVE CENTRE
338 KING STREET
ABERDEEN AB2 3BJ
0224 638970 FAX: 0224 637990

GLASGOW COLLEGE OF NAUTICLE STUDIES
21 THISTLE STREET
GLASGOW G5 9XB
041 429-3201

DIVE SHETLAND
YAAFIELD, MAYWICK
BIGTON, SHETLAND ZE4 9JF
09502 314 FAX: 09502 321

ISLE OF MAN

SOUTHERN DIVING LODGE
4 ATHOL STREET
PORT ST MARY, ISLE OF MAN
0624 832943

WALES

PREMIER SCHOOL
ANGLESEY DIVER TRAINING COLLEGE
ASSC, PORTH DAFARCH ROAD
HOLYHEAD, ANGLESEY
GWYNEDD LL65 2LP
0407 764545 FAX: 0407 763636

PREMIER SCHOOL
DIVING SERVICES ANGLESEY
HEATHERCLIFFE, RAVENS POINT ROAD
TREARDDUR BAY, HOLYHEAD
ANGLESEY, GWYNEDD LL65 2AQ
0407 860318

DIVERS AIR
THE POPLARS, ROSSETT ROAD
HOLT, CLWYD LL65 9SY
0829 270985

WEST WALES DIVING SCHOOL
HASGUARD CROSS
HAVERFORDWEST, DYFED SA62 3SJ
0437 781457 FAX: 0437 781093

NORTHERN IRELAND

DV DIVING
24 FIFTH AVENUE, BAYLANDS
BANGOR, CO. DOWN
NORTHERN IRELAND BT29 5JP
0247 464671 / 861686

ISLE OF WIGHT

SCUBA TECHNIQUES IOW LTD.
ELMSWORTH LANE, PORCHFIELD
ISLE OF WIGHT P030 4LR
0983 529023

SOLENT SUB-AQUA SCHOOL OF DIVING
GABLE END, PLAYSTREET LANE
RYDE, ISLE OF WIGHT P033 3LJ
0983 812033

DIVING AND MARINE SERVICES IOW
75 STAPLERS ROAD, NEWPORT
ISLE OF WIGHT P030 2DG
TEL/FAX: 0983 525169

CHANNEL ISLANDS & ISLES OF SCILLY

GUERNSEY SCHOOL OF DIVING
QUATRE VENTS, RUE DES MONTS
DELANCEY, GUERNSEY
CHANNEL ISLANDS
0481 47664

ISLES OF SCILLY DIVING SCHOOL
HIGHERTOWN, ST MARTINS,
ISLES OF SCILLY TR25 OQL
0720 22848

Special Interest Training

PHOTOGRAPHIC

BKSTS TRAINING
547-549 VICTORIA HOUSE
VERNON PLACE
LONDON WC1B 4DJ
071 2428400 FAX: 071 4053560

DIVE FORCE MARINE
10-10A CHEAPSIDE
NORTH CIRCULAR ROAD
PALMERS GREEN
LONDON N13 5ED
081 8030241 FAX: 081 8840801

MARTIN EDGE
238 REMPSTONE ROAD
MERLEY, WIMBORNE, DORSET BH21 1SY
0202 887611

TECHNICAL

AQUATRONICS
42 MARSH ROAD
TATCHAM, BERKSHIRE RG13 4DR
0635 869185

IANTD : BAS-N, TECH-N, TRI

BLACKPOOL AREA DIVING CENTRE
32 BEECHWOOD DRIVE
THORNTON CLEVELEYS
NR BLACKPOOL
LANCASHIRE FY5 5EJ
0253 869188 FAX: 0253 869188

IANTD : BAS-N

CHRIS EDGE
THE STONE BARN
GRAVEL LANE, DRAYTON
NR ABINGDON
OXFORDSHIRE OX14 4HY
0235 529888 FAX: 0865 275216

IANTD : BAS-N

CURRENT STATE DIVING
8 KELLAWAY AVENUE
REDLAND, BRISTOL
AVON BS6 7XR
0272 247030 FAX: 0272 245009

IANTD : BAS-N, TECH-N, TRI

DIVE IN GILDENBURGH
GILDENBURGH WATER
EASTREA ROAD, WHITTLESEY
PETERBOROUGH, CAMBRIDGESHIRE PE7 2AR
0733 351288 FAX: 0733 351299

IANTD : BAS-N
ANDI : BAS-N, TECH-N

DIVE RITE
PO BOX 498, LONDON SW19 6BX
081 7890961 FAX: 081 7802018

IANTD : BAS-N, TECH-N
ANDI : BAS-N, TECH-N, ST

DIVER TRAINING SCHOOL
THO OLD BAKERY
5 CAMPERDOWN TERRACE, EXMOUTH
DEVON EX8 1ES
0395 266300 FAX: 0395 276341

IANTD : BAS-N

DORSET DIVING SERVICES
UNIT 7 WEST HOWE INDUSTRIAL ESTATE
ELLIOT ROAD
BOURNEMOUTH, DORSET BH11 8JX
0202 580065 FAX: 0202 593529

IANTD : BAS-N

FORT BOVISAND UNDERWATER CENTRE
PLYMOUTH OCEAN PROJECTS LTD
FORT BOVISAND, PLYMOUTH
DEVON PL9 0AB
0752 408021 FAX: 0752 481952

IANTD : BAS-N

MIKE SEARES
90 HARBUT ROAD, LONDON SW11 2RE
071 5852589

IANTD : BAS-N

PETER PATTERSON
6 WARREN COURT
CASTLEBAR COURT, EALING
LONDON W5 1BX
081 9987294

ANDI : BAS-N

SCUBA WORLD DIVE CENTRE
LANGLANDS BUSINESS PARK
UFFCULME, DEVON EX15 3DA
0884 840001 FAX: 0884 841770

IANTD : BAS-N

SEA AND SKI SPORTS
3 COLVILES ROAD
KELVIN INDUSTRIAL ESTATE, EAST KILBRIDE
STRATHCLYDE G75 0RS
03552 21514 FAX: 03552 41241

IANTD : BAS-N
ANDI : BAS-N, ST

TECHNICAL DIVING LTD
NEIGHBOURNE COTTAGE
NEIGHBOURNE, OAKHILL
SOMERSET BA3 5BQ
0749 840685 FAX: 0749 840685

IANTD : BAS-N, TECH-N, TRI, REB, WP

THE DIVING INITIATIVE
143 HOSPITAL STREET
NEWTOWN, BIRMINGHAM B19 3XA
021 3334312 FAX: 021 3596043

ANDI : BAS-N, TECH-N

WIMBLEDON DIVING CENTRE
WHITE HORSES (AQUASPORTS)
574 KINGSTON ROAD, RAYNES PARK
LONDON SW20 8DR
081 543 4576 FAX: 081 543 3830

ANDI : BAS-N, ST

FIRST AID

BLACK ROCK DIVING
4 THE BROADWAY
WHITEHAWK ROAD, BRIGHTON
SUSSEX-WEST BN2 5NF
0273 571402 FAX: 0273 602870

DAN OXYGEN PROVIDER COURSE

UNDERSEA MEDICINE TRAINING SCHOOL
FIRST ACTION (MARINE)
PO BOX 1448, CHELMSFORD
ESSEX CM1 3LU
0245 421782 FAX: 0245 421782

COMMERCIAL (HSE approved)

COMMERCIAL DIVING CENTRE
UNIT 12
25 COWLEY ROAD
NUFFIELD INDUSTRIAL ESTATE
POOLE, DORSET BH17 7UJ
0202 667111 FAX: 0202 667997

C-TCA : PARTS I, III, IV
C-ERCA : PARTS I, III, IV
CONSULT : STUART MONRO

DIVER TRAINING SCHOOL
THO OLD BAKERY
5 CAMPERDOWN TERRACE
EXMOUTH, DEVON EX8 1ES
0395 266300 FAX: 0395 276341

C-TCA : PARTS III, IV
C-ERCA : PARTS III, IV
CONSULT : TIM STEVENS

FORT BOVISAND UNDERWATER CENTRE
PLYMOUTH OCEAN PROJECTS LTD
FORT BOVISAND, PLYMOUTH
DEVON PL9 0AB
0752 408021 FAX: 0752 481952

C-TCA : PARTS I, III, IV, IV (TANK DIVING)
C-ERCA : PARTS I, III, IV
CONSULT : LTN CDR ALAN BAX

HERRIOT-WATT UNIVERSITY
INSTITUE OF OFFSHORE ENGINEERING
RESEARCH PARK
RICCARTON CAMPUS
EDINBURGH, LOTHIAN EH14 4AS
031 4493393 FAX: 031 4496254

AREA : SPECIALIST-SCIENTIFIC
C-TCA : PART IV
CONSULT : ROBERT FORBES

INTERDIVE
THE DIVER TRAINING CENTRE
WEST HOE ROAD, PLYMOUTH
DEVON PL1 3BH
0752 255665 FAX: 0752 255344

C-TCA : PARTS II, I, III, IV
C-ERCA : PART II
CONSULT : JOHN RABONE

NORTHUMBRIA POLICE NATIONAL DIVING AND MARINE SCHOOL
PIPEWELLGATE
GATESHEAD
TYNE & WEAR NE8 2BJ
091 2323451 FAX: 091 2323451

AREA : SPECIALIST
C-TCA : RESTRICTED PART III (POLICE), PART IV COURSES
CONSULT : CI D THOMPSON

PRODIVE LTD
SERVICES AREA
FALMOUTH DOCKS
FALMOUTH, CORNWALL TR11 4NR
0326 315691 FAX: 0326 315716

C-TCA : PARTS I, III, IV
CONSULT : ED WILLS

RGIT LTD
338 KING STREET
ABERDEEN
GRAMPIAN AB2 3BJ
0224 638970 FAX: 0224 637990

AREA : SPECIALIST
C-TCA : RESTRICTED PART IV (TANK DIVING) COURSE
CONSULT : JOHN MACDONALD

ROYAL ENGINEERING DIVING ESTABLISHMENT
HMS NELSON (GUNWHARF)
QUEEN STREET, PORTSMOUTH
HANTS PO1 3HH
0705 822351 Ext 24605

AREA : SPECIALIST
C-TCA : PARTS III, IV COURSES
CONSULT : CAPTAIN RUTHERFORD

ROYAL NAVY DIVING SCHOOL
HMS NELSON (GUNWHARF)
QUEEN STREET, PORTSMOUTH
HANTS PO1 3HH
0705 822351 Ext 24861

AREA : SPECIALIST
C-TCA : PART III COURSES
CONSULT : CPO (D) N CHRISTIE

STRATHCLYDE POLICE NATIONAL DIVING SCHOOL
SPRINGBURN POLICE OFFICE
755 HAWTHORN STREET, GLASGOW
STRATHCLYDE G22 6AY
041 5581113

AREA : SPECIALIST
C-TCA : RESTRICTED PART III (POLICE), PART IV COURSES
CONSULT : INSPECTOR D HIGGINS

THE DIVING INITIATIVE
143 HOSPITAL STREET
NEWTOWN, BIRMINGHAM B19 3XA
021 3334312 FAX: 021 3596043

AREA : CITY & GUILDS - NATIONAL VOCATIONAL TRAINING

THE UNDERWATER CENTRE LTD
FORT WILLIAM, HIGHLANDS PH33 6LZ
0397 703786 FAX: 0397 704969

C-TCA : PARTS I, III, IV
C-ERCA : PARTS I, III, IV. PART II WITH INPP, FRANCE
CONSULT : DOUG SHEARER

Magazine Publishers

AQUACORPS
618 ASHE STREET
KEY WEST, FL 33040 USA
010 1 800 3652655
FAX: 010 1 305 2947612

PUBLISHER-AQUACORPS TECHNICAL DIVING MAGAZINE

EATON PUBLICATION
55 HIGH STREET
TEDDINGTON, MIDDLESEX TW11 8HA
081 9434288 FAX: 081 9434312

PUBLISHER-DIVER MAGAZINE

FREESTYLE PUBLICATIONS LTD
18 MARKET STREET
POOLE, DORSET BH15 1NF
0202 682699 FAX: 0202 682987

PUBLISHER-SCUBA WORLD

MARKET LINK PUBLISHING
MARKET LINK HOUSE
TYE GREEN, ELSENHAM
BISHOPS STORTFORD, HERTS CM22 6DY
0279 647555 FAX: 0279 815300

PUBLISHER-SPORTS DIVER

OCEAN REALM
342 WEST SUNSET ROAD
SAN ANTONIO, TX 78209 USA
010 1 210 8248099
FAX: 010 1 210 8203522

PUBLISHER-OCEAN REALM

RODALE PRESS INC.
33E MINOR STREET
EMMAUS, PA 18098 USA
010 1 215 9675171
FAX: 010 1 215 9678963

PUBLISHER-RODALES SCUBA DIVING

SKIN DIVER MAGAZINE
8490 SUNSET BOULEVARD
LOS ANGELES, CA 90069 USA
010 1 310 8542222
FAX: 010 1 310 8542121

PUBLISHER-SKIN DIVER

SUB AQUA JOURNAL
750 WEST BROADWAY
LONG BEACH
NY 11561 USA
010 1 516 8891208

PUBLISHER-SUB AQUA JOURNAL

UNTERWASSEFOTOGRAFIE (UWF)
T. FLEISCHMANN VERLAG KG
POSTFACH 13 01 54, D-8500
NURNBERG 13,
GERMANY
010 49 9 11563501
FAX: 010 49 9 11515783

PUBLISHER-UWF

Book Publishers and Distributors

CORAL MARINE
BROADWAY HOUSE
21 BROADWAY
MAIDENHEAD
BERKS SL6 1JK
0628 810654 FAX: 0628 810669

DISTRIBUTORS OF MARINE PUBLICATIONS

IMMEL PUBLISHING
20 BERKELEY STREET
BERKELEY SQUARE
LONDON W1X 5AE
071 4911799 FAX: 071 4935524

PUBLISHER-MARINE & WILDLIFE FIELD GUIDES

INIGO PRESS LTD
24 POLAND STREET
LONDON W1V 3DD
ENGLAND
071 434 3807
FAX: 071 434 3799

PUBLISHER-UK DIVERS SOURCE

Diving Books

DIVE GUIDES - UK

#4755
Dive Sussex - Kendall McDonald
#4760
Dive Wight and Hampshire - Martin Pritchard, Kendall McDonald
#4756
Dive Dorset - John and Vicky Hinchcliffe
#4757
Dive South Devon - K McDonald, D Cockbill
#4758
Dive South Cornwall - Richard Larn
#4759
Dive West Scotland - Gordon Ridley
#4773
Dive North-West Scotland - Gordon Ridley
#4829
Dive Scotland - Northern Isles and East Coast
#4761
Dive North East - Dave Shaw, Barry Winfield
#4762
Dive Yorkshire - Arthur Godfrey, Peter Lassey

USA

#4841
Ned DeLoach's Underwater Florida
#3004
Upper Florida Keys Diver's Guide - Shlomo Cohen
#4515
Florida Keys - Diving & Snorkelling Guide - 2nd Edition
#4562
Stephen Frink's Underwater Guide - Florida Keys
#4514
Florida's East Coast - Diving & Snorkelling Guide - 2nd Edition
#4775
Diving Offshore California
#4522
Channel Islands: Calif. - Diving & Snorkelling Guide.
#4524
South California - Diving & Snorkelling Guide
#4523
North California - Diving & Snorkelling Guide
#4598
Texas - Diving & Snorkelling Guide
#4731
Great Lakes - Diving & Snorkelling Guide
#4616
Pacific Northwest - Diving and Snorkelling Guide

AUSTRALIA

#4599
Australia - Diving & Snorkelling Guide
#4615
S.E. Australia - Diving & Snorkelling Guide

BAHAMAS

#4521
Nassau/New Prov. Island - Diving & Snorkelling Guide - 2nd Edition
#4513
Bahama Family Islands - Diving & Snorkelling Guide

BELIZE

#4519
Belize - Diving & Snorkelling Guide

BERMUDA

#4596
Diving Bermuda - Jesse Cancelmo & Mike Strohofer
#4701
Wonders of the Deep: Underwater Bermuda

BONAIRE

#4595
Diving Bonaire - George Lewbel & Larry Martin
#4728
Bonaire - Diving & Snorkelling Guide

CAYMAN ISLANDS

#3002
Cayman Island Diver's Guide - Shlomo Cohen
#4518
Grand Cayman - Diving and Snorkelling Guide - 2nd Edition

CURACAO

#4568
Curacao - Diving & Snorkelling Guide

HAWAII

#4700
Diving Hawaii - Steve Rosenberg
#4517
Hawaiian Islands - Diving & Snorkelling Guide
#4750
Hawaii Below: An Island by Island Guide - Rod Canham
#4893
Dive Maldives - Expected 1994

MICRONESIA

#4785
Diver's Guide to Guam and Micronesia - Tim Rock

MEXICO

#4777
Diving Cozumel - Steve Rosenberg
#4520
Cozumel - Diving & Snorkelling Guide

RED SEA

#3001
Red Sea Diver's Guide - Shlomo Cohen
#4705
The Egyptian Red Sea - Eric Hanuer

TURKS AND CAICOS

#4614
Turks and Caicos - Diving and Snorkelling Guide
#4703
Diving the Turks and Caicos - Bob Gascoine
#4729
British Virgin Islands - Diving & Snorkelling Guide
#4776
Diving British Virgin Islands - Jim & Odile Scheiner
#4730
U.S. Virgin Islands - Diving & Snorkelling Guide
#4528
Best Dives of the Western Hemisphere - J & J Huber
#4741
Caribbean Diver's Guide

SHIPWRECKS

#4866
The Ultimate Wreck Diving Guide - Gary Gentile
#4713
Advanced Wreck Diving Guide - Gary Gentile
#4525
Shipwreck Diving - Dan Berg
#4620
Sunken Treasure - World's Greatest Shipwrecks - Gaetano Cafiero

UK

#4764
Great British Wrecks Vol 2
#4765
Great British Wrecks Vol 3
Shipwreck - John Fowles

USA

#4720
Treasure of the Atocha - Duncan Matthewson
#4529
Florida Shipwrecks - Dan & Denise Berg
#4542
Famous Shipwrecks of the Florida Keys
#4746
Andrea Doria - Gary Gentile
#4747
U.S.S. San Diego - Gary Gentile
#4604
Shipwrecks of New York and New Jersey
#4852
New England's Legacy of Shipwrecks - Harry Keatts
#4546
Wreck Valley Vol 2 - Dan Berg
#4594
Guide to Shipwreck Diving - N. Carolina - Roderick Farb
#4833
Shipwrecks: The Graveyard of the Atlantic - Roderick Farb
#4603
Shipwrecks of Southern California - B Cardonne & P Smith
#4597
Guide to Shipwreck Diving - S. California - Darren Douglass

#4710
Dive into History - Vol 1: U.S. Warships - H Keatts & G Farr
#4711
Dive into History - Vol 2: U.S. Submarines - H Keatts & G Farr

CARIBBEAN WRECKS

#4544
Tropical Shipwrecks - Dan & Denise Berg
#4545
Bermuda Shipwrecks - Dan & Denise Berg

MICRONESIA

#4714
WW II Wrecks of the Kwajalein & Truk Lagoon - D Bailey
#4845
WW II Wrecks of Palau - D Bailey
#4880
Hailstorm Over Truk Lagoon - Klaus Lindemann
#4881
Desecrate One - Klaus Kindemann

PHOTOGRAPHY SYSTEM MANUALS

#4552
The Nikonos V Handbook - Jim & Cathy Church OUT OF PRINT.
#4551
Choosing & Using Underwater Strobes - J & C Church
#4830
How to Use Sea & Sea - Joe Liburdi & Cara Sherman

PHOTOGRAPHY TECHNIQUES

#4555
Howard Hall's Successful Underwater Photography
#4825
Underwater Photography - Charles Seaborn
#4828
Mastering Underwater Photography - Carl Roessler

VIDEO TECHNIQUES

#4709
Shooting Underwater Video - Steve Rossenberg
#4872
Jim Church's Essential Guide to Underwater Video

MARINE LIFE

#4770
British Sea Fishes - Dr Francis Dipper
#4742
Sea Life of Britain & Ireland - Elizabeth Wood
#4743
Guide to Inshore Marine Life - D Erwin & B Picton
#4736
Red Sea Reef Fishes - Dr John Randall
#4737
The Diver's Guide to Red Sea Reef Fishes
#4735
Red Sea Invertebrates - Peter Vine

FISH AND INVERTEBRATES IDENTIFICATION

\#4802
Reef Fish Identification - Paul Humann
#4846
Reef Creature Identification - Paul Humann
#4898
Reef Coral Identification - Paul Humann
#4899
Reef Identification Boxed Set
#4797#4854
Reef Notes & Slate - Paul Humann
#4533
Guide to Corals and Fishes (Waterproof) - Jerry Greenberg
#4800
Diver's Guide to the Fishes of the Maldives - Dr John Randall
#4706
Fishes of the Great Barrier Reef & Coral Sea
#4564
Sea of Cortez Marine Invertebrates - Alex Kerstitch
#4541
Beneath the Tropic Sea
#4847
Watching Fishes - Roberta & James Wilson
#4873

Marine Biology - Peter Castro & Michael Huber

CORAL IDENTIFICATION

#4898
Reef Coral Identification - Paul Humann
#4533
The Coral Reef - Jerry Greenberg
#4894
Divers' Guide to Corals - Elizabeth Wood
#4609
The Greenpeace Book of Coral Reefs - Sue Wells, Nick Hanna
#4782
Great Reefs of the World - Carl Roessler

SHARKS, DOLPHINS, WHALES, ETC.

#4845
Master of the World Oceans - Michael Bright
#4726
The Undersea Predators - Carl Roessler
#4534
Sharks and other Dangerous Sea Creatures - Jerry Greenberg
#4623
Sharks, Silent Hunters of the Deep - Ron and Valerie Taylor
#4739
Sharks of Arabia - Dr John Randall
#4719
The Pictures in the Dolphin Mind - Frank Robson

MEDICAL

#4740
Red Sea Safety - Peter Vine
#4707
Medical Guide to Hazardous Marine Life
#4769
Diving Emergency Handbook - John Lippman & Stan Bugg
#4895
Advanced First Aid Afloat - Peter Eastman, MD
#4896
Scuba Life Saving - Albert Pierce
#4897
Underwater Ear And Nose Care - N Roydhouse, MD

TECHNICAL DIVING

#4868
Deeper into Diving - John Lippman
#4867
Essentials of Deeper Sport Diving - J. Lippman
#4843
Deep Diving - Bret Gilliam & Robert Von Maier
#5013
The Underwater Investigator - Corp R G Teather
#5012
Man In The Sea - Yu Chong Lin & K K Shida
#5005
NITROX Manual - Dick Rutkowski
#5004
The Application of Enriched Air Mixtures - Edward Betts
#4550
Mixed Gas Diving - Tom Mount & Bret Gilliam

CAVE DIVING

#4605
The Darkness Beckons - Martin Pritchard
#5007
NSS Cavern Diving Manual - Zumerick, Prosser & Grey
#5006
Basic Cave Diving - Sheck Exley
#5008
Cave Diving Comms. - J Prosser & H Grey
#5008
Basic Underwater Cave Surveying - J Burge

BOATS, NAVIGATION, ETC

#4909
Rigid Inflatable Boats - Colin Jones
#4607
Coastal Navigation - Gerry Smith
#4608
Simple Electronic Navigation - Mik Chinery
#4610
Marine VHF Operation - Michael Gale
#4611
Weather at Sea - David Houghton
#4613
Knots and Splices - Jeff Toghill

All titles available from various outlets or from Coral Marine on 0628 810654 quoting catalogue number.

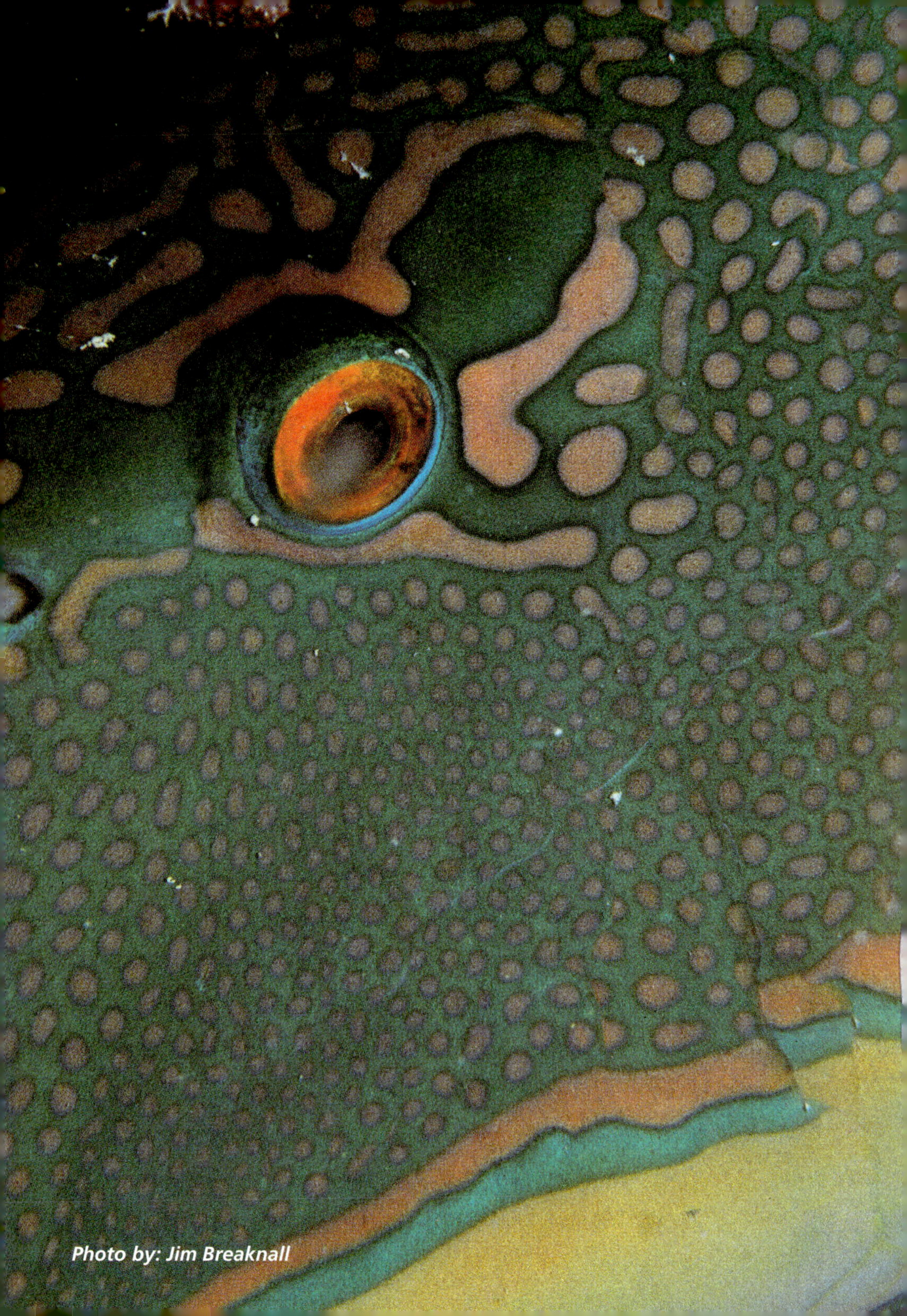
Photo by: Jim Breaknall

Travel

Getting your Visa right from the start

Worldwide Visas are based at Charing Cross in London and advise on a wide range of visa and travel requirements.

It is a familiar resonant tone at Heathrow Terminal Three as the information system calls the name of yet another beleaguered passenger experiencing visa and passport difficulties. It is unlikely that this traveller to the Indian Ocean will ever cross that customs line, let alone unwrap the innocuous boiled sweet as he prepares to equalise at the point of no return.

What distinguishes this passenger from the traveller who has already purchased his essential duty free's and is currently relaxing in the departure lounge? Clearly the latter is not suffering from stress, he has organised this trip, down to the last tube of his favourite toothpaste. He uses his time to anticipate the challenging dives that await him at his destination and to ensure that throughout his trip he can meet a demanding and comprehensive itinerary.

Furthermore, this trip will involve crossing several international borders, achieving successful re-entries and having the correct currency in hand to meet all financial obligations. He will also have taken care to find out the latest health requirements applicable to the countries he plans to visit.

All these plans and preparations may seem a nightmare to the uninitiated. Similarly, the regular traveller is not infallible. It is easy to adopt a blase approach to overseas travel and overlook fundamental requirements for entry and exit to the countries in question. Certainly, one of the main stumbling blocks to smooth and efficient travel, is gaining access to that all important visa whether it be for work purposes, residency, a working holiday, business or purely for pleasure.

How long will the visa take to issue? The length of stay and validity of the visa is important. Are there any problems associated with a particular category? Do we require more than one entry and can we extend this visa on arrival?

The number of forms and photographs need to be precise. Is the form current, do the photographs need to be black and white or in colour, do they need to have precise dimensions? What supporting documents are required and, in particular, what form should an invitation take in order to be accepted?

Visitors to parts of Africa and the Far East will be expected to produce a letter from their sponsor clearly outlining full immigration responsibilities for the duration of the stay. In some cases visa requirements include certified and legalised general medical forms, contracts of employment and sometimes educational certificates and proof of a negative HIV test.

For travel throughout Africa, South America, Asia and the Far East, visas may not be granted unless evidence of vaccination certificates are available. Countries like Nigeria will require photocopies of travellers cheques and China will ask for evidence of airline tickets.

The former Soviet Union will expect to see proof of visa purchase as well as letters and telex invites for business travel from approved/official organisations. In general terms, copies of bank statements, the itinerary, proof of travel insurance and letters confirming repatriation issued by employers may all be necessary in supporting a visa application.

Consular staff are familiar with most of the requirements for those travelling to their country on the host country's passport. However, their Foreign Affairs Manual or computer will dictate precise documentary requirements and approximate time scales for processing. The manual or computer is updated periodically, and with rare exception, must be adhered to.

We can curse and swear and complain about what may appear to be time wasting, bureaucratic procedures but the individual official has limited scope to adapt or change the rules laid down. Certain foreign nationals applying in the UK will have their application referred. This may be a diplomatic reaction or one of reciprocity. This process can take between seven days and three months.

Having determined the category of visit and the requirements for visa issue, it is time to check that the passport also meets the Embassy/Consulate requirements for visa issue and will not restrict the validity of a visa or prevent entry at the border. Is the passport signed? Thailand will not issue a visa to an unsigned passport. We need to check the expiry date. Most countries will not issue a visa unless the life of the passport exceeds the normal minimum entry validity time. Thailand and Egypt require six months passport life irrespective of your period of stay and Papua New Guinea requires one year. Each country has a slightly different view on permitted stay periods, which must not be confused with the overall life or validity of the visa.

The visa validity will also determine how far in advance the application should be made. There is no point in obtaining a string of African visas all valid for three months from the date of issue only to discover that at least half will have expired before entry is made.

Returning to the passport check, ensure that adequate pages exist, not only for visas issued in the country of departure but for visas issued en route and the inevitable entry and exit control stamps. Some countries require a clear left and right hand page for visa issue. It is considered undiplomatic to issue more than one visa on any one passport page. Does your passport photograph still reflect a true likeness? Even radical hair style changes can create problems. Did you collect a sensitive stamp on the last business or holiday trip abroad? Or have you forgotten about the last visa denial stamp which both India and United States have a habit of placing in the passport.

Once your visa is issued check thoroughly for accuracy. Check that family dependants have been acknowledged. Check that you have received the correct passport. The new EEC-style document lacks personal identity on the outside cover.

The irony of international travel is that it symbolises freedom but binds us in red tape. So where and to whom should we turn to for valuable and informative advice. There are many sources offering up to-date information on health requirements, visa and passport matters, local customs, weather and climatic guidance and many others. You can spend ages trying to obtain information from Embassies, Consulates and Government departments by phone. Travel agents are a useful source of information but despite EEC-Directives expressing travel advice procedures, they have to concentrate on that all important multi-sector air travel booking.

There is an alternative however. You can try a specialist visa agent. These guide customers through the sometimes complex jargon, ensure forms are correctly filled in and matched with supporting documents. Fees currently range from around £l5 to £50 depending on the complexity of the work involved.

Staff experienced in immigration can take the headache out of organising visas including work and residency permits and supply comprehensive information packs, medical and dental kits covering most countries of the world, by post. Visa and Passport applications can often also accepted by post or courier and foreign currency can be purchased at rates often more attractive than high street vendors.

While you are planning that dream trip to dive the crystal waters of some of the farther flung sites around the world it is worth considering the advantages of arranging the necessary documentation through a specialist agent.

They are not prohibitively expensive and, as visa requirements have a habit of changing at short notice and embassy information lines are often overloaded, talking to the right people in good time could save you no end of trouble.

Coral Reef diving

by Mark Caney

Coral reef, Red Sea. Picture: Mark Caney.

Sooner or later all divers will probably dive a coral reef. Maybe you are dreaming of a trip to the Red Sea or the Maldives and swimming amongst fantastic clouds of coloured fish and gardens of coral - well maybe you need to start to change the way you dive right now so that you are ready for that trip.

Coral is an animal, closely related to jellyfish. A coral head is made up of many individuals known as polyps, each one looking like a miniature sea anemone. There are two basic kinds of coral, soft and hard. The hard corals have a limestone "skeleton" which supports their bodies. Millions of years of coral growth have resulted in such massive structures as the Australian Great Barrier Reef, but it is a painfully slow process.

All corals are covered in a slimy mucus substance which protects the organism in

TRAVEL

much the same way as your skin protects you. Any form of contact with the coral can remove this layer which can then allow bacteria to attack the coral which may result in sickness or death of the affected polyps. Worse still, the branching forms of hard corals are very brittle and easily broken off by a careless diver.

The simple fact is that you must not come into any contact with the living reef. Don't fall into the trap of thinking "well it won't make any real difference what I do".

Thousands of divers visit the reef each year and if they all shared that attitude the reef would soon die. I am not exaggerating here, there are places in the world where large numbers of divers have hurt the one they love and devastated large areas of coral through ignorance and bad practice.

The best way of limiting the harm done to the reef is through proper buoyancy control. Yes, I know you can pivot up and down on your fintips in a swimming pool for a minute, but are you sure you can spend one hour underwater without ever touching the bottom? That is exactly what you will have to do if the sea-bed is covered in coral.

Don't overweight yourself. This results in a very poor posture underwater and unnecessary work for you.

Your BC will lift your head and you will need extra effort to swim horizontally. PADI produce an excellent video on the subject of buoyancy which can give you a lot of useful hints about truly mastering buoyancy control, something that surprisingly few divers actually achieve.

I have seen many Brit divers arrive at a tropical resort for a dive, put on their 3mm shorty and then a pair of 6mm heavy-duty gloves! They might just as well wear a T-shirt with the slogan "go ahead polyp - make my day".

You don't need those gloves in most warm waters unless your buoyancy control is so bad that you keep falling on the reef; in which case stay on the novice diver's site until you get it right!

Check you have no trailing gear. Octopus regulators, consols and torches cause a lot of damage as well as creating drag, so attach them to your rig somehow.

Obviously don't throw litter in the water, and if you see a plastic cup or beer can down there, why not bring it up and put it where it belongs? If only one diver in ten did this the dive sites would soon look a lot more attractive.

If you are boat diving, you certainly must not drop an anchor on a reef. This causes a fantastic amount of damage and must be avoided at all costs. All good dive operators use permanent moorings in this situation.

Finally, if you are a photographer this issue becomes even more important. Imagine you want to take a photo of a 3 cms nudibranch on a totally covered coral seabed.

You have to hover with your lens 5 cms away from the subject and remain perfectly stationary within your depth of field which is about plus or minus 5mm. Is your buoyancy control really that good?

Please do aim to dive in coral waters, the marine life is incomparable, but treat it with real respect, the reef took millions of years to grow and takes seconds to destroy.

Red Sea diving

by Hossam Helmy

Hossam Helmy is a law graduate from Ain Shams University in Cairo. Following some 14 years working for the Egyptian government in presidential security he chanced upon a Dutch geologist/diving instructor who changed his life by teaching him to dive. Now five years and 2500 dives later, his love for the Red Sea remains undimmed. To further his ambition to dive the whole of the region and to share its unique pleasures, he started the Red Sea Diving Safari Company.

Many people believe that the Red Sea offers superlative diving. It is not hard to appreciate why. Stepping from a land steeped in history into waters that were already well charted by 1500 BC when Queen Hatsheput of Egypt sailed its length, this sea provides an underwater environment as rich in wild life as the land above appears barren. An area of only 169,000 square miles of water contains over a thousand species of fish and many thousands more marine invertebrates. With the advent of scuba this underwater realm is now open to almost any one with the appropriate qualifications.

Sports diving in the Red Sea is concentrated predominantly around the Sinai. The majority of dives are from boats - which are employed either as transportation from land bases or as liveaboards. As the entire western border of the Red Sea is fringed by a reef system that runs more or less continuously along its entire length it is clear that there must be many more miles of coastline which for reasons of logistics are not often dived or explored at all.

A simple and convenient way of diving these remote sites which is gaining in popularity, particularly along the southern Egyptian Red Sea coast, is on a shore diving safari. As the name implies, housed in tents for mobility, the dive party moves along the coast as and when diving opportunities in individual sites are exhausted. With all the required amenities and many luxuries provided for, the diving is leisurely and safe.

To fully appreciate this form of diving it is interesting to learn a little of the geology and physical geography of the region.

The Red Sea stretches from Suez in the north and extends some 1300 miles in a south easterly direction to the Straits of Bab el-Mandeb where it joins the Indian Ocean. The sea lies in a fault depression that forms part of a complex rift system that stretches from Tanzania, Kenya and Ethiopia in the west through to the Gulf of Aqaba in the north east.

Cutting through a central mass of Precambrian igneous and metamorphic rocks, it reaches a maximum depth of 2947m while in contrast the land on the surrounding coastal plains can rise to over 2018m - indeed the outcrops of this mass, known as the Arabian-Nubian Massif, now form the rugged mountain ranges clearly visible in the region. Surrounding the massif are marine

The Red Sea Diving Safari
Pioneering Safaris ~ El Quesir ~ Marsa Alam ~ Ras Banas & The Brothers
Red Sea Diving Safaris
Tel: 020-2-701833/709942
Fax: 020-2-3494219
UK contact: Amanda Levick
Tel: 0323 648924
Fax: 0323 738356
RED SEA DIVING SAFARI

sediments from the Palaeozoic through to the Early Tertiary eras.

The Red Sea valley has been formed by complex phases of land movement - the first separated Africa from Arabia some 50 million years ago, the second created of the Gulf of Suez and the northern part of the sea. The Gulf of Aqaba and the southern half of the Red Sea are the most recent additions and date back only 3 - 4 million years. Today the region remains in motion, separating at a rate of 0.59 to 0.62 inches a year. Considering the geological youthfulness of the region, combined with the lack of precipitation, it is not surprising that the geographical features both on land and underwater retain the legacy of their rugged past.

Shore Diving

These geo-physical actions have left four easily identifiable physiographic characteristics on the western shoreline of the Red Sea. These are *Marsa, Sharm, Ras* and *Dahar*. While diving opportunities along the shore will depend on factors such as weather conditions and tidal movements, a knowledge of the characteristics common to these formations can be of help in predive planning and local orientation.

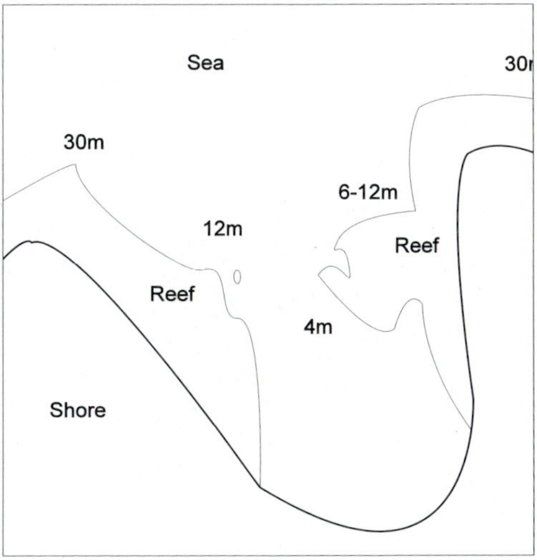

Marsa Wisr is located approximately 42m south of El Quesir. In common with marsas in the region, its northside is rich in coral while its southside is richer in fish. It is not unusual for pelagics like dolphin and manta rays to enter the bay.

(Map not to scale)

Preparing for a dive

Marsa *(Arabic - anchorage for small boats).* Marsas are U shaped bays formed when wadis (now dried river beds) originating from the surrounding mountains reach the shore and cut through the fringing reef formation. They are characterised by a sandy entrance in the

TRAVEL

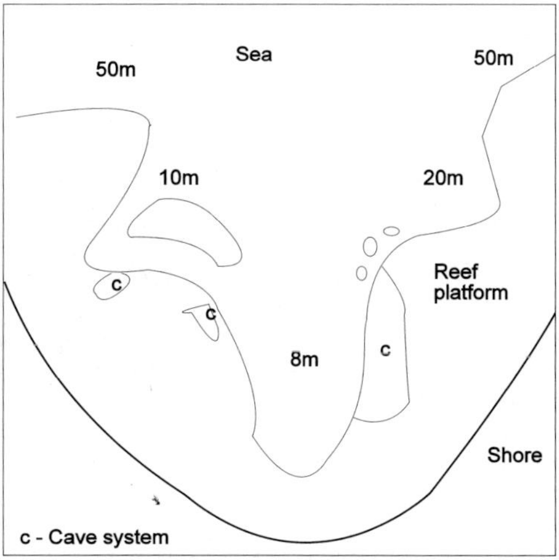

Sharm Abo Dabbor, 100 km south of El Quesir, is a typical Red Sea sharm formation. Apart from rich marine life features include cave systems and free standing coral encrusted pillars.

(Map not to scale)

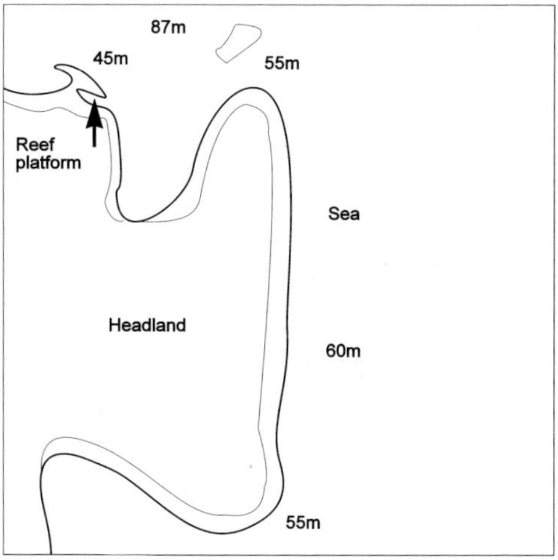

Ras Abo Soma lies 42 km south of Hurgada. It stretches some 11 km in length and protrudes roughly 10 km out into the sea. Being subjected to currents, pelagics, soft and hard coral are common.

(Map not to scalc)

middle of the U and bordered on both sides by a reef platform. Changes in depth are gradual; it increases from sea level at the entrance to some 35 - 40m at the outer edges of the bay. Sandbars, resulting from wave action and local currents, are common in the shallows.

Sharm *(Arabic - lips of a camel).*
Sharms, like marsas are formed when an inland wadi or wadi system reaches the coast. However unlike marsas they do not cut through the reefs. Sharms are characterised by a V shaped groove on the outer edge of the reef formation and are so called as this channel resembles the grooves in the upper and lower lips of a camel. Depths range from 8 - 15m inside the point of the V to 35 - 45m at its outer edges.

Dahar *(Arabic - back of an object).*
Dahars are the land connections between marsas, sharms and ras'. They are characterised by having an unbroken reef platform. Depths vary from 10 to 45m.

Ras *(Arabic - head).*
A ras is simply a headland. Underwater its edges can slope steeply downwards, sometimes almost vertically, to reach depths of 60-70m.

Entry Techniques

At sharms, ras' and dahars, and on occasions at marsas, the fringing reef platform has to be crossed before reaching open water. Care has to be taken when doing so as whilst the main part of the platform is more or less flat it can be peppered with holes and slippery with algae growth. In certain areas potentially hazardous marine life such as sea urchins can be found and require additional care.

Furthermore the whole of Egypt's coastal reef system is designated a marine park and though the coral on the reef platform is normally dead and eroded, there can still be live coral pockets which should not be disturbed. Towards the seaward side of the

Camping on the shore of the Red Sea.

reef healthy hard corals are usually present and final access to open water should be made swimming with the aid of a snorkel or demand valve to avoid damaging the reef. At windward sites, surf entry and exit techniques may have to be used.

Temperature

While the temperature on land remains consistently warm during the day the water temperature varies with the time of the year. In winter, a drysuit or a wetsuit of 6mm or greater thickness may be needed while in the summer, thermal protection equivalent to a 3mm wetsuit will probably suffice. Consideration should also be given to thermoclines and the amount of time spent underwater.

Gulf of Aqaba

Currents are common along the shore of the Gulf of Aqaba and flow in a roughly southerly direction. Such currents can reach high speeds and though hard corals dominate the region, soft corals can be abundant in areas subjected to these currents.

With a north northwest prevailing wind, hard corals tend to be best developed on the northern leeside of marsas and sharms while fish are more evident at both the outer and southern edges of these formations where current and wave action carries abundant sources of food.

Picture: Paul Naylor

Ras' however have an opposite distribution of marine life - the northern windward side will normally have more fish while the southern leeside of the headland provides a more suitable environment for hard coral development.

The dahars are generally poor in marine life when compared to marsas, sharms and ras' especially if they are associated with greater depths. A lack of current along the dahars combined with short exposure to sunlight - dahars tend to be east facing - may be contributory factors.

Hurgada to Ras Banas

Along the shoreline south of Hurgada currents are generally localised and can be unpredictable.

Funnelling along the sandbars in marsas and at the narrow inner end of the V in sharms can result in currents when heavy winds and tidal movements are present. These currents run into the open sea from the sandbar and will tend to end outside the funnel area.

Local currents may also be encountered at ras' and at the outer edges of marsas and sharms. Caused by a combination of heavy wind and/or tides the direction of these currents will vary depending on the wind direction and local tidal movements. Again these currents will weaken and disappear with distance from the reef.

Marine life is generally most abundant in sheltered areas - in marsas, sharms and the leeward side of a gently sloping ras. Such places offer relatively quiet waters and a greater catchment area for sunlight promoting hard coral growth and therefore richer marine life.

South of Ras Banas

Little is known about diving between Ras Banas and the Sudanese border as the Egyptian government only recently sanctioned scuba activities there. However there is no reason to believe that the generalisations made above do not apply.

Formalities

In theory, given time and perseverance, a diver should be able to organise a private shore diving holiday in the region. However in practice, for reasons outlined below, the logistics of such an exercise will tax all but the most dedicated.

Much of coastal Egypt is designated military controlled area. Without an understanding of the language and procedures, applications for access permits can prove tricky. Secondly the Arabian desert, wildly beautiful as it is, is rather sparsely populated. As it encompasses virtually the whole of the coast all necessary provisions and water will have to be carried. The third and perhaps the biggest consideration to be made is personal safety in the event of illness or a diving accident. Without the infrastructure present to cope any private venture can best be described as foolish.

If the above sounds daunting salvation exists in the form of a few commercial safari operators who can provide access and shore dives in this region both safely, effortlessly and without the headaches. It will take supreme willpower to forego such convenience.

• *Please note that the generalisations above are made as a result of the author's diving experience in the region. While the author believes them to be valid and of help in planning a dive, it neither can nor should replace proper predive procedures.*

Diving around Gibraltar

by Dennis Santos

Dennis Santos is one of Gibraltar's most active and widely experienced divers. He has served as a club officer for the Joint Services SAC and was a founder member of HMS Calper RNVR diving unit. Dennis is a volunteer tender with the Gibraltar Hyperbaric unit.

Gibraltar, because of its unique position at the entrance to the Mediterranean, offers excellent diving to both the novice and the accomplished diver alike.

Gibraltar forms a neck of land connected to the Spanish hinterland but otherwise is surrounded by water. On the western side of the rock is the Bay of Gibraltar into which flows the Atlantic whilst to the east is the Mediterranean sea. The middle of the bay to the west is approximately 400m deep and the fact that this mass of water flowing in from the straits has to fill in this massive basin dictates that the maximum tidal range be no more than 1m.

However, for this reason also, the currents especially at Spring tides, can be quite fierce. This accounts for the difficulty experienced in predicting slack water correctly. Consequently the flood tide may be flowing into the bay at the same time as the ebb tide is still trying to find its way out into the straits. The result is either no slack water period at all in certain parts of the bay or a current that is found to be flowing in completely the opposite direction to that expected. However local knowledge and a bit of trial and error ensures some periods of slack water.

Most of the diving is concentrated on the western side of the rock. The bay is littered with wrecks, some of which are accessible from shore. More adventurous diving is always available on the eastern side where several reefs provide refuge for numerous species of marine life, some of exceptional proportions.

The underwater visibility can vary from about 1m to anything up to 10, and exceptionally up to 20m though this type of visibility is only likely during the months of September and October when plankton levels are at their lowest. The underwater temperature can vary between 5°C in winter and 18°C at the height of the summer months. However most dives can be comfortably carried out in a wetsuit irrespective of the season.

It would be impossible to cover every diving site around Gibraltar in a single article but one or two locations deserve a mention.

Camp Bay on the western side of the rock is a sheltered beach where no more than approximately 50m offshore runs an artificial reef originally started by divers

The Rock of Gibraltar

from the Gibraltar Sub Aqua Club. This artificial reef constructed from old barges, tyres and so forth boasts a multitude of marine life at depths from about 10 to 16m. The fish which inhabit this reef have become accustomed to visits by divers since access to this site is very easy from shore and fish feeding constitutes one of the highlights of this location. For the novice diver this area is a perfect introduction to open water diving.

The southern-most tip of Europe (Europa Point) provides diving on two reefs with awesome drop-offs and the chance to spot the odd Roman or Phoenician anchor. These two reefs protruding up to within 19m of the surface and within a mile of one another are definitely the domain of the experienced diver.

For those with an inclination towards artifacts of archaeological value, there are various sites around the rock which have yielded gin bottles, inkwells etc. Some of the wine bottles found have dated from between 1690 and 1820. Similarly some clay pipes have been uncovered belonging to eras between 1580 and 1880. There are a few sites still to be surveyed for historical remains and the recent interest taken by the Oxford University MARE's Sub team working with the Gibraltar Museum bodes well for the future conservation of Gibraltar's historical heritage.

Organized diving is catered for by various bodies, though they all come under the banner of the BSAC. There are two clubs on the rock, the Gibraltar Sub Aqua Club (branch 888 of the BSAC) and the Joint Services Diving Club (branch 317/s of the BSAC). There are also two commercial operators on the rock, which provide diving and tuition primarily for the visitor. Many individuals on the rock dive either on their own or with friends since the law in Gibraltar precludes the need for certification prior to taking up diving. It goes without saying that this practice should be discouraged, especially amongst our younger divers who, despite their affinity with the sea as a result of its proximity, should still be encouraged to seek proper training prior to taking up this fascinating sport.

The Maltese Islands

by Phil Jackson

The Maltese archipelago is an all-year round centre for the diver. Even in a severe winter the sea temperature seldom falls below 13°C and in stormy weather sheltered coasts offer a number of interesting dive sites.

Diving in the winter is enjoyable as many species of fish move inshore to the shallower, slightly warmer waters. As they are rarely disturbed by swimmers, you can observe and photograph them in conditions that are often more favourable than those found in the peak seasons.

Sea temperatures in summer are around 23°C and you will be comfortable in a light 3mm diving suit although you can dive without one.

The islands are within easy reach of the European mainland - two to three hours at the most - and their facilities compare favourably with other more distant and expensive resorts. They have a well developed infrastructure which is capable of coping with sophisticated diving demands.

Diving schools have organised themselves into the "Association of Professional Diving Schools". All of these lease up-to-date equipment with a good follow-up service at favourable rates.

The seas around Malta are virtually tideless. Underwater currents are very rare in the summer and more frequent in winter though, due to the small size of the island, you can shift to an alternative site without too much trouble. Some locations are more comfortable to dive from a boat, especially as there is always somebody on hand to assist or direct divers.

Ramla - Gozo.
Picture: Courtesy of Malta National Tourist Office

TRAVEL

Requirements

You will need to buy a permit to dive in Maltese waters. This is issued by the Department of Health and costs around one Maltese Lira. A medical certificate, two photographs and your logbook must be presented.

You should note that unless you hold an advanced qualification (PADI Advanced\BSAC Sports Diver\CMAS 2-Star or equivalent) you

Picture: Courtesy of Malta National Tourist Office

will be required to dive with an instructor. All diving schools will handle this paperwork for you and even the experienced diver would be well advised to apply through them rather than to try dealing with it independently. Diving is strictly prohibited in some areas as a result of environmental and archaeological considerations - your school or instructor will advise you on these.

If you are taking a courses under control of an authorised instructor you will require only a medical certificate.

Getting wet

If the year round diving and professional services together with the benevolent attitude of local officials are not in themselves reasons enough to consider a trip to the Maltese Islands then the waters may be.

By Mediterranean standards the waters are still extremely clear and clean and are home to a number of rare species of fish, including the "Anthias Anthias", which unfortunately have vanished from other parts of the sea. Visibility varies between sites but thanks to the rocky coast it reaches 30m on average which makes Malta a natural venue for underwater photography. Colours, especially shades of orange and red, reproduce naturally in depths of 10-12m, even without a flash.

Marine life

The rugged contours of the Maltese islands continue underwater and this bizarre undersea landscape harbours numerous caves (some as large as sports halls), holes, grottos and crevices all of which are home to a rich variety of animal life.

Besides these natural habitats there are the wrecks of ships and aeroplanes around Malta which have become home to fish, crayfish and a multitude of other marine life though the chances of meeting big-game fish or certain species of sharks is almost nonexistent. A few sea animals in these waters are beautiful to watch but dangerous to touch. Though seldom deadly the scorpion fish, bristle worm, weaver and stingray can prove very painful.

You are likely to encounter groupers, amberjacks, bream, wrasse, damsell fish, octopus, squid, flying gurnard, stingrays, meagre, bogue, red mullet and more. Occasionally will you see moray eels as the structure of the coast and the rocks offer ideal living conditions for them, although they tend to be more active during night dives.

Picture: Courtesy of Malta National Tourist Office

Night Diving

Night diving opens a whole new dimension to the experienced diver. After dark in Malta the diver sees an entirely different assortment of fish and colours are more vibrant under a diver's torch. Most diving schools feature

Picture: Courtesy of Malta National Tourist Office

night diving in their programme and under the right conditions every competent diver should enjoy this thrilling experience.

The resort

The islands however are not purely a diving haven. They are islands of history with many interesting attractions - a 6,000 year-old temple built by the earliest inhabitants, many artifacts dating back to the times of the Phoenicians, Greeks and Romans, the proud buildings and cathedrals of the Knights and many remnants of the last war in which Malta was once again the centre of activities in the Mediterranean.

Malta has much to offer - just about everything you want in a holiday and a lot of what you need from a dive.

Dive Cyprus

by Mark Caney

Mark Caney holds the highest level Instructor qualification with PADI, BSAC, SAA and ANDI. In addition to running PADI instructor courses he also provides Nitrox instructor courses and advises dive centres on Nitrox production techniques. Mark has been heavily involved with Training Through Diving, a team of diving professionals who are aligning sport diving qualifications to NVQs (see training section). He currently runs Scubex in Cyprus and specialises in running Instructor level training courses worldwide.

Cyprus has been a popular destination for divers from Europe for many years now. It offers clear water diving and plenty of things to do when not diving. It is also one of the best places to see antiquities underwater, remnants of the ancient civilisations of Greece and the Romans.

The Republic of Cyprus is located in the eastern end of the Mediterranean and has a population of about half a million people. The island is bigger than Malta but you can drive across it in about three hours. In the south of the island, where most of the tourists congregate, the language is Greek, but almost everyone can speak English. Even the driving is on the left so the Brits feel at home right away.

It is easy to arrange holidays from the UK, either through specialised diving travel companies or by booking the holiday separately, and contacting the dive centre yourself. During the high season Cyprus is not a cheap place to travel to but you can get some very good deals during the winter, especially if you make a last minute booking.

The most popular areas are Paphos, Limassol, Larnaca and Ayia Napa. All of these are seaside towns and all have dive centres. The better diving tends to be at the extreme west or east of the island, so Paphos and Ayia Napa are the preferred destinations of most divers.

The water temperature varies considerably according to the time of year. It is at it's warmest from July to early October at 20-25 degrees when a thin wetsuit or half of a thick one will keep you comfortable on most dives. During the rest of the year a full wetsuit is needed, especially for January to April when it can drop to about 15 degrees.

All of the better dive centres offer gear for hire, but it is usually cheaper to bring your own equipment except for cylinders and weights. Most of the hire cylinders are aluminium 10 or 12 litre sizes. If you prefer to use nitrox, Cydive in Paphos is now offering courses and fills.

You must take your qualifications and logbook in order to hire gear or dive. If you and your buddy are reasonably experienced most of the dive centres will allow you to dive without a guide. The diving is about equally divided between shore dives and boat

Vera K. Cyprus. Picture: Mark Caney

dives. Boats are usually anchored so you need to be able to find your way back underwater if you want to avoid long surface swims! Hard sole boots are needed for any shore dives.

The majority of the dive centres are PADI but there are a few that are also BSAC. Cyprus is an ideal place to upgrade your qualifications during your stay and the local conditions are perfect for training. The big dive centres offer all courses right up to instructor level as well as covering most of the speciality areas such as underwater photography.

The diving is usually good with visibility typically in the 15-40 metre range. There are virtually no currents and the sea is calm for most of the year. The marine life is typical of the Mediterranean; a lot of small, colourful fish and the occasional big Grouper. Octopus are often seen, especially on night dives. Most dives are on rocky bottoms, and underwater caverns and archways are common. The majority of dives are between 5m and 30m, but there are a few that are a little deeper.

A special attraction of Cyprus is the variety of remains from ancient times. These usually take the form of fragments of amphorae, the large clay jars carried on the trading vessels of that time. Large stone anchors and occasional bronze artifacts may also be seen. These are normally found in a concentrated area where a ship has been driven into shallow water and subsequently broken up, leaving it's cargo scattered on the seabed. Paphos was the capital of the island in Roman times so there are especially high concentrations of ancient wrecks along the nearby coast.

If you are taking your underwater still or video camera, you will enjoy the clear blue water and ample light. You can easily get

Amphorae, Cyprus. Picture Mark Caney.

print films developed in a few hours but slide processing is harder to find. There are plenty of macro subjects around, many of which can be found in the most unlikely sites such as harbours. The best place to take your wide angle lens is on the wreck dives. Two well known wrecks in the Paphos area are the *"Vera K"* and the *"Achilleas"*, both very interesting dives in around eleven metres, which means plenty of light and bottom time.

The most famous Cyprus wreck is the *"Zenobia"*, in forty metres of water near Larnaca. She is a was a huge RORO ferry with over one hundred lorries still on board. She is a recent wreck and is still in excellent condition. The wreck is just a ten minute boat ride from Larnaca marina and trips are arranged from a number of dive centres in Cyprus. The acknowledged expert on the wreck is Englishman Ian McMurray who runs Octopus Divers, a PADI dive centre in Larnaca. Ian has logged well over a thousand dives on the wreck and explored her enormous interior further than anyone.

Zenobia, Cyprus. Picture: Mark Caney

Because the site is so close to the shore the usual procedure is to make a single dive in the morning and then return in mid afternoon. This also allows divers to have a reasonable bottom time on the second dive. Typically, open, high speed boats of around ten metres are used to reach the wreck.

This is mainly a dive for the experienced due to the depth range, but the highest parts of the wreck are at around 18m. The bottom is fairly level at 40m. Obviously this depth range makes the site ideal for Nitrox, and Octopus Divers are planning to start producing it later this year. The wreck now lies on her port side, and you can see most of the outside of the ship by restricting your maximum depth to 30m. A computer is very useful to maximise your dive time as you can easily plan a multi-level dive on a wreck of this size.

Another famous dive site is Kakoskaliou Island which is located near Latchi in the Paphos district. It has the best underwater scenery of any dive in Cyprus with sheer walls dropping to over 35m and particularly clear water. The easiest way to access it is through Cydive in Paphos or Atlantis Divers in Lachi.

When you have finished diving for the day you will find one of the best features of Cyprus is that there is still plenty to do. This makes it especially popular with non-diving spouses! There are many good bars, nightclubs and restaurants for the evening. During the day you can lie on the beach or try one of the many watersports such as water skiing, parascending or sailing. If you are there in the winter you can even go snow skiing in the Troodos Mountains, but don't try that straight after a morning deep dive, they rise to 2000m!

Corsica - The Scented Isles

by Caroline Cameron

An area of the Mediterranean that is relatively unknown to the UK diver lies between the shores of Corsica and Sardinia.

They are stunning islands: an extension of the Alps that rises suddenly from the seabed, with deserted white sandy beaches and clean, clear waters. The mountains continue beneath the sea as underwater cliffs and coral caves, offering some outstanding dive sites.

Visibility is excellent, and there is a surprising abundance of marine life due to the large sea areas that are designated reserves (in 'Merouville' you will find the largest concentration of Groupers in the Mediterranean). Corsica is French; and prices may seem a little high, but the quality of diving coupled with the beauty of the islands and variety of non-diving activities available make this a dive/holiday destination well worth exploring.

One of France's top diving schools, Club Atoll in Southern Corsica, offers comprehensive packages and a wide range of courses (BSAC).

Details of other dive organisations and tour operators for both Corsica and Sardinia may be obtained through the French and Italian tourist offices. There are now direct flights to both islands.

Around the USA

by Colin Taylor

The Florida Keys is the most popular dive destination in the USA and the diversity here is endless; deep diving, wreck diving and abundant coral reefs to name a few options.

Key Largo, the northern most key and the most densely populated with dive stores, offers a variety of dives. Most dive stores offer two types of dive trips; a two tank dive for sport divers, usually a deep dive of 80 to 110 ft followed by one or two shallow reef dives which are usually full of student divers finishing their training. The best time to dive in Key Largo is during the week. Some of the best sites are the wrecks of the *"Duanne"* and the *"Bibb"*, US Coast Guard cutters sunk in around 100 to 110 ft and a couple of reef sites in about 30 feet called the Molasses and Frenches reef. Another point of interest is a sunken statue of Christ.

Islamorada, Marathon, Looe Key and Key West do not have as many dive stores as Key Largo but the diving is even more spectacular. The wreck of the *"Eagle"* is well worth a visit when you stop in Islamorada. Looe Key Marine Sanctuary is a must for those looking for marine life and a chance to swim with dolphins.

Key West has some great reefs and wrecks and a nightlife to suit all tastes. There are a few liveaboard dive boats that leave Key West for a three day trip to the dry Tortugas, a series of islands you can only reach by boat

Inside 'Atlantis' at Apra Harbour. Picture: Courtesy of United States Travel & Tourism Administration.

Ocean City, Maryland. Picture: © Heinz Steenmans; Courtesy of United States Travel & Tourism Administration.

or by plane. The reefs are abundant with marine life and have suffered very little diver damage. This is a must for the serious diver. The visibility is usually 80 to 100 ft.

The east coast of Florida offers some diverse diving, from deep wrecks sunk to make artificial reefs, to great drift diving.

Miami and Fort Lauderdale have some of the best wrecks in Florida. Most stores have boats and run trips daily to these sites. The best time to dive is during the week, among some of the best wrecks are the *"Mercedes"*, the *"Atria"* and the *"Rebel"*.

A little further north is West Palm Beach. Here the drift diving is excellent. Turtles are a common sight and there is plenty of coral. If you have never done drift diving before make sure you pay attention at the dive boat briefing.

The Gulf Coast has some great wrecks but is very shallow and it can take quite a time to get to these sites. Visibility is not as good as on the east coast. Diving at West Palm Beach, Tampa or the Springs could easily be combined with a trip to Orlando and all the Disney attractions. Crystal River is famous the world over for its Manatees; during the winter months the creatures come in from the gulf to live in the perennial 72° water.

It is best to see these during the week, as just like the Keys, hundreds of soon-to-be-certified divers visit the Springs to complete their training and to see the manatees.

This is shallow water diving and one, maybe two days is the all that you would need to spend here. Nearby are various springs where a number of cavers train and dive. Sport divers take to the fresh water springs and rivers daily and the Blue Grotto is a must for fresh water spring divers.

The Florida "pan handle", Panama city, is about 600 miles from Miami and is also a great destination, particularly for wreck divers. This is a popular site for many taking a long weekend as well as divers from the surrounding states.

Florida has some great diving. For those who like the coral reefs and wrecks then the Keys and southeast Florida are for you. A week here and a week in Orlando will satisfy you and please the whole family.

North and South Carolina, the scene of a lot of the American civil war naval battles, are a must for those interested in finding old artifacts. Who knows what you might discover on your next dive.

Charleston, Hilton Head and Myrtle Beach are some of the lead off points in South Carolina as are Wilmington and Nagshead in North Carolina. Visibility can vary from day to day, between 15 and 50 ft. Saturday and Sunday are the best days to get on boats going out to the wrecks.

New York has some of the best wreck diving in the US. It is very similar to the UK with respect to visibility and depth. The best time to dive is at weekends during the summer.

Texas and Louisianna have some diving, mainly a little off the coast. There are a number of oil rig platforms with great coral formations, one of which is called the "flower gardens", a must if you are in the area at a weekend.

Not only is California home to the headquarters of many a dive training organization and equipment manufacturer, it also boasts a wide variety of diving. Beach diving is very popular and most dive stores arrange shore dives regularly. Beach diving in California requires surf entry so a dive guide might be advantageous.

Just off the coast of Los Angeles is the island of Catalina, a good 2-3 hour trip by boat. These boats have cooking facilities for breakfast on the way out and snacks on the way back. This is an all day trip and means an early start due to the traffic in Los Angeles. The diving here is mainly in kelp with sea lions visiting you on nearly every dive. The water temperature is colder than in Florida but diving in the kelp forest is a unique experience due to the colours beaming through the plants and the surge action. Diving in kelp is also prevalent in Northern California.

The Hawaiian islands are way out in the Pacific ocean, a 4-5 hour flight from California and were formed by volcanic eruptions. This is a popular dive destination for the divers from the west coast of North America. As a result of the volcanic action you will find lava tubes here. Although the coral is relatively young compared to the Caribbean you will meet large sea turtles, nudibranch, and loads of eels as well as several varieties of fishes that are found only around these islands. Between December and March whales visit the islands and you can see and hear them on dives. Dolphins and reef sharks are not unusual all year round.

The waters of the United States offer the seasoned diver a thrilling variety of environments and the novice some vibrant experiences. The common language is surely an advantage for a trouble free trip and landbound partners or family will find no end of activities to keep them occupied.

The US Virgin Islands

by David Patterson

The islands of St Croix, St John and St Thomas lie at the eastern end of the Greater Antilles about 60 miles east of Puerto Rico between two seas. St John is surrounded by the Atlantic and St Croix by the Caribbean while St Thomas separates the two.

The landscape varies between arid, rocky terrain, lush rain forests, rolling pastures and white sand beaches. Lying directly in the path of the subtropical easterly trade winds humidity is low while the weather is perennially warm and sunny with the odd tropical shower and no specific rainy season.

The water temperature makes wetsuits and skins unnecessary for thermal protection though many choose to wear them against stings and cuts. Visibility of 60 to 80 feet is commonplace and days with 100 foot visibility are not unheard of. Storms in the Atlantic sometimes bring swells, pushing in plankton. As a result of this visibility can fall to 50 or 60 feet though as a plus point, the plankton attracts large filter feeders to the area.

There is a great deal of good diving from all of the US Virgin Islands with a large number of sites that are rarely visited. If you're happy to co-operate with the local operators a little, you can find an abundance of the kinds of marine life that you only rarely see in other Caribbean destinations.

When the plankton is flowing, coral polyps can be seen fully deployed in broad daylight. Big pelagics are common visitors to the islands, although large groupers and snappers are rare. Even though spearfishing on scuba is legal, huge jewfish and nurse sharks can be found on wrecks south of St. Thomas as can large grey angels, queen angles, goatfish, blackbar soldierfish and morays.

The volcanic rocks of St. John and St. Thomas are dappled with multicoloured sponges and make for dramatic diving as does the north wall of St. Croix.

All three islands boast superb shallow reefs and St. Croix has a true wall along its north and west shores. Hurricane Hugo hit St. Croix in 1989 damaging Buck Island marine park but leaving the vast majority of sites unscathed. Even at 50ft the fragile stag horned coral that decorates the North Wall seems intact. Where giant Elkhorn has been toppled the processes of nature are rebuilding the reef as polyps of star coral and other varieties recolonise the area.

Although the Islands are not renown as a wreck diving destination there are several to be found. The *"North Wind"* lies in about 45ft off St Croix. A short swim away is a North Sea trawler the *"Suffolk Maid"* in about 65ft and close by lies the *"Rosaomaira"* in about 100ft. The *"Witshoal"* were it elsewhere in the Caribbean, would draw divers from all around the world.

The sandy beaches and the night life around the islands will ensure that the holiday is enjoyed by sun and fun lovers alike, making this a destination that is sure to please all members of the party.

Dive Australia

by the Australian Tourist Commission

In Australia it is possible to dive from most shores of the continent - from the Great Barrier Reef to the wreck filled waters of South Australia. Beginners and advanced divers have a multitude of choices, from off-shore, week long charter boat trips to land based day trips. This article has been compiled by the Australian Tourist Commission, Peter Christopher, Kevin Deacon and Neville Coleman.

DIVING HINTS

Wear protective clothing when diving. Scratches from coral can cause infection. Wear sun-screen lotion to protect your skin from too much exposure.

Always seek local guidance and advice about sea conditions before going onto new dive sites.

Check with local authorities to see if you need written permission to go into a protected area.

Many parts of the marine coastline of Australia are wildlife sanctuaries or marine reserves and as such most underwater flora, fauna and shipwrecks may not be hunted or taken from their locations.

CERTIFIED divers must be able to produce their international certification card and log book. Make sure that the company that takes you on a dive checks your log book.

DIVING IN NEW SOUTH WALES

Sydney Harbour

Sydney Harbour is the world's largest natural deep water harbour, but a diver should always watch the weather and sea conditions in this area. There are lots of good off shore dive sites - such as, Campcove, Little Manly and Lady Jane Beach - as well as good boat dive sites throughout Sydney.

NORTH COAST

Newcastle

Newcastle, 171km north of Sydney, has tremendous diving. Just off Newcastle itself are literally hundreds of shipwrecks, ranging from a paddle steamer lying in 35m of water to a completely intact World War II tank. In Swansea Channel, a very popular shore dive, the remains of an old bridge in 15m of water is home to a huge array of marine life. Schools of bream and luderick constantly sweep through and groups of large kingfish are often sighted. The area also shelters fish usually found in more tropical climates.

The gutters and caves of nearby Catherine Hill Bay and the wreck of the *"Bonnie Dundee"* also provide excellent diving as do the reefs that run off from Moon Island.

Port Stephens

206km north of Sydney, Port Stephens offers both good shore dives and brilliant boat dives at Broughton Island.

Broughton Island with its large protected bays provides easy diving with visibility of 15m. The Looking Glass is a huge split right through the middle of the island teeming with marine life. Two other popular dives are the Bubble Cave and the Sponge Gardens on the northern side. The wreck of *"Oakland"* which sank in 1903 is almost intact and is easily accessible in just 28m of water.

Fly Point is an easily accessible dive within Nelson Bay. Its main feature is a 100m long ledge in 10-15m of water, covered in sponge with schools of bream, luderick and blue groper. Marine life on the sea bed includes sponge crabs, sea horses and sea dragons.

Halifax Park, also within the Bay, is a similar dive with an average depth of 20m. The water is often clearer here and the colourful sponge life is more prolific, covering a wider area.

Forster / Tuncurry Seal Rocks

Tuncurry, 327km north of Sydney, has everything from large plate corals and beautiful sponge gardens to granite-like formations creating sheer drop offs. Latitude Rock is a famous bommie (large coral outcrop under water) where hundreds of blue groper and other large fish can be hand fed. Taurus Reef is different again, with beautiful Butterfly Cod, crayfish, coral and sponge gardens.

In the gutters of Seal Rocks divers can often see grey nurse sharks. Experienced divers can dive the wreck of the SS *"Satara"*, over 400ft long and covered with marine life. The enormous prop is intact and many artifacts remain an board. The dive has a starting depth over 35m and is not for novice divers.

Southwest Rocks

South West Rocks, 496km north of Sydney, boasts one of the largest ocean caves in Australia. Dives in this area include: Fish Rock, The Wall, the Aquarium, the reefs off Green Island, Black Rock and the wreck *"Agnes Irving"*.

Just past the opening of Fish Rock the sandy bottom hides beautiful cowrie shells; a

The Great Barrier Reef from the air. Picture: Courtesy of the Australian Tourist Commission.

narrow chimney leads deeper into the rock in almost complete darkness before the light of the exit is seen.

The last 15m are spectacular - the walls lined with gorgonia, crayfish, ascidians, sponges, starfish and shells all in rainbow colours. Air spaces trapped under the roof allow you to "talk underwater".

Near Fish Rock is a 50m deep wall where monstrous grouper, cod, kingfish and jewfish school. The "Aquarium" is well-known for the density of its beautiful tropical fish.

There is easier diving on the shallow reefs off Green Island, home to the shovel-nosed ray. Black Rock is a good dive for those who have not seen coral before and wreck divers can dive the *"Agnes Irving"* a 19th century paddle steamer.

Byron Bay

Byron Bay 813km north of Sydney, offers the diver a host of different sites where hundreds of different species of animals and plants can be seen. Within the Bay there are two kelp reefs - Wilsons Reef and Bait Reef - inhabited by thousands of yellowtail, whiting and herring.

SOUTH COAST

Jervis Bay

Jervis Bay, 190km south of Sydney, is a popular diving area. An abundance of marine life inhabits the waters of the bay - sponges, sea ferns and fish - all in waters that generally give visibility of around 20m. The underwater terrain contains huge boulders, caves and tunnels from the surface down to around 50m.

Picture: Courtesy of the Australian Tourist Commission.

Batemans Bay

Batemans Bay, 282km south of Sydney, also offers good diving. Lighthouse Reef has a magnificent wall and the bottom is covered in sea sponge gardens, sea whips, gorgonian fans, hydroids and sea tulips.

ISLANDS

Norfolk Island

Norfolk Island situated in the South Pacific is almost 1700km north east of Sydney. Its 32km of rugged coastline consists almost entirely of steep cliffs which rise sheer from the water's edge. There is coral on the reefs around Norfolk Island, however what distinguishes this location is its exciting caves and tunnels, chasms, chimneys and grottos.

Visibility always exceeds 30m and is often as good as 50m. More than 30 dive sites have been documented around the Island. One of the deepest dives is at South Rock, a large rocky outcrop where there is a constantly breaking sea. Here the diver can descend as far as 40m to enjoy the prolific growths of black coral and fish life.

Lord Howe Island

Lord Howe Island is 700km north east of Sydney. This tiny island's isolation has allowed it to develop a unique, endemic animal and bird life. In these waters marine species typical of New South Wales waters mingle with tropical species common to Queensland. Deep-sea currents ensure a constant flow of crystal-clear water and allow a visibility which ranges between 30-60m. The diving season on Lord Howe is strictly limited to the period between September and May.

Diving in the Northern Territory

Tropical temperatures mean that diving in the Northern Territory is great all year round. However, during October and May sea wasps are present in the waters off the coast.

Although visibility in the Territory's waters ranges from 3-30m, the area still offers an array of tropical fish, and a rich and prolific range of invertebrate life as well as dives in freshwater.

Expert training is available throughout Australia.
Picture: Courtesy of the Australian Tourist Commission.

Darwin Harbour has several wrecks such as the *"Megis"*, a 15,000 tonne freighter, and the *"Peary"*, an old destroyer dating back to World War II.

There are also many coral reefs, some with outstanding soft coral gardens. All these sites are easily accessible by boat.

The Cobourg Peninsular is located at the north western corner of Arnhem Land, about 200km north east of Darwin.

The Cobourg Peninsular Marine National Park is a haven for coral fringed reefs, mangroves, turtles and crocodiles. One should beware of crocodiles and box jelly fish particularly during the wet season (November to March) and wetsuits must be worn.

Diving in Queensland

Queensland is home to the Great Barrier Reef Marine Park, which is on the world heritage list. The marine park has many areas which are off limits to divers.

Most diving in Queensland is done from the major centres of Cairns, Townsville, Port Douglas, the Whitsundays and the Capricorn Bunker group (that is, Heron Island, Lady Elliot and Musgrave Islands) from Bundaberg or Gladstone.

Heron Island

Heron Island can be reached by helicopter flight or by catamaran from Gladstone. The journey takes two hours.

Heron Island is renowned for spectacular diving just minutes from the beach. There are 17 specified and moored dive locations around the Heron Reef, including three on nearby Wistari Reef which incorporate not only some fabulous drop offs but also some great lagoon dives. Night diving on Heron is an experience not to be missed, especially a trip to the famous Heron Island Bommie or Gorgonia Hole.

Lady Elliot & Musgrave Islands

Lady Elliot is the most southerly island on the Great Barrier Reef and is 90km north east of Bundaberg. Charters depart Bundaberg daily every half hour. It offers good diving and its resort is frequented mainly by divers and snorkellers. The island, and nearby Lady Musgrave Island, are home to a large family of manta rays.

Lizard Island

Towards the far north end of the Great Barrier Reef, near Lizard Island, is a series of unique reef formations. Lizard Island is 27Okm north of Cairns.

The most popular site in the area is known as Cod Hole. It is not really a hole but the edge of a pass between two coral reefs - Cormorant Reef and Ribbon Number Ten. It is home to a group of about 20 giant potato cod, one of the most bizarre looking of tropical fish, and a protected species that is rarely encountered.

Coral Sea

The Coral Sea, part of the South Pacific Ocean, is dotted with a number of remote reefs. The diving is exciting and unpredictable with visibility from 30-60m. One of the best areas in the Coral Sea for diving is the Flinders group of reefs off Townsville.

The Rock Arch is a dive on the western side of Flinders. Here the reef drops from 4-1,000m, a sheer wall decorated with gorgonians, sea whips and brilliant soft corals. Divers encounter sharks, mackerel, tuna and other fish. The Patches consists of a series of bommies rising from 35m to within a few metres of the surface. Between these coral bommies are row upon row of large gorgonian fans that stretch out into the current to collect food.

China Wall is a sheer wall that drops vertically from 3m to 1000m. The wall is covered with soft corals, gorgonians and sea whips. Large fish constantly move through - tuna, mackerel, rainbow runners and trevally to name a few. After the wall you can swim into the shallow lagoon through any one of the numerous caves that cut into the face. The water here is only 6m deep and is home to parrotfish, triggerfish, surgeonfish, coral trout and anemonefish.

The SS *"Yongala"* sits in 28m of water and is a haven for marine life, an artificial reef in a desert of sand. On a typical dive you find tuna, mackerel, barracuda, coral trout, turtles, eagles rays, olive sea snakes, batfish and the list goes on. The hull of the Yongala is fully encrusted with hard corals, soft corals, sea whips, oysters, daisy coral and black coral trees.

DIVING IN SOUTH AUSTRALIA

Port Noarlunga

Port Noarlunga is only 34km south of Adelaide. A natural reef forms part of an aquatic reserve with depths ranging from 6-20m. The southern end of the reef is broken by a gap, where the depth reaches 20m. The reef is 300m off shore, and is accessible by a jetty running out to it. The jetty itself is quite an interesting dive in its own right. The area abounds with marine life, and is worth a visit as either a day or night dive.

Port Willunga

Port Willunga is only 40km south of Adelaide (50 minute drive). Off the shore of Port Willunga lies the wreck of the *"Star of Greece"*. This iron ship was lost in 1888 and its skeletal remains rest in 6m of water. Very little marine life is present, but the wreck itself offers an interesting time.

Victor Harbour

Only 84km south of Adelaide is the beautiful seaside resort of Victor Harbour, providing a variety of diving options. Granite Island, connected to the mainland by a causeway

Diving the Great Barrier Reef. Picture: Courtesy of the Australian Tourist Commission.

has an interesting variety of marine life. A horse drawn tourist trolley located at the edge of the jetty saves carrying gear to the Island.

The following sites can be reached only by boat but are still only day trips from Adelaide:

Picture: Courtesy of the Australian Tourist Commission.

Glenelg

The suburban seaside resort of Glenelg is easily reached by tram from Victoria Square in the city centre. The harbour shelters a number of yachts and boats which can be chartered.

A tyre reef, sand hopper and a barge sunk approximately 6km west of Glenelg provide divers with magnificent artificial reefs. Both vessels and the tyre reef are now homes for many varieties of reef fish.

Aldinga Drop Off

Aldinga is 43km south of Adelaide. The Aldinga Reef provides one of the most spectacular dives. Less than a kilometre from shore, it drops off from 5 to over 20m, and is a mass of caverns, crevasses and overhangs.

Fish of almost every kind, gorgonia coral and soft sponges make this a photographer's paradise.

The South East

The South East of the State offers divers the opportunity to explore both a rugged coastline and the tranquil, crystal clear, waters of famous sinkholes.

Robe

Robe is located 350km south of Adelaide. The main sites to visit are the reefs just offshore and South of Cape Dombey.

A pass with an echo sounder almost anywhere up to 1km from shore will reveal massive crevasses ranging from 5-15m in depth. Apart from crayfish, the colourful sponge growth and normally clear water makes this area good for photography.

Godfrey Islands and The Black Pigs, 8km north of Robe in Guichen Bay, provide diving up to about 6m in depth.

Once again the main interest for many is crayfish, but the area has patchy reefs and sea grasses which are home to numerous varieties of reef fish and shells.

Mount Gambier - The Sink Holes

Mount Gambier is 486km from Adelaide. Kendell Airlines fly from Adelaide to Mount Gambler. The flight takes just over an hour.

The area is well known for its freshwater sink holes - the most famous being Piccaninny Ponds which descends more than 60m into the earth. Inside, tall strands of algae are a habitat for freshwater crayfish, eels and other fish.

A permit system exists to ensure that divers visiting the area meet necessary experience and equipment standards.

Picture: Courtesy of the Australian Tourist Commission.

SOUTHERN EYRE PENINSULA

Port Lincoln

Port Lincoln is 662km from Adelaide and is pleasantly situated on Boston Bay. The Bay is mostly sandy but good diving is available at Cape Donnington and nearby Donnington Island. The wreck of the fishing vessel *"Degei"* is located 100m from the southern end of the island.

Tumby Bay, 45km north of Port Lincoln, is a good base from which to visit the Sir Joseph Banks Group of Islands.

Coffin Bay, 40km west of Port Lincoln, offers two types of diving. The inner harbour is well protected and is good for scallops and oysters. Some shallow reefs extend from two small islands, The Brothers. Venturing out of the inner bay there is stunning diving at Point Sir Isaac. Depths are in the order of 10m and the area abounds with many varieties of fish, including large groper. The area can be accessed by land but only by using four wheel drive vehicles.

Northern Eyre Peninsular

Most diving along the Peninsular takes place on the east coast, particularly between Whyalla (396km north west of Adelaide) and Port Augusta (317km north of Adelaide).

The two most popular dive locations are Point Lowly, 42km south of Port Augusta and the old iron ore jetty at Whyalla. Point Lowly offers an excellent shore dive, dropping into 18m depth within 200m of the shore. A tyre reef has been established in 18m depth, with lots of fish and scallops. The old Whyalla jetty drops to 10m depth, and the pylons and bottom are heavily overgrown with marine life.

Kangaroo Island

Kangaroo Island is the third largest island off the Australian coast and is about 80km south west of Adelaide. Transport to the island is by air and sea. It is a 30 minute flight. Airtransit fly from Adelaide to American River, Parndana, Kingscote, Penneshaw. Lloyd Aviation also fly to Kingscote Airport.

Diving around the jetty at Penneshaw is worthwhile both as a day or night dive. Although only about 5m deep the jetty is covered with many colourful varieties of sponges and corals.

Further west, reefs of up to 20m can be found at Cape D'Estaing and Cape Cassini. As well as the usual reef fish, snapper and salmon can be found in these locations. These areas are best visited when based on the Island, using larger boats.

Kangaroo Island has over 60 wrecks along its rugged coast, but access to most of these is difficult. The *"Lock Vennachar"* and the *"Portland Maru"* at the western end of the Island are two of the most famous.

DIVING IN TASMANIA

Bicheno

Bicheno, situated on the East Coast of Tasmania is the gateway to some of the most picturesque diving. An early 19th century sanctuary for sealers and whalers, Bicheno is now a busy crayfishing and abalone port.

In winter when diving is best with water visibility reaching 30m, many have the pleasure of diving amongst schools of dolphins or swimming alongside whales which use Bicheno as a stopover during their migration.

Picture: Courtesy of the Australian Tourist Commission.

The Castle, 30m in depth, offers drop offs with 15m long swim throughs. The overhang has wall-to-wall Bulls Eyes and Butterfly Perch with resident Boarfish.

The entire dive at Muirs Rock can be spent in swim throughs and caves. Cave walls are carpeted with Zoanthids and Jewelled Anemones.

The Hairy Walls, 40m in depth, is known for its countless seawhips, jewelled anemones, basket stars and huge sponge gardens.

The Giant Kelp, 18m in depth, has extensive kelp forests which are home to much of Tasmania's marine life.

At Trap Reef a diver can drop off the top of reef at 2m and swim down the crevasse to the sponge garden and clouds of Butterfly Perch.

At Bird Rock, 21m in depth, one can swim into caves adorned with jewelled anemones and hand feed the masses of tame fish. This dive is classed as the best all-round dive in Bicheno.

The Rock, 16m in depth, is the best shallow water shore dive in Tasmania. Boar fish, octopus, squid, leather jacket, morwong and sea horses abound.

Sorell

Sorell is 26km north east of Hobart, only a 30 minute drive. This area offers everything - 30m visibility, giant kelp forests, caves and swim throughs. There are shipwrecks galore and prolific fish life abounds at every dive spot.

Tasmania's pristine wilderness enables divers the very real possibility of experiencing whale and dolphin encounters. Southern Fur Seals are also common in the area. One of the most popular locations is Deep Glen Bay which offers cave dives, swim throughs and a huge variety of marine life. Dive in the "Shipwreck Graveyard" - home to 11 wrecks including freighters, tugs, ferries and barges all of which lie in a small protected area.

Wynyard

Situated on the North West Coast of Tasmania, Wynyard has its own aerodrome in Burnie and is only a 40 minute drive from the Bass Strait Ferry Terminal in Devonport.

Wynyard is on the doorstep of some of Tasmania's most accessible and exciting diving. Diving is available for groups or individuals to premium dive spots such as the Pinnacle and the SS *"Southern Cross"* which has been on the sea floor for a 100 years.

King Island

Within just forty minutes of Melbourne you can experience wilderness diving in water with up to 35m visibility. The area is known for its concentration of wrecks and crayfish and its spectacular giant kelp forests, drop offs, swim through caves rich with gorgonians, sponges and prolific fish life.

DIVING IN VICTORIA

Bass Strait

The ocean which lies between the northern coast of Tasmania and the mainland of Australia is known as Bass Strait. The Strait is one of Victoria's popular diving areas. It caters for the wreck diver and underwater photographers with its extensive reefs and shipwrecks.

Port Philip Bay

Port Philip Bay is a large inlet on the central Victorian coast on which the cities of Melbourne and Geelong stand. The entrance to Port Philip Bay is the most popular area for divers.

The Bay's appeal lies in the fact that it provides varied diving to enthusiasts of all standards and interests. There are vast areas of largely unexplored reefs, a number of shipwrecks and a large range of marine life. Fishlife in this area is protected and there are unusual types such as gobies, shore eels, snapping shrimps, juvenile flounder and red cake bryozoans.

Access to all dive sites is good, especially from the coastal resorts of Queenscliff and Portsea. Both resorts are south of Melbourne and are approximately 1.5 hours drive. Good shore diving is available on the reefs from Point Gellibrand to Point Cook.

The best time to dive is after a long period of dry, calm weather, usually during April and May. Visibility varies depending on the weather conditions, but on most days it is at least 10m.

A short power boat ride out the entrance of the Barwon River at Geelong, south-west of Melbourne, puts divers within range of kelp forests, reef formations and shipwrecks. Chimney Rock has become a very popular dive location. This underwater feature, approximately 1km south of Barwon Heads Bluff, rises 10m from the sea bed in a reef formation supporting a wide variety of fish.

Wilsons Promontory

Wilsons Promontory, 225km south east of Melbourne (3 hours drive) is classified as a national park and is extremely picturesque with large mountains of thick granite jutting out from the waters below. Divers without a boat need to base themselves at Tidal River which has good amenities for campers with showers and a general store.

The best diving is approximately 9km from Tidal River at Shellback Island, or there is Norman Island at 5km, and the Glennies at 6km. The most effective way to dive the promontory is by charter boat.

Phillip Island

Phillip Island is 124km from Melbourne. A ferry service runs from Stoney Point on the mainland to northern shore of the Island. At San Remo on vehicle bridge connects with Phillip Island

Its southern coast borders Bass Strait while its northern coast, in contrast, abuts the more tranquil waters of a bay. These calmer waters are excellent for diving.

Phillip Island is best known for its wildlife, particularly its fairy penguins. Off the southwest tip of the island, a rocky island called Nobbies is home to a noisy colony of seals.

Apollo Bay

Apollo Bay, the name of a bay and holiday resort, is 187km south west of Melbourne. The area is known for its large crayfish and ship wrecks.

DIVING IN WESTERN AUSTRALIA

Western Australia offers a wide range of dive sites and marine environments. There are four outstanding sites in the State - Perth, Esperance, Exmouth and the Rowley Shoals (Broome).

Perth

There are three major diving areas within the greater Perth Metropolitan area. They are Marmion Marine Park, Shoalwater Bay and Rottnest Island.

Marmion Marine Park off Perth's northern beaches contains within its boundaries a range of limestone reefs, sea grass beds and caves. Little Island is a resting place for Australian sea lions and bottle-nosed dolphins can be regularly seen in the area.

Shoalwater is off the southern suburbs of Perth and offers an array of small islands, sea grass beds and a wide range of marine plants and animals. The largest island, Penguin Island, has a breeding colony of little penguins and is also a resting place for sea lions.

Rottnest Island has numerous dive sites, the best of which are Porpoise Bay, Jackson Rock, Transit Reef and West End. Rottnest is well known for its coral gardens and spectacular caves.

Diving at Rottnest Island can be booked through any dive shop in Perth all of which offer equipment hire and tank refilling facilities.

Esperance

Esperance, 725km south east of Perth, is the gateway to the Recherche Archipelago which contains hundreds of islands. These islands offer a multitude of dive sights with good diving available in all weather. The granite rocks that make these islands provide majestic drop offs from 3-60m. Esperance can be dived all year round but the best conditions are from February to April.

The islands are home to the Australian fur seal. Fish life is also abundant - salmon, kingfish and blue groper. The Esperance jetty is considered one of the best night dives in Western Australia.

Exmouth

Exmouth, a town on the most north westerly shore of western Australia is 1,264km north of Perth. Based in Exmouth, a diver can access both Ningaloo Reef and the Muran Islands.

Ningaloo Reef is a 200km long coral reef ranging between 200m and 6km from the shore and running along the western side of the Exmouth Peninsula.

Made up of a wide variety of corals with the associated tropical marine life, the reef is also home to sharks, manta rays, sea snakes, sail fish and marlin. There is also a range of large fish such as coral cod and coral trout. Between the reef and the shore are large lagoons with white sand bottoms and coral bommies. The depth in these lagoons varies from 3-8m and is ideal for snorkelling and shore dives.

The Muran Islands and other smaller nearby islands offer a superb range of coral and marine life. On the ocean side of the islands, large gutters are carved up through heavy corals and are frequented by large fish. On the leeward side of the islands more delicate corals and bommies exist with a wide range of smaller fish. The islands are home to turtle colonies and these may be seen all year round as may humpback whales, whale sharks and manta rays.

Dive Travel Companies

Dive travel arrangements can also be made through some dive retailers. ***See page 93.***

AGGRESSOR FLEET
PO DRAWER K
MORGAN CITY, LA 70381 USA
0101 504 3852628 FAX: 0101 504 3840817

CARIBBEAN, PACIFIC

ALIGN SPEED TRAVEL
FIRST FLOOR
40 EAST STREET, BROMLEY, KENT BR1 1QU
081 3139081 FAX: 081 3139080

SEYCHELLES

AQUA NUTS
102970 OVERSEAS HIGHWAY
KEY LARGO, FL 33037 USA
0101 305 4510414 FAX: 0101 305 4514892

FLORIDA

AQUASPORT INTERNATIONAL
80 ALCESTER ROAD
MOSELEY, BIRMINGHAM B13 8BB
021 4494148 FAX: 021 4494148

JORDAN

AQUATOURS
7 CRANES DRIVE
SURBITON, SURREY KT5 8AJ
081 3996953 FAX: 081 3996953

SEYCHELLES, RED SEA, CUBA, MEDITERRANIAN

BAREFOOT TRAVELLER LTD
204 KING STREET
HAMMERSMITH
LONDON W6 0RA
081 7414894 FAX: 0932 845772

CARRIBEAN, INDIAN OCEAN

BARFIELD TRAVEL & TOURS
14 CHAIN LANE
NEWARK, NOTTINGHAMSHIRE NG24 1AU
0636 705612 FAX: 0636 707600

WORLDWIDE

BASKIN IN THE SUN
PO BOX 108
TORTOLA, BRITISH VIRGIN ISLANDS
010 809 4942588 FAX: 010 809 4942385

BRITISH VIRGIN ISLANDS

BEQA DIVERS
FIJI GPO BOX 777
SUVA, FIJI
010 679 361088 FAX: 010 679 361047

FIJI

BUD AND MARY'S DIVE CENTRE
PO BOX 1126
ISLAMORADA, FL 33036 USA
0101 305 6642211 FAX: 0101 305 6645592

FLORIDA

CLUB ATHOLL SARL
CAVALLO MORTO BP3
20169 BONIFACIO, CORSICA
0460 55326 FAX: 0460 53627

CORSICA

CLUB SARDIVE
TAGS BOAT YARD
44 SUMMER ROAD, THAMES DITTON
SURREY SM5 3NL
081 3980905 FAX: 081 3984402

SARDINIA

CORAL CAY CONSERVATION LTD
THE IVY WORKS
154 CLAPHAM PARK ROAD,
LONDON SW4 7DE
071 4986248 FAX: 071 4988447

BELIZE

CYDIVE
1 POSEIDON AVENUE
K PAPHOS, CYPRUS
010 357 6 234271 FAX: 010 357 6 235307

MALTA

DEAN JOHNSON'S CARIBBEAN DIVING
BUCCANEER MALL
SUITE 106-208, ST THOMAS
US VIRGIN ISLANDS
0101 809 7757610 FAX: 0101 809 7742030

US VIRGIN ISLANDS

DEEP SEA DIVERS
PO BOX 5264
CAIRNS, QUEENSLAND 4870
AUSTRALIA
010 61 70312223 FAX: 010 61 70311210

AUSTRALIA

DEREK EDWARDS DIVING WORLD
55 OLD CHURCH STREET
CHELSEA, LONDON SW3 5BS
0708 444421 FAX: 0708 457664

RED SEA, CARIBBEAN

DIVE & SAIL
NASTFIELD COTTAGE
THE GREEN
FRAMPTON ON SEVERN
GLOUCESTERSHIRE GL2 7DY
0452 740919 FAX: 0452 740943

RED SEA

DIVE ISLAY
139 OLD HALL LANE
FALLOWFIELD MANCHESTER M14 6HL
061 2249845 FAX: 061 2249845

NORWAY, FALKLANDS, GOA, NEW ZEALAND

DIVE MED UK LTD
130 GREENCROFT GARDENS
LONDON NW6 3PJ
071 3287828 FAX: 071 3287828

CYPRUS

DIVERS WORLD
26 TEMPLE FORTUNE PARADE
LONDON NW11 OQS
081 4585115 FAX:

RED SEA, AUSTRALIASIA

FRONTIER EXPEDITIONS
77 LEONARD STREET
LONDON EC2A 4QS
071 6132422 FAX: 071 613 2992

TANZANIA, MAFIA ISLAND

GOZO AQUA SPORTS
79 GROSVENOR TERRACE
LONDON SE5 0NN
071 7031384 FAX: 071 7031384

MALTA

H2O SPORTS
PO BOX 19
HAMILTON ISLAND
QUEENSLAND 4803, AUSTRALIA
010 617 9 469888 FAX: 010 617 9 469888

AUSTRALIA

HARLEQUIN WORLDWIDE TRAVEL
HARLEQUIN HOUSE
2 NORTH ROAD, OCKENDEN
ESSEX RM15 6QJ
0708 852780 FAX: 0708 854952

CARIBBEAN

HOLIDAY MALTA COMPANY LTD
314-36 UPPER RICHMOND ROAD
PUTNEY, LONDON SW15 6TU
081 7853255 FAX: 081 7800833

MALTA

LONGWOOD TRAVEL & HOLIDAYS LTD
182 LONGWOOD GARDENS
CLAYHALL, ILFORD, ESSEX IG5 0EW
081 5514494 FAX:

RED SEA

LUXURY DIVE CHARTERS LTD
WHITEFIELD ROAD
BREDBURY, STOCKPORT
CHESHIRE SK6 2SS
061 4306818 FAX: 061 4307928

RED SEA, OMAN

MALDIVES SCUBA TOURS LTD
6 FRONT STREET
MENDLESHAM, SUFFOLK IP14 5RY
0449 766116 FAX: 0449 766069

MALDIVES

MELDIVES
MARFA ROAD
MELLIEHA BAY, MALTA
0276 20382 FAX: 0276 63431

MALTA

OCTOPUS DIVING CENTRE
PO BOX 24
LARNACA, CYPRUS
010 3574 650266 FAX: 010 3574 650266

CYPRUS

ONE EARTH TOURS
12 STRATFORD ROAD
LONDON W8 6QD
071 3760516 FAX: 071 3762320

EAST AFRICA

OONASDIVERS
23 ENYS ROAD
EASTBOURNE, SUSSEX BN21 2DG
0323 648924 FAX: 0323 738356

RED SEA

POSEIDON NEMROD DIVERS LTD
PO BOX 152
READING, ST JAMES
JAMAICA WEST INDIES
010 1 809 9523624
FAX: 010 1 809 9523079

JAMAICA

RED SEA AQUARIANS
59 LONDON ROAD
HACKBRIDGE, SURREY SM6 7BJ
081 6690068 FAX: 081 6696531

RED SEA

RED SEA DIVING SAFARI
53 EL HUSSAIN STREET
DOKKEY
CAIRO, EGYPT
UK AGENTS: OONASDIVERS

SHORE DIVING SAFARIS, SOUTHERN EYGPT

RED SEA SPORTS CLUB
PO BOX 390
EILAT, ISRAEL
010 972 7376569 FAX: 010 972 7374083

RED SEA

REGAL DIVING & TOURS
22 HIGH STREET
SUTTON, ELY, CAMBS CB6 2RB
0353 778096 FAX: 0353 777897

WORLDWIDE

S'ALGAR DIVING SL
PASEO MARITIMO
S/N SALAGAR, SAN LUIS
MENORCA, SPAIN
010 3471 150601 FAX: 010 3471 150601

SPAIN

SCUBA CUBA
27 LANCASTER ROAD
NORTH HARROW
MIDDLESEX HA2 7NN
081 4240712 FAX: 081 4249549

CUBA, CARIBBEAN

SCUBA CYPRUS
515A KINGSLAND ROAD
LONDON E8 4AU
071 9232085 FAX: 071 9231597

NORTH CYPRUS

TRAVEL

SCUBA SAFARIS
14/11 PARK HOUSE
SOUTH BANK COMMERCIAL CENTRE
140 BATTERSEA ROAD
LONDON SW11 4NB
071 4980003 FAX: 071 4980009

WORLDWIDE

SCUBEX
PO BOX 2158
PAPHOS, CYPRUS
010 357 6246680 FAX: 010 357 6247977

CYPRUS

SEA TRADE LTD
SUITE 505
CROWN BAY MARINA SUB. BASE, ST THOMAS 00802, US VIRGIN ISLANDS
010 1 809 7742001
FAX: 010 1 809 7779600

US VIRGIN ISLANDS

SEYCHELLES UNDERWATER CENTRE
PO BOX 384
CORAL STRAND HOTEL, MAHE
SEYCHELLES
010 248 44223 FAX: 010 248 44223

SEYCHELLES

SIMPLY TURKEY
8 CHISWICK TERRACE
ACTON LANE, LONDON W4 5LY
081 7471011 FAX: 081 9955346

TURKEY

SM HENSHAW & CO
59/7 DEVILS TOWER ROAD
010 350 73616 FAX: 010 350 73616

GILBRALTAR

ST ANDREWS DIVERS COVE LTD
SHOP 1 & 2
ST SIMON STREET, XLENDI BAY
GOZO, MALTA
010 356 551301 FAX: 010 356 561548

MALTA

STRAND DIVING SERVICES
PO BOX 20
ST PAULS BAY, MALTA
010 35 6 574502 FAX: 010 35 6 240834

MALTA

SUNVIL HOLIDAYS
UPPER STREET
ISLEWORTH, MIDDLESEX TW7 7BJ
081 5684499

CYPRUS

SUPERSTAR HOLIDAYS
185 REGENT STREET
LONDON WC1R 8EU
071 4379277 or 061 8346553
BROCHURE LINE 0303 250250

RED SEA

SUREDIVE LTD
6 PERSHORE GROVE
AINSDALE, SOUTHPORT
0704 573714 FAX: 0704 570555

AUSTRALIA, TRUK LAGOON

SYMON MARTYN HOLIDAYS
17 NORWICH ROAD
IPSWICH
SUFFOLK IP1 2ET
0473 280910

SPAIN. BY COACH

THE DIVING SITE
12399 OVERSEA HIGHWAY
MARATHON
FL 33050 USA
010 1 305 2891021
FAX: 010 1 305 7434251

FLORIDA

THE SCUBA BASE
PO BOX 394
NISSI AVENUE
AYIA NAPA 17.1
CYPRUS
010 357 3722442
FAX: 010 357 3722882

CYPRUS

TWICKERS WORLD
22 CHURCH STREET
TWICKENHAM
MIDDLESEX TW1 3NW
081 892 7606
FAX: 081 892 8061

WORLDWIDE

WAKEFIELDS
38 CHARTER HOUSE SQUARE
LONDON EC1M 6EA
071 4549454
FAX: 071 4549646

MALTA

WORLD EXPLORERS
35 FARREN ROAD
LONDON SE23 2DZ
081 6998268 FAX: 081 6991559

WORLDWIDE

TRAVEL ADVICE

FOREIGN TRAVEL ADVISORY SERVICE
CLIVE HOUSE
PETTY FRANCE
LONDON SW1H 9HD
071 2704129

WORLDWIDE VISA
9 ADELAIDE STREET
LONDON WC2N 4HZ
071 3790419 FAX: 071 4972590

INSURANCE

CHRISTOPHER HINDLE
INSURANCE BROKERS
10 CORNMARKET
WORCESTER
WORCESTERSHIRE WR1 2DR
0905 612944 FAX: 0905 611108

DIVE MASTER INSURANCE
CONSULTANTS LTD
PO BOX 146
LEIGH ON SEA
ESSEX SS9 1SZ
0702 76902 FAX: 0702 471892

FAIRMAY INSURANCE SERVICES LTD
MAYFAIR HOUSE
20-22 BELMONT ROAD
WALLINGTON, SURREY SM6 8TB
081 7730033 FAX: 081 7734006

VISASPORTS (UK) LTD
62 PRINCE STREET
BRISTOL
AVON BS1 4QD
0272 308654 FAX: 0272 308601

WESTFIELD (INSURANCE BROKERS) LTD
56 WESTFIELD ROAD
WESTFIELD, WOKING
SURREY GU22 9NG
0483 721299 FAX: 0483 770214

International Airline Details

Airline	Code	Admin	Reservations	Fax
Aberdeen Airways	SM	0224 724782	0224 771177	0224 770488
Adria Airways	JP	071-734 4630	071-437 0143	071-287 5476
Aer Lingus	EI	081-569 4646	081-569 5555	081-569 4410
Aeroflot	SU	071-491 1584	071-355 2233	071-355 2323
Aerolineas Argentinas	AR	071-439 6288	071-439 6288	071-734 4166
Aero Lloyd	YPO	0293 567811	0293 567811	0293 567815
Air Afrique	RK	071-493 4881	071-629 6114	071-493 2037
Air Algerie	AH	071-487 5709	071-487 5903	
Air Canada	AC	071-465 0090	081-759 2636	081-564 7644
Air France	AF	081-759 2311	071-499 9511	071-493 7212
Air India	AI	071-493 4050	071-491 7979	071-493 4050
Air Lanka	UL	071-491 0444	071-439 0291	071-629 4968
Air Malta	KM	081-785 3199	081-785 3177	081-785 7468
Air Mauritius	MK	071-434 4370	071-434 4375	071-439 4101
Air New Zealand	TE	071-930 1088	071-930 3434	071-930 1333
Air Seychelles	HM	0293 36313	0293 542101	0293 562353
Air UK	UK	0279 755950	0345 666777	0279 680012
Air Zaire	QC	071-434 1152	071-434 1151	071-734 1699
Air Zimbabwe	UM	071-499 8947	071-491 0009	071-355 3326
Alitalia	AZ	081-745 8200	071-602 7111	071-603 1095
All Nippon Airways	NH	071-493 3322	071-495 7667	071-493 3326
American Airlines	AA	081-577 4802	081-572 5555	081-572 8646
Ansett Australia	AN	071-434 4071	0800 747767	071-734 4333
Ansett New Zealand	ZQ	071-434 4071	0800 747767	071-734 4333
Ariana Afghan Airlines	FG	071-629 1611	071-493 1411	
Aurigny Air Services	GR	0481 822804	0481 822886	0481 823344
Australian Airlines	TN	071-434 3864	081-897 4400	071-494 0858
Austrian Airlines	OS	071-439 1851	071-439 0741	071-437 0343
Avianca	AV	071-408 1889	071-437 3664	071-494 3786
Balkan Bulgarian Airlines	LZ	071-631 1263	071-637 7637	
Biman-Bangladesh Airlines	BG	071-439 0362	071-439 0362	071-287 9120
B'ham European Airways	VB	021-782 0521	021-782 0711	021-782 0296
Britannia Airways	BY	071-388 2881	0582 405737	0582 458594
British Airways	BA	081-897 4400	081-897 4400	081-562 0596
British Midland	BD	0332 810741	071-589 5599	0332 852662
Brymon Airways	BC	0752 705151	0345 717383	0752 793067
BWIA International	BW	071-839 7155	071-839 9333	071-839 5396
Cameroon Airlines	UY	071-734 7676	071-734 7676	
Canadian Airlines Int.	CP	081-686 5255	081-667 0666	081-688 2997
Cathay Pacific	CX	071-930 4444	071-930 7878	071-839 4597

Cayman Airways	KX	071-581 9960	071-584 9960	071-584 4463
China Airlines	CI	071-494 1261	071-434 0707	071-439 4888
Continental Airlines	CO	0293 771681	0293 776464	0293 773726
Cook Islands International	KC	071-494 1655	071-494 1655	071-734 4333
Cubana De Aviacion	CU	071-930 1138	071-930 1138	071-839 5379
Cyprus Airways	CY	071-383 4831	071-388 5411	071-388 9055
Cyprus Turkish Airlines	YK	071-930 0725	071-930 4851	071-930 1046
Czechoslovak Airlines	OK	071-255 1366	071-255 1898	071-323 1639
Dan-Air Services	DA	071-378 6464	0345 100200	0293 774717
Delta Air Lines	DL	0293 826100	0800 414767	0293 773325
Dragonair Hong Kong	KA	071-930 4444	071-930 7878	071-839 4597
East West Airlines	EW	071-734 4917	0800 747767	071-734 4333
Egyptair	Ms	071-580 5477	071-734 2395	071-287 1728
El Al Israel Airlines	LY	071-439 2506	071-437 9255	071-439 2920
Emirates	EK	071-930 5356	071-930 3711	071-930 9647
Ethiopian Airlines	ET	071-839 3694	071-930 9152	071-839 2642
Faucett Peruvian Airlines	CF	071-930 1136	071-930 1136	071-839 5379
Finnair	AY	071-629 4349	0800 282832	071-629 7289
Garuda Indonesia	GA	071-935 7055	071-486 3011	071-224 3971
GB Airways	GT	0293 664239	081-897 4400	0293 664218
Ghana Airways	GH	071-499 0201	071-499 0201	071-491 1504
Gulf Air	GF	071-409 0191	071-408 1717	071-629 3989
Hamburg Airlines	HX	0293 29885	0293 29885	0293 512229
Hawaiian Air	HA	0293 774412	0293 774412	0293 786497
Iberia Airlines of Spain	IB	071-437 9822	071-437 5622	071-434 3375
Icelandair	FI	071-388 5346	071-388 5599	071-387 5711
Iran Air	IR	071-491 3656	071-409 0971	071-408 1360
Iraqi Airways	IA	071-930 0982	071-930 1155	071-839 8559
Japan Air Lines	JL	071-629 9244	071-408 1000	071-499 1071
JAT Yugoslav Airlines	JU	071-629 2007	071-493 9399	071-493 8092
Jersey European Airways	JY	0392 66669	0345 078400	0392 66151
Kenya Airways	KQ	071-409 3121	071-409 0277	071-499 2973
KLM Royal Dutch Airlines	KL	081-750 9200	081-750 9000	081-750 9090
Korean Airlines	KE	071-930 1957	071-930 6513	071-925 2390
Kuwait Airways	KU	071-486 6666	071-935 8795	071-487 5647
Lan Chile	LA	071-487 4335	071-487 4335	071-487 5905
Libyan Arab Airlines	LN	071-499 1016	071-499 0381	071-491 0339
Lloyd Aereo Boliviano	LB	071-930 1442	071-930 1442	071-839 5379
Loganair	LC	041-889 1311	041-889 3181	041-848 1087
London City Airways	11	071-474-2230	071-511 4200	071-511 1043
Lot Polish Airlines	LO	071-631 1539	071-580 5037	071-323 0774
Lufthansa	LH	071-408 0322	071-408 0442	
Luxair	LG	081-745 4255	081-745 4254	
Maersk Air	DM	071-638 1249	071-638 7920	071-256 6258
Malaysia Airlines	MH	081-862 0770	081-862 0800	081-862 0117

Malev Hungarian Airlines	MA	071-439 0577	071-439 0577	071-734 8116
Manx Airlines	JE	0624 824111	071-493 0803	0624 824578
Mexicana	MX	081-440 7830	081-440 7830	081-449 5504
Middle East Airlines	ME	071-493 6321	071-493 5681	071-629 4163
Monarch Airlines	ZB	0582 424211	0582 422922	0582 405059
Netherlines	WU	081-750 9200	081-750 9000	081-750 9090
Nigeria Airways	WT	071-493 9726	071-629 3717	071-491 9644
NLM City Hopper	HN	081-750 9200	081-750 9000	081-750 9090
Northwest Airlines	NW	0293 574553	0345 747800	0293 574546
Olympic Airways	OA	081-846 9966	081-846 9080	081-846 9709
Pakistan Int. Airlines	PK	081-741 8066	071-734 5544	081-741 9376
Philippine Airlines	PR	071-836 0828	071-836 5508	071-379 6656
Pluna	PU	071-930 1138	071-930 1138	071-839 5379
Polynesian Airlines	PH	071-494 1655	071-494 1655	071-734 4333
Qantas Airways	QF	081-846 0466	0800 747767	081-748 8551
RFG Regionalflug	VG	0293 567557	0293 567557	0293 512229
Royal Air Maroc	AT	071-439 8854	071-439 4361	071-287 0127
Royal Brunei Airlines	BI	071-402 0472	071-402 2047	071-706 4369
Royal jordanian Airlines	RJ	071-437 9465	071-734 2557	071-494 0433
Ryanair	FR	071-794 0636	071-435 7101	071-435 1983
Sabena World Airlines	SN	081-780 2270	081-780 1444	081-780 1502
SAM	MM	071-408 1889	071-437 3664	071-494 3786
Saudi Arabian Airlines	SV	081-995 7755	081-995 7777	081-995 8444
Scandinavian Airline Sys.	SK	071-734 6777	071-734 4020	071-434 2595
Scenic Airlines	YR	0992 441517	0992 441517	0992 467731
Singapore Airlines	SQ	081-995 4901	081-747 0007	081-742 1701
South African Airways	SA	071-437 9621	071-734 9841	071-734 2218
Suckling Airways	CB	0473 718346	0473 729091	
Sudan Airways	SD	071-499 8105	071-499 8101	071-499 0976
Swissair	SR	071-734 6737	071-439 4144	071-439 7375
TAP Air Portugal	TP	071-828 6599	071-828 0262	071-828 1742
Thai Airways International	TG	071-491 7953	071-499 9113	071-409 1463
Transavia	HV	0293 29883	0293 38181	0293 512229
Tunis Air	TU	071-437 6236	071-734 7644	071-734 6763
Turkish Airlines	TK	071-499 9249	071-499 9247	071-495 2441
Uganda Airlines	QU	071-409 1121	071-409 1121	071-499 9919
United Airlines	UA	071-495 2424	0800 898017	071-493 3652
US Air	US	071-734 3001	0800 777333	071-434 2099
UTA French Airlines	UT	071-493 4881	071-629 6114	071-493 2037
Varig Brazilian Airlines	RG	071-629 9408	071-629 5824	071-495 6135
VIASA Venezuelan Airways	VA	071-493 5573	071-493 3630	071-493 2915
Virgin Atlantic Airways	VS	0293 562345	0293 562000	0293 561721
Yemenia Yeman Airways	IY	071-409 2171	071-491 7186	071-355 3062
Zambia Airways	QZ	071-491 7521	071-491 0658	071-491 2795

Worldwide Destinations

For international dialling codes see reference section.

ANTIGUA AND BARBUDA

Capital: St. John's.
Time: GMT - 4.
Climate: Sub-tropical, sunny and warm.
Temperature: 21 to 30°C.
Rainfall: 85mm (monthly average).
Population: 80,000.
Language: English.
Currency: East Caribbean dollar
Requirements: No visa required by most nationals. Yellow Fever - if arriving within 6 days of leaving or transiting infected areas. Driving Licence - local permit required.
Airport: St. John's - V.C. Bird International - Tel: 30082.
UK Visa Office: 071 486 7073.

AUSTRALIA

Capital: Canberra.
Time: Capital Territory, New South Wales, Tasmania, Victoria GMT + 10 (summer time GMT + 11), Queensland GMT + 10, South Australia GMT +9.5 (summer time GMT + 10.5), Northern Territory GMT +9.5, Western Australia GMT + 8 hours.
Climate: Tropical north. Sub tropical east. Temperate south-east. Mediterranean south and west. Semi arid interior.
Temperature: (south-east) max. January and February 13 to 28°C / min. July 1 to 11°C.
Rainfall: (south-east) max. October 56mm / min. April 41mm.
Population: 16,500,000.
Language: English.
Religion: Church of England and Roman Catholic.
Currency: Australian dollar
Requirements: Visa required by all. Cholera - recommended if arriving via countries where cholera occures. Yellow Fever - if arriving within 6 days of leaving country in former endemic area. Driving Licence - International Driving Permits.
Airports: Canberra Airport - Tel: 062 731514; Sydney - Kingsford Smith Airport - Tel: 02 667 0544; Melbourne - Tullamarine - Tel: 03 338 221 1; Brisbane Airport International - Tel: 07 26 891 1; Adelaide Airport - Tel: 08 432211; Perth Airport - Tel: 003 277 0770.
UK Visa Office: 071 438 8698.

BAHAMAS

Capital: Nassau.
Time: GMT - 5 (summer time GMT - 4).
Climate: Sub-tropical. High humidity July and August.
Temperature: max. August 24 to 32°C / min. February 18 to 25°C.
Rainfall: max. September 175mm / min. December 33mm.
Population: 240,000.
Language: English.
Religion: Anglican, Baptist, Roman Catholic.
Currency: Bahamas dollar.
Requirements: Onward or return tickets and document permitting entry to another country. Yellow Fever - if arriving within 14 days from or via infected area. Driving Licence - Valid foreign licence useable for three months for drivers over 17 years.
Airports: Nassau International - Tel: 809 77281; Freeport International - Tel: 809 3526020.
UK Visa Office: 071 408 4488.

BARBADOS

Capital: Bridgetown.
Time: GMT - 4.
Climate: Sub-tropical.
Temperature: max. June, August, September 23 to 31°C \ min. February 21 to 28°C.
Rainfall: max. November 206mm \ min.

February 28mm.
Population: 250,000.
Language: English.
Religion: Anglican, Methodist, Roman Catholic.
Currency: Barbados dollar.
Requirements: Yellow Fever if arriving within 6 days from endemic or infected area. Driving Licence - International or foreign - Must be registered and fee paid with Ministry of Transport and Telecommunications or proprietor of car rental firm.
Airports: Christ Church - Grantley Adams International - Tel: 73149.
UK Visa Office: 071 636 9448.

BERMUDA

Capital: Hamilton.
Time: GMT - 4 (summer time GMT - 3).
Climate: Sub-tropical.
Temperature: max. August 23 to 30°C \ min. February, March 14 to 20°C.
Rainfall: max. October 149mm \ min. April 104mm.
Population: 60,000.
Language: English.
Religion: Christian.
Currency: Bermuda Dollar.
Requirements: Onward or return ticket and any necessary visa. Driving Licence - Bermuda licence valid for residents only. No self-drive cars available to visitors.
Airport: Kindley Field - Tel: 80929 31640.
UK Visa Office: Tourist Office - 071 734 8813.

BRAZIL

Capital: Brasilia
Time: East GMT - 3 (summer time GMT - 2); West GMT - 4 (summer time GMT - 3).
Climate: North-west -topical; North-east - sub tropical; coastal plains and central uplands - temperate; South - cold.
Temperature: (south-east coast): max. February 23 to 29°C / min. July 17 to 24°C.
Rainfall: (south-east coast): max. December 137mm \ min. July 41mm.
Population: 138,490,000
Language: Portuguese, English, French, German.
Religion: Roman Catholic, Protestant
Currency: Cruzado.
Requirements: Business visa and company letter required when signing of contracts or money transactions involved. Yellow Fever - if arriving within 6 days of leaving or transiting infected areas. Malaria - precautions recommended. Driving Licence - International, validated by Automovel Club de Brasil. Credit card and passport required when renting a car.
Airports: Brasilia - Tel: 2420069, 2424597; Rio de Janeiro - Galeao - Tel: 398 6060; Sao Paulo - Congonhas - Tel: 61 6666.
UK Visa Office: 071 930 9055

CANADA

Capital: Ottawa.
Time: (Central) GMT - 6 (summer time GMT - 5).
Climate: Various depending on altitude and proximity to sea and lakes.
Temperature: (south-east) max. July 11 to 33°C / min. January to -18 to 6°C.
Rainfall: (south-east) max. July 74mm / min. February 61 mm.
Population: 25,610,000.
Language: English, French.
Religion: Roman Catholic, Protestant.
Currency: Canadian dollar.
Requirements: Return or onward ticket. Driving Licence - International.
Airports: Ottawa International - Tel: 613 998 3269; Toronto International - Tel: 416 676 3030; Montreal - Dorval - Tel: 514 636 3223; Newfoundland - Gander International - Tel: 709 256 4417; Vancouver International - Tel: 604 273 2311; Calgary International - Tel: 403 276 0254.
UK Visa Office: 071 929 9492.

CAYMAN ISLANDS

Capital: Georgetown.
Time: GMT - 5.
Climate: Sub-tropical. High temperature moderated by winds.
Temperature: Max. July, August 24 to 30°C / min. January, February 18 to 24°C.
Rainfall: Monthly average: 119mm.
Population: 21,036.
Language: English.
Religion: Christian.
Currency: Cayman Dollar.
Requirements: Return or onward ticket. Driving Licence - Local licence required.
Airport: Grand Cayman - Owea Roberts - Tel: (9) 2811.
UK Visa Office: 071 581 9960

CHINA

Capital: Beijing (Peking).
Time: GMT + 8.
Climate: Widely ranging.
Tem perature: (Beijing) max. July 21 to 31°C / min. January -10 to 1°C.
Rainfall: Max. July 240mm / min Dec. 3mm.
Population: 1,072,220,000
Language: Mandarin (north) plus local dialects.
Religion: Confucian, Buddhist, Taoist, Moslem.
Currency: Ren Min Bi (yuan)
Requirements: Visa - letter of invitation required for business visa. Yellow Fever - if arriving within 5 days of leaving or transiting infected area. Malaria - precautions recommended. No car hire facilities.
Airports: Beijing - Capital Airport - Tel: 555531; Shanghai - Hung-Chaio Airport - Tel: 536530.
UK Visa Office: 071 636 5637.

CUBA

Capital: Havana.
Time: GMT - 5 (summer time GMT - 4).
Climate: Sub tropical, perennially warm.
Temperature: Max. July-August 24 to 32°C \ min. January-February 18 to 26°C.
Rainfall: Max. October 173mm \ min. February-March 46mm.
Population: 10,250,000.
Language: Spanish, English.
Religion: Roman Catholic.
Currency: Cuban peso.
Requirements: Visa - company letter for business visits. Personal letter for tourists onward or return tickets. Yellow Fever - if arriving within 6 days of leaving or transiting infected area. Driving Licence - Foreign or International.
Airport: Havana - Jose Marti - Tel: 70 9119.
UK Visa Office: 071 240 2488.

CYPRUS

Capital: Nicosia.
Time: GMT + 2 (summer time GMT +3).
Climate: Mediterranean. Hot, dry summers. Coastal areas humid.
Temperature: Max. July 21 to 37°C \ min. January 5 to 15°C.
Rainfall: Max. January 76mm \ min. July 1mm.
Language: Greek, Turkish, English, German, French.
Religion: Greek Orthodox, Moslem.
Currency: Cyprus pound.
Requirements: Driving Licence - international or foreign, must be presented to Registrar of Automobiles for authorisation. Full British licence accepted without further requirements.
Airports: North - Ercan (Tymbou). South - Larnaca - Tel: 041 53017.
UK Visa Office: 071 629 5350

EGYPT

Capital: Cairo.
Time: GMT + 2.
Climate: Winter - cool and dry. Summer - hot and dry. Intense heat in the north.
Temperature: Max. July 21 to 36°C \ min.

January 8 to 18°C
Rainfall: Max. December 5mm \ min. July, August 0mm.
Population: 49,610,000.
Language: Arabic, English, French, Greek.
Religion: Moslem, Christian.
Currency: Egyptian pound.
Requirements: Visa - company letter for business visa. Cholera - if arriving within 5 days from infected countries. Yellow Fever - if arriving from any endemic areas. Malaria - precautions recommended. Driving Licence - International.
Airports: Cairo International - Tel: 64381; Alexandria - El Nhouza - Tel: 71260.
UK Visa Office: 071 229 8818.

FIJI

Capital: Suva
Time: GMT + 12.
Climate: Tropical. Heat and humidity tempered by sea breezes.
Temperature: Max. January-March 23 to 29°C \ min. July, August 20 to 26°C.
Rainfall: Max. Mar. 368mm \ min. July 124mm.
Language: English, Fijian, Hindi, Cantonese.
Religion: Christian, Hindu, Moslem.
Currency: Fiji dollar.
Requirements: Onward or return ticket. Cholera - if arriving from infected area. Yellow Fever - required if arriving from infected area. Driving Licence - International.
Airports: Nadi International - Airport Tel: 72500; Nausori International Airport - Tel: 48344.
UK Visa Office: 071 584 3661.

FRANCE

Capital: Paris.
Time: GMT + 1 (summertime GMT + 2).
Climate: Temperate north. Mediterranean south.
Temperature: (north) max. July 14 to 25°C \ min. January 1 to 6°C.
Rainfall: (north) max. August 64mm \ min. March 35mm.
Population: 55,400,000.
Language: French, Breton, Basque.
Religion: Roman Catholic, Protestant, Moslem.
Currency: Franc.
Requirements: Driving Licence - International or Foreign.
Airports: Lyon - Satolas - Tel: (7) 8719221; Marseille - Marignane - Tel: (42) 899010; Paris - Charles de Gaulle - Tel: (1) 4862 12120; Paris - Le Bourget - Tel: (1) 862 5306; Paris - Orly - Tel: (1) 884 5498.
UK Visa Office: 071 823 9555.

GIBRALTAR

Capital: Gibraltar Town.
Time: GMT + 1 (summer time GMT + 2).
Climate: Temperate. Warm summers, cool winters.
Temperature: Max. August 19 to 34°C \ min. February 3 to 20°C.
Rainfall: Max. Jan. 152mm \ min. July 1mm.
Population: 30,000.
Language: English, Spanish.
Religion: Roman Catholic, Moslem, Anglican.
Currency: Gibraltar pound.
Requirements: Driving Licence - International or Foreign.
Airport: Gibraltar Tel: (350) 63852.
UK Visa Office: 071 836 0777.

GREECE

Capital: Athens.
Time: GMT + 2 (summer time GMT +3).
Climate: Mediterranean. Cold winters in the north.
Temperature: (central) max. July 23 to 33°C \ min. January 6 to12°C.
Rainfall: (central) max. December 70mm \ min. July 6mm.
Population: 9,970,000.
Language: Greek, and most European

languages.
Religion: Greek Orthodox, Moslem.
Currency: Drachma.
Requirements: Yellow Fever if arriving within 6 days of leaving or transiting endemic area. Driving Licence - International or foreign for EEC nationals.
Airport: Athens - Athinai Airport - Tel: (01) 97991.
UK Visa Office: 071 727 8040.

INDONESIA

Capital: Jakarta
Time: Western Zone GMT + 7; Central Zone GMT +8; Eastern Zone GMT +9.
Climate: Tropical. Warm and humid.
Temperature: Max. April-May 24 to 31°C \ min. January-February 23 to 29°C.
Rainfall: Max. January, February 300mm \ min. August 43mm.
Population: 166,940,000.
Language: Bahasa Indonesian, Dutch, English.
Religion: Moslem, Hindu, Christian.
Currency: Rupiah.
Requirements: Visa - required for business visit. Onward or return tickets and documents. Cholera - precautions recommended. Yellow Fever - if arriving within 6 days of leaving or transiting infected areas. Malaria - precautions recommended. Driving Licence - International.
Airport: Jakarta - Halim Peranakusuma International - Tel: 801108.
UK Visa Office: 071 499 7661.

ISRAEL

Capital: Jerusalem
Time: GMT + 2 (summer time GMT +3).
Climate: Mediterranean. Coast areas humid summers.
Temperature: Max. August 18 to 31°C \ min. January 5 to 13°C.
Rainfall: Max. January-February 132mm \ min. July-August 0mm.
Population: 4,300,000.
Language: Hebrew, Arabic, English, French, German.
Religion: Jewish, Moslem, Christian.
Currency: Israeli Shekel.
Requirements: Driving Licence - Foreign or International.
Airport: Tel Aviv - Ben-Gurion International - Tel: (03) 972610.
UK Visa Office: 071 937 8050.

ITALY

Capital: Rome.
Time: GMT+ 1 (summertime GMT +2).
Climate: Mediterranean.
Temperature: (central) max. July 20 to 30°C \ min. January 4 to 11°C.
Rainfall: max. Nov. 129mm \ min. July 15mm.
Population: 57,220,000.
Language: Italian, French, English, German.
Religion: Roman Catholic.
Currency: Lira.
Requirements: Driving Licence - Foreign with official translation.
Airports: Milan - Linate - Tel: (02) 720342/5; Genoa - Aeroporto Cristoforo Colombo - Tel: (O1) 470374; Rome - Ciampino - Tel: (06) 600021; Rome - Leonardo da Vinci (Fiumicino) - Tel: (06) 601541.
UK Visa Office: 071 235 9371.

JAMAICA

Capital: Kingston
Time: GMT - 5.
Climate: Tropical coast. Sub-tropical inland.
Temperature: (coast) max. July-August 23 to 32°C \ min. January, February 19 to 30°C
Rainfall: (coast) max. October 180mm \ min. February 15mm.
Population: 2,375,000.
Language: English.
Religion: Protestant, Roman Catholic.

Currency: Jamaican dollar.
Requirements: Yellow Fever if arriving within 6 days from endemic area. Driving Licence - International.
Airports: Kingston - Norman Manley International - Tel: 938 6057; Montego Bay - Donald Sangster International - Tel: 952 3124.
UK Visa Office: 071 823 9911.

MALAYSIA

Capital: Kuala Lumpur.
Time: GMT + 8.
Climate: Tropical.
Temperature: Max. April, May 23 to 33°C \ min. December 22 to 32°C.
Rainfall: Max. April 293mm \ min. July 98mm.
Population: 16,200,000.
Language: Malay, Tamil, Chinese, English, Iban.
Religion: Moslem, Buddhist, Hindu, Christian.
Currency: Malaysian dollar or Ringgit.
Requirements: Confirmed onward or return ticket or sufficient funds. Yellow Fever - if arriving within 6 days of visiting or being in endemic areas. Malaria - precautions recommended. Driving Licence - Foreign.
Airports: Kuala Lumpar - Subang International - Tel: 54551; Penang - Bayan Lepas - Tel: 04 831411.
UK Visa Office: 071 235 8033.

MALTA

Capital: Valletta.
Time: GMT + 1 (summer time GMT + 2).
Climate: Mediterranean.
Temperature: Max. August 23 to 29°C \ min. January 10 to 14°C.
Rainfall: Max. Dec. 11Omm \ min. July 0mm.
Population: 380,000.
Language: Maltese, English, Italian.
Religion: Roman Catholic.
Currency: Maltese lira.
Requirements: Cholera - if arriving from infected area. Yellow Fever - if arriving from infected area. Driving Licence - Foreign.
Airport: Valletta - Luqa - Tel: 22921.
UK Visa Office: 071 938 1712.

MAURITIUS

Capital: Port Louis.
Time: GMT + 4.
Climate: Tropical maritime. High humidity on coastal areas in the summer.
Temperature: Max. January 23 to 30°C \ min. July, August 17 to 24°C.
Rainfall: Max. Mar. 221 mm \ min. Sept. 36mm.
Population: 990,000
Language: English, French, Hindi, Creole, Chinese.
Religion: Hindu, Roman Catholic, Moslem.
Currency: Mauritius rupee.
Requirements: Yellow Fever if arriving within 6 days of leaving or transiting infected area. Malaria - precautions recommended. Driving Licence - International or Foreign.
Airport: Mauritius Plaisance - Tel: 73531.
UK Visa Office: 071 581 0294.

MEXICO

Capital: Mexico City
Time: General Mexico GMT - 6; Lower California, N. Pacific coast GMT - 7; Baja California, Norte GMT - 8 (summer time GMT - 7).
Climate: Tropical, south. Temperate, highlands.
Temperature: (highlands) max. May 12 to 26°C \ min. January 6 to 19°C.
Rainfall: (highlands) max. July 170mm \ min. February 5mm.
Population: 79,560,000.
Language: Spanish, local Indian languages, English.
Religion: Roman Catholic, Protestant.
Currency: Mexican peso.
Requirements: All travellers must complete a Tourist Card. Yellow Fever - if arriving within 6 days of leaving or transiting infected area. Malaria - precautions recommended.

Driving Licence - Foreign.
Airport: Mexico City - Benito juarez International - Tel: 571 3030.
UK Visa Office: 071 235 6393.

NEW ZEALAND

Capital: Wellington.
Time: GMT + 12 (Summer time GMT + 13).
Climate: Temperate.
Temperature: Max. January, February 16 to 23°C \ min. July 8 to 13°C.
Rainfall: Max. July 145mm \ min. January-March 81mm.
Population: 3,290,000.
Language: English, Maori.
Religion: Christian.
Currency: New Zealand Dollar .
Requirements: Onward or return ticket and documents. Maximum stay 6 months. Driving Licence - Foreign (valid for 1 year depending on category).
Airports: Auckland International - Tel: 275 0789; Christchurch International - Tel: 584 029; Wellington International - Tel: 888 500.
UK Visa Office: 071 937 0363.

NORWAY

Capital: Oslo.
Time: GMT + 1 (Summer time GMT + 2).
Climate: Temperate south, Arctic north.
Temperature: South max. July 13 to 22°C \ min. January -7 to -20°C.
Rainfall: South max. July 95mm \ min. March 26mm.
Population: 4,170,000.
Language: Norwegian, Danish, Swedish, English, German.
Religion: Evangelical Lutheran.
Currency: Norwegian Krone.
Requirements: Driving Licence - International or Foreign.
Airports: Bergen - Flesland - Tel: (05) 2260-00; Oslo - Fornebu - Tel: (02) 5933 40; Stavanger - Sola - Tel: (04) 651000.
UK Visa Office: 071 235 7151.

PHILIPPINES

Capital: Manila.
Time: GMT + 8.
Climate: Tropical - March-June; Dry season - July; Wet Season - October, high humidity. November-February cooler.
Temperature: Max. May 24 to 34°C \ min. January 21 to 30°C.
Rainfall: Max. July 432mm \ min. Feb. 13mm.
Population: 56,000,000.
Language: Filipino, English, Spanish.
Religion: Roman Catholic.
Currency: Philippine peso.
Requirements: Return or onward ticket. Visa not required for visits under 21 days, extension to 59 days possible. Yellow Fever - if arriving within 6 days of leaving or transiting infected area. Malaria - precautions recommended. Driving Licence - International.
Airport: Manila International.
UK Visa Office: 071 937 3646.

PORTUGAL

Capital: Lisbon
Time: GMT (summer time GMT + 1).
Climate: Temperate north. Mediterranean south.
Temperature: Central max. August 17 to 28°C \ min. January 8 to l4°C.
Rainfall: Max. Jan. 111 mm \ min. July 3mm.
Population: 10,290,000.
Language: Portuguese, Spanish, English, French.
Religion: Roman Catholic.
Currency: Escudo.
Requirements: Driving Licence - Foreign or International.
Airport: Lisbon - Aeroport de Lisbonne - Tel: 881 101.
UK Visa Office: 071 581 8722.

ST. VINCENT & THE GRENADINES

Capital: Kingstown.
Time: GMT - 4.
Climate: Sub-tropical. Rainfall greater in mountains.
Temperature: Coast max. September 21 to 33°C \ min. January 17 to 29°C.
Rainfall: Max. Aug. 270mm \ min. April 86mm.
Population: 100,000.
Language: English.
Religion: Anglican, Methodist, Roman Catholic.
Currency: East Caribbean dollar.
Requirements: Yellow Fever if arriving within 14 days of leaving infected area. Driving Licence - International.
Airport: Kingstown - Amos Vale - Tel: 84011/84960.
UK Visa Office: 071 937 6570.

SEYCHELLES

Capital: Victoria.
Time: GMT + 4.
Climate: Tropical. Average humidity 76%.
Temperature: Max. April 25 to 30°C \ min. July-August 24 to 27°C.
Rainfall: Max. December 340mm \ min. August 70mm.
Population: 70,000.
Language: English, French, Creole.
Religion: Christian, Roman Catholic, Hindu.
Currency: Seychelles rupee.
Requirements: Onward or return ticket or adequate funds. Visitor's permit valid six weeks issued to all nationals, renewal thereafter every three months for period not exceeding one year. Driving Licence - any Foreign licence acceptable up to three months.
Airport: Seychelles International - Tel: 76551.
UK Visa Office: 071 439 9699.

SOUTH AFRICA

Capital: Pretoria (administrative capital) \ Cape Town (legislative capital).
Time: GMT + 2.
Temperature: Cape max. February 16 to 26°C \ min. July 4 to 17°C.
Rainfall: Cape max. July 90mm \ min. February 7mm.
Population: 33,225,000.
Language: Afrikaans, English, native African languages.
Religion: Christian, Hindu, Moslem, Jewish, Bantu churches.
Currency: Rand.
Requirements: Business letter from employers onward or return ticket. Yellow Fever - if arriving from infected or former endemic zone. Driving Licence - International.
Airports: Cape Town - D.F. Malan - Tel: (021) 93 2261; Durban - Louis Botha International - Tel: (031) 42 1164; Johannesburg - Jan Smuts - Tel: (O11) 975 1185.
UK Visa Office: 071 930 4488.

SPAIN

Capital: Madrid.
Time: GMT + 1.
Climate: Temperate, north. Hot and dry, south
Temperature: Central max. July 17 to 31°C \ min. January 1 to 8°C.
Rainfall: Max. Oct. 53mm \ min. July 11mm.
Population: 39,315,000.
Language: Spanish (Castilian), Catalan, Basque, French, English.
Religion: Roman Catholic.
Currency: Peseta.
Requirements: Driving Licence - International.
Airport: Madrid - Barajas - Tel: (1) 222 1165; Barcelona - Sabadell - Tel: (3) 317 0008.
UK Visa Office: 071 581 5921.

THAILAND

Capital: Bangkok.
Time: GMT + 7.
Climate: Tropical.

Temperature: Max. April 25 to 35°C \ min. December 20 to 31°C.
Rainfall: Max. September 305mm \ min. December 5mm.
Population: 52,650,000.
Language: Thai, Chinese, English.
Religion: Buddhist, Moslem, Christian.
Currency: Baht.
Requirements: Visa - company letter for business visa. Cholera - precaution recommended. Yellow Fever - if arriving from an infected area. Typhoid - precaution recommended. Malaria - precaution recommended.
Driving Licence - International.
Airport: Bangkok - Don Muang.
UK Visa Office: 071 589 0173.

TRINIDAD AND TOBAGO

Capital: Port of Spain.
Time: GMT - 4.
Climate: Tropical.
Temperature: Max. May 22 to 32°C \ min. January 21 to 31°C.
Rainfall: Max. August 246mm \ min. February 40 mm.
Population: 1,200,000.
Language: English.
Religion: Christian, Hindu, and Moslem.
Currency: Trinidad and Tobago Dollar.
Requirements: Visa required by businessmen. Yellow Fever - if arriving within 6 days from or via infected areas. Driving Licence - Foreign.
Airport: Port of Spain - Parco - Tel: 664 4806.
UK Visa Office: 071 245 9351.

TURKEY

Capital: Ankara.
Time: GMT + 2 (summer time + 3).
Climate: Inland, continental. Coastal, Mediterranean.
Temperature: Central max. August 15 to 31°C \ min. January -4 to 4°C.
Rainfall: Central max. December 48mm \ min. August 10mm.
Language: Turkish, German, Greek, French, English, Kurdish, Arabic.
Religion: Moslem, Christian minority.
Currency: Turkish Lira.
Requirements: Cholera, Yellow Fever and Malaria - vaccinations required if arriving or transiting from infected area. Driving Licence - International.
Airports: Ankara - Esenboga International - Tel: 241270; Istanbul - Yesilkoy International - Tel: 737964.
UK Visa Office: 071 589 0360.

UNITED STATES OF AMERICA

Capital: Washington DC
Time: Eastern Time GMT - 5 (Summer time GMT - 4); Central Time GMT - 6 (Summer time - 5); Mountain Time GMT - 7 (Summer time - 6); Pacific Time GMT - 8 (Summer time - 7).
Climate: Ranges from Arctic (Alaska) to sub-tropical (Florida).
Temperature: Washington max. July 20 to 31°C \ min. January -3 to 6°C.
Rainfall: Max. July 112mm \ min. Nov. 66mm.
Population: 241,600,000.
Language: English, Spanish, German, Italian, French, Polish, Yiddish.
Religion: Protestant, Roman Catholic, Jewish.
Currency: Dollar.
Requirements: Visa. Driving Licence - Foreign or International.
Airports: Baltimore - Washington International Airport - Tel: (301) 859 7100; Houston Intercontinental - Tel: (713) 230 3100; Los Angeles International - Tel: (213) 646 4267; Miami International - Tel: (305) 526 2000; New York City - J.F.Kennedy International - Tel: (718) 656 4520; Washington - Dulles Int. - Tel: (703) 661 8202.
UK Visa Office: 071 499 3443.

Plaice - Pleuronectes platessa

Safety

Emergency VHF Marine Radio Procedures

Coastguard Maritime Rescue Centres maintain a constant watch on Channel 16 - the distress, safety and calling channel.

Always call for assistance on channel 16

Turn the set on. Channel 16 will automatically come up. If it does not, push the channel 16 button. Your set will have one. To broadcast, push in the button on the handset. Finish your last sentence with the word "OVER". To receive, release the button.

If in an EMERGENCY situation - WHEN LIFE IS IN GRAVE OR IMMINENT DANGER - use the DISTRESS call as follows.

MAYDAY - MAYDAY - MAYDAY
followed by:

1) **NAME and/or CALL SIGN of your craft.**
2) **Your present POSITION (latitude and longitude or placename).**
3) **The nature of your PROBLEM (diving emergency/fire etc).**

If in an URGENCY situation - when NO IMMINENT DANGER to life exists (eg broken down or drifting), use the URGENCY call as follows:

PAN PAN - PAN PAN - PAN PAN
followed by:

1) **NAME and/or CALL SIGN of your craft.**
2) **Your present POSITION and INTENTIONS.**
3) **The nature of URGENCY.**

CONTINUE TO BROADCAST THE MESSAGE UNTIL AN ANSWER IS RECEIVED. NEVER TURN YOUR SET OFF. WAIT-YOU MAY RECEIVE FURTHER INSTRUCTIONS.

FOR EMERGENCY MEDICAL PROCEDURES SEE PAGE 333

The above guide is not intended to be a substitute for proper training in radio operation and procedures

Safety at Sea

HM Coastguard

We talk about safety at sea, but in the end there is no such thing. The sea is always out to catch the unwary. Balmy summer days are a rare bonus, weather conditions change very quickly and the set of the tide may be taking you towards the rocks, or a bank of thick mist may be creeping up.

Ensure that your boat is of good design, properly built, well maintained and equipped.

The Coastguard will advise about safety equipment and how to make sure your voyage is as safe as possible.

In this article we can do no more than offer a few hints, and perhaps encourage further study of seamanship. Yachtsmen, yachtswomen, or the sports diver while on his way to and from the dive site, all need to master the same skills of boathandling.

Boats are fun. They provide the kind of deep-rooted satisfaction that stems from the slow build-up of experience. Stay close by the home port at first and gradually extend your range as confidence comes. We will deal here primarily with recommendations for recreational divers before moving on to some topics of reference for the boatman.

ADVICE FOR DIVERS

The following diving routines are recommended by the Coastguard as the most advisable to take before, during and upon completion of the dive.

ACTION BY THE DIVE MARSHAL

Take local advice on dive site conditions and always get an up-to-date local weather forecast. Always inform the Coastguard of the intentions of your diving party and give clear information about diving profiles. Check that a comprehensive outfit of safety equipment is carried and confirm the location of the closest hyperbaric chamber and its current status. Last but not least, you should always discuss your intentions with the skipper of your boat before leaving harbour.

ACTION BY THE BOAT SKIPPER

Ensure that the boat does not exceed the licence limits for the number of people you are to carry and you should make certain that the boat is suitable for the diving operation.

You should always discuss the diving site conditions with the Dive Marshal and ensure that at least the minimum safety equipment is carried in accordance with current regulations. It is essential that you discuss emergency procedures with the Dive Marshal. Before commencing any diving operation you should ensure that you have communication with the Coastguard - carry out a radio check. The attendant craft must display a rigid replica of the International Code of Signals Flag A.

ACTION BY DIVERS

All divers should be qualified in all respects for the proposed dive and have verified that personal equipment has been maintained correctly and is fully operational. You should make absolutely certain that you understand your diving brief and that you know precisely what action to take in an emergency. Remember that safety is ultimately the responsibility of the individual.

Agree the recall to boat signal.

BEFORE AND DURING THE DIVE

Dive Marshal

On arrival at the diving site, you should have ensured that the location and dive profile are as planned and that all divers are fully briefed and have been appraised of emergency procedures - prior to entry into the water. You should maintain dive logging and continually check the location of divers throughout the dive period and carry out regular communications checks with the Coastguard - at one hour intervals. Remember to report any change of plans to the Coastguard. Also remember to inform the Coastguard when the dive is completed and all divers have been recovered.

Upon Completion

Report to the Coastguard when the diving boat is safe alongside and all activity has finished for the day. The Coastguard are also interested in any local effects which may prove valuable to other divers and would improve their local knowledge.

During the dive and on completion of the dive, activities should be carried out as arranged between the Dive Marshal and the boat skipper, bearing in mind that the Dive Marshal is responsible for the safe conduct of the dive and that the boat skipper is responsible for his craft and for those embarked.

Remember, Coastguard Rescue Centres hold details of emergency hyperbaric chambers and have access to 24 hour specialist emergency diving medical advice.

ADVICE FOR BOATMEN

Get Trained Join a recognised school or club.

Sail within your ability

Know the limitations of your craft and whether it is suitable for all weathers and sea areas, and has sufficient reserve buoyancy to support all on board without sinking if swamped. Do not overload or stand up in your boat; rough conditions can reduce its capability. Use dinghies only near the shore or in good conditions; they have little or no keel and are difficult to handle even when powered.

Learn the 'rules of the road'. Check local harbour bye-laws, and where there are restricted areas for windsurfers or water skiers.

Talk to people with local knowledge. Get charts and tide tables. Be aware of tidal race or other local peculiarities rocks, wrecks etc.

Let someone ashore know where you are going and your estimated time of return.

Speak to the Coastguard. They are always pleased to meet small-craft sailors and can offer you sound advice on local hazards, weather and sea conditions and on many other important aspects of going afloat. If you are going abroad, check with them about the Small Ships Register.

Enroll with the Yacht and Boat Safety Scheme. Let the Coastguard know your sailing plans and seek their advice.

ON BOARD

Sound signals and lights. All craft are required by law to have a means of giving sound signals and to display adequate navigation lights when at sea between sunset and sunrise. All craft must have stand-by means of propulsion. A small extra outboard motor is useful even on a small power craft. An engine tool-kit would also be useful.

You will need an anchor. A larger one is better than one too small; one heavy anchor should hold better than two small ones. Large boats may need a kedge anchor as well. Carry a suitable bailer. Larger boats need a fixed bilge-pump, and it is sensible on smaller ones.

Life jackets for all on board are essential and should be worn at all times. Life jackets that have to be inflated by mouth should be worn partly inflated. In sheltered waters or inshore, a buoyancy aid may suffice.

Safety harnesses. Carry safety harnesses for each working member, and one or more on a motor cruiser. Life jackets and harnesses should conform to British Standard specification BS 4224/75.

Clothing. Pay particular attention to fitting children and make sure you have the proper clothing for all weather conditions.

Radio. Carry an appropriate portable radio capable of receiving weather forecast (See Radio on board).

Identity. Display the yacht's name in bold lettering.

Flares and signals. Small craft, within three miles of shore, should carry two red hand flares and two orange smoke signals. Larger yachts in coastal waters, up to seven miles from land, need four two-star red signals (or two red parachute rockets) in addition.

Offshore (more than seven miles) they should carry four red parachute rockets, four red hand flares and two orange smoke signals. White handflares are used for collision warnings. Make sure everyone knows where they are and how to use them and that they are in good condition and in date. (See Pyrotechnic signals).

A radar reflector is essential for seagoing yachts. It is hard to improve on the old eight-sided type, the larger the better. Mount as high as possible, with an inner cone operating upwards vertically, for maximum efficiency.

Fire extinguishers. Motor yachts over nine metres with powerful engines should have fixed fire extinguisher installations. Others should hold two 1.4 kg (3 lb) dry powder extinguishers and a spare 2.3 kg (5 lb). A rope ladder or canvas strop will be useful in case of 'man-overboard' and take a boat-hook and two good lines.

Other necessities. You will need charts of the area, a nautical almanac and one of the pilot's books published especially for yachtsmen, an alarm clock and a radio receiver (See Radio on board). Don't forget a first-aid kit, water resistant torch with spare batteries, matches, knife, whistle, watch, blankets, food supplies and drinking water. Have a hand bearing compass which can be used for steering in an emergency, as well as a steering compass.

IN AN EMERGENCY

If you get into trouble and capsize, stay with the boat. Do not try to swim ashore. The rescue services can spot a bright coloured boat more easily than a swimmer. (See Distress signals).

WEATHER

You are advised to contact the Coastguard about local weather and sea conditions before you put to sea, by telephone. Sea area forecasts and strong wind warnings are also available from them. MARINECALL (see page 131) provides inshore forecasts (up to 12 miles to seaward).

Weather Forecasts are broadcast at regular intervals by all Coastguard Rescue Centres at 4 hourly intervals, (2 hourly when Force 6 or above). Broadcasts are on Channel 67 (after initial announcement on Channel 16) and also include weather 'actuals'. Your local Coastguard Centre will advise you on their radio transmission times for all weather information appropriate to their area.

Forecasts for inshore waters are broadcast on BBC Radio 3 (1215 kHz/247 m) every day at 06.55 and on Radio 4 (200 kHz/ 1400 m) immediately after the shipping forecast at 00.33. Shipping forecasts on Radio 4 are normally made every day at 00.33, 05.55, 13.55 and 17.50, but check with the Radio Times.

Local radio stations also broadcast forecasts so carry a transistor radio and listen carefully for changes in local conditions - the weather can worsen very quickly.

Certain British Telecom Coast Radio Stations also give shipping forecasts on the Radiotelephony Service. Times and frequencies differ between stations; a preliminary announcement is broadcast on 2182 kHz and Channel 16 VHF.

RADIO ON BOARD

You will be much safer at sea if your craft carries conventional marine radio telephone equipment capable of operating on the international maritime distress frequencies 156.8 MHz (VHF Channel 16) or 2182 kHz as well. MRCCs and MRSCs keep constant watch on VHF Channel 16; their call-sign gives the name of the Centre and the word 'Coastguard'- for example, 'Solent Coastguard'. Channel 67 is the Small Craft Safety Frequency and safety information can be exchanged with the Coastguard after first calling on Channel 16.

CB radio must not be considered a substitute for VHF. It is not monitored by the Coastguard and you cannot rely on your message being picked up by anyone. A false sense of security could have fatal results.

Emergency Beacons (EPIRBS)

Although conventional marine radio is the best means of alerting nearby shipping and SAR services to a distress situation, the carriage of an Emergency Beacon will much improve your chances of being located should conventional means fail. Beacons which operate on 121.5 MHz, 243 MHz and 406 MHz are now detected by satellite, in addition to aircraft, and re-transmitted to a Coastguard Rescue Centre.

However, it is important to note that Beacons:

- must be used for distress only.
- will be detected by satellite and maybe by passing aircraft.
- once activated should not be switched off- even if the situation changes for the better before you are located.
- are not substitutes for conventional radio.
- should not be dropped or knocked.

The carriage of EPIRBs requires a licence. The DTI's Radio Communications Division can offer advice and details.

DISTRESS SIGNALS

Even the best sailors get into difficulties and need to make their position known. All water users should also be aware of the different distress signals, what they mean, and which ones are suitable for them.

If you find yourself in grave and imminent danger, you should transmit the distress signal MAYDAY, MAYDAY, MAYDAY and give your name and callsign, position, nature of the distress and assistance needed, the number of crew and your intentions. The Coastguard will coordinate all the rescue services RNLI, RN and RAF helicopters and other aircraft, and other vessels in the area - but this should not be lightly invoked.

If you need urgent help but are not actually in danger - for example, broken down and drifting, you should use the signal PAN PAN, PAN PAN, PAN PAN. You should give the same information as for a distress call. In addition, use the International Flag Signal V or the Morse Code signal V: dot dot dot dash ('I require assistance'). A white flag may be used to indicate your position to an approaching vessel if danger of collision exists. The signal W (dot dash dash) is used when medical attention is needed.

Other recognised signals are slowly and repeatedly raising and lowering outstretched arms; the Morse Signal SOS (··· - - - ···) by lights; an article of clothing on an oar; the flag signal NC; or a square flag having, above or below, anything resembling a ball. You could hoist the ensign upside-down or make it fast in the rigging. Continuous sounding of a siren or whistle will also be recognised. Life-saving stations use orange smoke signals and, at night, three white star rockets fired at one-minute intervals as answering signals.

PYROTECHNIC SIGNALS

Inshore (up to three miles) use red hand flares and orange smoke signals; in coastal waters two-star red flares or red parachute rockets; and offshore, red parachute rockets.

In coastal or offshore waters, fire the first two signals within two minutes. Keep back at least one red hand flare (in darkness, gale or poor visibility) or orange smoke to signal your position. Hold flares down wind away from your body.

Out of date flares should not be disposed of at sea. Ask the Coastguard about local disposal arrangements; they can arrange for the Ministry of Defence Explosive Ordinance Disposal Teams to collect them.

The chandlers might also take your old ones when you buy new ones.

LANDING SIGNALS

'Land here' is an up-and-down movement of a white light, white flag or flare; or arms fully extended; or Morse Code letter K (dash dot dash) by light or sound. If two lights, flags or flares are shown at a lower level, approach with two lined up.

'Landing dangerous' is indicated by a side-to-side movement of a white light, flag or flare; or arms fully extended; or a Morse Code letter S (dot dot dot) by sight or sound.

After a 'landing dangerous' signal, 'go in the direction indicated' is shown by placing a flag or light in the ground and carrying a second light or flag in the safe direction, or by Morse Code letter S (dot dot dot) followed by R (dot dash dot) or L (dot dash dot dot) for 'right' or 'left'.

OTHER SIGNALS YOU SHOULD KNOW

The windsurfer

Windsurfers carry a recognised distress flare or smoke signal. An orange 'dayglow' flag is now recognised by the Coastguard as an effective distress signal; another is slowly lowering and raising outstretched arms. With training at a recognised school, they should be able to carry out the self-rescue technique quickly, but are advised to wear a life jacket and go to sea in groups.

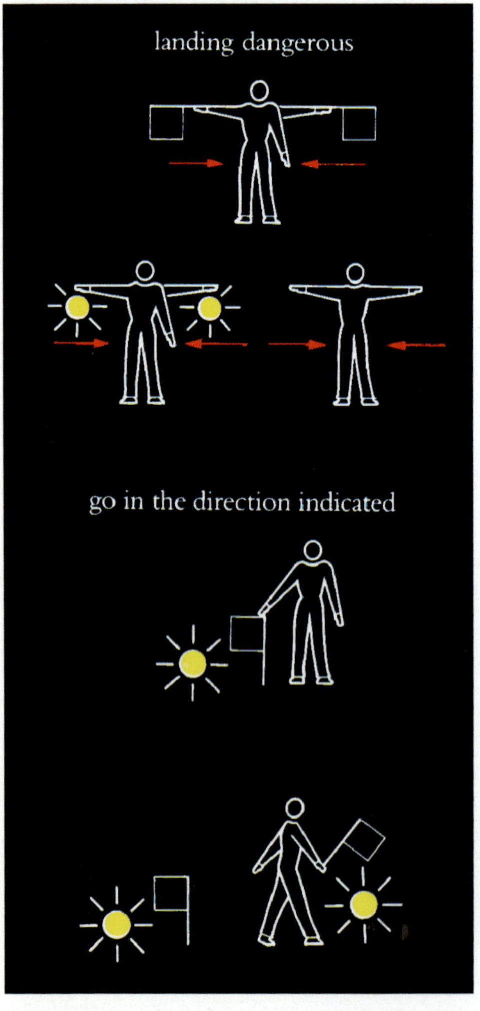

AT SEA IN THE DARK

Sailing in the dark has to be preceded by a lot of experience in daylight. Even in the most familiar waters, it will astonish you how different everything appears in the hours of darkness. Preserve your night vision by avoiding the use of torches. A good seaman is able to do everything as well in the dark as in daylight. Keep a good look-out. Make sure you can be seen.

Show green and red sidelights and a stern light. If under power show a white 'steaming' (masthead) light as well. A sailing boat of under 20 metres (65ft) may use a three-colour lantern (all lights should be Department of Transport approved). Crossing a shipping lane, out at sea, a ship's steaming' (masthead) lights will be visible long before you see her sidelights. As the after 'steaming' light is higher than the forward one, they tell you which way she is headed.

A single white light may be a ship's stern light and she is going away from you. It could also be the single steaming light of a small power vessel - less than 50 metres (164ft) in length - but if so, you will probably be able to see the sidelights as well, which tell you which way she's heading. Show a good white light (a powerful torch) in good time if another vessel approaches you and then use a white hand-flare to attract attention if you think that you have not been seen (Rule 36), but on the whole it is better not to 'stand on your rights' with a big ship. Should you lose the argument, the consequences could be disastrous.

The regulations governing the position, intensity and visibility etc. of navigation lights are to be found in the Merchant Shipping (Distress Signals and Prevention of Collision) Regulation 1989.

LATERAL MARKS

Used generally to mark the sides of well defined navigable channels.

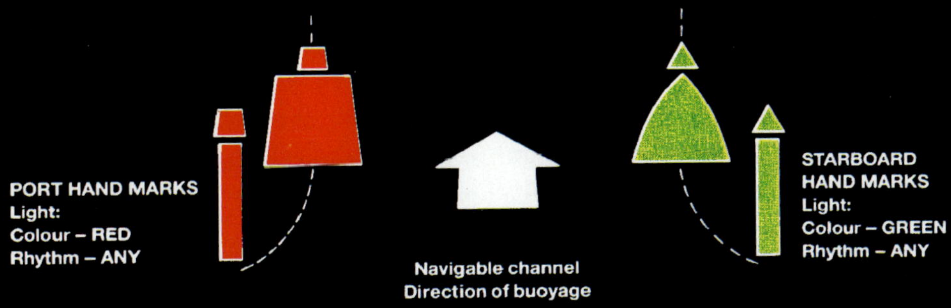

CARDINAL MARKS

Used to indicate the direction from the mark in which the best navigable water lies, or to draw attention to a bend, junction or fork in a channel, or to mark the end of a shoal.

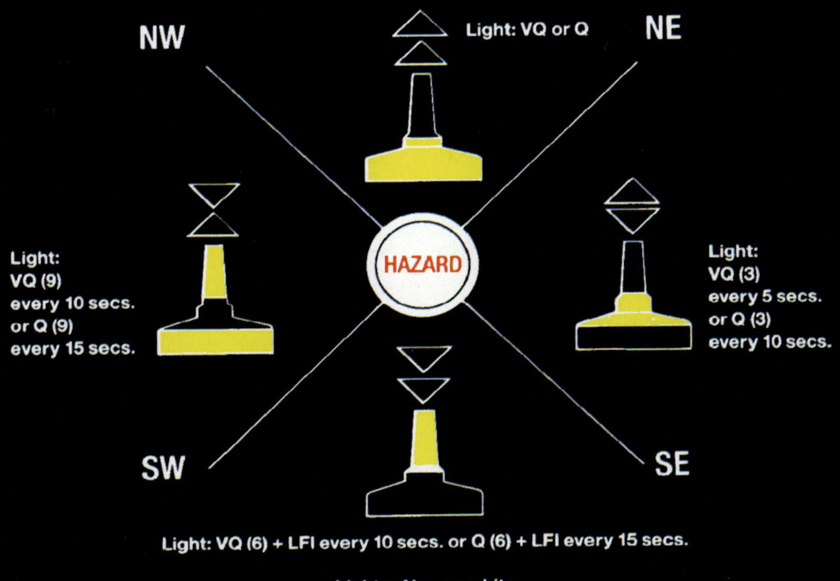

Lights: Always white

Q = Quick flashing (light flashing at 60 times a minute).
VQ = Very quick flashing (light flashing at 120 times a minute).
Fl(9) = Group flashing
LFl = Long flashing (flash 2 seconds or longer)

BUOYS

The system of buoyage now used around Britain and Ireland is the IALA Maritime Buoyage System for Region A.

This system is progressively introduced in all North West European waters and replaces the obsolete Lateral System of buoyage that may still be encountered in a few minor ports.

Cardinal Marks

There is a simple logic to the IALA system of buoyage which is easy to remember. The key to recognising cardinal buoys is in the topmark. North and South are obvious, points up and down respectively.

The West topmark appears Wasp Waisted and East topmark is equatorially enlarged. The position of the black colour on the body of the buoys corresponds with the position of the points of the cones.

The lights conform to a clock code, three at East, six at South and nine at West, with a long flash added to the South characteristic to reduce the chance of miscounting the flashes.

Isolated danger marks

(Red and black)

Indicates the position of an isolated danger with navigable water all round.

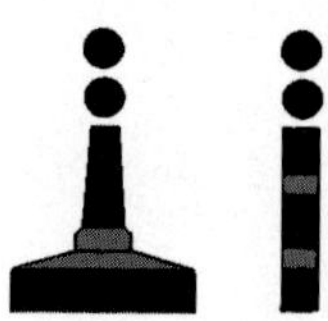

ISOLATED DANGER MARKS
Use: to mark a small isolated danger with navigable water all round. Light: Colour – white. Rhythm – group flashing (2).

Special and new danger marks

SPECIAL MARKS

Any shape not conflicting with lateral or safe water marks.
Light: Colour – yellow.
Rhythm – different from other white lights used on buoys.

These are not primarily intended to assist navigation but to indicate a special area or feature, ie. traffic separation zones, recreational areas, spoil grounds, military exercise areas, sewage out fall etc. New dangers (newly discovered hazards not yet recorded in nautical documents: shoals, sandbanks, rocks or wrecks) are marked with the combined systems described above.

Safe water marks

(Red and white)

Indicates that there is navigable water all round the mark; it is used as a centre line or mid-channel mark or as an alternative land fall mark.

SAFE WATER MARKS

Use: Mid-channel or landfall.
Light: Colour – white.
Rhythm: Isophase, occulting or 1 long flash every 10 seconds.

HM COASTGUARD RESCUE COORDINATION CENTRES

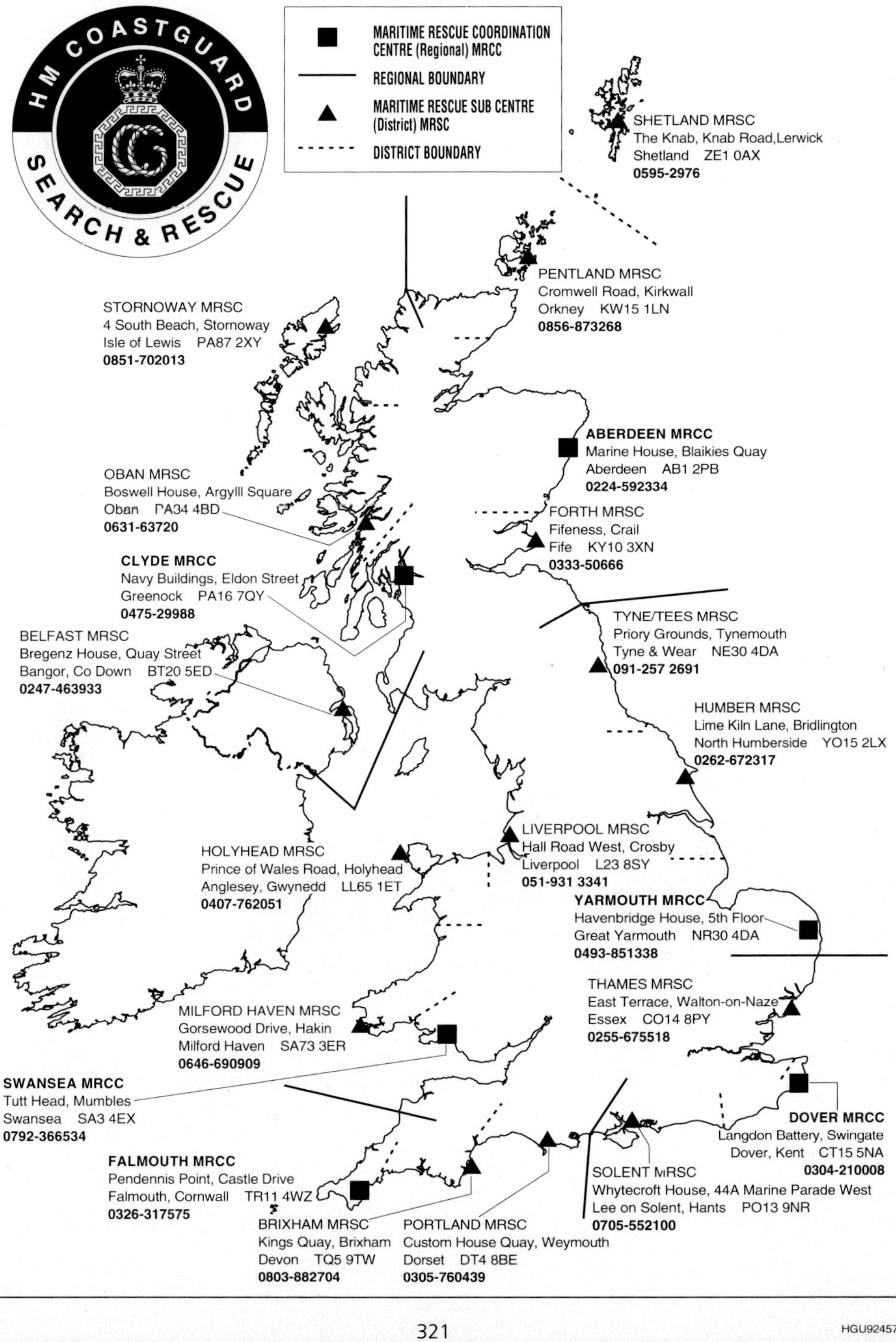

SAFETY

HGU92457B.DRW

Good Buddies

by Robin Sharp

Robin Sharp is assistant public relations officer with the Royal National Lifeboat Institution.

"It was the most terrifying experience of my life. When the lifeboat came, I was begging for life. It seemed as though we were in the water forever".

The words of a survivor, rescued from the icy North Sea by a lifeboat one dark February night. One more tale of a life saved, another rescue successfully carried out.

For 170 years, the Royal National Lifeboat Institution has maintained a seaborne rescue service in the varied and often treacherous waters around Great Britain and Ireland. In 1992 the number of lifeboat launches was an all-time record: 5,445 services (averaging around 15 every day), with 1,372 lives saved.

The rise in calls on the lifeboat service is due in part to the mounting number of people using the sea for pleasure, together with those who earn their living from it, on it, or beneath it. Services to divers are also on the

Aldeburgh's D class inflatable lifeboat launches through breakers. Picture: East Anglian Daily Times. Courtesy RNLI.

increase. For instance, there were 24 launches in 1982 with three lives saved; by 1992, the launches had gone up to 64 with 12 lives saved. In fact, in 10 years (1983-92) lifeboats have launched 561 times in answer to calls from divers in distress and saved 88 lives. This is in addition to another 100 or so who were "landed" - ie whose lives may not have been in immediate danger.

In 1824, there were 30 lifeboats run by the RNLI, powered by oars and costing around £100 each. Today, the fleet consists of 269 lifeboats at 211 stations, with a further 100 in reserve. To build and equip a 17m (56ft) Severn class lifeboat with the latest technological aids to navigation and rescue costs some £1.2 million.

Although lifeboats, equipment and types of casualties have changed over the years, the spirit of the service remains the same. Every spring the RNLI holds its Annual Presentation of Awards in London, when medals for gallantry are presented; an inspiring occasion which pays tribute to the finest human qualities. Among the medallists at the 1991 Awards was Assistant Mechanic Jim Dougal of the Eyemouth lifeboat, honoured as a result of the following episode:

Soon after 4.00pm on 6 October 1990, a sudden and dramatic change in the weather gave rise to southerly hurricane force winds along Scotland's east coast. Sub-aqua enthusiasts diving in the waters between Dunbar and Eyemouth were among those caught out.

Both Dunbar and Eyemouth lifeboats were launched, but a telephone failure caused by the adverse weather conditions meant that neither Eyemouth's coxswain nor second coxswain could be alerted in time. Assistant Mechanic Jim Dougal therefore took the helm. Dougal negotiated the narrow harbour entrance as 20ft waves whipped up by 100mph winds, ran in and crashed over the sea walls. Visibility was virtually nil in the rain, spume and spray. In heavy seas, the lifeboat was steered clear of dangerous rocks outside the harbour and out into the open sea towards St Abbs.

Meeting the 35ft seas head on, the lifeboat rolled violently, but Dougal resolutely drove forward. Within 20 minutes of launching, the lifeboat had arrived on scene, where a coastguard on the harbour wall had spotted two heads bobbing in the waves. Using the faint glimmer of the lifeboat's searchlight as his only reference, the coastguard directed Dougal to the casualties' last reported position.

Just 200 ft away, to port and starboard, lay Ebb Carr and Cathedral Rocks, neither visible and, due to heavy spray, undetectable on radar. On deck, secured by lifelines, the lifeboat crew scoured the sea for survivors. Suddenly, they saw them: still conscious, close to a buoy.

Twice Dougal battled to bring the lifeboat close enough for a line to be thrown, but failed. On the third attempt he won through and the casualties were hauled against the lifeboat's starboard shoulder. With difficulty, first one and then the second diver was pulled on board, to warmth and shelter. Both were suffering from shock and hypothermia.

Dougal turned south to search for two more divers, still missing, but the condition of the two survivors began to give cause for concern. Entry to St Abbs harbour was too dangerous in prevailing conditions and an attempted transfer to a helicopter had to be abandoned. Dougal made for the shelter of Burnmouth where, due to a power cut, the

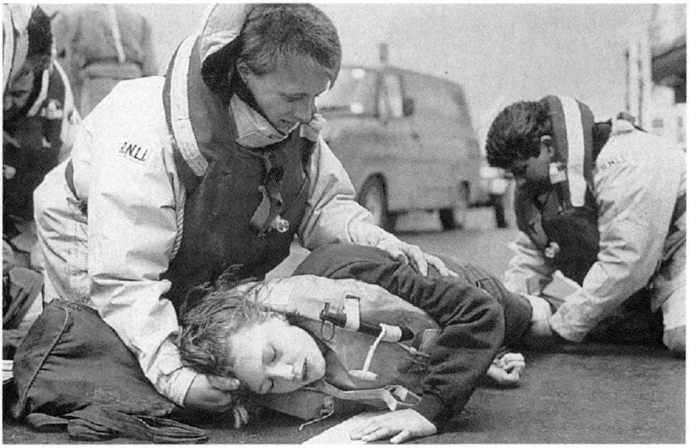

Medical exercise, Newcastle, Co Down. Picture: Colin Watson. Courtesy RNLI.

lifeboat's path into harbour was lit by car headlights. The survivors were landed safely into the care of waiting ambulance a little after 8.00pm.

Dunbar lifeboat followed the Eyemouth boat into harbour and as preparations were being made to put to sea again to resume the search, news came that, miraculously, the two missing divers had been washed ashore, unharmed, and recovered by a coastguard search party.

For his courage, tenacity and outstanding skill in atrocious conditions, Assistant Mechanic Jim Dougal was awarded the RNLI's silver medal.

The RNLI is supported entirely by voluntary contributions, and operates with volunteer lifeboat crews. The Institution is justifiably proud of this voluntary and independent status, free from external financial restraints and interference.

However, raising the funds necessary to sustain the lifeboat service is never easy: in 1993 alone it is estimated that it will cost around £46 million. It is thanks only to public goodwill and generosity that the service not only survives, but remains strong and active.

As proof of appreciation and that it is not all "one way traffic", members of the British Sub Aqua Club have been dedicated RNLI supporters for a number of years. Four lifeboats have been funded by the BSAC in the past decade - the Atlantic 21's at Whitstable and Harwich (British Diver and British Diver II) and a D class and a C class (III and IV) both placed in the RNLI's relief fleet and serving throughout the British Isles whenever a station lifeboat is away for overhaul or repair. In fact, over £100,000 has been subscribed by BSAC members to the RNLI in 10 years. Many lives have been saved thanks to that enthusiasm and generosity.

Everyone has the opportunity to contribute to rescue at sea, either by raising funds in their own area or by joining the national membership scheme with an annual subscription from as little as £9. There is even a special club for under 16's called "Storm Force".

Every survivor has a story to tell, their own reason to believe that money subscribed to the RNLI is well-spent:

"I couldn't possibly put a price on the feeling of relief and assurance on seeing the lifeboat and the crew. They put their lives at risk to come and pick us up - besides everything else, they were very brave men".

Plymouth Chamber

by Julian Roberts

Julian Roberts is a Volunteer Hyperbaric Medical Technician with the Diving Diseases Research Centre.

"Brixham Coastguard, Brixham Coastguard Plymouth Chamber, radio check, Over."

"Plymouth Chamber Brixham Coastguard you're loud and clear, Over"

"Brixham Coastguard you're loud and clear also Plymouth Chamber out...."

And so begins another day at Britain's busiest Hyperbaric treatment centre. Based at the Fort Bovisand Underwater Centre in Plymouth, the Diving Diseases Research Centre treats more divers than any other civilian chamber in the country. It boasts some of the most up to date intensive care facilities for the treatment of serious diving and non-diving related cases which can be mobilised within 10 minutes of receiving an emergency call, 24 Hours a day, 365 days of the year. In fact the centre has never been closed since it opened in 1979!

You may well have heard of us, but are you aware of all of the benefits which DDRC provides both the diver and non diver alike? For example did you know that if you got bent in Jamaica or Saudi Arabia, it would probably be DDRC that ultimately assists in your treatment? If not then maybe you should read on.

The Diving Diseases Research Centre was established in 1979 at Fort Bovisand. It originally started with two Fort Bovisand magazines and a small 42" chamber housed in a corrugated iron shed. This later expanded into a larger wooden shed which housed two (donated) "Comex" 1200 chambers. The facility, which was dedicated to undersea research, was the brainchild of Dr Maurice Cross. Ten years ago it outgrew the modest wooden shed and a further two "Comex" 1800 chambers were again donated and together with one of the old 1200's, were installed in their present location on the waterfront at Fort Bovisand.

In 1988 the facility treated its first four non diving illnesses after an unusually high radiation dose at a South West hospital x-ray department. The resulting condition, known as radionecrosis, was successfully treated and since that day the number of non-diving cases treated at the centre has almost doubled each year.

In order to maintain high standards of treatment the centre underwent massive improvements in 1991 and as a result became Britain's first and only registered Hyperbaric Nursing Home. It also successfully negotiated with the local health authority and won NHS funding for all emergency cases. This meant that 90 % of all running costs would be met by the NHS but despite this, DDRC has remained a registered charity and still relies on donations to fund the purchase of new equipment, thereby improving the treatment facilities available to you, the diver.

Achieving such high standards has not been an easy task and has been achieved through the commitment of a small number of dedicated staff. At present the staff comprises two doctors, two intensive care nurses, two chamber operators, two admin staff and a rather over stressed manager!

However, the centre owes much of its success to part time volunteer staff, the majority of whom are local sport divers. The small team of full time staff is supported by an equally small band of highly motivated and dedicated part time volunteers who have given up their time to train for the job and turn out at hours of the day when most of you may be dreaming about your favourite dive.

Indeed some of our volunteers are so dedicated they went all the way to the USA to receive their training! In addition to our local sport divers we also have a number of intensive care nurses, paramedics and diver medics who volunteer to help with our more serious cases.

Treatment

At this point it is probably pertinent to outline just what the treatment of a sick diver (or non-diver) involves. The purpose of the treatment is to apply pure oxygen at a higher than ambient pressure.......We get oxygen to the places others can't reach! This serves a number of purposes.

Generally in a decompression accident the body is affected by the presence of bubbles. Either of air in the case of Air Embolism or nitrogen in the case of Decompression Sickness. Initially placing the diver under pressure helps reduce the size of these bubbles but pressure on its own is simply not enough. The objectives of recompression therapy are:

1) To reduce the size of bubbles in the blood vessels therefore restoring blood flow to the tissue.

2) To promote the reabsorption of the gas in the bubbles by the blood and tissue.

3) To reduce the chance of further bubble formation by lowering nitrogen tensions in the blood and the tissues.

4) The oxygenation of hypoxic tissues.

In order to achieve 2, 3 and 4 the diver must breath pure oxygen while in the chamber. This oxygen is delivered to the diver via a face mask connected to a demand valve similar to that used in diving. In diving therapies the patient breathes oxygen for 20 minute intervals having a five minute air break to reduce the risk of oxygen toxicity. Diving treatment therapies can last from between approximately 2 hours 15 minutes to 8 hours. Every patient is monitored by an inside attendant and two outside chamber operators. A doctor is always close at hand on the outside. Most treatments prove very successful and many of our past patients have returned to full and active diving.

Although, as our name implies, the centre was originally established to treat divers, and still does, the majority of our present patients have never been under the water in their lives. In fact it is not only divers who can benefit from Hyperbaric Oxygen Therapy (HBO). There are actually 12 recognised conditions that are routinely treated in this way. We receive patients from all over the country (and even the world) who have medical conditions which respond very well to HBO therapy. These include Carbon Monoxide poisoning from suicide attempts, house fires and faulty central heating (have you had your boiler serviced recently?), problem wounds that will not heal properly, gas gangrene, bone and soft tissue necrosis and many others. It is a little known fact that HBO therapy can also be used in the treatment of Brown Recluse spider bites. However we are still awaiting our first victim of this little beast and since it is not indigenous to this country we could be waiting a long time! Having said that it is probably true to say that DDRC can boast the only successful HBO treatment of a domestic cat. The treatment followed a road accident that left the cat paralysed but that's another story. As a general rule DDRC does NOT treat animals.

So how can you, the diver, utilise the facility should you ever have the misfortune to need to do so?

Any diving accident whether at sea or shore based should be co-ordinated via the Coastguard. They can be contacted using VHF Channel 16 stating that you have a diving medical emergency and that you require a recompression facility. The Coastguard will then assume responsibility for co-ordinating the evacuation of the diver to the nearest facility and will contact the nearest and most appropriate facility available. Should a problem arise after leaving the diving site then the Coastguard can be contacted through the usual emergency channels by dialling 999 and asking for the Coastguard.

Alternatively we also provide an emergency number through which you can contact one of our diving doctors. The number is **0752 261910** and you will be asked to leave your number so that the duty diving doctor can call you back shortly afterwards. I must stress that this is an EMERGENCY number only, do not ring for any other purpose.

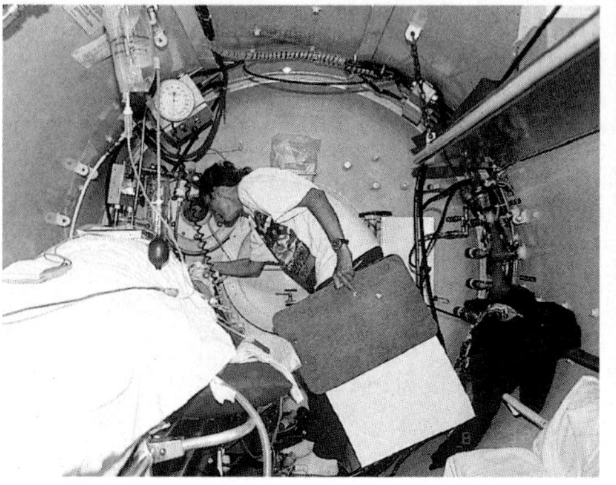

Intensive care layout.

In any event you should have the following information at hand:

The depth and duration of the dive.
What the signs and symptoms of the casualty are.
When they first appeared.
Whether oxygen was given on site and if so for how long.
Whether oxygen administration caused an improvement or not.

All divers should be aware of the first aid procedures for DCS and Air embolism. Oxygen should be administered at the earliest possible stage. The casualty should be kept in the lying position and in the case of DCS fluids should be administered if the diver is conscious and not at risk of vomiting.

Should you wish to view our facilities in more relaxed circumstances then groups can arrange for a tour and a "dry" dive in one of our chambers, for a small fee to cover our costs. Just call us during normal office hours and speak to one of our staff. If you are unable to visit the centre in person then why not ask for some of our information packs to be sent to you or your club. We also have a Club which anyone can join.

The aims of the club are primarily to raise funds for the purchase of new equipment and to fund research projects and to inform our members of relevant medical information in the diving field. So at the same time as supporting DDRC you will be continuing your diving education.

A further educational publication of the centre is the well known Underwater Diving Emergency Handbook written by Dr Philip Bryson.

The third edition of this very popular book is now in print and will be ready shortly. It contains information on how to recognise and treat all the major diving related emergencies and includes sections on resuscitation, emergency procedures, helicopter winch procedures and much more. It is printed on waterproof paper and fits neatly in any oxygen administration kit. Again the sale of this helps to raise funds for the purchase of vital new equipment. The DDRC is currently raising funds for a new Hyperbaric Unit based at a Plymouth hospital.

The cost of the new chamber alone is estimated at over £120,000 for the bare hull and the new building will represent a further million over the next 2 to 3 years.

"Brixham Coast guard Plymouth Chamber, Over"

"Plymouth Chamber Brixham Coast guard, Over."

"Brixham Coast guard Plymouth Chamber closing down for the night, Over."

"Roger Plymouth Chamber, Goodnight"

"Goodnight Brixham Coastguard, Plymouth Chamber out"

Divers Alert Network

by Dr Alessandro Marroni

Divers Alert Network (DAN), a non-profit organisation, exists to provide expert information and advice consistent with the current medical literature for the benefit of the diving public.

DAN is already well established in the United States and is making significant inroads into Europe. This is discussed later by Dr. Alessandro Marroni. Let us begin by looking at the organisation and the service that they provide in the States.

DAN's historical and primary function is to provide emergency medical advice and assistance for underwater diving accidents, to work to prevent accidents and to promote diving safety. It promotes and supports underwater diving research and education, particularly as it relates to the improvement of diving safety, first aid and medical treatment.

The organisation strives to provide accurate, up-to-date and unbiased information on issues of common concern to the diving public and to advocate diver's concerns, primarily, but not exclusively for diving safety.

The mission of the DAN training division is to provide comprehensive, educationally sound training in support of its mission and obligation to the diving community and to disseminate the latest information on topics related to diving safety through articles, reports, seminars, lectures and training programs.

It intends to develop programs and materials which will complement currently available dive safety training throughout the diving community and to foster co-operative efforts in dive safety in the worldwide diving and medical communities.

Fitness to dive

There are a number of medical conditions which could have a negative impact on individuals and whether they should be diving at all. These fitness to dive questions are a large part of the Medical/Safety Information Telephone Service.

Examples of such questions would include: those from prospective dive students who are concerned about their histories of asthma; the instructor who has a student with high blood pressure; or the experienced diver who needs to know how long to recuperate before diving after surgery.

The DAN medical staff can either immediately answer the question or can consult with a specialist. In some cases a consultation with a diving physician is deemed appropriate and DAN can provide a referral to a local physician. DAN maintains a list of over 500 such specialists in the USA.

By using this service the diving community is able to effectively educate and screen divers to help reduce the risk of injury to unsuspecting divers. This is DAN's leading service in the area of dive accident prevention.

Post-dive problems

When problems arise after a dive, the Medical/Safety Information Telephone Service can help determine the correct action, if any, which should be taken.

The majority of dive incidents are not "pressure related" and require no recompression. Divers with ear, nose and throat problems often call two or three days after a dive asking for advice. Consultation on the unique aspects of injuries from marine life is also provided. In some cases, very subtle symptoms of DCS develop after a dive. Initially DAN may receive questions about symptoms such as these on the non-emergency lines.

These questionable situations are handled with an appropriate physician referral and possible treatment.

There are many other types of questions that the Medical/Safety Information Telephone Service can answer. New research is a common topic on the Non-emergency Line. DAN can sometimes forward reference materials to DAN Instructors and others interested in a particular area of diving medicine.

Assistance in emergency preparedness plans is available, as well as consultation on oxygen equipment and evacuation plans. DAN conducts one-day, three-day and week-long seminars on diving medicine and hyperbaric medicine. DAN also offers a four hour Oxygen First Aid in Diving Accidents course to cover the basics of providing emergency oxygen as first aid in the event of a diving accident.

DAN EUROPE
by Dr. Alessandro Marroni

The history of Dan Europe dates to 1982, with the founding of International Diving Assistance (IDA), the first non-profit organisation dedicated to promoting diving safety, to furthering diver safety education, to fostering underwater diving medical and safety research, and to providing expert emergency and non-emergency medical assistance for underwater diving accidents.

My decision to initiate IDA was based on my previous experience in organising worldwide diving emergency medical services for offshore commercial diving, in my capacity as the medical director of the commercial diving division for the Italian National Oil Company. Being also an active recreational scuba diving instructor, it seemed natural to me that I should do something to the advantage of the recreational diving community and to further the safety of diving. IDA was born under the auspices of the Italian Society of Underwater and Hyperbaric Medicine and with the enthusiastic co-operation of the major national hyperbaric centres and underwater medicine specialists.

The support of the recreational diving community was immediately strong. Soon IDA started growing beyond the national borders and became quite active throughout the Mediterranean area and in the Maldives archipelago, because of the significant presence of Italian divers and scuba instructors.

In 1989 Dr. Bennett in the USA, Dr Gorman in Australia, Dr Mano in Japan and myself in Europe, almost telepathically considered that the times were right for an international organisation of the existing diving emergency networks.

In 1990 a historic meeting took place in Amsterdam which witnessed the birth of the International DAN concept and the decision to adopt the name of DAN internationally.

DAN Europe is now quite active and, due to the multiple European nationalities and languages, is organised in national branches, under the national directors. The headquarters are in Italy, with branches in France, Germany, Malta, Spain and

Switzerland. Almost all other European countries are represented by their leading diving medicine scientists who are members in DAN Europe's Scientific Committee.

Thanks to the cooperation and open-mindedness of a major European insurance company, DAN Europe developed a very comprehensive insurance plan that covers all possible diving related risk and insures timely assistance wherever in the world. Any European citizen is eligible for insured membership in DAN Europe.

DAN Europe's central hotline is in Milan, Italy, and it is planned to operate in coordination with a network of regional hotlines, organized by linguistic criteria, to ensure prompt and appropriate reply in all the European languages.

DAN Europe is also actively involved in research and educational projects in diving medicine, in cooperation with the European Undersea Biomedical Society, the European Committee for Hyperbaric Medicine and most of the national European scientific societies of diving and hyperbaric medicine. In particular we are now developing European standards for the emergency treatment of decompression injuries, European epidemiological studies on recreational diving accidents and a project for the continuous education in diving medicine of divers and of technical and medical health care personnel.

DAN Europe membership is presently over 4,000 and our goal is to reach the entire European diving community, by developing strategies which will overcome the typically European problem of language and cultural barriers.

Emergency Medical Procedures

THE LIST OF RECOMPRESSION CHAMBERS OVERLEAF (MINISTRY OF DEFENCE AND CIVILIAN), PROVIDED BY THE HEALTH & SAFETY EXECUTIVE, IS INTENDED FOR YOUR REFERENCE ONLY.

NEITHER THE HSE NOR THE PUBLISHERS IMPLY ANY APPROVAL OF A RECOMPRESSION FACILITY BY ITS INCLUSION IN THIS LIST.

IF YOU HAVE A DIVING MEDICAL PROBLEM:

CALL THE COASTGUARD ON VHF CHANNEL 16.

or

TELEPHONE 999 AND ASK FOR THE COASTGUARD.

or

CALL YOUR NEAREST COASTGUARD RESCUE CENTRE **(SEE PAGE 331).**

and

STATE THAT YOU HAVE A DIVING MEDICAL EMERGENCY AND THAT YOU MAY REQUIRE RECOMPRESSION FACILITIES.

The coastguard will then assume responsibility for:

- **Contacting the most appropriate facility available.**
- **Co-ordinating the evacuation of the diver.**

SAFETY

Should a problem arise after leaving the dive site the coastguard can be contacted through the usual emergency channels by dialling 999.

Alternatively the DDRC provide an emergency number through which you can contact a diving doctor. The number is **0752 261910** and should only be used ***in an emergency.***

CHAMBERS UNDER MINISTRY OF DEFENCE CONTROL

ENGLAND

Address	Chambers	Contact
Defence Research Agency Life Sciences Dept. Fort Road Alverstoke Gosport Hampshire P012 2DU	4 Chambers lxl5O bar lx67 bar lx25 bar lx35 bar	Portsmouth (0705) 582617 or 822351 Ext 41876 office hours only. 24hr. emergency No. 0831 573724
Plymouth Clearance Diving Unit (PCDU) Diving Centre HM Naval Base Devonport Plymouth Devon PL2 2BG	7 bar	Mountwise (0752) 555386/7 Ask for Staff Officer. Limited availability for civilians. Out of hours (0752) 501182

SCOTLAND

Address	Chambers	Contact
Clyde Submarine Base Clearance Diving Unit (CBSDU) HMS Neptune Faslane Dumbartonshire	7 bar	Helensburgh (0436) 74321 Ext 309/6361 Sick Bay 0436 886801 During working hours 0436 886834 outside working hours. Civilians only if indemnity form is signed.
Clyde Marine Services Base Great Harbour Greenock Renfrewshire PA15 2AR	8 bar	Greenock (0475) 87912 Ext 230/279 (08.00 - 16.30)
NSWU 2 RAF Macrihanish Campbeltown Argyll	6 bar	Duty Officer 0586 554307 Civilians as last resort

CHAMBERS UNDER CIVILIAN CONTROL

ENGLAND

Address	Pressure	Contact
Royal Victoria Infirmary Newcastle-on-Tyne NE1 4LP	4 bar	091 232 5131 Mr John Cook (No air call)
Northumbria Police Sub Division Underwater Search Unit Viking Park Blackett Street Jarrow	6 bar	091 232 3451 Ext 65016 091 510 2020 Ext 65207 65208 Limited availability to civilians
Hyperbaric Treatment and Training Services 12 Rowan Grove Bebington, Wirral, Merseyside	8 bar	051 355 7109 24 hours
Lancashire Constabulary HQ PO Box 77 Hutton Preston, Lancashire PR4 5ZB	8 bar	Longton 0772 614444 Ext 2442 or 2438 24 hours
Stoney Cove Marine Trials Stoney Stanton Leicester Leicestershire LE9 6DW	6 bar	Mr D Crouch, Sapcote 0455 273089 If no reply to above No. contact Hinkley Police 0455 637881 or 0455 842778
Stena Offshore Ltd Stena House Brinnel Way Harfreys Industrial Estate Great Yarmouth NR31 OLU	10 bar	0492 604445 office hours Health call 0493 667887 A Johnson 0493 780860 D Capps Jenner 0502 563753
Port of London Authority Marine services Denton Wharf Mark Lane Gravesend Kent DA12 2QB	6 bar	0474 560311 Ask for Duty officer Thames Navigation Services

Seaton Marine Services The Harbour Axmouth Seaton Devon	6 bar	0297 20616 (surgery) 0297 23344 (chamber) 0297 23230 (home) 24 hours
Diving Diseases Research Centre Fort Bovisand Plymouth Devon	1x12 bar 2x26 bar	Plymouth 0752 261910 24 hour State diving emergency or 0752 408093 office hours.
Prodive Ltd Services Area Falmouth Docks Cornwall TR11 4NR	6 bar	Falmouth 0326 315691 During day. Cannot give 24 hour service
Diver Training School 5 Camperdown Terrace Exmouth	6 bar	0395 266300 office hrs. 0404 815094 Limited availability outside outside office hrs.
Commercial Diving Centre Salterns Marina 38 Salterns Way Lilliput Poole Dorset BH14 8SR	6 bar	0305 760439 office hours or 0893 610775 0202 708999 24 hour call out

SCOTLAND

Aberdeen Royal Hospitals Trust Hyperbaric Medicine Unit Royal Infirmary Forester Hill Aberdeen AB9 2ZD	31 bar	0224 681818 Ext 53263 Emergency Hyberbaric Doctor
The Underwater Centre Ltd Fort William Invernesshire Scotland PH33 6LZ	2x6 absolute bar	Fort William 0397 703786 Contact diving Supervisor other times via Oban Coast Guard 0631 63720

Dunstaffnage Marine Research Laboratory Oban Argyll Dunbeg Argyll PA34 LAD	6 bar	0631 62244 Office Hours Other times via Oban Coast Guard 0631 63720
Kingdom Underwater Engineering Block 2, Unit 2 Forthview-Industrial Estate Newmills Fife KY12 8TL	1x1O bar lx8 bar	0383 880054 office hours 0383 830384 0383 733236 0506 827056 out of hours
University Marine Biological Station Millport Isle of Cumbrae Scotland KA28 OEG	6 bar	0475 530581/2 24 hours

IRELAND

Craigavon Area Hospital Craigavon County Armagh Northern Ireland	5 bar	Portadown 0762 336711 or 334444
Galway Regional Hospital Recompression Team Duty Medical Officer Galway, Ireland	8 bar	Galway 010 353 9124222

CHANNEL ISLANDS

Ambulance & Rescue Service Rohais St Peter Port Guernsey Channel Islands	5 bar	Guernsey 0481 725211 Ask for Duty Officer 24 hour availability
Jersey Association of Divers Next door to Harbour Office St Helier Jersey	7 bar	Dr A Ellison 0534 31421 or 34451 Dr S Hamilton 0534 73633

ISLE OF MAN

Hyperbaric Dept Fire Headquarters Peel Road Douglas Isle of Man	5 bar	0624 24589 Dr Richard Hamm 0624 626394 or 673333 Dr David Chalmers

SINGLE COMPARTMENT HYPERBARIC CHAMBERS

Hyperbaric Unit Whipps Cross Hospital Intensive Care Unit Whipps Cross Road Leystone London Ell 1NR	3 bar	081 539 5522 Ext 5846
Peterborough District Hospital Intensive Care Unit Thorpe Road Peterborough Cambridgeshire PE3 6DA	3 bar	0733 67451 Duty anaesthetic registrar
Manchester Monsall Hospital Regional Dept of infection and Tropical Medicine Newton Heath Manchester M10 8WR	3 bar	Dr Dunbar 061 205 2393
Vascular Dept Dept of Clinical Measurement Level 4 Ninewells Hospital Dundee DD1 9SY	2 bar	0382 60111 Ext 2869 Dr D K Harrison
*Glan Clwyd Hospital Bodelwyddan Clwyd, North Wales		0745 583910 2 bar

**Note:* although this is only a single compartment chamber the hospital possesses extensive diagnostic facilities for hyperbaric patients.*

Diving Doctors
(BSAC medical referees)

BERKSHIRE

DR N.J. MCFETRIDGE
16 BLAGROVE LANE, WOKINGHAM
BERKSHIRE RG11 4BA
0734 775384

DR R.G.TAYTON
THE HEALTH CENTRE, THATCHAM
NEWBURY, BERKSHIRE RG13 4HH
0635 67171

BUCKINGHAMSHIRE

DR F. PRESTON
WYNN INSTITUTE
21 WELLINGTON ROAD
LONDON NW9 9SQ
071 586 2266

DERBYSHIRE

DR S. KAY
2-3 THE SQUARE
BUXTON SK17 6AZ
0298 4046 SURGERY: 0298 3019

DEVON

DR P. DENSHAM
THE MEDICAL CENTRE
FORE STREET
ST. MARYCHURCH
TORQUAY
0803 35123 & 37773

DR P.J.S. FARRELL
TOWNSEND HOUSE SURGERY
49 HAREPATH ROAD
SEATON EX12 2LX
SURGERY: 0297 20616

DR W. HOUSTON
BEAUMONT ROAD
PLYMOUTH P14 9BL
0752 63776

DORSET

DR SALLY HODDER
VILLA SANTANDER
64 BUDMOUTH AVENUE, PRESTON
WEYMOUTH DT3 6QT
0305 834880

ESSEX

DR M. HUNT
THE HOLLIES
THE GREEN, GREAT BENTLEY
COLCHESTER, ESSEX CO7 8PJ
0206 250691

HAMPSHIRE

DR D.R. BATHAM
THE HEALTH CENTRE
CHARLTON ROAD
ANDOVER SP1O 3LD
0264 365031

DR B. ELLIS
18 HEATH ROAD
PETERSFIELD GU31 4DY
SURGERY: 0730 64011

DR I.P. STOBBS
TOTTON HEALTH CENTRE
TESTWOOD LANE, TOTTON S04 3AP
SURGERY: 0703 865051

DR C. JELLIFFE
TORRINGTON PARK HEALTH CENTRE
16 TORRINGTON PARK
NORTH FINCHLEY
LONDON N12 9SS
SURGERIES: 081 445 7622 / 081 445 4127

ISLE OF MAN

DR R. HAMM
46 LOCH PROMENADE, DOUGLAS
0624 73923 SURGERY: 0624 75490

KENT

DR M.J. FRANK
PARKWOOD HEALTH CENTRE
LONG CATLIS ROAD
PARKWOOD
RAINHAM ME8 9PR
0634 33491

DR L.H. VAN CLEEF
99 HARVEY ROAD
ASHFORD TN24 OAR
0233 628596

LANCASHIRE

DR J. PAGE
32 BRADSHAW BROW
BRADSHAW, BOLTON BL22 3DH
0204 592653

LINCOLNSHIRE

DR D.R. PRAGNELL
THE BUNGALOW
CHURCH FARM, CHURCH ROAD
HARBY, NEWARK NG23 7ED

DR M.R. POLLING
2 JAMES STREET
BOSTON PE21 8RF
0205 62556

LONDON

DR J. BETTS
32 GROVE AVENUE
MUSWELL HILL, LONDON N10
081 883 7413

DR S. DOMIZIO
515 WESTHOME AVENUE
ELTHAM
LONDON SE9 6DL
081 850 1613

DR E. JONES
138 HARLEY STREET
LONDON W1
071 935 0554

DR D.C. LINDSAY
68B ASHMORE ROAD
LONDON W9 3DG
081 969 3076
SURGERY: 071 351 8179

MANCHESTER

DR A. MAW
138 FRAMINGHAM ROAD
SALE, CHESHIRE M33 3RG
061 973 0069

NOTTINGHAMSHIRE

DR M. COLLEY
3 MANOR COURT
BRAMCOTE, NOTTS
0602 227351

OXFORDSHIRE

DR C.EDGE
THE STONE BARN
GRAVEL LANE
DRAYTON, OXON
0235 529888

SHROPSHIRE

DR D. LOWDON
PRESOOT SURGERY
BASCHURCH, SALOP SY4 2DR
(BASCHURCH) 260210

SOMERSET

DR P. GLANVILL
SPRINGMEAD SURGERY
CHARD
SOMERSET TA20 2EW
0460 63380

STAFFORDSHIRE

DR M. WOOD
ORCHARD COTTAGE
ASH FLATS LANE
STAFFORD ST18 9BP
0785 47744

SUFFOLK

DR A.W. O'MALLEY
HOLLY LANE, NUTFORD
BECCLES NR34 7RX
050 276 344
SURGERY: 0493 600611 EXT 356

TYNE AND WEAR

DR M.S. MULLEA
HEALTH CENTRE
FLAGG COURT
SOUTH SHIELDS
0632 560791

DR D. TALBOT
87 GLENTHORN ROAD, JESMOND
NEWCASTLE-UPON-TYNE NE2 3HL
0632 816996
SURGERY: 0632 328511 EXT 3160

WARWICKSHIRE

DR R.W. AWAD
17 WADEBRIDGE DRIVE
HONESTON GRANGE
NUNEATON, CV11 6SY
0203 385836

WEST SUSSEX

DR ANDERSON-UPCOTT
68 PARKSIDE
SHOREHAM-BY-SEA BN4 6HA
0273 452759

WILTSHIRE

DR H.E. WEHNER
THE AVENUE SURGERY
14 THE AVENUE
WARMINSTER
WILTS BA12 9AA
0985 846224

WORCESTERSHIRE

DR S.G. KING
ST JOHNS HOUSE
28 BROMYARD ROAD
WORCESTER WR2 5BU
0905 423612 SURGERY: 0905 421688

YORKSHIRE (SOUTH)

MR R. ELSON FRCS (SURGEON)
NORTHERN GENERAL HOSPITAL
SHEFFIELD S5 7AV
0909 562177 SURGERY: 0742 434343

YORKSHIRE (NORTH)

DR A. COLLING
ROUNTON HOUSE
EAST ROUNTON
NORTHALLERTON DL6 2LA
060982 339

YORKSHIRE (WEST)

DR J. CRABTREE
11 FLAPPIT SPRINGS
KEIGHLEY BD21 5PU
0535 273871

DR PETER WILMSHURST
TELEPHONE CONTACT ONLY
0484 422191

DR B.K. FINDAL
SPEEDWELL SURGERY
1 SPEEDWELL STREET
PADDOCK , HUDDERSFIELD HD1 4TS
SURGERY: 0484 531786

NORTHERN IRELAND

DR D. BOYD
77 CHURCH ROAD
NEWTOWN, BREDA , BELFAST BT8 4AN
0230 646284

DR J. GALWAY
TARA, BROMPTON PARK
DERRHALE, PORTADOWN
COUNTY ARMAGH
0762 871757

DR J. SWEETNAM
KILLYDUSH
38 DUNMORE ROAD
SPA, BALLYNAHINCH , COUNTY DOWN
0238 562642

SCOTLAND

DR J.D.M. DOUGLAS
TWEEDALE SURGERY
FORT WILLIAM
INVERNESS-SHIRE PH33 6EU

DR N. PIERCY
CASTLE GAIT
25 BRIDGE STREET , MONTROSE, ANGUS
0674 72554

DR K. STEWART
19 CLARENDON PLACE
STIRLING
0786 73776 SURGERY: 0786 73151

WALES

DR J. COSTELLO
6 WOODVILLE RD, NEWPORT, GWENT NP9 4JB
0633 267685 SURGERY: 0633 256337

DR M. O'KANE
3 BROADWAY, SKETTY
SWANSEA SA2 OTQ
0792 204922 SURGERY: 0792 653941

DR G. LLOYD
ROATH HOUSE
100 PENYLAN RD , ROATH PARK, CARDIFF
SURGERY: 0222 461100

DR N. LUPINI
39 HENDRE PARK , LLANGENNECH, LLANELLI
DYFED SA14 8UP

DR J. THOMAS
BARLOW HOUSE MEDICAL CENTRE
22 HAMILTON TERRACE, MILFORD HAVEN
PEMBROKESHIRE SA73 3JL
06462 78295 SURGERY: 06462 2674

DR CHRISTOPHER WALKER
'YEOVIL' HOLYHEAD MOUNTAIN
HOLYHEAD, ANGLESEY
0407 4791 SURGERY: 0407 2713

CHANNEL ISLANDS

DR A.J.H. ELLISON
2 LE ROUTE DU FORT, ST. HELIER, JERSEY
0534 31421

DR S. HAMILTON
21 GROSVENOR ST , ST. HELIER, JERSEY
0534 62876 SURGERY: 0534 73633

DR B.D. PARKIN
ROHAIS MEDICAL PRACTICE
ST. PETER PORT, GUERNSEY
0481 723322

Health & Safety Organisations

BRITISH ISLES GROUP OF HYPERBARIC THERAPIST (BIGHT)
HYPERBARIC UNIT
WHIPPS CROSS HOSPITAL
WHIPPS CROSS ROAD
LEYTONSTONE
LONDON E11 1NR
081 5395522 FAX: 081 5588115

BUPA HEALTH SCREENING
4 KNYVETON ROAD
BOURNEMOUTH
DORSET BH1 3TS
0202 290934 FAX: 0202 317828

DIVERS ALERT NETWORK (DAN)
BOX 3823
DUKE UNIVERSITY MEDICAL CENTRE,
DURHAM, NC 27710 USA
010 1 919 6842948
FAX: 010 1 919 2869208

DIVERS ALERT NETWORK (DAN) EUROPE
VIA PUGLIE 82
64026 ROSETO, ITALY
010 39 85 8930333
FAX: 010 39 85 8930050

DIVING DISEASE RESEARCH CENTRE (DDRC)
FORT BOVISAND
PLYMOUTH
DEVON PL9 0AB
0752 408093 FAX: 0752 404127

HEALTH & SAFETY EXECUTIVE
TECHNICAL AND HEALTH DIVISION
ROOM 301
MAGDALEN HOUSE
BOOTLE, LIVERPOOL 2O 3QZ
051 9514645 FAX: 051 9227918

INSTITUTE OF NAVAL MEDICINE
WATER MEDICINE DEPARTMENT
CRESCENT ROAD
ALVERSTOKE
GOSPORT
HAMPSHIRE PO12 2DL
0705 822351 FAX: 0705 504823

NUFFIELD HOSPITALS HEALTH SCREENING
NUFFIELD HOUSE
1-4 THE CRESCENT
SURBITON
SURREY KT6 4BN
0202 301600

RNLI HEADQUARTERS
WEST QUAY ROAD
POOLE
DORSET BH15 1HZ
0202 671133 FAX: 0202 670128

ST JOHNS AMBULANCE
EDWINA MOUNTBATTEN HOUSE
63 YORK STREET
LONDON W1H 1PS
071 2583456 FAX: 071 2583793

UK SPORTS DIVING LIASON OFFICER
HM COASTGUARD TRAINING CENTRE
HIGHCLIFF
CHRISTCHURCH
DORSET BH23 4JQ
0425 277621 FAX: 0425 278246

Purple sunstar - Solaster endeca

Reference

Key Codes to Listings

Equipment Manufacturers & Distributors

BASIC:
BCD = Buoyancy Control Devices
MFS = Masks, Fins and Snorkels
LT = Dive Lights
BD = Buoyancy Device (Lifting bags etc)
ACC = Accessories

AIR SOURCE:
REG = Regulators
AA = Alternate Air Sources
TNK = Tanks (Air cylinders)

INSTRUMENTATION:
CSL = Consoles
CMP = Computers
WCH = Watches

CLOTHING:
WET = Wet Suits
DRY = Dry Suits
SEM = Semi-Dry Suit
SKN = Dive Skins
THM = Thermal Undersuits
OUT = Outdoor Wear
CTM = Custom (made to measure)
BTS = Boots
GLV = Gloves

PHOTOGRAPHIC:
CAM = Camera
FSH = Flash
CSE = Casings (video, camera or light)
VID = Video Cameras
VLT = Video Lights
ACC = Accessories

Retailers

EQUPT: = Equipment
BAS = Basic (Masks, Regulators etc)
CTH = Clothing (Wetsuits, Dry Suits etc)
CAM = Cameras (Photographic & Video)
SFY = Safety
BKS = Books, Magazines & Videos
BTS = Boats & Boating Equipment

TANKS:
TST = Cylinder Testing
IDEST = IDEST Registered Testing House

Boat Charter

NAME = Name of boat
PASS = Number of Passengers
DL = Dive Leader on board
CREW = Crew on board
DKS = Hot drinks available to order
FD = Food available to order

EQUPT:
ES = Echo Sounder
RDR = Radar
GPS\DECCA = Navigation Systems
VHF = VHF marine radio on board

SAFETY:
EMG = Emergency equipment on board
AID = First Aid equipment on board
OXY = Oxygen on board

Education & Training

TECHNICAL:

IANTD = International Association of Nitrox & Technical Divers
ANDI = American Nitrox Divers Inc.
BAS-N = Basic Nitrox
TECH-N = Technical Nitrox
TRI = Trimix
REB = Rebreathers
WP = Wreck Penetration
ST = Nitrox Service Technician

COMMERCIAL:

C-TCA = Training and Competence Assessment
C-ERCA = Experience Route Competence Assessment
CONSULT = Contact name

1994

*Public holidays are shown in **bold**.*

January

Sunday		2	9	16	23	30
Monday		**3**	10	17	24	31
Tuesday		4	11	18	25	
Wednesday		5	12	19	26	
Thursday		6	13	20	27	
Friday		7	14	21	28	
Saturday	1	8	15	22	29	

February

Sunday		6	13	20	27
Monday		7	14	21	28
Tuesday	1	8	15	22	
Wednesday	2	9	16	23	
Thursday	3	10	17	24	
Friday	4	11	18	25	
Saturday	5	12	19	26	

March

Sunday		6	13	20	27
Monday		7	14	21	28
Tuesday	1	8	15	22	29
Wednesday	2	9	16	23	30
Thursday	3	10	17	24	31
Friday	4	11	18	25	
Saturday	5	12	19	26	

April

Sunday		3	10	17	24
Monday		**4**	11	18	25
Tuesday		5	12	19	26
Wednesday		6	13	20	27
Thursday		7	14	21	28
Friday	**1**	8	15	22	29
Saturday	2	9	16	23	30

May

Sunday	1	8	15	22	29
Monday	**2**	9	16	23	**30**
Tuesday	3	10	17	24	31
Wednesday	4	11	18	25	
Thursday	5	12	19	26	
Friday	6	13	20	27	
Saturday	7	14	21	28	

June

Sunday		5	12	19	26
Monday		6	13	20	27
Tuesday		7	14	21	28
Wednesday	1	8	15	22	29
Thursday	2	9	16	23	30
Friday	3	10	17	24	
Saturday	4	11	18	25	

July

Sunday		3	10	17	24	31
Monday		4	11	18	25	
Tuesday		5	12	19	26	
Wednesday		6	13	20	27	
Thursday		7	14	21	28	
Friday	1	8	15	22	29	
Saturday	2	9	16	23	30	

August

Sunday		7	14	21	28
Monday	1	8	15	22	**29**
Tuesday	2	9	16	23	30
Wednesday	3	10	17	24	31
Thursday	4	11	18	25	
Friday	5	12	19	26	
Saturday	6	13	20	27	

September

Sunday		4	11	18	25
Monday		5	12	19	26
Tuesday		6	13	20	27
Wednesday		7	14	21	28
Thursday	1	8	15	22	29
Friday	2	9	16	23	30
Saturday	3	10	17	24	

October

Sunday		2	9	16	23	30
Monday		3	10	17	24	31
Tuesday		4	11	18	25	
Wednesday		5	12	19	26	
Thursday		6	13	20	27	
Friday		7	14	21	28	
Saturday	1	8	15	22	29	

November

Sunday		6	13	20	27
Monday		7	14	21	28
Tuesday	1	8	15	22	29
Wednesday	2	9	16	23	30
Thursday	3	10	17	24	
Friday	4	11	18	25	
Saturday	5	12	19	26	

December

Sunday		4	11	18	25
Monday		5	12	19	**26**
Tuesday		6	13	20	**27**
Wednesday		7	14	21	28
Thursday	1	8	15	22	29
Friday	2	9	16	23	30
Saturday	3	10	17	24	31

Year Planner

January

February

March

April

May

June

July

August

September

October

November

December

REFERENCE

International Direct Dialling (IDD) and Time Zones

International dialling codes are made up of four sections which should be dialled in sequence (see note 2 below). These are :

1) the international code
2) the country code
3) the area code
4) the customers telephone number

Note :

1) Some countries do not have facilities for IDD and international calls must be placed through the international operator. Where applicable this will be represented by '*'.

2) In some countries a pause in dialling is required while awaiting for a second tone. This will be represented by '#'.

3) The international code for calling most countries from the UK is '010' while the international and country code for the UK from abroad is normally 00 44. These codes will not be listed unless it is different.

Country Codes

Country	IDD from UK	IDD to UK	Time Zone
Afghanistan	93	*	4.5+
Albania	355	*	1+
Algeria	213	00#44	1+
Andorra	33 628	0#44	1+
Angola	244	*	1+
Anguilla	1 809 497	001 44	4-
Antigua & Barbuda	1 809	011 44	4-
Antilles	599		4-
Argentina	54		3-
Aruba	297	*	4-
Ascension Islands	247	01 44	0
Australia	61	00 11 44	8/10+
Austria	43		1+
Azores	351		1-
Bahamas	1 809	011 44	5-
Bahrain	973	0 44	3+

Bangladesh	880		6+
Barbados	1 809	011 44	4-
Belgium	32	00#44	1+
Belize	501	*	6-
Benin	229	00#44	1+
Bermuda	1 809	1 44	4-
Bhutan	975		6+
Bolivia	591		4-
Bosnia	38	99 44	1+
Botswana	267		2+
Brazil	55		3/5+
British Virgin Islands	1 809	011 44	4-
Brunei	673		8+
Bulgaria	359		2+
Burkina Faso	226	*	0
Burma (now Myanmar)	95	*	6.5+
Burundi	257	90 44	2+
Cambodia	*	*	7+
Cameroon	237		1+
Canada	1	011 44	3.5/9-
Canary Islands	34	07#44	0
Cape Verde	238	*	1-
Cayman Island	1 809	0 44	5-
Central African Republic	236	*	1+
Chad	235	*	1+
Chile	56		4-
China	86		8+
Christmas Islands	672 4	*	7+
Cocos Island	672 2	*	6+
Colombia	57	90 44	5-
Comoros	269	*	3+
Congo	242		1+
Cook Islands	682		10.5-
Costa Rica	506		6-
Cote d'Ivoire	225		0
Croatia	38	99 44	1+
Cuba	53	*	5-
Cyprus	357		2+
Czechoslovakia	42		1+
Denmark	45	009 44	1+
Djibouti	253		3+
Dominica	1 809 449/44	011 44	4-
Dominican Republic	1 809	*	4-
Ecuador	593		5-
Egypt	20		2+

El Salvador	503		6-
Equatorial Guinea	240	*	1+
Ethopia	251		3+
Falkland Islands	500	01 44	3-
Faroe Islands	298	009 44	0
Fiji	679	05 44	12+
Finland	358	990 44	2+
France	33	19#44	1+
French Guiana	594	*	3-
French Polynesia	689		10-
Gabon	241		1+
The Gambia	220		0
Germany	49		1+
Ghana	233		0
Gibraltar	350		1+
Greece	30		2+
Greenland	299	009 44	3-
Grenada	1 809	011 44	4-
Guadeloupe	590	*	4-
Guam	671		10+
Guatemala	502		6-
Guinea-Conarky	224	*	0
Guinea-Bissau	245	*	0
Guyana	592	011 44	3-
Haiti	509	*	5-
Honduras	504		6-
Hong Kong	852	001 44	8+
Hungary	36		1+
Iceland	354	90 44	0
India	91		5.5+
Indonesia	62		7/9+
Iran	98		3.5+
Iraq	964		3+
Ireland	353		0
(Dublin)	0001		0
Israel	972		2+
Italy	39		1+
Ivory Coast	225		0
Jamaica	1 809	*	5-
Japan	81	001 44	9+
Jordan	962		2+
Kenya	254	000 44	3+
Kiribati	686	09 44	12+
Korea, North	850	*	9+
Korea, South	82	001 44	9+

Kuwait	965		3+
Laos	*	*	7+
Lebanon	961		2+
Lesotho	266		2+
Liberia	231		0
Libya	218		1+
Liechtenstein	41 75		1+
Luxembourg	352		1+
Macao	853		8+
Madagascar	261	*	3+
Madeira	351 91		0
Malawi	265	101 44	2+
Malaysia	60		8+
Maldives	960	*	5+
Mali	223		0
Malta	356		1+
Mariana Islands	670	*	10+
Marshall Islands	692	*	12+
Martinique	596	*	4-
Mauritius	230		4+
Mexico	52	98 44	6/8-
Micronesia	691	*	9/12+
Monaco	33 93	19#44	1+
Mongolia	*	*	7/9+
Montserrat	1 809 491	*	4-
Morocco	212	00#44	0
Mozambique	258	*	2+
Myanmar (Burma)	95	*	6.5+
Namibia	264	091 44	2+
Nauru	674		12+
Nepal	977		5.75+
Netherlands	31	09#44	1+
New Caledonia	687		11+
New Zealand	64		12+
Nicaragua	505		6-
Niger	227		1+
Nigeria	234	009 44	1+
Niue Islands	227	*	11-
Norfolk Island	672 3	*	11.5+
Norway	47	095 44	1+
Oman	968		4+
Pakistan	92		5+
Palau	680	*	10+
Panama	507		5-
Papua New Guinea	675	31 44	10+

Paraguay	595	002/003 44	3-
Peru	51		5-
Philippines	63		8+
Poland	48	0#044	1+
Portugal	351		0
Puerto Rico	1 809	135 44	4-
Qatar	974	044	3+
Reunion	262	19#44	4+
Romania	40	*	2+
Rwanda	250	*	2+
St Helena	290	*	0
St Kitts and Nevis	1 809 465	*	4-
St Lucia	1 809	0 44	4-
St Pierre and Miquelon	508	*	4-
St Vincent & Grenadines	1 809	0 44	4-
Samoa	684	144	11-
San Marino	39 549		1+
Sao Tome and Principe	239	*	0
Saudi Arabia	966		3+
Senegal	221	00#44	0
Seychelles	248	0 44	4+
Sierra Leone	232	*	0
Singapore	65	005 44	8+
Slovenia	38	99 44	1+
Solomon Islands	677		11+
Somalia	252	*	3+
South Africa	27	09 44	2+
Spain	34	07#44	1+
Sri Lanka	94		5.5+
Sudan	249	*	2+
Surinam	597	001 44	3-
Swaziland	268		2+
Sweden	46	009 44#	1+
Switzerland	41		1+
Syria	963		2+
Taiwan	886	002 44	8+
Tanzania	255	*	3+
Thailand	66	001 44	7+
Togo	228		0
Tonga	676	0 44	13+
Trinidad & Tobago	1 809	01 44	4-
Tristan da Cunha	*	*	0
Tunisia	216		1+
Turkey	90	9#944	3+
Turks & Caicos	1 809 946	*	5-

Tuvalu	688	*	12+
Uganda	256	*	3+
United Arabs Emirates	971		4+
Uruguay	598		3-
USA	1	011 44	5/11-
Alaska	1 907		
Hawaii	1 808		
USSR	7	810 44	3/12+
Vanuatu	678	*	11+
Vatican City	39 66982		1+
Venezuela	58		4-
Vietnam	84	*	7+
Virgin Islands, US	1 809	011 44	4-
Western Samoa	685	*	11-
Yemen, Arab Rep	967		3+
Peoples Dem	969		3+
Yugoslavia	38	99 44	1+
Zaire	243		1+
Zambia	260		2+
Zimbabwe	263	110 44	2+

Imperial to Metric Conversions

Travellers from Europe to other international destinations will often be faced with Imperial measurements. The following conversions should help:

LENGTH UNITS

LAND

Imperial		Metric	
12 inches	= 1 foot	10 millimetres	= 1 centimetre
3 feet	= 1 yard	10 centimetres	= 1 decimetre
22 yards	= 1 furlong	10 decimetres or	
5280 feet or		100 centimetres or	
1760 yards = 1 mile		1000 millimetres	= 1 metre
1 knot	= 1 nautical mph	1000 metres	= 1 kilometre

NAUTICAL

6 feet	= 1 fathom	1852 metres	= 1 international nautical mile
100 fathoms	= 1 cable length		
6080 feet	= 1 nautical mile		

EXACT CONVERSIONS

1 millimetre	=	0.03937 inches
1 centimetres	=	0.03281 feet
1 metre	=	39.3701 inches
	=	3.2808 feet
	=	1.0936 yards
1 kilometre	=	0.62137 statute miles
	=	0.53961 nautical miles
	=	0.53996 international nautical miles
1 inch	=	25.4 millimetres
1 foot	=	30.48 centimetres
1 yard	=	0.9144 metres
1 mile	=	1.6093 kilometres

QUICK CONVERSIONS

Miles to kilometres	=	multiply by 8/5
Kilometres to miles	=	multiply by 5/8
Miles to nautical miles	=	deduct 1/8
Nautical miles to miles	=	add 1/7
1 knot	=	1.7 feet per second
	=	0.51 metres per second
1 mile per hour	=	1.5 feet per second

SAMPLE CONVERSIONS (nearest 1/4 metre)

Feet		Metres
10	=	3.00
12	=	3.75
15	=	4.50
18	=	5.50
20	=	6.00
30	=	9.00
40	=	12.25
50	=	15.25
60	=	18.25
70	=	21.25
80	=	24.50
90	=	27.50
100	=	30.50
110	=	33.50
120	=	36.50
130	=	39.50

WEIGHT UNITS

Imperial (avoirdupois)

16 ounches	= 1 pound
14 pounds	= 1 stone
28 pounds	= 1 quarter
4 quartes	= 1 hundredweight
2240 pounds or 20 hundredweights	= 1 ton

Metric (mass)

10 grams	= 1 decagram
10 dekagrams	= 1 hectogram
10 hectograms	= 1 kilogram
100 kilograms	= 1 quintal
1000 kilograms	= 1 tonne

EXACT CONVERSIONS

1 gram	=	0.03527 ounces
1 kilogram	=	2.20462 pounds
1 tonne	=	2204.62 pounds
1 ounce	=	28.3495 grams
1 pound	=	453.592 grams

QUICK CONVERSIONS

Pounds to kilograms	=	9/10th (pound wgt/2)
Kilograms to pounds	=	11/10th (kilo weight x 2)

SAMPLE CONVERSIONS (nearest 1/4 kg)

Avoirdupois (lbs)		Mass (kg)
10	=	4.50
15	=	6.75
20	=	9.00
25	=	11.25
30	=	13.50
3	=	15.75
40	=	18.25
45	=	20.50
50	=	22.75
55	=	25.00
60	=	27.25
65	=	29.50
70	=	31.75
75	=	34.00
80	=	36.25
85	=	38.50
90	=	40.75

CAPACITY UNITS

Imperial		Metric	
5 fluid ounces	= 1 gill	10 millilitres	= 1 centilitre
4 gills	= 1 pint	10 centililitre	= 1 decilitre
2 pints	= 1 quart	10 decilitres	= 1 litre
8 pints or		10 litres	= 1 decalitre
4 quarts	= 1 gallon	10 dekalitre	= 1 hectolitre
2 gallons	= 1 peck	10 hectolitre	= 1 kilolitre
4 pecks	= 1 bushel		

EXACT CONVERSIONS

1 litre	=	61.024 cu. inches
	=	0.0353 cu. feet
	=	2.1134 US pints
	=	1.7598 UK pints
	=	0.2642 US gallons
	=	0.21997 UK gallons
1 UK pint	=	0.5683 litres
1 UK gallon	=	4.54609 litres
1 US gallon	=	3.785 litres
1 UK gallon	=	1.20095 US gallons

QUICK CONVERSIONS

1 pint	=	0.5 litre
1 quart	=	1 litre

SAMPLE CONVERSIONS (nearest 1/4 litres)

Imperial (UK pints)		Metric (litres)
0.5	=	0.25
1	=	0.50
1.5	=	0.75
2	=	1.00
2.5	=	1.50
3	=	1.75
3.5	=	2.00
4	=	2.25
4.5	=	2.50
5	=	2.75

TEMPERATURE UNITS

EXACT CONVERSIONS

Centigrade/Celsuis	=	5/9th x (Fahrenheit temperature - 32)
Fahrenheit	=	(9/5th x Centrigrade temperature) + 32

SAMPLE CONVERSIONS (nearest 1/2 degrees C)

Fahrenheit		Centrigrade/Celsuis
30	=	-1.0
32	=	0
40	=	4.0
45	=	7.0
50	=	10.0
55	=	12.5
60	=	15.5
65	=	18.5
70	=	21.0
75	=	24.0
80	=	26.5
85	=	29.5
90	=	32.0
95	=	35.0

PRESSURE UNITS

EXACT CONVERSIONS

1 pound per square inch (psi)	= 6.8965 kilopascal (kPa)
1 atmosphere (atm)	= 101 kilopascal
1 bar	= 100 kilopascal

QUICK CONVERSIONS

Pounds per square inch to atmospheres	=	divide by 14.7
Atmospheres to bars	=	near parity
Water depth (feet) to bars absolute	=	divide by 33 and add 1 bar
Water depth (metres) to bars absolute	=	divide by 10 and add 1 bar

by B Hugo.

SAMPLE CONVERSIONS (nearest PSI)

Bars		Pounds per square inch (psi)
50	=	725
75	=	1088
100	=	1450
125	=	1813
150	=	2175
175	=	2538
200	=	2900
225	=	3263
250	=	3625
275	=	3988
300	=	4350
325	=	4713
350	=	5075
400	=	5800

CLOTHING (Approximate equivalents)

MENS SUITS

UK/US	32	34	36	38	40	42	44
Europe	42	44	46	48	50	52	54
Metric	81	86	91	97	102	107	112

MEN'S SHIRTS (COLLAR)

UK/US	14.5	15	15.5	16	16.5	17	17.5
Metric	37	38	39.5	41	42	43	44

WOMEN'S DRESSES, ETC

UK	10	12	14	16	18	20	22
US	8	10	12	14	16	18	20
Europe	38	40	42	44	47	50	52

SHOES

UK	4	5	6	7	8	9	10
US men's	5	6	7	8	9	10	11
US ladies	5.5	6.5	7.5	8.5	9.5	10.5	11.5
Europe	37	38	39	40.5	42	43	44.5

Qualification Equivalences

by Steve Warren

The multitude of training agencies, clubs and associations offering diver education means that today's recreational diver has more choice than ever before. However with choice comes confusion. What happens if you begin training with one agency and then decide to continue with another? Suppose you arrive at a lush tropical diving resort only to find that the only dive centre on the island has never even heard of your prestigious certification?

When transferring from one training association to another, the usual protocol is to credit the diver's existing training towards the nearest equivalent rating on the new agency's scheme. Additional training will be given to ensure that the new diver is familiar with any theory or skills that he or she would have received had they had been trained by the new organisation from the start. Typically an entry level diver transferring to a British agency from a North American one would be introduced to basic rescue skills and small boat diving practices together with an orientation to their preferred dive tables. Going the other way, a mid level diver might be required to complete additional first aid and rescue training. Once these criteria have been met the diver can continue on to the next level of training and earn the new organisation's awards. One diving association will not ordinarily allow a diver to automatically receive their certification on the strength of being qualified through another. However most welcome divers from other camps and will gladly arrange for them to cross over as quickly and easily as possible.

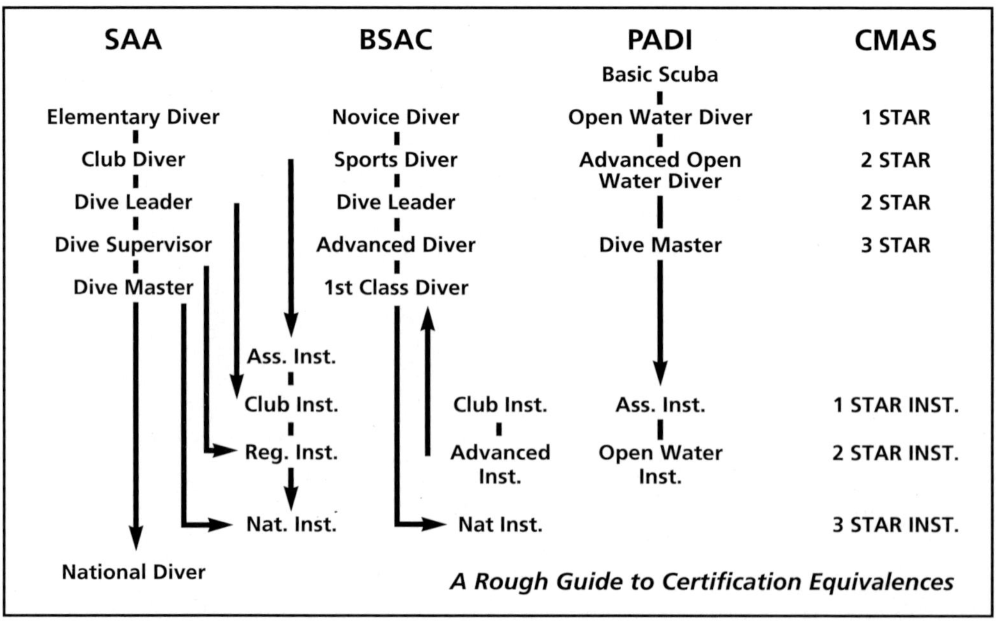

A Rough Guide to Certification Equivalences

Additional Diving Products & Services

AQUATEQUE LTD
33 PEERS STREET
BURY
LANCASHIRE BO8 2QF
061 7978148

PRODUCT: MINUTE FINDER-DEPTH VS REMAINING AIR CALCULATOR

GENESIS SCREEN PRINT
7 SANDY LANE
SOUTH WOOTTON
KINGS LYNN
NORFOLK PE30 3NX
0553 673401

PRODUCT: T SHIRTS WITH DIVING SCENES

I & EM NUTTAL JEWELLERS
18 STATION ROAD
SWANAGE
DORSET BH19 1AE
0929 426685

PRODUCT: DIVING JEWELLERY

KELVIN HUGHES
145 MINORIES
LONDON, EC3N 1HH
071 7099076 FAX: 071 4811298

PRODUCT: COMPREHENSIVE STOCKIST OF ADMIRALTY CHARTS

LOUISE WILLIAMS
SKYLARK STUDIOS
MAIN ROAD
TYDD GOTE
WISBECH
CAMBS PE13 5QA
0945 76403

PRODUCT: SCREENPRINT OF UNDERWATER SCENES

MARINECALL
TELEPHONE INFORMATION SERV. PLC
24 WEST SMITHFIELD
LONDON EC1A 9DL
071 975900

PRODUCT: WEATHER, TEMPERATURE AND SEA STATE INFORMATION SERVICE

NASSAU SCUBA CENTRE
EDEN COURT
93 INGLEBY DRIVE
DENNINGTON
GLASGOW
STRATHCLYDE G31 2PP
041 5541824 FAX: 041 5545905

PRODUCT: BATTERIES FOR COMPUTERS, LIGHTS

NITECH LTD
4-6 HIGHFIELD BUSINESS PARK
CHURCHFIELDS TRADING ESTATE
ST. LEONARDS ON SEA,
EAST SUSSEX TN38 9UB
0424 852788 FAX: 0424 851008

PRODUCT: RECHARGEABLE 6V LANTERN BATTERIES

NOONBELL SOFTWARE
REPPERSFIELD
BREAGE, CORNWALL TR13 9PG
0326 561316 FAX: 0326 561316

PRODUCT: COMPUTERISED DIVE LOG

NU CAST CRAFTS
57 TENBY STREET
NORTH HOCKLEY
BIRMINGHAM B1 3EG
021 2331854

PRODUCT: PEWTER DIE CASTED SCUBA OBJECTS

RAMPATCH LTD
HALLOM HOUSE
20 MARBOROUGH RISE
CAMBERLEY
SURREY GU15 2ED
0276 675044 FAX: 0276 675003

PRODUCT: REPAIR KITS FOR DRY SUITS

RS PUBLICATION MARKETING
6 LONDON ROAD
STROUD
GLOUCESTER GL5 2AA
0285 641953 FAX: 0453 752916

PRODUCT: HANDCRAFTS, OBJET D'ART OF SCUBA ITEMS

SCUBACAM LTD
17 RATHGAR AVENUE
EALING
LONDON W13
081 7423177

PRODUCT: PROFESSIONAL CAMERA HIRE

STANFORDS
12-14 LONG ACRE
LONDON WC2E 9LP
071 8361321 FAX: 071 8360185

PRODUCT: COMPREHENSIVE STOCKISTS OF MAPS

SURVIVAL AIDS
11-13 WEST COLONNADE
EUSTON STATION
LONDON NW1 2DY
071 3888353 FAX: 071 3873250

PRODUCT: SPECIALIST SURVIVAL SHOP

TAKE FIVE VIDEO
TWICKENHAM
MIDDLESEX TW2 6LS
081 8940218

PRODUCT: UNDERWATER VIDEO EQUIPMENT HIRE

TAURUS LTD
DERBY MILLS
THOMAS STREET
BOLTON
MANCHESTER BL3 6JU
0204 396555 FAX: 0204 361523

PRODUCT: T SHIRTS WITH DIVING SCENES

THE ROBERT STRATTON STUDIO
87 DEVON ROAD
WARLEY
MIDLANDS B67 5EL
021 4292562

PRODUCT: DIVING ART

Notes

Notes

Notes

REFERENCE

Notes

Notes

Picture by: Louise Williams

Index

Alphabetical index of entries

INDEX

Advertisers Index

The publishers would like to extend their thanks to the following companies for supporting the first issue of The Source.

INDEX

ipl

Competition & Questionnaire

In order to monitor and continually improve on the standards of the SOURCE, the publishers are holding a competition as an incentive for our readers to reply to the quality assessment questionnaire overleaf.

PRIZE

Vouchers to the value of **£1000** to be spent only with any of the display advertisers appearing in the publication. Spending may be split between eligible advertisers. No cash alternatives will be given under any circumstances. It is a condition of the competition that entrants who are not certified divers may only redeem the prize on scuba equipment once they have gained a valid certification.

HOW TO ENTER

Complete the quality assessment questionnaire in full, then answer all three questions and the tie-breaker. Send your answers to the **Freepost** address specified on page 384. All entries must be received no later than Monday, 28th February 1993 when the competition will close. The publishers may at its discretion and for whatever reasons extend the closing date without prior notice.

RULES

1) The competition is not open to employees of Inigo Press or advertisers appearing in the SOURCE, their families, agencies or anyone connected with the competition.

2) The conditions and instructions for 'Prize' and 'How to Enter' form part of the rules.

3) Only one entry per person is permitted and only one attempt per entry is allowed. Each entry must be made on the official entry form as printed in the SOURCE.

4) The winner will be the entrant who answers the questions correctly and who, in the judges opinion, completes the tie-breaker in the most apt and original way. The judges' decision is final. No correspondence will be entered into.

5) Proof of posting will not in any circumstances be accepted as proof of delivery. Responsibility will not be accepted for entries lost or delayed in the post. Incomplete, damaged and/or illegible entries will be disqualified.

6) Entries will not be returnable, and they, and the copyright in them will become the property of the publisher. The entries may be used by the publisher in any manner it chooses without fees or reward.

7) The competition judging will take place on the 14th March 1994 by a panel of 3 judges appointed by the publishers including one member independant of the publishers. The winner will be notified by post no later than 21st March 1993. Applications for the results may be made after 28th March to the publishers by enclosing a stamped self address envelope.

8) The winner may be required to become involved in further publicity or advertising. Photographs of the winner may be used in the press for publicity purposes.

9) The Judges' decisions shall be final in all matters concerning the competition and they reserve the right to declare void any entries or declare the competition void should no entries reach a required standard or declare that none of the entries worthy of a price should the anticipated response or standards not be achieved. Such decisions shall be unchallengable.

It is a condition of entry that the rules of the competition are accepted as final, and that entrants agree to abide by the rules.

Quality Assessment Questionnaire

To be completed by the entrant

READERS PARTICULARS

Name: ______________________________

Address: ______________________________

Town: ______________________________

County: ______________________________

Post code: ______________________________

Certifying Agency: ______________________________

Certification level: ______________________________

DESIGN

Are you satisfied with the design and physical construction of the book and materials used? YES /NO

Do you find the book well laid out? YES /NO

Do you find the lettering used easy to read? YES /NO

CONTENTS- articles *(delete as neccessary)*

Do you find the articles:

well written / interesting / informative / boring

Do you think the articles:

general / basic / avanced / technical / just right

Do you find the spread of topics covered:

narrow / wide / just right

What other areas or sectors of diving would you like to see covered?

CONTENTS - pictures

Are you happy with the:

standard of the pictures used YES /NO

quality of reproduction YES /NO

number of pictures included YES /NO

What other areas of photography would you like to see included?

LISTINGS & REFERENCE

Do you find the reference section easy to use YES /NO

Do you find reference material easy to find YES /NO

Do you find the reference section useful YES /NO

What other reference information and areas would you like to see included

GENERAL

How do you find the book in terms of value for money

very good value / good value / fair value / expensive / very expensive

If you find the book expensive what do you think it is an appropriate price for it

If you ordered the book direct from the publishers are you happy with the:

sales service received. YES /NO

despatch time YES /NO

packaging of the book YES /NO

Would you like to be informed of future publications YES /NO

Would you buy the SOURCE again YES /NO

Please comment or describe how you think the SOURCE can be improved:

If you have enjoyed the book or find it useful please spread the word around. Alternatively you could enclose the names of three divers of your acquintance for us to contact about the publication. The quality and price of future publications depends on your help. Please turn over now for the competition

Thank you for your time.

The Competition

Fill in this form and return it to:

The UK Divers SOURCE Competition
Free post 39 (WD5061)
London W1E 3DR

no later than 28th February 1994.

Questions:

1.

Who designed the first demand regulator that lead to the successful development of SCUBA?

____

2.

What does the acronym IDEST stand for?

____

3.

In what body of water are the US Virgin Islands?

____

Tie-breaker.

In not more than 30 words state how you think the UK Divers' Source will benefit you with your diving.

____

____

____

DECLARATION

I agree to be bound by the competition rules and confirm that I do not fall into the category of uneligible entrants as defined in paragraph 1 of 'Rules' page 381.

Name: ______________________________

Signature: ____________________ Dated: ____________________